Contents

About the Cover

The book cover is a picture of Lance Corporal Michael Paul Helton, First Marine Division, taken on December 25, 1967, at the north perimeter of the small MAG-36 helicopter and marine ground force (grunts) base at Quang Tri, northern I Corps, just about a dozen clicks south of the DMZ. Con Thien (pronounced "Kon Tee-in") is north about eight clicks, Khe Sanh (pronounced "Kay Sohn") west about twenty-two clicks plus. Hue (pronounced "way") is south about eight clicks.

Helton is a Wilson Street Boy from Monticello, Illinois, just turned twenty years old at the time of this picture, the consummate small town tough and determined Marine "Grunt." The Quang Tri River is in the background. Beyond the river, in the dense jungle landscape, was a major night battle with an NVA Division, about February 20. It was estimated that there were over two thousand NVA who were poised for a night attack to overrun the base of helicopters and about 250 marines. During the day, NVA movements were discovered. They became trapped under the wrath of PUFF and fast moving, high fire-powered marine tank units that were alerted and rolled in for the night, disappearing again before dawn. A sight to see!

The picture was taken by Wilson Street Boy, Sergeant Fox, also having just turned twenty years old at the time of the photo. Helton and Fox joined the Marine Corps in '66 on the "Buddy Plan" but had been separated since Boot Camp at MCRD San Diego. They met again preparing for night action, that December 24, in a foxhole which would have been about fifteen feet in front of Helton, toward the camera in this picture. Christmas day, a care package of US goods arrived from Helton's parents in Illinois. That Christmas night was calm, silent, and full of bright stars, at least a couple shooting across the sky as symbols of other places, perhaps brighter, safer, more angelic.

Helton is deceased. Fox wrote *The Domestic Vietnam* in Helton's memory, esteemed honor, and lasting regard. Read! Enjoy, absorb, drink in the accounts of this confused era of American history. Live with passion and high regard for those who served and serve yet today with faith, internal trust, and honor, completing duties as assigned. Live with respect and gratitude for the wives, girlfriends, and lovers who faithfully companion with veterans and often never truly know what is compounding inside of them. Live with forgiveness for those who could not, for whatever reason, be content with the doubts and uncertainties of relationships with combat veterans, for they can never grasp the nature of the boots walked within. Finally, live with conviction that the sacrifices made on America's behalf by those honored in this account will never fully be understood to anyone's satisfaction.

Author's Note

The work presented here is a novelized narrative, reflecting forty-five years of perspective. The writing is inspired mostly by true events, with predominately true characters, concerning the forever, ongoing saga of America's War in Vietnam. The unique composite of the perspective you will read is the first of its kind in print. We bring the reader from the early 1960s through the Vietnam War, into America today. You will see and feel the creek bed at Go Noi; look down the shadowy dangerous trails at Hill 881, Khe Sanh; ride Hueys into an exploded Con Thien; smell the burning blood and stench of the Battle of Hue; dive into a blackened underground bunker at Quang Tri; bounce through the war no one understood, often on the shoulders of two Marine Corps sergeants traveling war's realities in I Corps, into and through the Tet Offensive. The reader will read of and be blessed by Aunt Marge and suffer with Mrs. Slyhope in St. Louis as headlines of Tet in I Corps torture her family daily. You will feel America at its political, criminal worst *and, through the heroic troop's struggles and commitments, feel America at a best.*

This book relates ongoing relative points throughout, such as "Angels," "believe all the stories," "Lipsticks," Tet chaos, "the wake-up," and many other personal aspects of a soldier's tour of duty and pride of service in the confusing era. These recollections and opinions of Nam are written with dedication to, and for, the Vietnam veterans with grand attention to veterans' wives, family, neighbors, close friends, and those who care to study, feel closer with, and never forget the '60s Nam era. The connotation of "domestic" in the title is a constant theme throughout, at the base of and revealing rational answers to some of America's most troubling questions from that era, many of which are still quite lively, living with us yet today in many ways.

After a career of writing primarily business plans and a few far less intense books, I saw the opportunity to finally, deeply consider my thoughts and feelings about the war in Vietnam. This work took four years and combines a good deal of research with realistic perspectives and experiences. It is important for the reader to understand that my thoughts and energies led the progress of the writing in the beginning, but that didn't last long. Just as mysterious as many situations were in Nam, and are in this book, elements critical to writing progress (research, attitude, determination, etc.) seemed to take over the effort of the work, and soon the book itself was leading me and continued to lead me through to the finish. This completed work is not what I expected when I started the writing process. I am a changed person because of this writing experience, and I know that you will likely be changed and influenced from its reading.

Some of the stories and situations described are more outrageous than others, and those are, in fact, the ones that are probably more truth than "novelized narrative." I suspect a good deal of this book will stop you in your tracks. It should. The war itself stopped or detoured important elements of the American spirit individually and collectively. Some situations were very difficult for me to write. You the reader can decide if those situations are properly done. (Don't worry, you'll know them when you read them.)

Thank you for your interest in this work. I will be most interested in your thoughts and feedback, perhaps to be shared later in additional stories and conversations. God bless the Nam veterans. We and our friends, family, and network of loved ones are a special force in the heart and mainstream of America, not to be overlooked.

Semper Fi!

Sergeant Fox, USMC, Vietnam '67-'68

Contact: fox@domesticvietnam.com

Listen to Fox and guests on internet radio: Military Appreciation Channel, Domestic Nam Show.

Chapter 1

Veterans, Angels, and Nam

"Believe all the stories; Trust in the Angels:
Nam's hindsight perspectives."

An introductory statement as the entrée to an historical war write has seldom been as necessary as for *The Domestic Vietnam*. Forty plus years beyond the adventures of the Johnson/ Westmoreland deceptive actions as American and global tough guys (along with gangs of bureaucrats, politicians, and career military) subjecting American citizens and select allies to Vietnam's cultural fifteenth-century civil war traditions. This written work arises slightly differently and hopefully realistically enough, so that aging American veterans, their families, and all others concerning themselves with the Vietnam War may contemplate the actions and consequences of their own service and commitment or the honorable service of their fathers in a new, positive, full-circle manner. The Domestic Nam is a "come home to another point of ground level view."

The wretched period of American leadership insanity (1955 to 1965, then through 1974), political malfeasance, and military asset misappropriation, although not totally forgotten, seems to be remarkably repeating itself in Afghanistan yet today. This Preface (as chapter 1) is intended to be the face-to-face objective conversation with the reader about the intent and style with which this brief book is composed. This Preface is our *handshake* between you and me. It is our personal sincere introduction to one another and a commitment to candid conversation and retrospect views, favorable or not. Although the stories and insinuations written here have intended accuracy, admittedly certain details and the completion of dangling premises are novelized now and then to fill in unverifiable gaps or occasionally to just carry logic to a point of readable understanding.

Primarily on a target-market reader scale, *The Domestic Vietnam* is written specifically for veterans and the extended families of Vietnam veterans, especially for those whose family relations or close friends gave their lives to the vague cause of American warring during that confused, misunderstood, rather leaderless and politically criminal, disingenuous upheaval of a disgraceful time in American history. Secondarily, the book is composed for those curious about some of the realities of the domestic Nam war in general or the realities of the specific period, October '67 through October '68, known universally as the "defining year."

This time period (October '67-October '68) accelerated the always pounding pulse of the deadly actions having developed in Nam and exemplifies the waste of that awkward befuddled war venturing, punctuated with the early February '68 realities of the infamous "Tet Offensive." In this period, Nam rushed and cursed its misleading way in combination with the broad upheaval (the domestic part) throughout the United States, sea to shining sea. The combination of Tet (launched late January '68) and American displays of social anarchy (October '67-October '68), ten thousand miles separated, built a deep insecurity in political leadership and military command, in the general public and, more importantly, in the minds, hearts, and actions of most individual soldiers:

> What the hell was America fighting for in Vietnam? What cause or benefit?
>
> Who, really, were they to fight? Who is the enemy, and how would you tell who the enemy is on a daily basis?
>
> Fight for how long, with what?
>
> With what leadership support and structure or plan?
>
> And most importantly, what the hell is *winning*? What will winning look like? What fixed landmarks and population shifts will tumble as a signal that something has been won?
>
> What has to happen to win the effort and thus return home/cease the waste/stop the outrageous charade of nation saving, thus calming America back toward a unified nation of common sense and believable common goals?

When America prosecutes a war, based on false ideologies, impossible human goals, led by leadership imposters—you get such unanswerable questions. We get the timid, direction-changing, awkward, quasi-criminal implementation of wars like the Vietnam War. If not publicly recognized and made example of, we then lean toward useless, wasteful criminal wars into the future.

Our Preface handshake would logically include an explanation of why now? Why, after all these years, would a seemingly insignificant, slightly normal Marine Corps veteran come to a point in life that he would make a commitment to take on the writing of such an unrequested, open-ended undertaking? First, I guess it is because I can. I now have the time and feel the time-considered perspective and obligation to recall accounts with the career-earned writing and organizational skills to finally put the accounts and the ideas together in a meaningful, hopefully informative, understandable, even entertaining manner. Although I sincerely feel that no matter the depth of this write-up, it will conclude as another "understatement" about the war and warring events at large. Nevertheless, voilà, the stories, perspectives, as much logic as possible and occasional humor of a Nam experience is offered. Maybe the telling will round out the thoughts and feelings of many others just a little bit.

In addition, for the "grunt," the dedicated, never detached, committed warrior of that time or any other time, wars never really end. The feelings of duty, the circumstances, the internal embedded viruses from the actions, suspend themselves in bodies and minds, usually all too silently, no matter how long removed from the fight. A career of writing business plans, marketing strategies, and product summaries gave the confidence for quasi-prolific writing creativities and methods that I hope will lend to descriptions and explanations of this meaningful work and time-warped review, for each individual that concerns themselves with this historic subject matter and some individual stories from the Nam. *The Domestic Vietnam* is offered for those who feel any need or just curiosity to have a belated face-off with some of their own Nam realities or desire to approach that face-off within the Nam stories from others.

When I made the commitment to this humongous, vague, and controversial topic and writing effort, I allowed three winters for writing. The off months were for reading and thinking what might meaningfully be included or refined in the next writing session. The first winter was 2011/2012. Within the writing process, new ideas, thoughts, and perspectives would amazingly arise. "Amazingly" because after forty years, one would think the message and tone would pretty much be figured out and well set in a mind's writing framework. But it wasn't. One review and thought about a specific Domestic Nam segment led to a new or different thought about what I think is a reality of what was a wretched life and death process of that time period for individuals and aggregately for America. Many new ideas and views and frustrations seemed to come into the writing all along the way, even surprising myself. As new topics for chapters arose, I would simply try to understand what a veteran reading the account would be interested in. What pieces would be meaningful in their personal experiences? This question became the standard for which topics may be expanded. Such as *Dreams*. How many of us have that dreadful sweaty recurring dream, from a near death in-country action, real or just avoided, or partially real? The unreal dream parts carried forward by the awards or curses of dreaming imagination? My dream lasted from 1970 to 2001, then left, and has never returned. In those dreaming years, eventually, I could not actually recall which of the dream's details was the truth of the long past moment, and which was from dream creativity, which of course is from a subconscious we have no control over. I do not expect my dream to return. Somehow I outgrew it, but it took that long.

The Domestic Vietnam is for all of us, all of us that touched or had loved ones that touched the confusing, nationally self-deprecating actions or tremors of the exhausting, expensive, fatiguing Nam experience. Nam broke America's leadership agreement with its citizens! Nam stole the individual youthful dreams of a different type! My hope is that veteran groups and reunions can draw some satisfaction and retrospect entertainment from seeing our accounts in this new, bird's-eye perspective from "one of us," with another second, ongoing handshake of Semper Fi.

How and the hell did we get there? Southeast Asia of all places, a guttural ancient underbelly of mix-master rural cultures, so detached from America's daily views and progressive presence in the world that few American citizens knew anything about Vietnam's history, culture, people, let alone the working intricacies of Nam's shifting militia-oriented government bodies. Let's digress from the real message of *The Domestic Vietnam* to set a table that won't actually verify how we got there but might detail enough mix of fact and speculation so that a reader can at least have a "chance" to accept the unwelcome truths of our nation's '60s blunderings. (Chapter 8 becomes more specific about how we perfected the blundering into the Nam's confusing embattled national quagmire.)

OK, so let's take a brief shot at how and the hell America came to have over half million troops and hundreds and hundreds of billions of dollars in assets in a sub-Asian military investment in a country of undefined leadership and undefined borders with a sixteenth-century rural culture and apparently no global or regional influence whatsoever? (I think I kind of, finally, can figure it out. See what you think. Part of the Preface handshake thing.)

America was generally either in a war or an economic depression from 1898 (the Spanish American/Cuba war of Teddy Roosevelt fame, and "Remember the Maine" origination) through 1975. One could actually make a case that the warring period was much longer, including the Civil War and the conquest of the American West. In 1942, government created the OSS (Office of Strategic Services). By 1947, Truman felt the need for a fully functioning intelligence office and reorganized the OSS into the CIA (Central Intelligence Agency), as it is known today. The National Security Act of '47 gave the CIA broad powers concerning about anything to do with "national security." "About anything" is the operative leverage, which meant including assassinations. A new largely undefined government bureaucracy-embedded tool was born, the CIA, in a dangerous post-WWII world, growing more dangerous with vast quantum leap increases in weaponry technology and delivery systems, amidst more clear divisiveness in national ideologies to inevitably butt heads within power struggles for global or regional dominance.

After WWII, America became unanimously elevated to global leadership for international causes of democracy building and human rights. With such leadership, self-appointed, or globally consented, American political leaders automatically assumed broad responsibilities for democracy building wherever such an influence could be persuaded (or pursued?). Nation-building would then be exported in three parts, US style:

- electoral democracy
- private ownership
- civil liberties

While this new global ideology was developing, in no certain methodology from the actions of the freshly concluded WWII, America would clearly see the obstacle to its new benevolent ways and commitments. The obstacle was Russian-style Communism and, to a lesser degree (at that time), the new successful Chinese revolution installing Communism in a new Asian-made, potentially dominant manner.

Post-WWII in the Eisenhower administration, Ike made great issues of informing America and whoever else would listen about America's "military-industrial" complex. Ike's intention was to bring attention to the vast, powerful, and influential military, acting hand-in-hand with American industry, concerning all matters and global directions relating to foreign interventions. America had supported and built a huge global warring machine and was not likely to easily give it up (nation's don't), just because one war was over. Especially with a new empowered CIA that had to then be aggressively utilized in a dangerous interactive world of subjective threatening means and operations. What began theoretically as "military" and "industrial" soon added another ingredient "congressional," making the machine three pronged with influence and schemes far more powerful than ever before. The "military" and "industrial" (towed along by CIA revelations) could create scenarios of needed influence or intervention, trading kickbacks to their new third partner (Congress) for empowering decisions to act in the military-industrial way.

However, "three-pronged" soon wasn't good enough. "Three-pronged" left room for finger pointing and blame, back to a propaganda-ish naked Congress. The triad needed one more element; it needed an aloof, vaguely attached, fleeting, quasi-ghostly, but influential, fourth prong, like an assassination needs a patsy. The fourth prong would be very much like the Communist propaganda creators that were so wholly detested. We would come to call the fourth prong "Think Tanks" and see vague innocuous names for them such as, The Center for Fair Democracies. (Today, the Think Tank names spring up early and often to any ambiguous social cause and are prolifically positioned to avoid immediate exposure to their purposes and goals.)

With the four prongs wallowing within themselves, America was ready for the brave new world of Communism-chasing and challenging, global cold-warring.

OK, but how did we get to Nam?

Weary of French colonialism for early twentieth century decades and fully aware of new methods and means of a friendly Chinese Communist government bordering to the north, the Vietnamese public in the north began to rise up and challenge the French, who in the '50s were depleted, broken, and recovering from WWII. This was difficult to do among a poor, rural, unarmed society, and thus assistance with challenging the French was developed through underground methods utilizing the newly formed Communist

Chinese political machines to secure weapons, military assets, and leadership methodologies. Within these processes, certain elements of family dynasties in the South of Vietnam began to move away from the communist-leaning north who was mobilizing to remove the French.

To shorten a much longer, detail summary: In the South, a rising rural community leader named Ngo Dinh Diem would become prominent and spend two of his most formative years, '53-'54, in the United States. (These two years were coincidentally the awakening of the four-prong military/industrial/congressional/think-tank building process.) While in the United States, studying and learning the ways of "democracy," Diem became a personal acquaintance and earned the trusting influence of two American senators, Jack Kennedy and Mike Mansfield. Kennedy and Diem became friends and cross influential sources for one another, both finding odd-fellow kinship in their Catholic beliefs. This period was also the absolute height of the national United States mania called McCarthyism, the anti-commie years advocating war with, around, to, and for the defense of Communism where ever it arose, even domestically, often especially domestically, a nation's struggle that Diem was about to undertake upon return to Vietnam.

Communist threats advanced, Diem did return to South Vietnam, and, in '55, with the help of America's CIA, became elected president, having promised to divide the country between the Communist north and the Democratic south, which he did and then would lead. With CIA election manipulation, Diem managed to gain 605,025 votes in the Saigon area from four hundred fifty thousand registered voters. This remarkable sweep of votes secured Diem as the president for the time being. Until his assassination, most believe at the complicit hands of America's CIA.

Most interesting, as a significant side note, the US Ambassador assigned as the conduit to Diem's new South Vietnam government was the CIA's Henry Cabot Lodge, Jr. One cannot study, diagnose, or interpret early events of America's eventual commitment to the

Vietnam War, without substantial historic study. In the process of such research and study, inevitably strange parallels of history begin to reveal themselves. I have long felt the impetus of US military aggression in Vietnam was largely a reaction to a multitude of internal affairs from the Kennedy Administration. Namely pressures and activities in and out of Cuba, including the Bay of Pigs, gun-running, Caribbean assassinations, enormous and sweeping CIA deployments, emerging powers and activities, etc. We will read much more of that in Chapter 8. However, one little known fact connecting a realization between Cuba's Spanish-American War and the War in Vietnam remains unspoken, hidden in political weeds. It is rumblings of a Spanish-American War to liberate Cubans from the colonialist, expansion-minded Spanish in the late 1800s marked America's shifting from post-Civil War days and expansion of territories into the West, launched by the "manifest destiny" attitude of the new twentieth century. The attitudes focused specifically in Cuba but also concerned actions in the Philippines and other Spanish holdings of the era, including Hawaii. Many influential American leaders in politics and business led a screaming way to war with Spain to liberate Cuba. Three main figures behind the screaming and influence building for a Spanish-American War were Teddy Roosevelt and his Rough Riders (Roosevelt was a believer that wars were an ideal function of government), William Randolph Hearst (the inventor and master of "Yellow Journalism," growing his chain of city newspapers led by the San Francisco Examiner and the New York Journal), and an influential, intellectual senator from Massachusetts, Henry Cabot Lodge. America's entry and indulgence in such a war, needing a push, finally turned from speculation to commitment with the reporting, by Hearst through Lodge, of the demise in 1898 of one of America's few warships of the time, "The Maine," while harbored in a Cuban port. America would hear little but the war-cry of "Remember the Maine." In the end, the Maine was largely thought to have been destroyed by an on-ship mishap, regardless the cause for war with Spain quickly became a "fait accompli." A little over sixty years later, Lyndon Johnson, unabashedly seeking a wider, deeper war in Vietnam, appointed a CIA employee as ambassador to South Vietnam. The ambassador, soon after assuming his post, reported in August 1964 that North Vietnamese gunboats had attacked a US Navy ship in the Gulf of Tonkin: an act of War! The incident could not grasp a taken "Remember the Maine" catchy slogan for a fighting cause, so they called it The Gulf of Tonkin Incident. A charge that remained largely in confused speculation and opinion, never proven! That ambassador's name was Henry Cabot Lodge, Jr., the grandson of the former coining of "Remember the Maine," with Hearst. Both incidents are recorded in history as largely skeptical in origin, both propelling America into a "war justification" that the leadership of those separate times were seeking. (We know about Vietnam. Americans suffered four thousand dead in the Spanish-American War.) Hearst was able to solidify and expand his newspaper business by leaps and bounds.

We now have all of the elements for the intervention into South Vietnam and the beginnings of *The Domestic Nam*—and thus, in '56, America took its first steps into the war by assigning eight hundred US military trainers to lead the early development of a standing army for Diem. The year '56 was also the year that US aid would begin to pour into Diem's coffers and efforts, and thus, eight hundred advisors had $270M pocketed from a complicit Congress to drop into the process as needed. At this point, Diem had support in Congress, the first military presence, and a growing aid pool of hundreds of millions of US nation building communist fighting/$$$$$.

In the process, one more US mega-trend came into full force and effective in the anti-communist global deterring business. The US press became fully complicit in the process of building up the Democratic Diem regime, build up the "cause" (the justification), and build up army training devices and assets now increasingly exported to the Nam. Nam would, since Korea's stand-off, now become the face of the Asian anti-communist thin red line. All with the full propagandish daily support of the US press who for six years had only token surface coverage, never really looking at the depths of the coming sub-Asian quicksand.

In the process of Diem's nation building, Kennedy was elected President, and thus the progressiveness of the relationship between Kennedy and Diem had no developmental obstacles, especially with the new business of the four prongers now established and an aggressive growing CIA. With Kennedy and his aides, America was served and swallowed the Communist Domino Theory, which the military effort in Nam was to guard against. And blah, blah, blah, blah, America was in the pie and in the soup—with actual implementation and the work of real village to village progress ignored. (Eight years later, the CIA, who had grown in powers, would assist in assassinating Diem and his then cogoverning brother, and many believe would at least look the other way, later, in the assassination of Kennedy.) America's Nam commitment was made on a global anti-communist stage that would swerve, two-step, and dodge-ball for cold-war decades, perhaps still is today, domestically.

And here comes the good ole boy from Texas—LBJ. Johnson hadn't a clue other than Texas tunnel vision swagger and pomposity, and thus, the four-prong thing would ramp up uncontrollably and drive the momentum of US human and asset build-up in the face of what had openly become an internal Vietnam civil war. But one of the few openly, active internal "communist opposing" civil wars globally with which to intervene.

A few million troops later and a few jillion-billion dollars later, after running the French out of the north, Ho, yearning for a Trail, would set his sights on reuniting Vietnam into one country and commit their built-up North Vietnam armies and arms flow to the unification effort. Ho and the north would then spend three years planning for Tet, the North's new Dien Bien Phu project, to be launched in the defining year we speak of herewith.

So *that*, with a few million details bypassed, is the snapshot of how we got there. That era's "sucking sound" was Nam and its falling dominoes of dreadful unintended consequences which would eventually become nationally, domestically overwhelming. It is how the Wilson Street Boys and their families got from bikes to M-16s and little league ball parks to hot LZs in a snappy six years. It is how America politically and humanly wasted at least one decade of development opportunity and how the military-industrial complex perpetuated and then thrived and does so yet today. It is how the CIA of those times would grow unruly in influence. It is how a foundation of warring elevates to begetting more warring and the process becomes SOP (standard operating procedure) in an environment of incapable government SNAFU perfecting. It is why America in the '60s and '70s would erupt socially, subjected to the stupidity and corruption of it all. Nothing would make sense because it was senseless; the leadership was afoul, tangled, awkward, and corrupt. That time period in American history set today's standard for much of the press's influence and today's four-prong international conflict standards of intervention and espionage.

A central theme of America's Vietnam intervention was the theory of stopping Communist "dominoes" from globally dragging one poor nation after another into Communist clutches and circles of influence, imprisoning whole populations. Falling "Dominoes" was what the public was served through the build-up years. In retrospect, the "dominoes falling" theory had relevance but was "back-ass-wards" in insinuation and explanation. The real dominoes were falling one to another *Domestically*, creating the four-prong military/industrial/congressional/think-tank engine for actual causes unknown but to a few and unpredictable even to those few. With two global strands of falling dominoes, internal and external, to a dysfunctional government, diligent strategies of prevention, compromising, or defeating, are diplomatically impossible to control.

I write forty-plus years advanced from the perspective and experience of a twenty-year-old Marine Corps sergeant assigned to I Corps, First Marine Division helicopter group HMM-364, The

Purple Foxes, detached from Mira Mar, California, San Diego County. I set first foot just within a Vietnam south I Corps shoreline on October 17, 1967, largely skeptical, confused, nervous, head up, pretty frickin' tough and determined, by hometown standards, which ceased to count for anything from that moment forward. Attached to a premiere helicopter unit, Chinook (generally called Sea Knights) and Hueys, would give me a well-traveled, thorough I Corps view and experience the entire next defining year. I was literally from Phu Bai and Chu Lai to Khe Sahn, Donh Ha at the DMZs south line down highway one through Quang Tri and Hue for the entire next year, in and out of way too many LZs and Fire Base positions to recall. Three days of so-called R&R at Red Beach (just a click north of the infamous Go Noi) near DaNang was the only pause, and even that was a tense encounter with passing ROK's and shifting uncertain other GIs just in from the bush or just on their dazed way to the next bush. We flew in daytime, and at night, hot LZs, then a milk run to a bombarded pad. The bravest jockey pilots blazed the river ravines and followed the smoky flares and tracers into medevac emergencies on a daily basis. In the chapters to follow, the reader will feel well traveled, experiencing tense and yet sometimes gracious encounters through the tour of duty. They will read about a background that prepared us and close other boys on the same track and path from our tiny Midwest town for our USMC/Green Beret/Navy Pilot/Army Grunt duty from the time we were old enough to form the first bicycle street-frolicking gangs.

At first, I felt the forty-year separation from active duty to actual writing would be very difficult to manage. In the midst of the work, I found the time expanse to be just the opposite. With accounts and details partially lost in time, this forty years of lock-and-load writing time has justified the leeway to fill in the blanks as I see fit, unrestrained from bending a moment's now vague realities.

Here are the youthful revelations that led to survival and ongoing years of contemplation: The Marines dug into I Corps, the northernmost sector of the fought over South Vietnam, designated

I Corps by fleeting commands that must label such things in some leadership fashion, break things down to usable increments of command and control stuff. It was incoming hot and weather hot. Busy Chinooks and Hueys were our new bikes and '57 Chevys. I gathered the rhythm of the war ASAP, unlike some who never seemed to find a rhythm in the events they reluctantly were forced to become a part of. Being there, it was inexplicably dangerous not to feel the rhythm of your war and yet be in the middle of it. However, some just could not grasp and live within the dawn to dusk danger and the decisions and reactions required in between. Strong, fast, confident, I let the war come to me when it made sense, but I went to the war all too often when I saw the duty in it or admittedly sometimes just for the selfish adventure.

I hope this experience, but more importantly the broad writing perspective, will be meaningful for all readers as well as useful for the coffee shop commando still occasionally in such never ending, never concluding discussions with the groups of opinionated "townies" who remain unrestrained in comment, just because of ignorance, which in idle coffee shop talk begets more misleading self-adulation ignorance. For this type of modern-day community commando, this write will hopefully provide a next level of Nam profundity with the hometown, half spent good ole boys, still charging those beaches, dry creeks, hills, and hot LZs. May they now venture on more milk runs than hot LZ landings.

About forty to sixty days in-country, now in the mix of various in-country USMC soldiering actions and reactions, a dawn of startled awakening came personally over me. The practically tingly electric-like feeling was so strange and new in my young life, it could not only not be ignored but felt below the surface to be a sensation to be embraced, be inhaled and lived within as some grand, vague elusive meaning. The sensation was strangely very spiritual like nothing I had ever felt. It was way too spiritual for the combatting conditions faced daily. This personal feeling was as if a guardian angel had been soaring invisibly above to finally decide I was worthy of the angel's companionship for my remaining in-country tour of duty year. I somehow knew it was for the whole year (but have never known for how long in total life, still don't, although I have learned that some say it is for life). It was this heavenly feeling, still difficult to describe with confidence but no doubt present, with me, that in the midst of unpredictable Nam, daily chaos became reality for the moment and changed my soulful outlook for the entire tour of domestic Nam duty.

I actually felt like I became two people: one, a disciplined active aggressive marine in a sergeant's cause of fighting and leading when called upon. In addition, being another totally different person, who was a detached "observer" to the whole nervous, constantly flowing scene, which is the best way I can explain it. Crazy? The unavoidable strange personal "angelic" phenomenon was with me all day, every day in Nam, and I knew that. I never doubted my angel's presence. In forty years, until now, I had not spoken of this more than two or three times to Cynthia, maybe less.

I understand this must sound pretty strange now, but it is important to recall the sensation, in order to try to fulfill the "handshake" agreement stated previously. For those rightfully confused about the seriousness of the angelic moment, I can only add this faint effort of further explanation, provided by Cynthia's interpretation of her own angelic real experience:

> *The life of flesh angels is not directly available to human eyes. These Angels, for those selected, are "guardians" (guardians defined as—one who undertakes responsibility for someone who is incapable of managing their own affairs). These "Guardian Angels" do not seek to directly influence you—you chart your own course—the Angels only act to make the best possible use of the course you have chosen. Furthermore, the Angels do not ordinarily*

intervene in routine affairs of human life, but when instructed (by Jesus) to perform some unusual exploit (saving us from harm or death) rest assured these guardians will find the means to carry out the instructions. Angels are "beings," who are going to be with you for many years, and they continue to receive instructions toward their work with you through those years. Angels have and feel accountability for their association with us during their life.

That's as close as I can honestly come to a description, and that has taken four decades.

Myself and my angel was, who I was that year as strange as that may sound, the duty-bound marine with the silent, unseeable angel. With that sensation, outlook, and revived confidence, I did a lot of aggressive stupid things, such as follow ROKs into the edge of the Hue Citadel, the last of the major Tet hand-to-hand battles. Except with ROKs, my hands were not needed—those boys are ugly— killing, "bad to the bone." In addition, with my angel, I gathered the stupidity to once deliver a tray of refreshing salty dogs to bunkered bros just off the NCO Club, in a field of live mortar fire. In retrospect, that action should be recalled as an unnecessary ill-advised risk that I probably could have done without.

Allowing for there to be two of me, I felt was a godly gift and rather than doubt the strange insanity of that make-believe soulful venture, I embraced it. I'm sure at various points I had conversations between myself and the other me. Goofy? I think it is that leap of imaginative trust, in a time of mental limbo when a person can justify the strangest things that later seem quite silly but may now allow to write *The Domestic Vietnam* these many years later. I don't really know how an angelic confidence of survival helps a combatant dodge bullets and shrapnel and live in muck and dirt with the earth's insects or if it ever really does help in any ground-truth way. But I think it did then, and I have trusted that it helped these many years. At least that was the way I felt then and ongoing. I now believe those angels are out there with many of us in many ways, on many shoulders, largely unnoticed and not actually felt by many people, like I felt mine. I also now believe that the timing of an angel's arrival is totally unpredictable. One specific, undeniable post-Nam encounter solidifies the guardian angel encounters.

Certain core values are drilled into a soldier as a result of specialty training in "staging" processes. These core values are generally operational, emphasizing weapons and tactics training, as well as some cultural in-country clues about native people and their living, all of which become meaningless in about twenty-four hours when tracer's power and blaze within your personal air space and the next minute appears doubtful, dreadful at best. Then, there are the coincidental off-handed incidents that lend to the adoption of other core values to be carried along a tour of duty way. Available only if a person is aware enough of surroundings and what people are offering to catch the kind feelings and advice extended by others. I personally was given some advice by a returned veteran as I departed from Camp Lejeune, North Carolina, for staging training at Camp Pendleton, California. The gifting war veteran was from Boston; his name I have forgotten, but I will never forget his message.

He told me: "Believe all the stories that come from Nam."

The advice sounded strange to me at the time. His simple explanation was this: Nam is a gang fight, sides are not defined, nor will they ever be defined. Everyone is armed and dangerous, in terrain from mountains to thorny beaches, the land between is jungle-hot, sticky, infested with disease and things causing more disease. Vietnamese from the north fight Vietnamese from the south; Vietnamese from the south fight other Vietnamese from the south. Americans fight them all, and they all fight the Americans, and Americans fight among themselves. ROK (Republic of Korea) fights everyone and take no prisoners. You will only own the very ground you stand on, and the next day, it will be different ground. The war is mobile, fleeting, deadly, twenty-four hours a day. A friend is a friend, that moment only. So stories abound and are a part of learning to stay alive. Listen to all of the stories because quite simply and most importantly, "If it didn't happen to that person, it happened to someone else." Do not forget that lesson. All the stories are true. I haven't forgotten a word of that eye-to-eye pre-war instruction from what I felt was a master of the process. I can still see the sincerity of the reddened Irish face of the Boston veteran advisor and still appreciate his unselfish moment to a fellow departing marine.

As a writing process, most of the individual incidents and stories described are as true as can be recalled. Certainly, the major scenes and situations are all true. Admittedly, some liberties are taken in story telling detail and perhaps conclusions because if it didn't happen that way in that incident, it did happen that way or in a similar manner to that guy over there on the next hill or in the next tree line skirting a dry, tree-lined, dangerous creek bed. There is no way to emulate the thud of mortars, the cracks of small arms fire overhead in the middle of the night or the sizzle and WOMP of the many killing rockets that shook the earth and shook those close around to the rocket's collision with the Nam ground. We can feel those effects in the stories of the young determined soldiers and make one more sorting of our own issues.

Maybe *The Domestic Vietnam* will answer some questions for some people who concern themselves with the topic, but it certainly can't answer all the questions that will only fade with the fading of generations, replaced by other citizenry who will know nothing of

Nam or care. I will take a stab at one macro-issue, which is this: On whose shoulders did the burden of the war fall—the industrialist suppliers? Not a chance. Although I think Johnson basically grieved himself to death, it was done silently with no cleansing statement to an America who deserved an apologetic, cleansing statement. LBJ was logically the symbol of the consummate barrier to clear thinking of his time. (Politics generally overrides cleansings.) So the burden did not lie with the politicians. Their two-step side dance largely covers their tracks. Did military leadership, the McNamaras and Westmorelands bull-up to the commitment of the cause and live or die by tours of duty? No, they didn't. McNamara's self-cleansing documentary, "*The Fog of War*," neither lent focus to the mirror imaged culprits nor expelled blame to the leadership. The "burden" we have always searched for was on us, us folks in the small towns and fringes of society who followed the national system of traditional national gallantry to the cause. The burden also fell on our families. I think, these decades later, it is OK to be really pissed about the whole national debacle and waste of everything in the path of Nam. What was humanly given, or what was taken, is very different in a million ways with millions of post-Nam families.

Having a late or lasting "understanding" of the Domestic Nam, was never a part of *our deal*, for anyone. We did not go to Nam based on an agreement to actually understand anything, then or at a later date, and thus, we have to let "understanding" the darn place go from our minds and hearts. We must attempt then to live as contentedly as possible with what we know we accomplished or tried to accomplish, and love what we did and with whom we did it. (To the current younger post-Nam generations, anything here sound familiar? Afghanistan anyone? Amazing!)

Readers will meet the boys from Wilson Street and see how, in a life's blink, they became what they became: military-ready, fast, determined, able to see above any confrontational fray into the duty of a moment. This was the post-WWII generation, so close to the returning veterans of that monumental effort that osmosis could let one group down easily while ramping the next group up rapidly. The Wilson Street Boys averaged about six to seven years from bicycle gangs and little league baseball to boot camp, staging and then shipping out. The chapter "Wilson Street" will capture that small town society and associated elements and provide a sense of how America had the crop of humans, to match the upgrade in weapons and thus, again voilà, the war environment could be fed with obedient, patriotic, new, strong bodies. The Wilson Street description is real and symbolizes America at the time.

If you are historically curious about the Domestic Nam addressed in this book, load the garage fridge with Falstaff or Pabst, or the reminiscent beverage of your choice, put your feet up, and give yourself a couple years to follow these writings, with *The Domestic Vietnam*, of course. Maybe we can discuss the whole matter at some corner of some Vegas reunion someday or within our developing radio show on the Military Appreciation Channel.

The Domestic Nam seemed to be another war on its merry warring way, with politicians waving flags in the day and sucking the industrial goodies and deal-making dinners in their main body of evening work. For the military, who, in many ways, must have meant well, the Domestic Nam became a game of checkers bound by the grand delusion mentioned above from a good idea of Kennedy's, through stages of a make-believe escalation of years, drawing American commitment and lives deeper into an impossible Asian quagmire. The real Grand Delusion crashed upon heads and hearts in late January 1968 with the reality of the Tet Offensive, America's collective Dien Bien Phu. Stories by the thousands must be unrecorded. This book features a couple stories previously untold and substantially true. The Tet Offensive was the grand awakening in the midst of America's own internal turmoil and routine of body and asset supply, extract, resupply, all while perfecting the counts of KIAs, WIAs, and captured enemy supply tonnage. Killing King, killing Robert Kennedy, killing students at Kent State, with urban riots and the DNC's own Chicago revolution put the events of Tet even higher on the scale of military debacle as America internally continued to unravel along with the war, none of which made it easier in-country for the soldiers, and in fact, created a heightened ferocity of turmoil for each individual soldier to deal with in their own in-country way.

The actual language of this writing style is a natural mix of the simple thoughts of a rural American growing-up, with attempts at more intellectual composition, fueled by floods of ideas to make various points more understandable or more impressive to a reader's personal perspective. I have attempted to largely avoid the depth of distaste and rudeness that youth and soldiering can combine to create in forms of vulgar language and behavior. Soldiers in foul conditions, living in a bull's-eye, sharp-shooter world can come up with some collectively abnormal analysis and descriptions. What "matters" to them, and what doesn't matter, has nothing to do with life in the real world in the long run? The active soldier's world is necessarily distorted!

The Domestic Vietnam is written solely alone, never seeking content advice, but always looking for input that would strengthen points or make descriptions more understandable. The few friends and associates who are aware of the work provided macro guidelines that were meaningful. Parents of soldiers, including the Wilson Street Boys, made their contributions long ago, unknowing of the positive influences they provided to those who concern themselves with the detail of such things these many years later.

War's more modern, newest tactics in leadership and field maneuvers create a necessity for more modern killing weapons, change relationships within a nation and internationally, and provide the synergy for advances in many support necessities that then become civilian peace time advancements. Advances of innovation in these and many other disciplines and opportunities from implementation can become both evil and benevolent. The capabilities of the field communication options available to command and control leadership were an underexplained, underresearched reality of the Domestic Nam. About the time of Nam, in a nation now warring for most of three straight decades, military and political leadership communications had advanced to new levels of distanced command and control possibilities. Unlike Civil War days, military leadership no longer had to be in the field, at the front, with the troops, with a nose in the stench, smoke, and dying.

Decisions and orders could originate and be disseminated from somewhere other than in the action. Politicians, then officers, could in the time of Nam, direct ground troops and air support into a deadly confrontation such as Go Noi Island or a thousand other hot spots, without ever really understanding the detail of the terrain or strength of enemy opposition or the condition of the troops they order. Someone unattached to the blood and guts can provide "orders" for an ambiguous assault on some meaningless, clay-based hill whose official name is Hill 555, as if it were a lottery pick. Those orders to a real face and human wearing a silver bar or two came from someone else, even further away, who discovers a propagandish necessity for pumped up numbers, or more enemy KIA info, because someone else even further up the blind displaced command chain in Washington must defend the war effort in a public speech early next month. Think about how unreasonable, unruly, riotous that whole scenario is, but it was us, America, the backdrop of four-prong strategic Domestic Nam operations fueled by the money and ambition of the time. Sound scarily contemporary? Again, Afghanistan.

In chapter 3, we will go with a Private Burke to a dreadful place called Go Noi Island. We will share the loss of lives in that waste of a combat field undertaking, originated by communication of misguided orders from multiple sources of detached numb-skulls, with stars and stripe flag standards as a false display of fortitude in the corners of far away "command" offices. Private Burke is us. It is a story of a child of the small town prairie moved along an American assembly line of soldier making of the time. With Burke, we will move through rural American '60s times and then Nam's grind.

Eventually, we share Burke's battles and will ride with him on his true, personal, cooling angelic journey.

In the current version of the Domestic Nam, which is Afghanistan, the same innocuous methods and foul judgments are a daily part of the mismanagement, adding profusely ignorant, politically motivated new "rules of engagement" to restrict combat actions. Along the way, these command-down rules of engagement, designed to be nothing more than political-correctness, are imposed in the name of society cleansing for an ancient prototype of a society who has no idea that they need or want the cleansing. The modern day political-correctness versions again add another awkward anti-swagger imposed on today's soldiering.

America's current youth, now mature along their merry way with constantly changing broad society influences and wavering signals of what exactly is a good moral influence and path of good judgment. Youth are encouraged to grow up fast socially, so the adults can then regret the acceleration. Character diversification is considered good for children to not only contemplate, but to breathe and act upon: "Oh look, young Stanley likes to try new ways of challenging adults. Aah, isn't he precious." We call it being "liberal," as if that is a good progressive thing. It was not that way in the '50s, '60s, when discipline was a "given" family and neighborhood instrument of the day. Children of that time, the pre-prep-up Domestic Nam generation, were expected to act and relate in a certain way, with all adults. Acceptable behavior was expected and demanded especially in the small rural communities where everyone actually cared. Combine that process with the fact that the boys, at eighteen, would register for the draft, an inevitable transitional indicator to maturity, which then would require an individual plan. The reality of the behavior and draft requirements made fast adults, rapidly producing bodies for the Domestic Nam grind.

When a nation's power base is in a warring mood, that nation wants its youth to be tough, aggressive, operationally keenly visionary, fast, obedient, fearless, and bullet proof, like the Wilson Street Boys and Burke. When the warring mood passes, for whatever reason or outcome, and the nation's outspoken attitude shifts to the niceties of "liberal" non-boundaries of behavior, the warring characteristics that were previously appreciated and thought of as heroic, protecting, victorious, then often become despised by the convenience of the times just won, especially in a society flaunting social systems for new unrestrained "freedoms."

We love you, appreciate you in the moments of the struggle. Then, you are dangerous, practically evil, certainly touched with misguidedness in the moments after the struggles victory or times just passing as freedom and safety are handed back to a public good, and the new influence peddlers know nothing of struggles fought and/or won. And thus was the conclusion for many who served the misguided ways of the Domestic Nam routine. Those days are begrudgingly over. Since the Nam's confusing aftermath, there does seem to be a national momentum to recognize and tip a hat to those who have and do serve. I am not sure it matters any more to the Nam vet; I generally think not, although occasionally producing a quiet, cynical, false grin.

Chapter 2

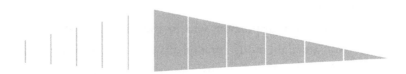

Wilson Street

"In America's late '50s and '60s, it was six to seven years
from
Little League to Boot Camp."

In the '50s every small, post-WWII United States town had a Wilson Street. Maybe not "Wilson," but they had a straight, harmless-looking street that anchored end to end an orderly and peaceful, quaint rural town, including a key intersection that gave people daily choices to take the three-minute trip to somewhere else in town. The Wilson Streets of mid-America would define the boundaries of the town's expansions, a smallish land parcel chunk here, and another one there added to the town's girth for those population growth years of post-WWII nationalized recuperation, generally considered to be 1945 through 1960-something. The "war recuperation time" being mostly the mid-'50s, long enough after WWII to allow some sanity of feelings to return without a begrudging attitude for personal sacrifices, and for common mid-America citizens to refocus priorities to marriage relationships, raising families, making a living within a goal-oriented career, and lending some sort of dedicated effort toward "community," for the good of the collective community at large. Citizens' contributions of time, expertise, and minor funding for community growth and unselfish prosperity were normal attitudes. It was a time when children of all the families were welcomed, observed, directed, or reprimanded by all the family sentries of each street or block of attentive neighbors. The '50s were generally good times! Ike was in charge, trusted, with honest, patriotic driven visions for all of America.

Those "times" became somewhat defined by what America use to call and still does occasionally refer to as the baby boom era. An era of more relaxed Americans, fresh from the tense waves of unpredictable living that flowed through America's '30s depression era to the monumental international WWII effort that drew human flesh from every town and street and redistributed those faithful bodies globally, treacherously, dangerously, and bravely in our military uniforms. WWII was a unanimous collective effort to save the world and America from Nazi Germany totalitarianism, then the same aggression from Japan in the opposite global direction from America's other coast, now commonly known as the "left coast."

Most of America generally understood the causes of that greatest war and eventually supported the effort unselfishly, trusting in America's depths of goodness and consistent leadership.

Inventiveness in domestic product concept and design, as well as in manufacturing and finance, and general mega-economics structuring, swept into place new homes and industry tools for an era of prosperity, bigger dreaming and an optimistically fascinating era of what "could be." The optimism, growth, and inventiveness were unprecedented in the history of America as well as broader global productivity. People could dream big in the '50s, and they did dream big. American muscle and ingenuity had just whipped the opposing axis of major evil powers of the world, literally saved Allied governments along the way and remained armed to the proverbial teeth to take on any more real or perceived enemies that may care to step forward in some fashion of regional injustice to isolated innocent others. The automobile industry invented fins for cars, which seemed to strangely define a time of "up, up, and away." Couples driving within the new fashioned, weighty steel on wheels could now see and feel America's expansion freely for the first time, ground level, coast to growing coast, seeing their USA in their Chevrolet, camping behind new highway billboards or in new Holiday Inns along the way, if they so chose.

In the small towns, on the Wilson Streets, people breathed easier from the war's conclusion and focused more on yard work, basement bar watering holes, tomato plants, L & M cigarettes, baseball, and newspapers being delivered on time by speedy coordinated kids on new red, white and blue bikes.

In reality, the world had not settled much in its wars or much that would actually last for very long, but the times felt good then, and that was good enough, then:

Europe was a landscape of broken buildings
and internal, hungry roaming refugees with all

governments in some phase of reorganization, verily able to concentrate on the essentials.

Japan was in worse condition than Europe, draped in radioactive atomic dust, having been "nuked to the threshold of the proverbial stone-age," as they would say in nuke-talk of the new emerging times.

Eastern Russia as well as all of Europe dove into a real search for family, reinvention of relationships with governments, and societies as uncertain as the momentum from the latest conspiratorial revolutionist rally. A split and splintered France had to reunite, forgetting the Vichy nonsense. England had to rebuild and reload completely.

The Pacific and Indochina stayed hot, much of Asia and sub-Asia still caught in ancient rapacious times. The same generations doing the agriculture based same things, decade after decade, largely avoided the big ideas of the rest of the world, except for advances in weaponry and the regimented uses of government's new weaponry, and isolated newborn Asian ideologies.

In the '50s, America had a chance to have babies, drink Jack, and travel new highways that Eisenhower was determined to build before the next world war that could be on American soil and thus require uninhibited troop mobility. Korea fussed up as a new war and was brutal for those in that dreadful rotation, but it was a mere blip on the peace-radar compared to the massive national and global undertakings of pre and post-WWII. Still, a Korean War was not to be missed by languid political leaders who had learned the art of industry with military, and all the production, delivery, resupply options amongst actual warring progress.

All in all, in the '50s America had time for looking more toward individual accomplishment, domestic morality, and structural rebuilding than did other countries slammed and staggered by the War of all wars. Tired of a foreign mind-set dominating fixed and intellectual assets, in America, it was OK and a good time to be selfish, build our own stuff, feed our own faces, and pop beautiful red, white, and blue twelve-ounce distractions in the late day breezes of a patio owned by a veteran, treating the neighborhood friends to local prosperity along the way, spontaneously, repeatedly, guiltless.

Treaties defined an end to the Big War, but trained warriors, hungry politicians and aggressive manufacturers of war essentials with fastened buyer relationships don't easily give themselves up in the minds and ambitions of those actually owning the warring initiatives. There is no switch to flip that turns off the WWII lifestyle or business-style. Small towns were filling with returning veterans. Mothers and wives, although often with the same spouses by name as in the prewar, experienced the return of men changed in character by unknown thoughts and unpredictable reactions to (what used to be) routine events of a day's work or leisure. Wars change men, and the ladies must take what they get upon the men's return. Perhaps the wars change the ladies also, more quietly, in smaller increments of change. Such are the "domestic" overlaps of any war.

American machines of many types had proven its global leadership. Certainly nationally and throughout the world's primary movers and shakers of the time, thought of these self-congratulatory times as proof of America's global superiority and leadership. Impressive exceptionalism beyond expectations, a time to unleash the economic hounds held back because of the demands of a unifying war effort and associated focus and expenditures abroad. These illusions of no regret and a focus of uninhibited accomplishment leading to riches previously not a priority could begin to expand in the '50s without limits or regrets, largely because dead people don't talk (beyond their cemetery monuments and Memorial Day flags) about what they miss and are more easily forgotten amidst the excitement of the ongoing, glamorous prosperity of busy nation-building now a priority once again as should be.

An America starved for domestic provocations that would be managed in a civilized manner not only began to build momentum in the cities, but also in the rural countryside, where good people were always patriots and ambitious, expecting some sort of rewards for sacrifices in one way or another. America built interstate highways and hundreds of small airports in hundreds of mid- and small-size communities that did not want or need small airports. Busy hands were happy hands. More building begets the good feelings and working prosperity of more building. The GI Bill mobilized and aided veteran's ambitions and provided a means for those ambitions, pulling together stimulus and visions to put people back to the good use of investing freely in "their own futures." Returning veterans were heroes, praised not only for what they did do (in winning the War), but what they would now do and could do, human potentials now unleashed in their communities and businesses. Homebuilding changed from the two-story barn-type gargantuan stick built boxes to what they called ranch homes. All the living quarters and living areas were on one stretched ground floor, with attached two-car garages for the five tons of steel on wheels that would inevitably roll into a family's growing mobile life.

Veterans of WWII were like veterans of all wars, having the deepest thoughts and feelings within, forever. Taking the veteran from the battle does not necessarily take the battle from the veteran. The luxury and comfort of new ranch homes included the first "official" American "man-caves." These were basement built bars, the alcohol drinking kind of bars, generally with a fireplace close by, and graced with a new invention: black-and-white televisions. The new man-caves were enhanced with flickering fireplaces, new exotic electrical gadgets to spiffy up drink mixing fun and fancy drinking glasses for every spontaneous social neighborhood drinking occasion. Having one of these new American-built man-caves, with the warmth of oak burning in the fireplace off to the side, was one of the war veteran's more delightful paybacks. The new black-and-white ten-inch portable bar TV gizmos were the glitziest, the bees knees. "Sit raht dawn there at the end of your own man-cave bar, and watch the Bears!" The best of times! Basement man-caves were the unofficial VFW or USO of the neighborhoods or that particular outpost on the edges of the town's otherwise outwardly organized living, where men and families escaped even further from the war and whatever rumors of the next crisis call to duty inevitably hung silently over the heads of a quieter America, still gasping for easier breaths from the last war.

A returning war veteran with their own stocked bar/man-cave had a safe-haven. Other thirsty roaming refugees of a neighborhood, separated from the day's community actions and demands, could drop in, also be separated from life's demands and did. Man-cave regulars could share war stories, attitudes, and experiences that needed sharing if the time and the audience was right for that moment, right for that round of drinks, right for that perfect football game on the man-cave black-and-white, which had little to do with who was playing, league, or conference standings. The veteran's stories were "magnanimous," unobtrusively embellished or not because they had been lived by the teller on the biggest global stage ever created. Stories of all kinds would be told, not to be missed: stories from marines on the ground in Italy, pilots prepping for takeoff from England, or army sergeants edging through France post D-day.

Very young sons of these ground, air, and sea heroes could perch quietly in the trusted arena of the veteran's thoughts and language, and listen, unnoticed, their young minds expanding by the intriguing wonderment of stories from across the world. On the well-kept small town streets and in the home man-cave bars of the ranch house built in the '50s, a seven-year-old could hear and feel the world's gigantic coordinated efforts and the flows of power-wielding super structures, suspecting the delicate dangerous balances that these men embraced for life or death in the clutches of defined military duties for love of country, or mom, or whatever.

These warring conversations were always controlled, practically rhythmic in the telling, expression, and conclusions. Naturally, the more the bar liquids flowed, the deeper in thoughtful meaning became the descriptions, conclusions, and inevitable analysis. These unofficial warring conferences would always come to unexpected sudden conclusions, usually as one or a group of wives finished snack support prep assignments and missions and descended to the war room to join the men. Even as a seven-year-old, one could feel the sudden shift of temperament from seriousness to light-heartedness with more actual concentration and discussion about the comparatively meaningless football game on the B&W or attention to comparatively meaningless concerns of the women now in the conversational presence. Rather than the previous descriptions of tenseness, in a B-17, taking off an English runway, as part of the Berlin Airlift, conversation toned down several clicks, then down a few more clicks, until nothing said mattered more than a single thought. As a seven-year-old, one could begin to feel that war stories are only for the veterans, largely not to be shared with those outside of the uniform. The stories, or at least their telling, was sacred territory, except for the occasional seven-year-old tucked in and off to the side, quiet in his awe of the men and their moments.

Home bars and support accoutrements did not have to be in the basement, but they did seem to have to be indoors, if war storytelling were to arise. As a seven-year-old, munching among the big boys, one could not find these glorious warring conversations in the summer outdoor drinking patio or as a part of cookout activities or out and around the yard. Outdoors must have been too open, too outdoorsy, not confined enough for adequate safety and trust among the post-war clan of the moment. Good war stories apparently are most meaningful only when shared with elbows on an indoor bar, the participant's posture over a fortifying drink, hunched-up shoulders never moving, with only the turn of a head to make a strategic point or the posture dip to yet another mouthful of the weekend's and war's favorite long-awaited relief and attitude adjustment.

As a seven-year-old, stocking the bar as a war discussion session moved along from Africa, to Italy, to England was a most honorable position but never ending in needs of one type of beverage errand or another ice bucket run up and back from the kitchen, as fast as possible to not miss some unpredictable analysis or emphasis that might be the best ever, and define a rarest combat stage that had been set. A seven-year-old story-stowaway-in-plane-sight could be speedy and stealth enough in bottle, ingredient, or ice fetching. He could be a child expert on the Berlin Air Lift, prisoner of war and refugee camp relief, England airstrips, and maybe English women by the time he was eight—a good start for a young, small town neighborhood lad, whose worldly visions could grow exponentially from a mere weekend.

Wars, cars, the Dodgers and Giants moving west, finance, real estate, a new family in town, and community growth and expansion shared the atmosphere with whatever the ten-inch black-and-white had to contribute in conversational pauses meant to be segues to other points that needed knocking around or further abstract analysis. The men relaxed, felt the safety and security of moments of trusted camaraderie within such a man-cave day, and then possibly the next day. The pains and the victories of their military service achievements accomplished, avoided, or survived by pure circumstance would be somewhat released for the moment but never gone. Apparently, the drowning of sentimental war incidents would beget more drowning.

The holidays were full of these impromptu war summits as the '50s winter weather socked 'em all in to be practically forced to the man-cave basement bars all day Saturday and practically every Sunday, if the men were in town. Any event or occasion seemed a good enough stimulus to circle the coolers and rattle the glasses. New Year's Eve and New Year's Day were marathons of discussions, drinking, and black-and-white football bowl game watching with minor gambling pools, with parades of inventive snack tray displays. The right basement bar was a magnet to these relatively new veterans, never losing the need to share this new or that old veteran thought, in a brave new world they were building and looked forward to living in, with a certain amount of ongoing peace and unlimited prosperity. Soon enough, the eight-year-old could sit as a cockpit copilot, call the drop of a bomb, walk through burnt villages of France, and ride home alive on an Atlantic troop transport through processing and home on a train to Wilson Street, finally unarmed.

In 1955, on the north end of this (and many other) small ordinary towns, anchored on the East by the town's landmark grade school built 1898, and anchored on the West by Dyson's pasture, was "Wilson Street." Wilson Street was eight-tenths of a mile long, half a click, east to west. An eight-minute energetic bike ride to the north was the Forest Preserve Park with the town's one little league baseball diamond. Six hundred and fifty paces on foot south from Wilson Street was the town square with a county seat, a drug store ice cream bar, and a Western Auto store. In the middle of this Wilson Street east to west was a main intersection with a north to south State Street and further west, just two skinny blocks, the rural highway made a statement of the town being some way connected to a bigger world. Two more blocks west was the railroad that noisily fussed up the neighborhood several times a day with displays of big things built somewhere else, being shipped for some great purpose, to build some great new contemporary monument, to some great new invented progress. State Street was an unofficial strategic north of the square runway point, although no one could really determine why. Maybe simply because it crossed Wilson Street, or perhaps it was because that was where the bigger/older houses were, probably both.

For years when the boys of East Wilson Street would meet and join up with the boys from West Wilson Street—the larger gang would form at the State Street intersection. West from State Street, just one long block past the tracks was Dyson's farm house. Boys in the '50s, unencumbered by video games, TV, and the wussificaiton of America, could turn a Wilson Street into a major magic gateway of growing up, sharing, exploring, challenging, sports, and parental harassment. For years, Dyson's pasture, behind the house and barn, was as close as the boys would get to the original Busch Stadium of the Cardinals, just a hundred and a half clicks down the road in a big city called St. Louis. In fact, for the times, Dyson's pasture was Busch Stadium! Sure, it had a few oak trees out there in fair territory, shrub lines, and wet spots, and included a turf of bumps, holes, and hundreds of nut carcasses the squirrels had bopped open and left in the field of play, but it was still a ball park for the imaginative, the competitive, and those tough enough to be accepted. The make-believe ball park was an early lesson in life's "true bounces."

In the '50s, for the taking by the inventive boys, a street could have a personality, an attitude, and become a worldly part of a life, usually on a bicycle. Just by being there, Wilson Street would become a first home field-advantage feeling. A biker gang was about eight to twelve in age, sporting no fenders or chain guards, often with one kid peddling and one kid on the handle bars, with most all of the bikes needing repairs from the last reckless chasing/tagging collision. In the '50s, the boys on bikes on Wilson Street defined the original youthful "fast and furious" for the town's fresh era of producing a new post-war generation that would not travel Europe with an M14 at arms rest and then at the ready and would not have to scramble for bunker cover at the scream of overhead "incoming" artillery or aerial bombardment.

In the summer, Wilson Street bubbled with little oil bumps from the sun's corn producing heat to produce thousands of small pops as the biker boys sped east and west, always in a hurry, going to, or coming from the adventurous competition of the hot day. Leaving Dyson's pasture at the last moment to beat the town's whistle home which erupted at precisely 5:00 p.m. was a daily uncertain moment, pressure unneeded. The whistle's main job was telling on anyone who was late beyond mom's clear orders to be home at five o'clock. Later the boys would individually petition parents to be home at 5:10, the five o'clock whistle being the starting gun that would set them off on their way in a race to be legally homeward bound. The petition worked for some, not so accepted for others in an era of tight discipline. Wilson Street was hot in the summer, every year. Chip and rock stuck to everything and flew off speedy bike tires in every direction. In August, when new rock was gracefully tail-gated from a lumbering city dumper for a new surface to be compacted by passing traffic, the traffic would throw the new rock in every direction before the surface compacted enough to be a sufficient bike track again. In August, the boys had to watch out for the flying rock from cars and their own bike tires. August kind of sucked, flying rock, hot, school only a few weeks away, which would be back in the confining indoors. In August, the boys had to adapt, put up with the town's inconvenient constructive side, and speculate gloomily over who would be there next home class teacher to be tortured. Hopefully not Mrs. Bruhn, with her infamous two-foot long, four-finger wide discipline paddle she seemed to love applying to the boy's backside.

In the winter, in the '50s, everyone lost sight of Wilson Street about December 10, maybe before, maybe a little after. By then, snow and ice accumulation had no intention of a meltdown, layering itself as if challenging any perceived warmness to whip its cold assets. In the upper Midwest, you said good-bye to the actual surface of Wilson Street and the earth in general in late December and longed for its return some time after news of the boys in Florida starting spring training. The street was gone, but not forgotten. The boys of the street retreated to a more confined indoors to grow in height and stature for the next year's challenges, which would be an expansion of their core Wilson Street dominance. For the parents, each coming year would be certain to include a little longer, deeper discussion of what America and broader issues would be about when the boy's time came. Always, with an eye and ear to whatever the next war would be about, where, why, as there seemed to always be one brewing up or melting down.

Wilson Streets of the '50s had no concrete gray rounded curbs paralleling the racing surface. The street had recessed ditches. Curbs aren't any fun. Curbs, like classrooms, confine. But in the fall, you can do all kinds of "boy's gang" innovative activities in ditches. When it rains a bunch, the ditches collect massive worm gatherings, handfuls of worms rise and gather in gooey clumps in the ditch puddles for the snatching. How many ways can a bike gang of eight- to nine-year-olds, get in trouble with hands full of worms to work with? And it wasn't just the worms from ditches that could be tossed or clumped. Worms attract birds, and birds attract BB guns. Ditches are also challenging for bikers to crash through, become airborne on the backside, dry or flooded (even more fun when flooded), and proceed without a wobble or wheel rim bending crash.

Seasonally, Wilson Street ditches were the best in the fall. In certain places east and west on Wilson Street, the ditches were deeper than other places. That means they held more fall leafs from the many large trees, which, of course, to a biker gang, means there would be places to hide, to be buried in the leafs, to spring out at any unsuspecting post-dusk neighborhood passerby, child or adult. Around Halloween, the ditches of Wilson Street were as deceptive as the caves of Okinawa. With an east to west biker gang, all dedicated to their ditch tricks in the fall, the entire Wilson Street could be a nightmare for trick-or-treaters, especially young ladies dressed as dancers or fairies or anything clean and pleasant looking begging for a scare and roughing up. Wilson Street ditches were there to be used, there for a reason. Jumping props or hiding, it all strategically worked to the favor and fun of a roaming platoon looking for or coming from the next or last skirmish.

There was not a season when Wilson Street did not have an underworld characteristic to the boys. Looking back, the town thought Wilson Street was a road of transportation for its citizens to ride dutifully to and from their routine errands and chores, here to there on various household or work missions, on a schedule and checklist of a day's progress. No such thing. Wilson Street was the road through Europe or the Burmese Trail or the transport from Okinawa to occupy Japan, Guam one day, Europe's "Bridge Too Far" the next. Wilson Street was the path across North Africa, the landings in Italy, and a training course to someday conquer the bluffs at Omaha Beach. Wilson Street was the track to raising the next generation, the connection of about anything connected to anything else, blending east end youth and families with those on the west end. Every family on Wilson Street knew every boy on every bike, sort of an unofficial underground of parental watchfulness and youth inventiveness. Veteran dads told stories the boys shared at the black top, translating as best they could the danger and heroism and returning faith. From bikes to baseballs, in the energy of trickery and exploration, the boys would grow and mature at various paces of maturing. Who would have known, just a bit later in the growing up, that it would only take the boys one-half of a fast moving decade to turn into uniformed United States soldiers themselves, dispatched in groups of thousands anywhere on the globe that America could rev up a new militarized interest, then commitment.

Wilson Street looked ordinary on the average summer morning to the average adult passerby, and it probably was ordinary until about 9:00 a.m. when the Boys of Wilson Street had finished home duties and area chores and set out for their day's rampaging, barn-storming work of growing up fearless and aggressive. In the summer, by midmorning, all or most of the more innocent women and children were off the street, occupied in their places of summer living. When the boys started, the street became more frantic. Speed mattered, especially in the mornings, when the small town day's activities always turned from anxious temptation, to then fall together as a worthy plan without much detail. Not much of a plan was ever really needed. Either a good idea spontaneously was reacted to in mass movement or the bikes went west to Dyson's pasture for another baseball pickup game.

As the mid-'50s years raced into the late-'50s years, adults could put the WWII-dominated thinking more on the back burner and concentrate more on building careers, holding on to stressed marriages, and attempt to participate in the excitement of growing American greatness. Being amongst American greatness of the times could be done in many ways and was. The parents of Wilson Street did what they could as workers and planners, union construction, fabricators, store owners, painting decorators, and gentlemen farmers. Or some as single moms, war widows, with their perpetual forced smiles and thankless straining broken hearts, never seen or suspected in nation-building business, quietly maintained their homes. Wilson Street was always an All-American picture of Midwest prosperity and stability on the outside in the daytime.

In the late '50s and for the next seven to eight years, the boys of Wilson Street spent all of their time together, with the complete approval of the parents of Wilson Street, apparently quasi-satisfied with just "the rid of them." None of the boys would recall much of a plea to stay at home as they launched out the door to their street adventures of the season and moment. The boys eventually realized and began to feel the shared foundation of their expanding lives together and thus endless journeys together, destined to create a bond that would deepen and potentially never disintegrate. Blood brothers of a sort that needed no further defining seemed the aggregate mutual feeling. The boys came to recognize that they not only all knew and "ran" with each other, but additionally realized that each boy was always totally welcomed in the homes and hearts of all the parents of the other boys. Eight boys and one home was a family's bigger family at a given moment until the boys were at another home, in which they were all made to feel totally welcome again. It was a trait of the times. Rarely did the parents of one family talk much to, visit much with, or make much of an effort beyond coordinating or policing the boys to know much better any of the other parents of other boys. It was just the boys who circulated. Parents were kind of parent-islands, fixed in their own post-war addresses, work demands, late-'50s priorities, inner thoughts, and outer community or career challenges. The parents always remained somewhat island-like for the boys and Wilson Street in the late '50s and stayed that way forever, even in times of more critical social challenges and national upheaval developing in the early '60s. What group of witted, young, up-and-comers could not make that puppy hunt for their adventuring advantage ("Hey, Mom, we'll be at Dyson's pasture!"), knowing full well that that promise would never be verified, afore, during, or later.

This type of unplanned circumstantial reality did two things. First, it drove the boys to feel like they had created a second family within themselves. After all, who does a boy become closer to? Mom, who lays out the milk, toast, and cereal in the morning? Or the embattled bike-jockey buddy who trusts timing and skills around second base to complete a double play, execute a hit-and-run, and defeat an opponent of a day? Or buddies who help challenge competitors at the school's blacktop in a deadly, swirling, frantic bike-game of hock-my-jock? In reality, laying out cereal, dusting, laundering bedding, and teaching the kid to restock the bar do very little in youthful bonding compared to bike racing, pasture baseball, rock throwing, or walking the riverbanks and bottoms to strategize the capturing of a frog or trapping of a muskrat. While the typical parents secured their place in the family service economy, the boys built bonds, skills, muscles, dependence on one another, and perfected the senses of risk-taking, conquering the crossing of an uncrossable high creek from recent rains to explore the other side, and then crossing back later in the day when the creek may have swelled even further.

The perpetual lack of accountability with parents drove the reality that no parents really knew what the boys were up to on any certain summer day, later to become year-round. When the boys of Wilson Street were not stuck to the strict rules of school attending, they could be anywhere, doing anything in a rain-swelled ditch, dry sand creek bed, or construction site brickyard. In a town of 1,400-ish population, six to fourteen boys on bikes could be from one end of the town to the other in a pancake flipping moment. Nothing was certain, secure, safe! With parent's concentrations of rebuilding a post-war America and stabilizing homes, the boys had sufficient free-reign hours to do their own creative extrasensory kid building.

Boys on the north end of town, just off Wilson Street hit the morning bike traffic east and west like new troops joining a marching platoon. Willis came from two blocks south on the east side, and Heacock from the same two blocks south and a little west of Willis. Bensyl and Helton had a conclave part of town of their own, just two blocks north of Wilson further over on the west side just east of the tracks. All boys, all the same age, processed through their youth all in the same school, in the same class (to a teachers regret), through the same creeks, parks, or pasture scrambles, all intent in their muscular inventiveness of bike ganging to the next Olympic-like event of the small town summer day. On this town's picture post-card perfect north end, the boys living on Wilson Street (sometimes two at a time per family) and the boys just off Wilson Street numbered in the teens at any one ganging moment. Even on the days where a troop or two had yard work or a dreaded dentist appointment or trapped at home on a tricky discipline issue, the gang was a worthy concern for the area's orderly part of the population.

Geographic fixtures along Wilson Street were an influence in daily adventure planning and implementation. The town's grade school, Lincoln School built 1898, was a squared brick mountain-like monument on the mideast side of Wilson Street. The grounds were perfect biking race track with crisscrossing sidewalks and blacktop walkways. The schoolyard was the perfect meeting place, open, blacktop with basketball hoops, swings, grounds for mischievous skill testing of all acrobatic types. The boys of Wilson Street rarely fought one another, but on occasion, certain scores were to be settled from a nasty bike wreck or an errant thrown rock one way or another, and that settling was always at the schoolyard. Other schoolyard settlements were more common when unsuspecting boys from other parts of town or from out of town had the unfortunate luck of "hanging" at the school yard at a bad time. Lincoln School was a maze of concrete walks, blacktop playground equipment, all blocked in sections—a perfect biking race track for warm summer evenings. Many a dexterity skill was learned in the speed and flashes of bike tag or a boys of Wilson Street invention that was called hock-my-jock, a rough riding, crashing game of perpetual bike chicken: kind of a soccer/hockey on street bikes kicking any sort of ball through double basketball supports like hockey goals without a net, at each end of the blacktop.

Another boy from off Wilson Street was a main character and person of great influence to the core gang. His name was Schroth, indicating his German heritage of which he regularly signified upon arrival with a pointed raised right arm, fingers extended together and his welcoming "Heil." Schroth was a physical specimen from birth. Dark eyes and hair, broad shoulders, calf muscles like medicine balls, and the attitude to go with it all, Schroth, at that time and through the years, was the best athlete in the world . . . on the whole planet. If the boys raced, Schroth was among the winners. Schroth ice skated, shot skeet, weightlifted, motorcycle raced, played billiards, pounded opponents on any pickup football game, shot baskets, played first base, and pounded the hell out of anyone who violated his perpetually at-the-ready nature. Later, Schroth would be the offensive center and defensive middle linebacker on the HS football team, then was one of America's first Army Green Beret advancing in the Central Highlands of the Domestic Nam.

Schroth possessed one other world-class unique usefulness to the boys on Wilson Street. Three point eight blacktop miles southwest from town, straddling the region's lazy, muddy, timbered, game infested Sangamon River, Schroth's family was the official employed caretakers and administrators of a six-thousand-plus-acre Allerton Park, complete with hundreds of acres of never cut forests, rolling hills, winding creeks, attack trails, all cut down the middle by the Sangamon River. The park was whatever a youthful bike gang needed it to be on a particular day of rampaging: Civil War battles, Indian warfare, or wars yet to be fought on unidentified fields. If you rode with Schroth, you road the park fast and fearlessly! The miles and miles of virgin timbered forest with hidden trails among thick foliage and waterways had never been disturbed by civilized development progress of any kind or by farming. Virgin timber, it was called. Other parts of the park included numerous ponds or watersheds from flooding, cabins for the States 4-H'ers, occupied all summer long with a different group each week. Allerton Park was a protected wildlife refuge of Central Illinois, with a central park area of world class gardens, walls dividing famous statuary brought from Europe, a true million square foot European-style "mansion" in the glorious middle of it all. Schroth and his Wilson Street buddies had a paradise at their fingertips, and the best thing about it was this: Schroth's caretaker parents were always eager to open the gates to the Wilson Street Boys.

A cold Saturday in early December? Come iceskate on the mansion's frontyard pond.

Fall? Strap on a .22-caliber pistol and flank both sides of the river to bang bunnies or pick off a riverside duck, all among the thick foliage beauty of an upper Midwest changing of the seasons and magnificent forestry colors.

Dead of winter? Sneak through the eloquence of the mansion rooms where the public often was allowed and find the back steps to the attic, where the boys had built an indoor basketball court.

Spring? Observe the foliage wake-up of a new season. Meet at dusk at the gate house, tape your pant leg jeans as tight as possible, grab a club, and tromp through the woods a quarter mile north to the park's dump, where as darkness fell, the rats began to invade and meet the clubs of rat grim reapers for a boy's killing field of scampering rat varmints.

Ohhhh, the good times were endless to think up, strategize, execute.

Summers, outside at Allerton Park, were of course the best, most rewarding devilishness of undertakings for Schroth and the Wilson Street angels loose about the park. In the summer, the boys could plan multi-level attack plans of all inventive sorts. The two dozen park cabins weekly and all summer housed visiting 4-H'ers from all over the Midwest, a week at a time for all types of youth development of goodness and 4-H honorable activities. Every Monday, a new group would arrive, eight to fourteen years old, with volunteer adult supervision among them. Late each week, the 150 or so new campers would routinely venture from the familiar safe cabin camp ground areas to an open hillside for campfire songs, readings, brotherly 4-H love-in stuff, and general camping-outdoor safe and well planned companionship, sharing all sorts of wonderful youth and guidance counselor fellowship. The Thursday evening special event was perhaps a 4-H camper's most rewarding time of the week to look forward to. Thursday evening's outdoor camp fire experience away from home, and away from the now familiar cabins, providing an exclamation to the week's memories to take home. The Thursday evening camping experience complete with bonfire was more or less their finale of the week's 4-H living and learning. By the late '50s and early '60s, the Wilson Street Boys and Schroth knew every inch of the park terrain, day or night. Stealth, silent movement among the gardens, within the walls and statuary, or around the rat dump had been perfected. And thus, new, adventurous, fun things to do with these new skills were always being considered, invented, and put into planning. Not much the boys wouldn't think up, and of course, there were no boundaries to the implementation.

To this day and forever, no one was ever sure who actually hatched the idea, and no one ever stepped forward for the credit (nor could they; it was too devilish). As happy, pleasant 4-H youngsters went through their week of outdoor park and cabin-living, carefree camping experience, the Wilson Street Boys would begin to infiltrate, visit the camping outskirts and the mess hall areas, greeting the campers and making them feel welcome and at home in their week of camp away from home. The pleasantness extended was kind of like being friendly unofficial park ambassadors from the general community to each week's new arrivals.

About Tuesday in each 4-H-ing week at the Allerton Park and 4-H campground, a few Wilson Street Boys would lend a happy woodland tip or two to the campers, including a slight warning about the park's hunchback, who reportedly had lived in the woods for years since arriving in the area from someplace way south. Guarantees were made that the hunchback was harmless and had not been even seen for several years, but nonetheless as just a courtesy of the park's camping area unofficial ambassadors, the boys wanted the estranged campers to be slightly "aware" of the tale of the Hunchback.

> *No big deal, probably nothing, just a courtesy heads-up. But he's probably out there somewhere! See ya. Have a good week. Have a great campout and fire Thursday evening on the open knoll northwest of the cabins, next to the thick, dark timber, where the hunchback was last seen a few years ago.*

Having laid the pipe, Schroth and the Wilson Street Boys harmlessly disappeared back into their woods or the mansion attic or the river's trails and waited for the Thursday evening 4-H camping/bonfire/Yippy ya-who—weekly finale of camper's events.

Each week would generate a new kind of hunchback story telling fun, if the hoax was properly managed.

The fun of Thursday evening's focus of the week's highlight campfire always arrived soon enough. The entire hoax process needn't be hurried as the suspense building of a couple days of hunchback stories was part of the scare building and perfecting. Early in each darkening of a Thursday evening, Schroth and the boys would proceed to assigned points of attack at the edges of the forest line and begin to stuff pillows in the back shirt of whoever would be the night's hunchback, an appointment of great honor. The hunchback would be positioned at the edge of the woods, a little west of the 4-H-ers evening open sight of campfire festivity. As the campfire caught stronger flames, rising in a quiet still summer night, the flickering, darting firelight reaching higher and higher, the whole evening atmosphere became 4-H surreal, a perfect evening, in a perfect week, relaxed.

The boys began to move in, placing themselves in a scattered perimeter along the tree lines and low in the tall grass along the north knoll, to watch the frantic reactions and screams of the unsuspecting 4-H-ers as their hunchback would move out toward the innocents in scary Hunchback moving fashion.

As fire flames and evening 4-H songs of goodness and blessing of America, led with the leadership of camping counselors and chaperones, rose from the unsuspecting 4-H'er hearts and innocent lips, the hunchback would be poised, then begin a low monotone screeching of a woodland monster trapped in death's struggle, just yards off the campsite, inside the dark edge of the timberline. Some of the Wilson Street Boys later confessed it even scared them, and they knew it was just one of their own pranks. Half bent over, one arm dangling outward as if mangled in a bear fight, dragging a right leg that followed the heavy clomping of the lead left foot, their hunchback began to slowly appear from the edge of the woods. A scene of flickering uncertainty, glimpses of "monstering" with stroboscope blinking flames on a pitch black background.

> *Clomp, low grumbling, gurgling screech, scan the area with hungry cruel eyes, drag a back leg toward the fire. Clomp! Drag! Boy's gang quietly, cautiously, excitedly poised on the sloping hillsides for the fun terrorizing about to be on display.*
>
> *Clomp! Drag! Gravely toned, night-groaning bellows of crazed, terrifying, hunchbacking sounds, coming first from the dark timber's edge, then more open, toward the fire and the victims.*

The innocent revelry of the campsite regularly occupied all of the attention and senses of the 4-H'ers, early in the hunchback's clomping/dragging/screeching task. Then, the fun: slowly, in small group's whispers, campers would begin to murmur amidst one another that something didn't seem right.

"What's that sound?"

"You hear something?"

It was never predictable how long it would take for a camper community to actually see the boys' hunchback of the night and then sound a frantic warning to all the otherwise preoccupied less attentive campers, camp chaperones, and heavens above or beyond. When the warnings of imminent hunchback danger finally sounded loud and clear, the hounds of Baskerville could not have more awakened the dead. Screaming, rampaging for cover, and saving innocent lives or help of any kind, mommies were instantly in huge demand. Chaos filled the evening's atmosphere, reverberating through the park as if whole towns or nations were under attack.

Once the campfire chaos was supreme, at a highest frantic chaotic level, it was the job of the night's hunchback to escape as best he could, hopefully unharmed. If pursued or threatened with pursuit or outright attacked, the plan was for the Wilson Street Boys to launch from their hiding places to interfere in the confusion enough that the hunchback would escape unharmed through the woods to meet later at the park's obstacle course behind the creek's dam. Each Thursday week night, the hunchback escapes became better executed and more fun, as campers ran one direction and the Wilson Street Boys, in a victorious state of another successful hunchback ambush escape, launched in another direction to their obstacle course temporary hideout and retreat gathering point. Only once in three years did the campers rise in spontaneous reaction of enough violence to attack and beat the hell out of the hunchback before the Wilson Street Boys could get to the fight and save the evening's hunchback. A small price to pay for three years of weekly camper riotous fun! Besides, Schroth himself was often the hunchback, and he couldn't be hurt by a bunch of sissy campers.

So what does an organized group of Wilson Street Boys do after exploiting the safe, spiritual, educational week of innocent 4-H campers? Often, it was too late to tape blue jean pant legs, grab clubs, and beat rats but too early to call it quits. Most often, they would hit the back trails to the hidden back basement door at their European mansion, which led into the kitchen. In the kitchen was enough ice cream to lock and load a major bowl for each boy, quickly, efficiently, and thus allow the boys timely exits back out the basement, up the pine tree trails, across the road to the cabins, and stretch innocently in the grass while terrified 4-H-ers returned from the campfire séances and experiences with lifesaving stories of spotting the hunchback they had been warned about. The camper stories of heroism veiled the night in fictitious armor. A hunchback scam executed with perfection was a thing of adolescent beauty. Never, in all those years, were the Wilson Street Boys caught or reprimanded for their malicious hunchbacking, and the tales lay dormant until now.

When you stop to think about it, the whole exercise was a character builder for everyone—valuable lessons difficult to come by—memoirs to be 4-H-er cherished. The 4-H'ers likely told and retold the story of the night they escaped the infamous hunchback. The whole hunchback chaos invention was about as much fun as a bunch of Wilson Street Boys could come up with on a given Thursday summer evening.

By the ages of thirteen-ish, the Wilson Street Boys were nocturnal, woods-savvy, monolithic hometown versions of Special Ops professionals skilled in setting up an attack (or prank) or penetration of any target's perimeter. Confident, stealth, unified, self-proclaimed indestructible, and sometimes a little mean, what didn't test the boys, the boys would test eventually. The DNA had been set, limitations analyzed and largely overcome, and obstacles conquered. Soon, 4-H-ers were too easy prey, the fun had gone from teasing children and naive chaperones. Beating rats at the dump was always fun, but even that got boring as rats needing beating became scarce. With Schroth as an indestructible anchor, park exploring, terrain busting, and general terrorizing went on for years. Normal park visitors always seemed startled when family hiking adventures would pass a group of eight to ten boys all armed with side arms, .22 rifles, bayonets, machetes, and general military-style survival gear.

The boys didn't even mind the visitors to their park as they missioned on conniving the next counter insurgency or special ops plan. If the day was slow in town, the boys could always go to the park and gig frogs, shoot skeet, or take potshots at river log jams where the numerous rattlesnakes blended into the log jammed branches and sunned for that summer day.

The boys (or their parents) never really knew it or felt it at the time, but the park was one long never-ending boot camp. The park was infantry training, stealth movement with starter-kit gear for killing or defending. Certainly, the group itself was a preplatoon potential fighting unit. To launch from the back door of the Schroth's "House in the Woods" into the dense timberland and surrounding elements at daybreak, maneuver to follow creekbeds and hilly terrain usually into the late afternoon, was rarified light infantry youth training experiences that would eventually be quite valuable.

Allerton Park adventures aside, Wilson Street was normal stability to the parents and citizens, but rank-and-file adventure to the boys scattered up and down the street. On the far east end of Wilson was the Parsons family. Mr. Parsons was a house painter, and Mrs. Parsons worked in the grade school cafeteria two short blocks west from their small foundationless home on Wilson Street. The oldest Parsons son was a Wilson Street Boy. The Parsons family was known within the boy's gang as a greatest of places where everyone was always welcome, any time, any way, as long as needed. This very modest one-story home had one major signature phenomena. As the boys piled in on a normal winter weekend, the house was always full of cooking game: rabbit, pheasant, quail, squirrel, whatever was shot and cleaned from the generous Illinois prairie countryside, maybe even a turtle or two boiling in a large steel kettle off to the side. At the centerpiece was always Stag beer in a most prolific flow to the adults surrounding the kitchen table. In the boys' minds, the Parsons' home had to be the Stag beer center of the universe. Stag! There was no "Stag" at any other house. There was a deep meaningful lesson in the presence and flow of the Stag, but no one young at the time knew what the lesson was at the time. The silver-legged kitchen table hard metal top was always full of dedicated Staggers. The boys would filter in, fill the small kitchen perimeter as an obedient audience as the Staggers carried on with their stories of America and their own adventures and challenges about the town, and what the big war had done or not done in a thousand different Stag-supported ways. The boys grew, older, bigger, but the Staggers held tight to their proud kitchen positions.

The Parsons' Wilson Street Boy was a trusted regular in the group and would eventually trade-in his youthful bike, fishing pole, shotgun, and townie notions for the US Army and would be one of the first Wilson Street Boys to enter the Domestic Nam tour of duty process. Ron was the oldest son of the Parsons, with a faithful dog named Freckles. In those great days, when a boy left home on his bike, Freckles was alongside. In the Wilson Street days, Ron's nickname was "Goose," nick-named after Goose Tatum of Harlem Globe Trotter fame. Ron was good on a bike but best with his shotgun or rifle on the trails at Allerton and the creeks and tree lines outside the city's limits where pheasants, rabbits, and quail waited to be flushed from hiding.

Two blocks west from the Parsons house, literally in the backyard of the north end grade school, was the Jordan house. So close to the school were the two Jordans (single mother and son) you could spot the empty fifth-grade seat in the second floor of the school, look out the back school windows, and see the Jordan boy on his back porch shooting the infamous fingered-bird to the teacher he was hookying from. Some days, Jordan went to grade school; some days, he sat on his back porch. It was that simple, and it only changed when Jordan turned sixteen, at which time he never attended the community schools again. But for the time being, in the late '50s into the early '60s, Jordan was a Wilson Street Boy.

Jordan was a huge boy and had huge arms, huge head, huge chest, huge chub-o, huge, huge, huge. But there was no one more agile. Mrs. Jordan's equally huge green Packard often chauffeured the boys to the Friday night movies downtown, and although the rest of the boys would just as soon gang up and walk home after the Friday night movie, the Jordan boy preferred to have his mom, Rosey, pick the boys up in the giant Packard so he could smoke a cigarette in the car on the ride home. Mrs. Jordan was a single parent, working, probably frustrated as hell, but would never let on and always open to the boys of Wilson Street. The north grade schoolyard was a butt-flip from their back porch, so the boys were often there, at the Jordan house, even when they weren't there, the house by proximity to the school was just in the loop. Jordan was always ten going on twenty or twelve going on twenty-four and bigger. At sixteen, he could shoot pool for dollars with the big boys at the downtown pool hall with a cigarette dangling, as did the true grownups. To be sixteen and not have the rising fag smoke irritate his young eyes hovering over a next pool shot was a talent way ahead of his years. In younger years, Jordan was with the Wilson Street Boys but not usually in the speed games unless it was backyard football at the school yard so he could mash people who were stupid enough to try to tackle him. As a youth, could have easily carried three hundred pounds on his fourteen-year-old tanker frame, unheard of size for a young teenager in those years. He always tried to work out and lose weight when he was in jail later in his teens, and he did lose weight, eventually until he was about 240 lbs. of pissed-off muscle on a 6'3" block muscle-battering-ram-cement structure with arms, legs, and medicine ball of a head. Jordan leaped into the army just in time, escaping numerous area police raps and with great fighting reputation in the southern Delta IV Corps survived the Domestic Nam. Some suspected he just ate the bullets shot his way, spat mortars, and squeezed to death any stupid Gook that might be in the wrong place at the wrong time. On the backside of a Nam tour, before an honorable discharge, Jordan was a street fighter at and around a German Army base, taking on all comers as his scarred face would later attest. If you were gonna go to war, go with Jordan. A big target with a deep, natural, buddy-system heart from Wilson Street, raised closest to the north end school that straddled Wilson Street, of which he would have no interest in attending. Nor would the school and town give much of an effort to attend to Jordan.

Between Parsons on the east end and Jordan, at the same age and of the same north/south street off Wilson, was Willis. Mr. Willis built cable at the local cable manufacturing plant. He worked at the same plant, a stable employment host for the community, his entire life. The son was regularly on Wilson Street and attained the same taste and adventurous flavor as the rest of the boys to the chagrin of his quiet conservative father. Young Willis joined the Marine Corps and also tasted Domestic Nam grit, although hardly trench-bound. In all roaming boy gangs, someone must be the base, the body for right field, the guy that holds the sign that says they went that-a-way, the grunt of perpetual dependable rank. Good guys come in all shapes, latitudes, intensities, forms of service. Willis was simply his own style but always loyal to any cause.

A block west of Willis, still a block south of Wilson, Heacock was a Wilson Street coheart for the youthful years, then not quite as much in early teen years as the family wisely moved a half mile out of town, to the near west, just off the always enticing Sangamon River country. Heacock was a genius, and no college had a curriculum that Heacock could not complete at a glance, literally one of the top academic achievers in the entire United States. He would figure anything out and was a great classroom help to the generally challenged, dunce population of a few other Wilson Street Boys. Later, Heacock did Nam in the navy, off-shore brain trusting radar work for the night pilots and copter crews. Others in the Nam always hoped Heacock was loading copper mail with warheads in a ship's long range cannon to support some hillside ops chaos that lifelong buddies from the street were dug into for the fight of the moment. Heacock rode Wilson Street with the fastest of them, never backed off a fight that needed fighting, and was always a loyal friend. Another buddy-system heart to go to war with.

In the second block, going west from the Jordan house and the north end school, literally in the middle of the Wilson Street small town '50s and '60s maturing of America was the Fox house, unique in every aspect, with three sons on the upbringing. The patriarch of the Fox house was not the father, but Grandpa Fox who actually lived about nine blocks straight south and a couple clicks back east. Grandpa Fox was the only real Grandpa that was present and in the mix with the growing ups of the Boys on Wilson Street. Retired by the late '50s and into the '60s, Grandpa Fox was an iconic figure, large in stature and presence, uncompromising in his immigrant ways and core values. Grandpa Fox was a German immigrant from his age of sixteen and would live by the standards of an appreciative immigrant, standards and life's lessons acquired through America's depression years and hard work of his future Americanizing into a successful career business-building into appreciative community stature. Grandpa Fox was what they used to call a city father. Whatever was going on stopped when Grandpa Fox showed up, had to. The Boys knew the risk was too great.

The Fox household was the biggest, newest home for the Wilson Street Boys, the closest to the key State Street intersection junction just a half block west, but within the house itself, there was never a true comfort zone, even for those that lived there. The Fox house local fame came largely from the events concocted at the basement bar when WWII neighborhood veterans camped for a day's or evening's drinking and conversation, recalling or sensationalizing battles fought, or that should have been fought, with thoughts, expressions, descriptions, and discussions far beyond basement or small-town confinements. The summits would often pause on a late Saturday but not end. Sunday morning regroupings added the exclamatory conversational points and vague closure inadvertently left dangling from the night before.

Mr. Fox was never home, or almost never home, as he claimed to travel a six-state Midwest territory, selling East Coast-manufactured clothing goods to the small town haberdashers of postwar, middle-

America building. Small towns were in the retail age then, before midsize city sprawling malls with Walmarts, Targets, and other megastores that now suck up all of the expendable rural dollars. Besides the dashing white brick new ranch home, Mr. Fox drove the newest, flashiest cars that Detroit could come up with in the creative expansion age of auto industry design and engineering. A new car yearly made some sort of community statement in those days. Styles and sleek lines of new Thunderbirds or big engine Plymouths of the times made a constant driveway announcement that Mr. Fox was home, off the road, and thus, the basement bar was probably open or soon would be. Neighbors need not wait for the fall new car displays from Detroit. Just go by Foxes and see at least one of the latest and fanciest.

Here's a forgotten, rare piece of American history that was a bunch of fun in the '50s for small town folks and bike gangs. In those quieter days of American development, in the early fall, auto manufactures would release the next year's models of new design and open road, auto power. Everyone, young and older, could not wait to see the new Cadillacs, Bonnevilles, Chevy Impalas, Fords, Buicks, or big-engine Dodge models that Detroit had designed and would soon become available at dealerships across America. These new models were normally shipped by railroad, right through small towns, like a moving show room or car show, before car shows actually existed. Wilson Street Boys could bike up alongside the tracks and watch one rail car after another pass slowly through town, full of two layers of brand-new two-tone shiny Caddies or any model. The cars sparkled, glittered, looked powerful, like something to grow up for, work for. Then, the next day, rail cars of other new models from a different auto company going slowly by in the other direction would provide the next free car showroom on rail wheels, a big black powerful train engine leading the way. The transport rail carriers were open-sided creating a free car show wherever the rails went to whomever was lucky enough to be trackside.

In retrospect, the railside, slowly moving, passing car shows were truly about much more than new cars. The events were about postwar reorganizing and American brilliance and exceptional-ism, a time and promise of endless growth and opportunity. Nowhere else on the planet was there such a display of manufacturing and engineering perfection. It was a fun, natural big deal that built a national expectation of bigger deals, always begetting bigger and bigger creative, inspirational deals guaranteed for America's future.

America lost that free autumn display of design and manufacturing gracefulness later in the '60s, when others trackside, in other locations could not resist bashing the new cars in transport with trackside rocks or other convenient throwing debris. Car companies were forced to enclose the sides of the transports, so no one could see the car shows any more. Since that loss, America has lost much more than free auto shows at railside. But it was fun while it lasted, right there on Wilson Street.

Meanwhile, back at the Fox household, if Mr. Fox was home for a visit for very long, without some visiting dignitary from the town's northend veteran buddies, Mr. Fox would grab a martini and canvas the yard, flowerbeds, and general grounds for anything to poke and fuss with until a suspect would stop on Wilson Street and join him for the effortless dance of drinks and chatter. Staying home and then indoors was grueling for Mr. Fox, for one stark, constant, agonizing realistic, elastic reason: Mrs. Fox.

Mrs. Fox would expertly, clinically personalize any broad issue into a neurotic adventure, overemphasizing any negative details that escaped a natural thought process for most people. For Mrs. Fox, the perfecting of dramatic crisis-building into a personal burdensome tragic-edged saga of challenge and eventual imminent defeat was as routine as a next breadth.

By the late '50s, Mr. Fox had been home from WWII for only a little more than one decade. Three sons later, his war as a B-17 bomber pilot was still fresh in his mind and at the very top of his personal list of life's accomplishments for self, family, and love of country. Daily missions from bases in England, through Holland, Germany, then to Berlin were still alive, real, and no less deadly than just fourteen or so years ago, a platform one does not step off of into easy living small town tree-lined streets and manicured lawns, with a wife whose daily premiere frustration could be as simple as a misplaced glance.

A few actual notes and accounts as written by Lt. Robert Fox, B-17 pilot, United States Air Force, 1944, notes brought home and hidden away until just now, can lightly describe the flying war life of a bomber pilot, who, at the time, was in his earliest twenties.

Final processing and equipment completed, shipped for the boat February 26, 1944—the ship was the Queen Elizabeth, in NY Harbor, the ship sailed February 28, arrived Clive River Scotland, March 6, disembarked at Greenorlt, Scotland, caught a ten-hour train ride to join the 130th Replacement Battalion, in Central England, twelve miles from Stratford and twenty miles from Hanley. We had one night out, the beer was good.

The thirteenth of March we arrived at our new station, the Thirty-Fourth Bombers at Mandelsham,

England. This is fifteen miles north of Ipswich; we were part of the Eighteenth Bomb Squad. A week of ground school I checked out on landings, instruments, emergency procedures. The twenty-fourth, we flew six hours, testing new engines.

March 27—Flew practice missions today, tried new formation in threes tacked down in trail—tomorrow I fly my first mission as co-pilot with experienced crew.

March 28—Bombing Hanover, Germany: 6 hrs. 50 min. 8-500-lb. general purpose bombs, 4- 500-lb. Inc. Very bad weather, I was copilot. We were on instruments four hours, to 18,000 ft. before we broke out. Bombed from 25,000 ft., hit targets, the crew called the enemy flak moderate.

March 30—Hamburg, Germany: 5 hrs. 45 min. 12-500 lbs. general purpose bombs, flew at 24,000 feet. Target was oil cracking plant. Very heavy flak. Attacked by 262 (jet) German fighters, but weren't hit, some others were. Engine No. 1 went out, came home lower on three engines. Rough mission.

April 4—bombing Keil, Germany: 7 hrs. 55 min. 6-1,000 lbs. general purpose bombs, flew at 23,000 ft. First mission for my complete crew. Bombed ship warehouse, heavy cloud cover, bombed HX seemed to miss target. Flak heavy and accurate. Saw two ships of 385th Battalion have mid-air collision—no one got out.

March 8—Nuremburg, Germany, 8 hrs. 55 min. 8-500 lb. G.P. 4-500 lb. Inc., at 15,000 ft. Bombed hell out of Engel. Bombed supply depot and army barracks. No flak, no fighters. Saw lot of war damage and country severely torn up.

> *March 9—Munich, Germany, 8 hrs. 25 min.*
> *38-150 lb. G.P. at 23,500 ft. Bombed airfield seven*
> *miles north of Munich. Attacked by four jet fighters,*
> *moderate flak. Fine results on target.*

The war progressed for bomber flight Lieutenant Fox for eighteen more months, mission after mission, flak upon flak, copilots and crew members in and out of the war's bombing theater until the Berlin airlift:

> *April 20* [Lieutenant Fox's birthday]—*to*
> *Berlin, Germany—on bomb run they turned into*
> *me while my HS was low and I had to pull out and*
> *drifted across whole squad.*
> *May 25, Linz, Germany—saved 85 French*
> *civilians took to A-55 Paris.*

The war went on! Rotterdam, Holland; Utrecht, Holland; Amsterdam, Holland; and finally the Berlin airlift, surrounded by Russians intent on their own occupation.

Mr. Fox more or less flew his ass off, along with thousands of others committed to the deadly WWII cause of defeating Germany throughout Europe. Whether at twenty-five thousand feet or on the ground back home, Lieutenant Fox would never really put the events of a bomber pilot behind him. The missions and crew loyalties would prioritize his life forever, perhaps rightfully, logically so, who is to say. Returning to the small Midwest town with the clean neat Wilson Street, to a wife always on the verge of a next fuss-up of some sort, Mr. Fox opened a men's clothing store on the town square, then later gave the store up to be constantly on America's new roads, selling wholesale the very same haberdasher items he was selling retail from the store. He would later build a state-of-the-art ranch house basement man-cave in the new home, white pine paneled, white brick fire nest, seating for six at the bar, and seating for plenty more out and about the cave.

How does a WWII wife/stay-at-home mom fit into the post-WWII pilot's life and the stories of bombing airfields through deadly flak, skirting enemy fighter jets intent on helping the bombers blow apart or crash? They don't! The whole process of loved ones receiving veterans' home from war was then and forever will be an uncertain, often self-deprecating, awkward, thin process. It certainly was for the Foxes. Life soon, and for a good while, becomes a matter of "perspective," relating past objects and events to changed, conditioned lives to be lived.

The intense training for such military missions does not just happen in the solitude of a dedicated pilot's mind and body and then exit with a handful of bye-bye papers as a discharge and the experiences to be simply set aside. Bomber pilots in war zones are responsible for a plane, the lives of the crew and responsible to perform a mission that will hopefully contribute to a warring victory for country and home. The monumental responsibilities are intensely lived to become an ongoing part of a pilot's mind and body.

Upon returning home and into the small community, alcohol would not only be a saving-grace subsystem crutch for Mr. Fox; it was downright essential Friday through Sunday until the next selling trip off in Missouri or Kansas or Iowa. With significant nagging irritations from Mrs. Fox a certainty, the alcohol created a tolerable weekend wedge of "nag-intervention," the nag-fest always relieved on America's new open, top-down, highways come Mondays. The uncomfortable wedge between Mr. and Mrs. Fox would widen and deepen and was often quite harsh with each year's travels, especially when the lipsticked shirt collars tumbled from the unpacking of last weeks traveled luggage. Ouch!

Despite the parent's constant contentious airings, the three sons at the Foxes were real, and Grandpa Fox's enormously strong and present right hand enforced realism, structure, a work ethic unsurpassed, and senses of duty and with living responsibility. Grandpa Fox was an anchor, heavy, steady, unwavering in judgment, quite tutorial with three maturing grandboys, skills learned from migrating across a vast ocean at the age of sixteen to a new language into an American prerecession largely closed to new arriving immigrants, an environment that pushed him further west in search of work and his American dream and into the small Illinois town of Decatur, then to Monticello. Grandpa Fox learned the lessons of a migrant as well as a pilot learns a bomber flight pattern lesson amidst exploding flak from hungry enemy ground fire. Once stabilized, Grandpa Fox grew a pride of American nationalism second to none, an appreciative patriotic pride that included the three grandsons. Grandsons that would later in their own times serve a nation's needs and demands, beyond what he was allowed to do as a German immigrant, in a nation at war with his birthplace motherland. Serious stuff for any German immigrant of the '40s and forward.

The younger two sons were part of the Wilson Street Boys, as different as corn and soybeans, but there was an older Fox son who was largely self-imposed aristocracy. Perfect in dress, movement, grades, breathing, music, and class leadership qualities, the oldest son lived largely on his own, in and amongst the real, less-worthy lives of others of the family, street, and town, but largely aloof on a single pedestal. This oldest son was actually liked by both of the Fox parents, held in high futuristic regard, anointed to some higher post to be identified later. Political office was mentioned now and again. Somehow, these types of preferred youth never seem to have to feel the dirt, blood, and tears that the other reckless kids naturally fall into, and thus the oldest of the Fox boys never was in the military. He was too busy as class president at one of the largest universities in the United States before a post-graduate job with a major US company in a major city. Success levels that at the time slightly stretched Wilson Street boundaries of expected accomplishment.

The middle-aged Fox son was an at large, ad hoc Wilson Street groupie, but Grandpa's dead ringer for a future high-ranking military officer. Not as adept at bicycle rodeoing or blacktop hock-my-jock dare-deviling, this middle Fox son made significant adventuring contributions. Strong enough but not strongest, fast enough but never fastest, middle Fox was like a trusty stagecoach shotgun, never feeling the need to bash himself against things that wouldn't move from his bashing. Middle Fox, because of his obvious natural good judgment, was able to keep himself largely out of the trouble that others dove toward with uninhibited youthfulness and would emerge as an iconic local figure of leadership and carry the trait forward, yet today. Matching the older boy's good grades with a work ethic that was unequalled, middle Fox set high standards on Wilson Street and then continually exceeded them, all while Mr. Fox was traveling with the T-Bird top down across Kansas with a martini-mix sidekick suitcase, while looking for the next small town single and vulnerable hairdresser. All while Mrs. Fox churned over another pack of L&Ms, with a number dialing snag in morning phone calls searching for a back porch happy-hour buddy employing the "misery loves company" concept.

Grandpa Fox knew what he had in middle Fox. Forever wise from the immigration survival requirements, the recession challenges, and building a local successful manufacturing business, Grandpa Fox could single-handedly watch middle Fox on Wilson Street and, from sheer "will and force," make certain middle Fox would be his military icon or at the very least have the opportunity to be. With such a predictable future set for him, middle Fox was allowed only as a Wilson Street substitute boy. He could be there but only temporarily so as not to absorb too much of the frolicking, risky, bad reputation building side of boyish human nature nonsense. Grandpa Fox wanted no character scars to live down, as "Academy" entry and future honors were imagined.

As our nation's light-headed leaders in Washington, DC, built a deadly case for a Domestic Nam, middle Fox paced through ordinary youthful tasking and into the Naval Academy, Annapolis bound, with a foundation set by a 1920s German immigrant and by what fell his way from being among hard-charging Wilson Street Boys. Middle Fox entered the Naval Academy in the fall of 1964, in the simmer and quiet escalation of a far off, under the radar Nam. Emerging from the Academy, four leadership years later, middle Fox went to jet-fighter/aviator training as a Naval Academy graduate, Lieutenant First Class, and was later assigned as a carrier A-6 Intruder fighter pilot on the USS *Enterprise*, home-based in Coronado, California, before shipping across the Pacific to the South China Sea, off the coast of Vietnam. His warring ship was the "storied" USS *Enterprise*, retired in December of 2012 after serving for an historic fifty-one years. Lieutenant Fox's flight bombing missions over North Vietnam in the early '70s, would largely be later confirmed as bomb dropping numbers and mission counts to be fed up the line of command for various shifting reporting needs. Many, many things happened to these Wilson Street Boys in those warring years of the Domestic Nam, and middle Fox's stories are mountain high and granite in stature, having executed over three hundred combat missions from the flight deck of a moving, bouncing out-to-sea carrier existence. Lieutenant Fox later assumed additional duties as officer of the deck of the *Enterprise*, in charge of the flight deck.

Grandpa Fox knew the flying stakes of war. Mr. Fox glided through a growing America with his top always down thinning hair in the changing breezes, tini-case a convenient reach away, from state to state. Mrs. Fox became buried in useless thoughts and fictitious scenarios of her own imaginative making. The youngest Fox boy was making a mark in other devilish but endearing ways on Wilson Street, nearly always in some sort of trouble, but somehow appreciated by the neighborhood watching hawks and always observant of the Wilson Street parental underworld.

In later years, one story could define and summarize middle Fox's Enterprise Aircraft Carrier Domestic Nam, one dangerous mission after another. The story could also characterize the true feelings of hundreds of thousands of veterans returning from about any war, but especially Nam. A Naval Academy degree requires an "active" Navy service agreement for six years, for those conquering the grueling academy process in the first place. Middle Fox loved the navy, loved his nation-representing, and loved Grandpa Fox for steering his appointment through state political processes, making it all possible. In combat action, just as ground marines were ordered to present their lives on the deadly line daily for the purpose of taking or holding some nowhere, nondescript random hill, Flight Officer of the Deck Fox, just like his father before him in England, was ordered on bombing mission after bombing mission targeting nondescript North Vietnamese assets, that were shattered to smithereens on Monday night bombing raids and rebuilt by the Friday night bombing raids. That sort of a life-risking, air-balanced, win-nothing/risk-everything routine experience affects the body, the outlook, the attitude, and the vision of:

Just what and the hell are we trying to Do? How can this be a war with a plan, a goal, an end-game for America?

Middle Fox served his obligatory post-academy six years as an A-6 Intruder Navy fighter pilot with a superior reputation and record numbers of combat flight missions, never avoiding a mission order or plan. In the times of Nam, many young military men in the early stage of their service held visions of career military, especially officers of the academies. The sins and awkward confusions of Nam often knocked the "career path" intentions from thousands of veterans who by the time they had survived Nam could not bring themselves to reup. A reup would just be too close to endorsing the Nam means and methods that were so obviously awkward and counterproductive for individuals, families, a nation, and a world at large.

So middle Fox returned home, although not on Wilson Street, returned to university life for a doctor of veterinary medicine degree, kept his mouth shut, was just as associated with or aloof from the old Wilson Street Boys as ever, and thus lived his postwar life having done as asked, and more, in and for the dangerous Domestic Nam never defined cause. Keeping largely to himself about the war, its undefined politics and lack of leadership, middle Fox simmered inside while multitasking outside to start a new career, again as an overachiever, in the technical field of veterinary medicine. The emotional balance of having managed over three hundred air "combat missions" from a moving carrier in the South China Sea, with the civilian garnishing of the ho-hum '70s population to which he returned, was generally an exercise in self-restraint for these types of shelved warriors who had been asked a great deal of.

A Battle of Perspectives

The word "perspective" largely refers to our outlook on life. A perspective is our personal interpretation of actions around us. It is how we derive actionable and action-less meaning from events that have happened to us, or might happen to us. Perspective mixes up our personalities and our subconscious, with our realities and forms attitudes about what is all around us, which results in behavior.

Perspective is how two witnesses in court can see the same crime and resolve two vastly different interpretations in relation to cause, guilt, or responsibilities. Perspective is why a married couple can confront one issue and retain two different wants, needs, demands, preferences, or excuses, concerning that same issue.

Perspective is why immigrant citizens from Cuba or Iran can look skeptically at one set of US national policy issues and circumstances and feel threatened by creeping government power or public suppression and average US citizens from birth, going about their daily business and duties cannot even "suspect" the creeping.

The perspective of a national leader can, and has, created havoc on international scenes throughout modern times, and will continue to, perhaps quicker, at a more in-depth pace.

Perspective is why veterans will scream and sweat from their sleep and struggle to be let go when the old subconscious unleashes and merges with a new life. Perspective is why veterans may then function in a personal quasi-trance, trying silently to interpret one or many perspectives of a day or arising situation. Common situations or comments can mean one thing to one person and appear vastly annoying, dangerous, or just silly to the passing veteran, who was forced to mentally process situation choices or just "things in life" differently.

The wicked or sublime crossroads in human perspectives occur individually or in large or small groups. Two hundred people can look at, hear, be persuaded, or suspended by a diatribe of criticism or self-pity or woe-is-us catastrophe building while the veteran sits quietly in restraint of an attitudinal middle finger as his calculated reaction to the same diatribe that has scrambled the brains of others.

Perspectives are often frustrating for the more simple minded not tested by battle but liberating for those who think and process events with deeper thoughtful reaction flexibility. A good lesson in perspective is

invaluable for the good listeners who have a curiosity for perspective, on how to embrace perspective, or how to change a direction for the better from a sudden new surprise perspective.

For folks generally of a positive nature, with no recognizable nadir of imminent defeat, perspective is fun, mind expanding, an inner talent to be anticipated. For others, perspective is a personal ball and chain.

Perspective

Is vital in love and war and is often why one person blends deeply with another, when others around them do not see the blessings, positive influence, or talent to be worth the blending.

Following is the best story of "perspective" that I have ever heard. The story is a real, live, explainable insight to a veteran's view of living and functioning perspective!

Occasionally, inside a war veteran's reorganizing of a life and priorities, circumstances can pile together that no longer allows the shelved warriors to remain shelved.

One of those instances for Wilson Street boy middle Fox occurred in Starkville, Mississippi, on the campus of Mississippi State University, 1980, in the conference hall of the School of Veterinary Medicine and is the valuable "perspective" lesson I refer to:

After four years at the Naval Academy and six years in combat flight training and active duty from an aircraft carrier, middle Fox invested six additional years and obtained his doctor of veterinary medicine degree, from a major Big Ten University. Uncertain of post-graduate veterinary opportunity in the broader private marketplace, middle Fox accepted a temporary post-graduate teaching assignment at Mississippi State University in Starkville, a university who had just been successful in acquiring the State funding to start, build and sustain the growth of their brand-new College of Veterinarian Development. Middle Fox arrived on the new deep South campus scene, mature from war hardening, but eager to contribute and possibly (but not mandatory) actually fit in socially. America was marching into the post-Jimmy Carter economic uncertainties, and struggling with all fundamental living and building issues, not seen since the times were tough tests in '29. Fuel prices were not just sky high, fuel was often unavailable. The Domestic Nam war and the Carter years of illusionary fake profundities had created such a vibrational uncertain economic foundation, that American direction in new career building began to become more brakes applied than acceleration employed. These uncertain times were nearly America's first serious economic national bumps and barriers since post WWII and thus were intolerable for the movers and shakers, simply off-balance for ambitious newbies. Carter's presidential reign of terror was so fundamentally the opposite of American growth and prosperity that those years eventually became most noted for the managing and manipulation of a national "misery index." From a shifting national perspective, few groups, businesses, or institutions could actually foresee a clear future, rich or poor, right side up, or upside down in the Carter era. (Much like the current Obama years.)

Carter single-handedly proved America was obviously leaderless (again), not particularly broken, but certainly waiting at the door for the entry or exit of ideologies that would normally promote growth or grass root, foundational shifts of some positive or progressive outcome and would build opportunity dominoes for normal institutional public goals. In the era, individuals, companies, institutions, population, and enterprise segments in between were forced to consider largely empty, rhetorical options built on undefined political illusions and fleeting what ifs. Therefore, Mississippi State University funding leadership, via the State of Mississippi capital in Jackson, began to set in motion the options of closing or defunding institutions throughout Mississippi, including the newly established College of Veterinary Development, now including Dr. Fox.

To start that unpopular ball on an uncertain roll, the dean of the Starkville, Mississippi State School of Veterinary Medicine called an assembly of all veterinary school employees and staff into the new main auditorium—mandatory attendance. Within that largely, outwardly dejected group was now Dr. Fox—previous warrior, combat pilot, midshipmen/ Lieutenant Fox and previous to that, a Wilson Street Boy, all to his crowded lonesome second row/center aisle self.

The gathering was of the dean's doing, his reaction to the negative trickle of defunding news out of Jackson, for "his" new vet school. The ordinarily well-meaning dean certainly thought all emotions, along with his own emotion flood, would run high and thick, and any assembly consensus would be unified, hopefully to a pleading, but not begging response of reconsideration back to Jackson for his beloved new school. Audience support for the dean's pleading would be assumed that gloomy day of decrepit news and thus a safe platform for any dean to self-promote and bleed the group agony opportunity into a unified pity party. Deans of college schools get that way; they tend to believe they are in charge of more than the Xs and Os of deaning, a schedule of curriculums and department unanimity. Another mistake that deans can make is to believe that emotion alone can carry a cause, any cause, especially in the liberal world of college campus academician ass-kissing. (Much like many coaches swagger into a false mental state of thinking a team is about a coach, separate from the team.)

Although appropriate commentary is added and a bit of reading between the lines is included, reports in the state's leading newspaper suggested the exchange in the auditorium that day went somewhat like the following: an incredible human lesson in "perspective" for anyone still confused about a Veteran's inner relationship between warring, and civilian living:

The excited dean began: "Oh, beloved coworkers of the School of Veterinary Medicine, within the esteemed higher institution of learning here at Mississippi State University. Today, we have learned that the wrath guided, misdirected political imposters [perhaps a Yankee or two among them], a few short miles from this very spot in the state's capital in Jackson, largely graduates of Ole Miss, are threatening to balance their ill-sighted/ill-advised state budget on the backs of this productive, loyal group in our brand new advancing, and already accomplished School of Veterinary Medicine, led by me, and the families and friends we so fervently and auspiciously assist to guide pro-actively forward. . ."

(Seeing the woe-is-us or woe-is-me, self-pity pouring, Dr. Fox, now gliding years backward into Lieutenant Fox mode, begins to sink in his second-row, aisle-side, auditorium seat—in full view of the Dean's come-forth to me for comfort flock. At a third sentence, pour-on-the-pity breath, the dean's low glance appeared to catch in his line of weeping vision the slumping nature of middle Fox posture, now Dr. Fox, in the past Lieutenant Fox.)

The dean anguished on, "May we show collective strength [by propping me up even further in the eyes of university and state institutions] in a collective determined rebuttal to the wayward politicians who see not the decades of state reputation building so needed as Mississippi struggles with a contorted past of other types of unfairness to other single targeted helpless victims toward good standing for all . . ."

(At which time Wilson Street took over, and the past middle Fox, the now Dr. Fox, but the former Lieutenant Fox, lazily and temporarily slightly elevated his entire presence from a second row, mid-auditorium seat with world-class body language speaking volumes and a larger than life "Up Yours" yawn, then settling even lower within the auditorium's new cushy seat. No one could miss that move, as center second row became the audience focus and the dean himself gave momentum to the immovable, unemotional display, being unable or

unwilling to follow his own dread of emotional nothingness on exhibit.)

The dean moved on, clearly distracted and unsure if he had a flock violator to his self-pity adulation party or just someone from another department temporarily displaced and mocking rival funders who have dodged the budget cannon-balls for now. "We will begin immediately to form department committees within our ranks in an effort to divide and lobby State legislators, teaching the deep values and enormous potential of our new institution," the distracted dean pronounced to an audience now awaiting middle Fox's next physical screw-you.

(The struggle of dean vs. Fox-swagger was in the dean's court, but not in the dean's wheelhouse. The dean halted with a queasy breath—gained another uneasy breath of intended fortitude— and pointed with an accusing finger, right at the boy from Wilson Street, previously harmless by comparison of force and influence—which was surely one of the dean's biggest career mistakes ever. Do not awaken the war weary, the Domestic Nam heroic survivors—but the dean had no experience with this sort of background. Humans are all rank, number, and "who do you know" to his pompous, comfy-ass ways. Cut your own throat, Dean. Just get a hammer and pound your own thumbs. You'd be better off. The audience of near two hundred colleagues fully understood the standoff in process, the tense situation and delicate balance of the event and collectively rose in their seats to witness whatever would happen next—between a now sweating dean and the Wilson Street veteran. The audience had

cautiously, and within themselves, turned on the dean and sat back to enjoy the inevitable ass-kicking they could feel coming.)

Like a country boy from Wilson Street, now half Wilson Street and half lieutenant, zero institutionalized collegiate doctor, middle Fox was forced into an unfortunate retort to the pointed finger—with an anti-rhetorical groining:

"Wellllllll, Mr. Dean-O. You see, it's like this!" *("Dean-O," slang in the tense situation, was the dead give-away, no more political departmental gimmies!)*

(Wooooe Nelly—folks: spineless dean sir, had awakened aircraft carrier, night bomber, Wilson Street Vet, middle Fox—and the reporters from Jackson covering funding battles, were poised—and another big ole "Auditorium Gosh," floated up from the audience as a pretense to the now drawn thin-red-line of a stand-off, campus politics out the window for the moment. Any observer could see that all of Dr. Fox was gone, imploded, exploded, self-extra-super-ploded . . . boomed-away and bombs-away; common sense, department hierarchy didn't matter. No more Dr. Fox, meek, unnoticeable Nice Guy.)

(The audience attention went back to the dean for the next meaningless counter cheer of resurrection pleading as the dean glanced down to the second row, middle seat, then paused again, glanced down again, paused, glanced, looked for a cab—seeking a direction to his pinning-down, that was not to come forward.)

(No one in the audience knew, had a clue, could possibly guess, that their best, once-in-a-lifetime "perspective" lesson was on the brink . . . free

to the group as a whole but character and reputation expensive for the ego-draped, now queasy perspiring dean, who was never used to real face-offs from real veterans of war.)

Lieutenant Fox began in a low fierce groan, "Ya' see, Dean, it's like this" . . . meaning . . . now you've done it—you have forced me to respond—to your silly pronounced over emotions of gloom and doom that in the big-pic, amounts to squat. So as a fair-minded colleague and a boy of Wilson Street, I'm gonna take a long pause of a breath, which will be your last chance to shift your impending ass-kicking in a direction that might just allow you to save your sorry self from the most embarrassing incident of your ass-kissing career. So, hey lily pad, you got one more chance. I'll pause so you can weasel away.

But deans don't understand the trenches, even knee-deep in the mud, they generally keep wallowing, often not realizing they are even in a trench—so the dean pressed his selfish point forward, having wiggled to a defenseless position anyway.

"Well, Dr. Fox, what do you have to say for your [insubordination] self?" Then, to make it worse, the dean insisted, "Stand up, Dr. Fox, speak to our friends and colleagues. Explain your careless attitude for the future of our fine and growing school and the hardworking dedicated staff within its productive confines."

Wilson Street Fox/veteran pilot warrior Lieutenant Fox: "OK! I will! I'll try. I'll give it a Go, so to speak. It's really very simple. You see, no matter what happens [in Jackson], all of us are going to get up when this sob session ends, exit, go back to our jobs, and go home to a warm, well-furnished home, generally with friends and family, and have a safe, carefree, good dinner and clean night's sleep, perhaps with episodes of entertainment sprinkled in the festive secure American style evening. And probably do the same thing tomorrow, with the same or better pleasures, regardless of how much useless degradation, fear and career danger you profess is imminent, but which is really not imminent, and you know it."

A silenced auditorium of colleagues, braced, frozen, mouths stitched closed, if not already dropped! Auditorium mental seatbelts clicking tightly, click-click, all shoulders and minds leaning into the next pitch, middle Wilson Street Fox with Lieutenant Fox, continued, "In a learned vision of comparative reality, this fabricated, makeshift opportunity for your plea-seeking has no relevance whatsoever, compared to thousands of America's brave military on the ground in America's latest war or within a combat night flight that includes:

—Racing in an A-6 Intruder fighter jet loaded with state of the art bombing weaponry to the quick instant ending of an aircraft carrier flight deck, where the fighter plane in full throttle, drops like a weight off a table to within a few feet of a hungry ocean surface, all of which is on a ship moving at twenty-six knots against a windy, bouncing South China Sea, immediately gaining altitude for night instrumentation direction to first group with other pilots off the deck who will form to locate a refuel cargo ship also to companion the mission, and then locate an enemy target over two hundred miles somewhere in the dark and is surrounded by defensive rocketry and surface-to-air missile (SAM) installations

built to latch onto your bright shining jet stream, now responsible for enough weaponry delivery and dropping accuracy to blow the hell out of any enemy North Vietnamese strategic installation that happens to be a target-piece of the mission, and then, while barely avoiding passing rockets intent on killing the night-flying pilot, guiding a two-hundred-mile-an-hour moving explosion machine called a fighter jet in a violent drop of thousands of pounds of bomb explosive killing technology, before sharp evasive flying maneuvers to the hilly lowland countryside to escape pursuing SAM killing rockets and dense flak, and then turning back east to a dark ocean scene to hopefully find a moving aircraft carrier ocean location that is now nothing close to where it was at mission launch, more than two hours before, while watching for new enemy rocket launches to blow my ass out of the sky, and simultaneously checking location instruments and throttling down, so that if the carrier actually is located, the aircraft can make a reasonably controlled crash landing on the deck, all while running out of fuel at a suicidal rate of descendancy.

Nights work not concluded, refueling, new weapons loading, and doing it all over again before a first eastern glimmer of a new day in Warville, because some jerk-off career turd in Washington needs a bigger, better, longer aircraft night jet strike assets-destroyed report. All while the other boys from Wilson Street sweat it out on some useless dirt hillside perimeter, waiting for the next Gook sneak-up and blast their ass target practice.

"And Good Ole Dean—compared to all that, I don't see a damn thing here today to worry *about . . . and furthermore, I'll just head on over to my brick block, cutesy light green cubicle and pick up my belongings and be on my merry way (before I strangle your sorry, wimpish ass in the hallway by an impromptu happenstance meet-up that neither of us will like).*

This kind of real life dean of school/subordinate faculty staff exchange, although providing terrific bystander entertainment, can seriously quiet an auditorium gathering, otherwise intended as a constructive exchange of helpful ideas. Darn it!

You can take the boy from Wilson Street, but you can't take the Wilson Street from the boy. The Domestic Nam created all kinds of domestic character backlash of which this is a true life example. Multiply the episode ten thousand times for the many confrontations like this that were avoided but should have happened!

Perspective can be a beautiful thing!

Perhaps one glue that was binding, tying the east end of Wilson Street with the west end, was the young Fox. The Fox family lived in the middle, east to west, and thus on the rare days of limitations, or more likely restrictions from disciplines, young Fox could always hookup one direction or the other, either an innocent one and a half block school yard visit or a ball's toss to State Street. The youngest Fox was outwardly likable, quick, strong, visionary, attentive to daily street situations, and a strikingly poor student for having two older brothers constantly on every honor roll that a school system could invent.

Besides near riotous daily street gymnastics, young Fox had special traits within his own submerged true personality. Young Fox was a good listener and spent as much time as he could listening with interest to all older people, especially within the basement bar room war story seriousness but also in the jovial exchanges in other houses such as the Parsons regular Sunday Stag beer conferences. Agile, adventurous, young Fox never missed a 4-H'er night raid at Allerton. He was a friend to every kid on Wilson Street and a friend to every scrutinizing parent. "Wilson Street worldly" in an "I get around" fashion one could surmise. Young Fox was built within a special relationship with Grandpa Fox, largely because of a strong natural work ethic shared outwardly by both.

One outstanding personal young Fox characteristic drove ever increasing challenges and occupied a good deal of his attitude for consistently bigger and better competition: He was a natural baseball player. There were no parental or up-generation baseball players in the Fox family, and neither older brother would crack the bottom of a baseball lineup, ever. Nevertheless, from the very beginning, young Fox seemed to understand the game, see right through the fundamentals, and transfer those unique visions to unique play on the field, always knowing where balls were going to be.

In the bicycle-dominated years (late '50s to about '61) of boys on Wilson Street, life was always about the Little League schedule of the evenings or the pickup game at Dyson's pasture on many afternoons or the impromptu game of Indian ball at Burgess' empty lot right across the street from the Fox white brick ranch home. Mrs. Fox was generally subdued with some self-inflicted obsession and of course Mr. Fox was coasting with the top down, through town after Midwest town.

Young Fox grew to have priorities in stone:

- play baseball any time, any place;
- listen to war stories from the WW II veterans, neighborhood heroes;
- plan and execute day and nighttime military-style raids at the Schroth-managed vast ka-million-acre private country club called Allerton Park; and
- obey, learn from, and work with Grandpa Fox.

None of the above options present, on any given day, the action would be on Wilson Street, the real school for the slightly less academic oriented. Often, it seemed that young Fox was in one of two predicaments with his fleeting parental concerns. He was either in trouble for something he had done or might do or was not yet in trouble as the facts of whatever violation occurred had not or would not yet have been detailed so as to become factual enough for the fragile, disconnected home regime to act upon with ranges of discipline.

At age twelve, young Fox rode through little league play with a wildish fast ball and consistent left-handed bat. His team, including six others from Wilson Street, tortured all the other teams with youthful gamesmanship before the games and then with strong play in the games. Seasonally undefeated to the end of a league schedule, the team would then challenge an all-star team from all the other teams in the league put together and sailed through that spirited mismatch year after year, posting more *W*s and deepening reputations. At thirteen, still a Wilson Street anchor, young Fox was recruited to play second base on the local American Legion team, normally populated with players seventeen and eighteen years old, and thus, young Fox joined that team of older players with some skills but mostly guts. These were the kind of teammates wise in broader travels, cars, near full-figured babes, and post-game ceremonies on hot double-dip Sunday afternoons. What thirteen-year-old wouldn't get a little bent from this sort of youthful fast track?

Such a quantum leap through overall adolescent living can cause lots of issues. Field competition was one thing, and young Fox held his own within some major area matchups with bigger towns and far away legends in their own towns. Young Fox's core concerns began to rally beyond the bicycles and play grounds of Wilson Street.

Young Fox would jump in the back of the legion team Bonneville convertible on a Sunday morning with coplayers older than his two older brothers, sometimes with the more exotic of available area babes and disappear into baseball heaven for entire days and weekend tournaments. A thirteen-year-old, not yet into high school, can learn a lot of things riding with eighteen-year-olds already graduated from high school, especially with his father on the road in Kansas and a mother hidden in the back bedroom twenty-two hours a day with some sort of sleep or nerve disorder requiring an impressive variety of medication.

Eventually, family interaction was largely confined to the war stories at the basement bar and stocking enough liquid fortitude to keep the veteran's stories rolling and expanding. One could simplify the lessons from such an upbringing: "Kill enemies and pound opponents." Thirteen years old going on sixteen, then fourteen going on twenty-something, what a classroom! The proverbial teenage baseball hit-and-run dream life, racing to games or tournaments, moving with a class act team, stealing second, seeing around corners, recovering, moving faster against bigger better competition, work a map, and then always looking ahead to new skills, get better, stronger, faster.

Fun years like those fly, and all the boys on Wilson Street developed their own stories and their own skills together and slightly apart. No matter what direction the boys worked toward, they all had one ever-binding reality in common: a war was brewing somewhere in a place referred to as Southeast Asia, a funny-shaped strange country, called Vietnam, way, way "over there" someplace. The intersection of the Vietnam warring political conflict and the development of the Wilson Street boys seemed impractical in the early '60s. Impossible, surely not. In fact, the adult gatherings, always "on the rocks," never failed to include the hopeful mindless noncommittal speculation, usually from the women of the group but always supported by the men, that this far away, little understood fussing up of a war between Asian tribes could never affect the boys of Wilson Street. America had been to war too long in WWII and had compromised with a barely satisfactory resolution to the Korean War, largely because Chinese regulars poured over the northern border helping to push US troops south to a compromising thirty-eighth parallel, where the war had originally started. In the '60s, as is the case yet today, the Korean warring venture against the Communist Dragon is not yet fully settled. Surely, a challenged government with a worn army would not get involved again, not with our boys, not in a meaningless, faceless place called Vietnam:

Why would our US government become militarily spent in a place like Vietnam?

For what would we send boys of those days or any other days to a 110-degree mountainous jungle pit to again fight and die for a foreign cause undefined, that is a regional civil war at best?

Surely there would be some middle ground of political support for such a country and situation, rather than massive military intervention, even if a cause were the great ideology of the moment, wouldn't there?

In the small towns on the Wilson Streets, the years flipped by, as years always do. The boys grew, as boys will always do. The US government seemed to get more paranoid about foreign proactive defense of fabricated global American interests, as the US government seems to always do.

Until post-Nam, within the brilliance of the Carter presidency, America traditionally employed a mandatory armed-service draft system, where every capable male body would have to, in some fashion or another, contemplate, calculate, and plan their time in the so-called "service" of the Armed Forces. Like all gargantuan national systems, there were flaws and bottlenecks, but generally, the system worked for the purpose of national defense and for the good of the individuals. The system worked from the macrosense for a country's defense as well as for training, educating and, showing the broader worldly ways to the young men of America. In the '60s, the draft system converged with Nam, at which time Wilson Street Boys from across America would have their duties before them and then their orders. The boys were fed into the Nam formula, along with the hard assets for the fighting. The '60s were a time when all young men had to contemplate individual choices toward their maturity, immediately upon turning eighteen years of age, graduating from high school, or in some cases, instead of high school. These would be choices "owned" by the individual, forever a part of a personal background of experiences and hopefully of accomplishment. (When America shifted to an all-volunteer military system, there were many consequences within the social sector, some unintended and are most obvious today.)

However, life for young Fox and all Wilson Street friends was within a civil service obligation, and thus, decisions must be made. From Wilson Street Boys flying east and then west, buddying up for the current activity, to post high school, which in the mid-'60s was an era of balancing personal ambitions with an armed forces draft obligation reality. In the forefront was the fact of growing military commitments of some sort in Southeast Asia, Vietnam (the place no one had heard of or knew anything about), where war's potential would quickly escalate to front and center reality.

The potential of the Nam war became unavoidable as a force of or obstacle to shifting speculations of subjective national interests. All of America's youth soon had to plan their maturity phases, scrutinizing options more seriously: college, the National Guard, farming, marriage, intentional personal injury. Some options included a draft deferment; some didn't, if a deferment status was of interest to a particular individual. Rapidly, it became obvious that everybody would have to deal with something called Vietnam that our nation was tumbling gracelessly toward.

Thus, young Fox with perhaps a closest Wilson Street friend, Helton, met frequently in the summer of '66 to talk of their personal armed forces draft status or enlistment options. Everybody had those conversations, some with buddies in the same pot, some within families at their kitchen tables. It was an era of tentative individual status, of which the family and the individual were only partially in control. Wilson Street boys like Fox, the son of a B-17 WWII bomber pilot, and Helton, the son of a US Navy veteran of the infamous Pearl Harbor December 7 attacks, now young men, would sit outdoors on a rotting couch placed at a Sangamon River bend in the depths of Allerton Park that they had run hundreds of search and destroy missions in, hunted in, scared 4-Hers in. These always enterprising Wilson Street boys had managed to steal away with a couch offered up for grabs and placed the rotten outdoor club house by their familiar back woods river bend, not realizing that old torn couch, in the isolated Allerton woods, would be a decision making staging location for their turn in America's next war. The two boys came to their conclusion.

One warm backwoods day in the early summer of '66, young Fox and Helton decided they would join the Marine Corps on the buddy system and become "active duty" that coming fall. Come what may, they would set a summer's preparation pace to enter the military service and, in so doing, plunge fearlessly toward their generation's war, together, one way or another, for better or worse, answering many calls and obligations in their course of those actions. They made this decision, fully not realizing that they sat in the midst of their own wild challenging training center in the vast acres, streams, and hills of good ole Allerton Park. Schroth was already a Green Beret in Nam, Parsons was already in Nam in the Army, Jordan was in the Nam Delta, and middle Fox was already in the Naval academy leading to A-6 Intruder flight training.

From the east moving west on Wilson Street, every one of the boys was to become committed to a service obligation, smack in the face of a growing, confusing, deadly Domestic Nam war that government leaders themselves could not, would not explain, and never has been sufficiently rationalized. Back porch happy hour conversations within the adults subtly changed from Nam warring that "can't be," to Nam warring that "appears to be," to Nam warring that "is." An ordinary short street had raised and accelerated rates of youthful maturity to uncannily match the rising human needs of a fog of a war on a far off horizon and treacherous landscape, within someone else's civil war.

Young Fox and Helton, joining at ages eighteen, shipped off in mid-October '66, for USMC wartime boot camp at Marine Corps Recruiting Depot (MCRD) in downtown San Diego, a baseball throw from the San Diego International airport. Helton soon enough would plunge into the war's deepest most violent depths in northern I Corps, on firebases at Dong Ha, then Con Thien, then other bald dirt knobs just as deadly in the midst of Tet killing.

Young Fox found his Marine Corps boot camp training rhythm immediately, and thus, by day two, he was appointed squad leader, first squad, one of five in a platoon to lead the 115 other boots through the grueling wartime MCRD boot training. Marine Corps boot camp training that punished normal kids who were not from Wilson Street, or not from the nighttime park raids over hundreds of dark acres, was a challenging individual test of strength, fortitude, commitment, especially punishing for the other less prepared recruits from cities or suburbs. Wilson Street boys had been training and crashing through one terrain obstacle after another, for prime hunting positions and advantaged objectives within changing terrain their entire youthful lives. Now they could do it with someone else's gear, weapons and ammo, and a uniform insignia of globe and anchor; pretty fricking official, it was. Scared 4-Hers would now be replaced with armed Viet Cong. Campfires would soon be replaced with artillery, rocket, and mortar flashes. Sparklers would be replaced with machine gun and small arms tracer fire. This was to be the big leagues, the biggest league on the planet at that time, ready or not, a quick six years from the frantic playful bike races around Lincoln School and out to the Little League diamond for the summer's evening games.

Marine Corps boot camp itself, in a wartime environment is one long twelve-week challenge of adapting to a new, structured, potentially violent world of self-evaluation and self-testing, led by seemingly screaming maniac drill instructors who hate everything about the very skin you live in, hate your sister, and hate your lonely dog at home. Those in charge, the drill instructors, have no curiosity about such things as opinions, alternative methodologies, or a thing commonly called an excuse. Head down, shut up, and grow eyes in the back of your head kind of summarizes the talents required immediately by fresh recruits stepping on to the boot camp parade ground. Drill instructors have one goal in mind and one goal only: "Upon graduation, can you properly defend your country?" That's all they care about, and they do their boot training jobs well. Boot camp battles for the recruit are largely within one's self, handling and adapting to the schedules and physical requirements, and adapting to the absence of any personal stature while expecting an uncertain probable violent future, sometimes as near as "tomorrow." In boot camp, "*no one cared who you were*" or "*what your daddy does.*" That's one of the great things about it! Young Fox and Helton stomped their Wilson Street way through boot camp, albeit now and then with certain boys-will-be-boys extra-curricular episodes under the DI radar and thus moved on with their military service obligations. Marching in a direct collision course with Domestic Nam escalations was the order of the day for about every recruit, and every recruit and DI understood that would be the demand, very soon for some, a little later for others.

Young Fox was promoted in boot camp from private to private first class, promoted twice in NC's Camp Lejeune, both promotions for no apparent reason that he was suspicious of, and promoted again upon landing on the white sand coast line of the South China Sea, I Corps, Domestic Nam. By a twentieth birthday, young Fox was Sergeant Fox, USMC, armed, fit, testy, aggressive, competitive, disciplined, and pretty frickin' dangerous, in a small town teammate trigger-happy kind of way. Night raiding would now be his Marine Corps/US business, although mostly from the side door of a Huey, the ultimate vantage point, having been upgraded to a .50-caliber machine gun of target destroying excellence, blast the countryside, bad-ass weaponry. The recoil sound and feel of a .50-caliber rattles teeth, vibrates the air, speaks volumes below, and lends a sometimes false sense of invincibility to the user.

The year '66 rolled contentiously into '67, and by '67, the Wilson Street boys were all over Nam. In fact, Wilson Street boys were also in the Philippines, Germany, Cuba, Hawaii, and on aircraft carriers and training toward jet cockpit seats. A new younger boy Burke, just eighteen, a friend of Wilson Street had joined the Marines Corps and prepared for his boot camp and Corps journeys that would land him within the newly reformed USMC Twenty-Seventh Marine Division at a hellhole called Go Noi, just a few short clicks south of Da Nang. At home, Wilson Street itself must have seemed strangely quiet in contrast to the bike gang days of learning physical skills and mental reactions to dozens of weekly impromptu situations. Perhaps the street still is comparatively quiet, now and forever.

By '67, every Wilson Street boy, middle to east on the street, was in some sort of military uniform, going to or coming from, following orders from somewhere up a command chain.

Three good baseball throws west of the Fox house was another Wilson Street boy at the Sumner house, the second single parent family, sometimes an unofficial member, sometimes mainstream. One son, the same age as the other Wilson Streeters biked, ran, competed with the rest of the boys but was always quick to recede from the marathon actions that the main body of Wilson Streeters dove toward, perhaps from good judgment. Individuality was his own characteristic, as if on an imaginary leash that the rest of the boys did not recognize or had already broken free from. That trait was never more obvious than when his time came to face draft options, and the Sumner boy chose to serve his military obligation in the National Guard. No one belittled the National Guard choices of anyone; it was an honorable alternative, and many others across the small county would choose that direction, just not normally from Wilson Street. Choices like that usually send characteristic signals outward, have repercussions, and so it did for Sumner, a great guy, but one who never again seemed to fit deeply within the group, but there could have been other reasons for that. At the adult post-WWII basement bar gatherings, there was no serious stories of some National Guard danger in piling sandbags as a flood barrier on a local swelled river. National Guard guys did their jobs as asked, but at the time, it was just kind of an unusual option, understood, accepted, but allowed the exclusionary card to be played later if that kind of card was thought to be needed. (Those type cards quickly faded from lack of need. It could be that no one ever criticized National Guard decisions because no one of the times could reconcile the other active duty choices. That's how much of a confused Nam war hair ball it was—nothing made sense, except live through the choice of options.)

Past Sumner, moving west just two more blocks were two Wilson Street boys, unique from most others, but much alike between themselves: Helton and Bensyl. Poised on their bikes as twelve years old, leaning into the wind over handlebars with bent solid forearms, looking east for the morning arrival of the east side Wilson Streeters, Helton and Bensyl from the very beginning looked and lived like young Spartans ready to join the daily conquering. Both from great families, Mr. Bensyl being a county cop and Mrs. Bensyl being the quintessential attractive momma of that part of the street, always with her welcome mat out for the boys. Like many other moms, Mrs. Bensyl and Mrs. Helton knew the perfect kind gestures to all the kids that needed gesturing, early and often, feeling inside that someday soon enough, the bike gang days would all too soon be over. The moms knew this vivacious grinning bike gang would wear boots and jungle fatigues, carry loaded M-16s as a normal part of a body.

Bensyl joined the Marine Corp in '67 and, within a year, was at Marble Mountain, Da Nang, Domestic Nam, a few clicks east of Red Beach, and just north from Go Noi Island, a Viet Cong and NVA stronghold of waiting vast destruction potential. Another Wilson Street boy in the war's mix doing his obligated best as assigned. Just outside Da Nang, up the bay coast, at a desolate nowhere type stop called Red Beach, April '68, Bensyl wandered into a tent, which at the time was serving as a sergeant's club, complete with cold Ballantine beer, which means a rare cold beer in the heat of Nam could be served on a plywood board on top of whatever would get the whole beer-holding, elbow-leaning scene off the sandy tent bottom and appear as a crude but usable "bar." Also at Red Beach, alone at that very makeshift Red Beach bar, as Bensyl approached, was Young Fox. Two Wilson Streeters had connected, against million-to-one odds, in a war zone on the other side of the earth. A grand cold splash of a reunion it was, before Bensyl's unit, pressed to move on toward some mission that seemed a good idea at the time to some low-ranking officer answering to some high-ranking officer. The two very young marines from Wilson Street clung to a few final moments and parted, secure in their destiny to meet again under better conditions, at home with Mrs. Bensyl serving up whatever made her the happiest.

Au contraire, it isn't that simple with Wilson Street Boys. Less than an hour past the surprising coincidence of the Bensyl/young Fox Red Beach reunion, young Fox was still leaning on the trusty welcome plywood bar, staring at a brand new can of cold Ballantine. Bensyl again appeared at the tent's opening, smiled his way forward with a typical Wilson Streeter howdy and made way for Willis who he had run across on his first bar retreat. The odds of three of the Wilson Street boys now briefly sharing a Red Beach plywood bar moment were incalculable—in a war that seemed uncontrollably unpredictable, chaotic, unmanaged, in a plywood bar place on no map, just a tent plopped on another pile of Nam coastal lowland sand. There was no reason for anyone in their right mind to be there, at that spot, at that time. Perhaps that is why three Wilson Streeters found it.

Who really knows what intuitions human chemistry includes that would bring these three friends from the other side of the planet to such an impromptu reunion for a moment of support or just general goodness, always with an undertow of adventurism. A strange Asian world it was, the Nam countryside now loading rapidly with five hundred thousand more Wilson Street boys from across America, coming and going in constant foreign warring tag teams.

Can such moments be emotionally made to really mean anything or just another Nam one in a million for the storytelling later in new man-caves yet to be created by new waves of America's vets?

In a violent world of soldier strangers, constantly crisscrossing an ever shifting landscape, one can never love a neighbor from down the Street, any street, more than when it is a brief respite from life and death daytime steps, and nights of dark holes and shadow movements lit by tracers and crashes of mortars.

Bensyl survived Nam, returned home, taking some Domestic Nam with him. Twenty-five years later, he was a highly honored state police detective. His violent death from a convict's bullet while on a night stakeout and arrest assignment ended his useful life prematurely, forever taking parts of many others from Wilson Street with him. Bensyl's memorial statement lives today for the public to contemplate, just a few clicks north of Wilson Street, as the boys never forgot, and have made Bensyl's memorial a part of the home town forever, building and naming Bensyl Commercial Park in his honor, just off the passing interstate exit, at the north end of their rural town.

Practically next door to Bensyl was Helton, the "Helton," Michael Paul. Helton's father was a WWII navy veteran, a December 7, Pearl Harbor survivor, a tough nut. Everyone called Mr. Helton "the dude," and he looked like it. Men of post-WWII resettlement are not called "the dude" because of kitchen and yard skills. Helton's mother, Margaret, was a mother to all. Blessed with the patience of a nun to tirelessly assist the Wilson Street boys and her Dude, year after year, no matter what cards were dealt. There was just no one like Helton and never would be. An average student, limited athletically, Helton created the "dancing to his own drum" that others could not emulate or resist. He was never flashy, generally quiet, not out front, but always there, like a hidden sentinel that everyone trusted. Those characteristics never changed. A personification of dry humor, Helton could turn fantasy to usable reality with the most casual comment or natural movement of an understatement. The boys could literally not tell what Helton would come up with next, ever, nor would they, ever. Helton joined the Marine Corps with young Fox, and thus, his trepid war adventure began and truthfully would never end. Helton was the quiet, thoughtful, giant personality whose characteristics could not be taught, hardly even explained. People of Helton's era, time, and acquaintance felt his power and depth but would always be hard-pressed to explain the true personality and deep goodness. Perhaps he was just too above it all.

From the buddy system USMC boot camp with Young Fox, Helton's MOS was ground-pound, grunt, infantry, (in the Nam era often called "bullet bait"), and he moved in a direction straight through Camp Pendleton staging to the Domestic Nam, I Corps. Boot training, Camp Pendleton staging, and Helton flew against a passing sun, straight to the I Corps action at the time the toughest, meanest, most deadly neighborhood on the planet; his Wilson Street special angel, Janet, partially in tow, partially waiting for his return. Helton and his M-16 dug in at Dong Ha, Con Thien, Hue, dozens of hot LZs once named and now long forgotten, "grunting" it wherever the I Corps action was the hottest, and the longer he booted it in Nam, the stronger and warring smart he got. Helton's life, mid-'67 through mid-'68, was in the mud one day, in unbearable heat the next day, then monsoon rains (that wetted him internally forever) and thick dampness, more depressing heat, the blood of wounded, and leeches of Nam. Wilson Street and hometown friends of all neighborhoods missed Helton. Many prayed and waited for any word, that violently long defining war year, that started for Helton a good while before Tet. Loved ones, neighbors, and friends waited daily for any news. TV transmissions of hundreds of Americans killed or wounded in action on unknown Nam hills, in valleys, dry sniper-held creekbeds, on dead-end dry roads, and ancient villages of total insignificance then and now would trickle to skeptical public attention.

A gauge of life's friendships is who did/would/will stay with you, around you, support you, risk their lives for you, when things are tough in war. Who would you go to war with? It is the Helton's who stay with fellow soldiers, face duties unselfishly, with a second nature of righteous confidence that spreads and lifts others in the fight. Helton would prove his loyalty over and over to those privileged to be in his circles of friendship and trust. Helton's bronze and purple medals hardly suitable recognition for his sacrifices.

Back in the World, on the other side of the globe, halfway around the unbalanced rotating earth, November 1, 1967, just a click north off the west half of Wilson Street, Mr. and Mrs. Helton packaged in a single box, small gifts, including a bottle of Jack Daniels, and mailed the gift box across the Pacific to their son who was moving unpredictably with his unit someplace in I Corps. The Helton's hopes were that their package of deep love, faith, and nervous sentiment, would act as temporary relief from the warring of a day and as a signal of eventual homecoming. As the confusing, meaningless war heightened to a worldly open exhibition of frustration and misallocation of lives, with a nation's insanity on full display, soldiers soldiered, and parents clung to homebound prayers and hopes, which was all they could really do. Working its way through an uncertain mail system to a war front, the packaged love, sentiment, fortitude, and hope made it to Helton, arriving on an isolated sandy knoll to a sandbagged foxhole with a few strings of barbed wire as the only defense, less than ten very short clicks above the slow-flowing and winding Quang Tri River, I Corps, Domestic Nam personified.

That package, touched by Dude and Margaret, from their humble, small, rented home arrived exactly Christmas Eve '67 to their only son, Michael Paul. Also arriving that day, expected as a holiday Christmas greeting from the Gooks, was a peppering of enemy mortars and rockets from hidden locations across the dark flow of the mysterious, jungle-lined Quang Tri River.

In Nam, especially in I Corps, explanations and circumstances are useless to try to take to logical reason, nothing makes sense or is seemingly connected, and thus "circumstance" is a stand-alone endeavor daily, often hourly. So much makes no sense, and the senselessness becomes so swirling and overwhelming that eventually, a tour of duty can adopt an attitude of nothing matters, nothing fits, don't try to make it fit, just do it, and live through it, tomorrow will be just as senseless.

As the mortars from enemy spotters and positions unknown, exploded along the leaky Marine Corps perimeter, Marines 150 clicks off the small Quang Tri heli-strip tarmac dug in, or took new positions, orders flying, ammo passing, and the reality of a long Christmas Eve night settled into hardened bodies expecting little other than another fight or hardship, which was usually a correct assessment. Helton had been living such moments for the past seven months of his infantry/grunt I Corps existence, from one hill and hole to another, in a world where you don't wash rotting skivvies or socks—you throw them away, do without, eventually hoping to find new.

New blood, manpower, weapons ammo, additional armed marine bodies would arrive into the short airstrip that Christmas Eve at the small Quang Tri helicopter pad and camp. Choppers up from Phu Bai whirled to a landing, expelling more armed marines to scatter to tarmac or perimeter positions. The choppers would quickly depart before enemy mortars could calculate brief positions. Reinforcements would arrive to help defend the perimeter and airstrip assets that threatening night of December 24, 1967, and for a few days after (five weeks before the official start of the simultaneous explosions of Tet). In a predusk rush to reenforce Quang Tri perimeter defenses, another flying marine delivered by a Huey literally dropped into Helton's river front foxhole. It was Sergeant Fox, young Fox, another Wilson Street boy of the original Helton-Fox boot camp, buddy-plan combo.

December 24, 1967, Tet awaited (lots awaited), and suddenly to Helton and Fox, the unknown hungry Cong or NVA-Charlies just across the river seemed to offer little threat, perhaps sensing they were now outnumbered by Wilson Street boys. With a new holiday gifted bottle of Jack Daniels awaiting their unexpected reunion, both startled marines had their perfect war in the trenches, holiday surprise style, in the poised violence, mud, sand, filth, chaos, and confusion of the Domestic Nam at its sneaking best. Wilson Street, boot camp/buddy system, a foxhole on the Quang Tri River, enemies just across the river, other side of the globe, loaded M-16s, *"a barbed wire Christmas,"* bull-up time, Jack Daniels touched by Margaret— it's just unpredictable stuff, Wilson Street stuff.

That one-in-ten-million reunion, with a slight delay, created an inspiration up and down Wilson Street, as eventually, word returned home through letters from Nam that the boys had guarded a perimeter together for that important Christmas holiday moment. Touched with a special spirit of hope, in a violent war torn routine, the boys could become temporary optimists concerning their uncertain destinies and thus enhance the feel of guardian angels watching their uncharted violent paths to a tour of duty rotation countdown.

Not much unusual in the way of the war happened at the river front perimeter that night. In the spirit of Christmas, the boys chose not to blast a passing putt-putt motorized river vessel out of the murky water, in spite of standard orders to the contrary. Reminiscing was the order of the night; the more Jack, the more reminiscent spirit of good ole times past and yet to be. The sun would eventually light the next day's warring. The shared moments and the Jack gone to time. Hopefully the numbing of tensions to let in a quick dose of relief would replace the night. Helton and young Fox stayed put at the opening of the foxhole for all of the next Christmas day, December 25, out of Jack, but that didn't matter. It was time to wake up anyway. (Life in them there parts was a little iffy to dive into a bottle of Jack for very long.)

Helton moved further north in I Corps on December 26, his embattled unit strung with weaponry, disappearing into surrounding jungle trails with his assigned grunt unit of the Seventh Marines. Off with new orders to defend or search and destroy in the most active

NVA strongholds within I Corps. Helton's unit would move into Dong Ha, narrow clicks south of the DMZ, then east to Con Thien. Then further to nameless creeks, useless hills in dense leech-infested jungles between wherever marines planted themselves for the night's warring and whatever Charlie had waiting for them, all in a war of confusion and inevitable US attrition.

While Helton moved with his eyes open, head up, eventually into and through Tet, back on the West Coast, new marines were beginning to be hustled into fighting units at Pendleton, where the Corps was gathering new young fighting bodies, with new friends of Wilson Street to get into the fight. By the day of that Christmas Eve foxhole reunion for Helton and Fox, Wilson Street boys were all over Nam, with more on the way.

> *(One marine to be on a Nam way was Robert C. Burke, who, as you will learn in the chapter to follow, would live his small-town determined life within Nam for less than a month, dying in a hellhole called Go Noi, giving his life to save the lives of many others on a mission ordered by Da Nang. Also from Monticello and a friend of Wilson Street, Burke dove into his war, earning the* Congressional Medal of Honor, *fighting with the reorganized Twenty-Seventh Marines, directly saving the lives of an estimated sixteen other marines, in so doing leaving a heroic epitaph that will forever mark his contributions of "service" and his time with us.)*

Helton survived the turmoil, upheaval, violence, confusion, and distraction stupidity of the Domestic Nam, rotated according to his leatherneck countdown with orders to Quantico, Virginia, serving further to complete his USMC active duty enlisted obligations. Helton and the youngest Fox would meet again, late October '68, as Fox's rotation date flashed on his scoreboard. Two more Wilson

Street boys had served and returned from warring missions as had been assigned.

As time passed, amidst careers, growing families, and weekend football games, it would become increasingly clear that Helton left the Nam, but the Nam would never totally leave Helton. Nam was forever Helton's internal virus but now outwardly visible. Many shelved warriors naturally have embraced their combat struggles and confrontations in their own private minds. To emotionally, mentally survive (and then perhaps justify) Nam battles, a soldier must bring his mental state to a point where he can inhale and ingest the personal surviving process. The post-Nam surviving process for many grunts or copter jockeys would seem natural, the easy part of the whole military service obligation. However, the subconscious imprints are indelible, forever invisible, to the point that the desperate wartime impressions become an internal part attached to the veteran's subconscious and inner soul, forever. Today, forty-plus years from Nam, they have a name for the lingering, postscript anxieties, fears, and subconscious, personality. They call the condition posttraumatic stress disorder (PTSD). Maybe that term is a plausible description, maybe not. It does sound a little too clinically generic, but in the halls of government administration, having a universal term does give the condition a useful "official" category.

No one knows to what extent, nor will they ever know, but many of Helton's dearest friends and family believe his premature death had a deep, darkened direct relationship to his war experience, as if a gnawing, rooting plague of a feeling would just never let go of a part of his ever being, like a dreadful virus clinging behind or within each day's real work of just living. Dreams from the filth and damp of an insect-crawling jungle floor, where shadows stare back, silence breaks at any second with the crack of AK-47 sniper assaults, and incoming mortars eagerly killing or crippling whatever moves in the killing field with total random selection of a target. Those kinds of *dreams* don't just drift easily away. Those *dreams* and their impressions burrow into a soldier's soul unspeakably, individually, and they are unexplainable. Over time, they can eat away to the point that a moving shadow or a flashing guide wire from an innocent roadside pole can whip a latent experience into a jerking reaction.

No plaque other than the graveside American Legion veteran's marker proclaims a thing about Helton, the Domestic Nam hero, nor will a plaque or badge probably ever likely come forth (other than the cover of this book). He simply grew up ready to serve, served, and returned to his Wilson Street roots. Helton lived for nearly thirty-five years after his return from Nam, married his hometown sweetness and grace angel Janet, raised a beautiful family, and then, when nearing his wholly earned final career retirement, he took his own life. No one will ever really say exactly why. Family and Wilson Street brothers can only speculate to the pieces of his psychological puzzle that would leave them all prematurely behind, mourning his passing yet today.

One old Wilson Street buddy recently said, *"Just think the fun we'd have today if Helton were still around!"*

Only another block west from the Bensyl and Helton households were the Baker brothers—tall and tough as zombie heels. Rumor was the whole family moved to Illinois after whipping all the bears in Kentucky. Older Baker was a charter member of Wilson Street, the younger brother not so much. That's OK. It only took one. Two would have been calamitous at a pace unsustainable. Older Baker biked hard, was at every pickup pasture baseball game, and was a walking danger to whatever passed north or south through Wilson Street boundaries. Baker's Domestic Nam purple hearts are probably in a drawer, forgotten, maybe just as well, maybe not just as well. Who knows what his subconscious gates prefer.

Once armied up, the pipelines full of weaponry and draftees aplenty, countries find it difficult to stand down from a speculative, confusing war of any kind. The bright lights gleaming on inflated grins and then studious looks of the stand-backish politicians, Congressional funding contraptions once flowing, apparently cannot be easily relinquished. Such power corrupts powerfully, seems to block out grassroots priorities with growing self-imposed disillusionment, and cannot seem to be broken as long as a country's infrastructure of supplies, greed, justification nonsense, and useful bodies remains intact and flowing to serve their squishy, underdefined purposes. As long as public opinion is not too violently opposed, the roads to war may continue practically unopposed.

Baker also did his duty, returning home to Wilson Street prematurely with arm and elbow pins and scars from his own leaps of aggression from desperations somewhere in the midmountain, Montagnard highland region of the Domestic Nam. Not a word of the experience or setbacks has ever crossed Baker's contemporary relationships with the world and civilian challenges ahead. Nor was there a word from Bensyl, Helton, the Foxes, Jordan, Heacock, Willis, Shroth, or Parsons. Strange how that works!

Wilson Street contributed one more soldier, Dyson of Dysons' pasture pickup baseball fame. Dyson lived in a small farmhouse at the complete west end, which, in those days, also marked the west end of the small-town boundaries. Starting on the east with Parsons, picking up the summer boys in a bike ride west, that gang landed at Dysons' farm and pasture for the pickup baseball games, with baseballs of torn red stitches verily holding their leather wrappings.

When the boys skidded to a sideways stop in the Dyson gravel drive, a young always grinning Dyson would pop out of the side door, and the boys would yell, "Hey. Hi, Hank!" Then young Dyson's older brother would likely come out, if not already out, and the boys would yell, "Hey. Hi, Hank!" Dyson's dad was likely around somewhere, and upon being recognized, the boys would yell, "Hey. Hi, Hank!" You see every male Dyson back in the day, and apparently, for the near future was Hank. They all had names but were all called Hank. No one really knew why, but it was such a silly Wilson Street habit that it was too much fun for the boys to concern themselves with real names and why they did it. Newcomers were hopelessly confused by the isolated ritual. Dysons appeared another relatively modest family for the times, with superior character and work ethic, always dabbling in small livestock projects, area seed sales, and local dairy deliveries here and there around the town and outskirts. If there was a herd of chickens to be killed and plucked at the Dysons' small farm, then first the heads of the chickens needed pulling off under a broom handle. An announcement of thinning the chicken flocks would spread east on Wilson and was sure to bring the bikes for the killings. The boys just could not get over the way chickens flopped around the Dyson's yard for a couple minutes with no heads. That sort of summer fun was right up there with smacking rats with baseball bats at the Allerton dump. Young Dyson, Hank, armed up, and with his quiet intellectual confidence, he served as a mapping expert (cartographer), a spotter for the Army Air Cavalry, 101st, based in and out of the Central Highlands vantage points. And he also returned home to degree up and teach for thirty-five years in the local grade school system, now retired, farming part-time with "Hank."

Dysons' small farm, with all the Hanks, was the end of Wilson Street. The street went no further and still doesn't today, although the back pasture, once an active cheering ballpark, is now a subdivision of middle class homes.

By late '68, so many Wilson Street boys were coming and going from military service and the mental and physical quagmires built by the Domestic Nam assignments, it was impractical for the adults to keep track of who was home and who wasn't or who was on what continent and who was wounded and what would be the eventual results. The boys matured, changed, built strong reliable personal characters for their future contributions, but the war itself never seemed to shift in a winnable or reasonable direction. Reported progress in the war became understood as pure fantasy, pure domestic propaganda, fed shamelessly to the public by confused politicians more and more certain of nothing war related. Every move or strategy seemed to be a strategic guess. The war became a rooting, eating cancer within America, merely to be tolerated until a plug could be pulled, relieving an embittered nation of the costs in lives and the international embarrassment.

One very small, ordinary, but unique Midwest town, with one short, ordinary quiet street had molded all-star Americans, doing a duty to country and fellow citizens as asked, in a government invented, unwinnable, and sustained FIASCO of the times. For causes right or wrong, from speeding bikes and pasture ball to loaded weapons and deadly hot LZs, a nation spent much of the youth of that era. Many of those not in the fight on the homeland domestic side were "spent" or just bent in a different way. Looking back, it seems impossible to believe such a small piece of a town's unknown history with its boys could even have happened. But the war with the boys did happen, creating new versions of veterans along the way, different from the returning WWII anchors of America's rebuilding. With their own basement bar stories never to be told, and their own visions of personal ambitions, ventures in productivity just ahead for their new worldly futures, the veterans of the Domestic Nam bit their bullets and tried to be mainstream, but with a different sort of perspective. In addition to Wilson Street, the small rural Monticello loaned dozens of others to the Domestic Nam cause: Myer, Miller, Murdock, McCann, Ashby, Kelly, Coon, and many, many more served, within "duties as assigned."

> *One story, counter to normal Nam in-country human struggles and atrocities was with Coon, a very close Wilson Street friend. A local football, farm-boy legend, Coon was "drafted" into the Marine Corps, a curious beginning to a draft obligation. To be drafted into the Marine Corps is very unusual, but done in Nam times, in order to fill the many boots rotating or just lost, in Tet-heightened warring. Coon was soon enough booted up in '68, immediate post-Tet, MOS'd, and remained west in California to "stage" for his Nam tour of duty. Soon enough, off*

he went, on the big silver wings again headed so far west, it becomes east. Coon's silver transport United bird, as was routine, stopped in Hawaii to refuel, for the final solemn flight to join the uncertain I Corps fighting fray. While in Hawaii, Coon's flight buddy marines exited the transport plane during refueling, milled casually about and eventually were "formed up platoon style" to reenter the plane and complete the back-end of the dreadful flight. While on the Hawaii commercial airport tarmac, awaiting orders to reboard, local marine high-command Major General Monahan unexpectedly appeared, in one of those noteworthy jeeps with a red license plate, two gold stars announcing the way. The marine base CO dismounted, surveyed the tarmac formed marines in slowed precise motions, talked with the officer in charge and, with weighted superiority, came to a halt, eye to eye in front of Coon, now at skeptical "attention." The general and Coon captured all tarmac attention. With a smooth transfer of papers, Coon was then ordered to remove himself from the formation, grab his duffle from the plane's underbelly, and join the base CO in the general's jeep for the short ride back to the hilltop, ocean view headquarters. Coon's Vietnam venture toward the Nam war was over as he was assigned to be the general's personal driver in Hawaii for the rest of his noncommission, enlisted days! Hawaii, of all places. Luck and angels, beyond luck and angels! That's not all. Coon later met the general's daughter-in-law and they later married. Coonie and Ms. General's Daughter—now Ellen Coon—eventually fulfilled the Corps obligations, in Hawaii, returned to the same small town near Monticello to farm and raise a family, and moved along quite nicely, always best of friends with Wilson Street Boys and is so yet today, an "almost" Nam story that is a most inspiring, unusual Nam story. What an angel Coonie must have had! Now that's an angel working big-time!

It has never been clear why WWII veterans openly and candidly, without self-adulation, would routinely talk about missions of WWII, and the boys back from Nam would never ever discuss the Domestic Nam. There was never even the discussion to discuss or not to discuss the Nam. I think it is because it was just that nasty, that inconclusive, that nonsensical. Being in the Nam warring was like being a part of an evil farce, perpetrated by a gang of puppeteers orchestrating a global scam or sham, or whatever malfeasance term is the nastiest. No national leader ever rose above the Nam pretense, never could step out in the sun, toward a wanting natural flow of public opinion and successfully influence a new direction that had taste, honesty, dignity, and an appreciation. But what the hell, that wasn't our deal!

The journey from the youthful/childish Wilson Street bike gangs to the deadly trenches of war in the turmoil of the Domestic Nam took six years. Prepared by the hills and terrain challenges of Allerton Park, disciplined by loyalties to one another, they served as did millions of other US youth of the times. Neither recognition nor reward was part of the deal, a condition known going in.

The Domestic Nam was an iconic national embarrassment of a struggle, outwardly with an enemy never really defined and inwardly with families and individual relationships and society at large. In fact, in truth, to the core of the issue was a deeply nagging inward reality that the real enemy was us, the United States itself. Nam was just the unfortunate third-world proxy-war stage provided for the inner American soul-searching struggle. The prodigious internal battles that it took to make a military commitment to a place called Vietnam and the sustained grumblings, misrepresentations, and vast waste of lives and money required to keep US troops in Nam as a sustainable effort of self-strangulation was America's turning point.

Was there no blame to make, no identification of the devilish figures responsible for such unabashed destruction? Would it all just go away? How long would that take before Nam is to be forgotten or just whitewashed to nothingness?

The massing of young troops, uniformed, armed, and shipped to a battle front, in retrospect, was no different than the warlords of bourgeoisie Europe cattle prodding French and German Huguenots as a paid army of vagrants to a foreign sixteenth-century English front, for someone else's princely, aristocratic warring boondoggle.

Patriotic troops of Nam, returning from the duties of foreign warring were not less loyal to their effort then than they are now. Yet returning from the Domestic Nam was a thankless, often berated, exercise for US troops, at the time still very young, enlisted as well as lower-ranked officers. Compared to the parades and accolades of today's veterans from the Middle East warring nonsense, the Domestic Nam veterans had an experience between shame, keep your head down, and the self-incrimination of how to fit in, how to not be renoticed as not so bad. Such a low profile was not because of Nam itself. Nam itself was a series of fulfilling duties while sustaining a vague sense of accomplishing something kind of big that needed accomplishing. The challenge of coming home, rotating at the end of a tour of duty, was another domestic part. The United States itself had changed significantly and was ramping up the pace of change '68 through '74 in all sorts of angry, reactionary, degenerative change ways that would restructure society. The nicety coats of societal Teflon were off after the '70s. The malicious nature of much of a nation's leadership was exposed, and American citizenry was reacting with more and more force into a human wave of having had enough, the misdirection political speak could no longer be overlooked, suspended, or double-talked to preposterous logic that would hold off or restrain loud public opinions. In the final Nam years, America was at the epitome of awkward, from government and military, into the core of families and friends, schools and industry, race relations, and longer range national intent. (Very much like today.)

The Wilson Street boys were met family by family and met individually between themselves with their special brands of reunion. WWII veterans in their clumps of kinship leaned and lectured war's older issues over swirls of vodka and bourbon-graced fortitude year after year. Domestic Nam veterans never shared or relived their war with one another, or the closest of family, largely for their entire lives yet to this day (with the exception of other various books and articles, or this modest write that may break a little more ice). Individual Nam experiences would never come up, like the whole thing didn't happen, feelings and attitudes forever sealed as in red hot tombs. Helton and young Fox enlisted on a Marine Corps buddy system, ate the same dirt and sand with the same sweat through boot camp, plopped in the same dangerous foxhole on a dangerous incident of discovery along the Quang Tri river, yet once they returned home, spent the next thirty years around one another with families and business building and never once did the Domestic Nam or that strange Christmas Eve meeting and war at Quang Tri ever come up in conversation. Not once! Ever!

> *How had America drawn that line between its government and population, and the veterans of the Domestic Nam? The politicians themselves, responsible for Nam, never seemed to hold an ounce of shame or regret.*
>
> *What then unidentified force, set the Domestic Nam veterans aside as "the baby killers" of the US military forces history?*

The boys of Wilson Street were ready to go to their war and did. They were trained from the time they could gang together on bicycles, in parks and pastures and running local tree lines and creeks on summer nights. Those boys took the community relationship baggage of small town civilization with them, and thus a common sense of what was truly right and what was wrong in life and behavior was in their DNA. In a year's tour, that positive kind of hometown baggage disintegrated as it had no function within the daily violent, constantly moving demands of Nam war essentials. On the ground, in the mud and mix of Nam's war, there wasn't much need for Wilson Street niceties . . . Being housebroken had no value or place.

Through a year's tour of duty, the baggage of civilization in America had little application. New baggage was loaded on to all the boys.

The baggage of war with strength, fearlessness, the ability and propensity to kill or be killed in a moment of distraction was not required but was a damn good idea. The temperament of acquiring and sustaining "hate" were new traits of increasing character importance.

Within the war's demands, hating something seemed to help various types of troops feel better about staying alive. The hating providing a haunting silhouette of self-passion for payback someday, payback eventually, even if the payback is far into the future and mostly undefinable at the time and generally unrecognizable by most. Hate could help the veteran's logic of progression to know the hate would hang on, could be used at their own private digression whenever a future moment required a hateful ingredient.

When a US Army funnels its teenage youth into a "prepare for war processing institution," those living, thinking bodies assume there is a civilian government behind them providing logic and planning to aspects of all missions casual or desperate. Not so in the late '60s, particularly '67-'68, the year of the real Domestic Nam. There was no publicly redeeming civilian government in existence. LBJ, the most pompous of the pompous, was at the wheel, driving the train wreck while surrounded by every yes man that could be uncovered from every self-serving military/industrial rock.

At this time in American history, committed to a war that no one could explain, the American military had been deeply "politicized" and the American politicians had been completely "militarized," partially as a result of near three continuous decades of warring. And both the "politicized" military and the "militarized" politics were continuously intoxicated from the kickbacks and privileges extended in the dark world of troop supply acquisitioning and weapons development and disbursement. "Amateur hour" of leadership was rampant. The norm was mutual admiration of the head-in-the-sand ostrich leadership.

While a nation's population spent more effort celebrating college bowl game victories than they did the return of those fighting for a country's professed causes, the nation as a whole slumped, sunk to its twentieth century low, practically eliminating the routine honors and glories of just twenty years prior from a World War. The nation could no longer be as good as it could be; too much mudslinging had become the main course of ass covering, and worse, had become our nation's institutional standard operating procedure. The lives of those brave smart young privates, corporals, sergeants, and lieutenants could not be replaced to rebuild the country's lost innocence or historic passions for excellence. Holes in the '70s deceived America could sit largely unnoticed or intentionally overlooked except for the hearts and emotions of the families related to, and receiving returning body bags. The decline into the Domestic Nam abyss took a bite out of America's existence and goodness that America has never recovered from and never will. One could make the argument that the decrepit standards set to justify and implement the Domestic Nam have created a national internal virus eating away at a nation in decline yet today, just as the individual Veteran's Nam virus eats slowly away at an unsuspecting subconscious.

Did the United States and scarce allies "win" a Domestic Nam war?

Most assuredly, *no!* But what is it that we didn't win? Was America to occupy a small unindustrialized third-world country with an ancient culture? No! Never!

Was just the strength of our presence going
to civilize or educate a population already content
in their own village agrarian existences? Never!

America never knew what it didn't win because we didn't know
what it was we wanted to win in the first place. All we knew was that
we *could* dominate a moment, suspend a phantom enemy aggression,
blow things up, break things, bully other things, and draft endless
numbers of mass American-Hessian youth for half training and
full fighting! America had unmatched wealth. America had the
Wilson Street populations and had the "militarized" politicians and
"politicized" military, fed by profiteering industrial complexes—and
thus, we *could*, and therefore we *did*. (There was another deep, dark
reason "*we did*." That is explained in chapter 8.)

What we lost was mostly at home within the soil of the United
States: losing pride of judgment and more than fifty-eight thousand
young brave Wilson Street boys from all over America were lost,
dead in every warring manner conceivable, countless others
wounded—the mass amount of these troops dying in every brutal,
unexpected, unaccountable, lost in action manner that could be
dreamed to be possible.

America spent its near future of that era in a waste of spending,
economic, human, and in institutional reputation:

Billions of dollars lost, hundreds and
hundreds of billions of dollars lost to the
vagrancies of useless warring, for the four-
pronged modern version of democracy.

America lost invaluable conventional
baggage of good decent social value population
standards and with it went a little thing called
civilian *trust*, all of which had taken near two
centuries to build.

America lost the calculable future and lost a realistic grasp of the times domestically and globally.

America lost the right to stand up in the world and say, "Follow us. We are stout, honest, good, trustworthy people."

America lost a disposition of contentedness as a united population, turning away from a good-natured population not to be angered because of the big stick. America has not been a united population since.

America turned inward into an angered population looking for a way to be reawakened in renewed accomplishment and legitimate leadership once again, but there was no social or political leadership mechanism to regain lost values. The concepts of national united goodness and global leadership are even more shattered today as Obama and company socialize their way through a divisive second term with little resistance.

The returning veteran of Nam was forced to balance his returning baggage with the baggage of an America imploding with urban and street riots, political assignations, campus bombings, and general unwelcome public attitudes. The weaker segment of returned veterans never did recover or become productive. Some laid about the streets and in the parks for decades, having become dependent on someone else carrying the new baggage they acquired but did not understand. Of course, in true life, no one carries your baggage, not really, and when they pretend to, it is at a cost of self-esteem that cripples individual ambition and thus begets more carrying of baggage that need not be carried because of the actual uselessness of the baggage itself.

By 1969, enough Domestic Nam veterans had returned home and applied for the GI Bill that college campuses were beginning to show fairly impressive campus enclaves of stout veterans, some a little testy. Assume most college kids attend immediately post high school, age eighteen to twenty-two and assume most returning Domestic Nam veterans heading for campus were older, twenty-two to twenty-five. Assume also that veterans were bigger, trained, a little mad, and have that middle Fox drilled in human "perspective of their times." In addition, a veteran's perspective was one prepared to work harder at life, have a sharper focus, and might also have a little more money than mommy's boys unsuspecting students in the normal ranks of college tuition payers.

Assume also that the traditional college kids were a little full of themselves. Armed with their first freedom from home confinements and their homeboy nature, they were ready to exercise America's righteous freedom of expression and biased, uneducated opinion about current events, especially about a war they so desperately hoped to avoid with one deferment effort or another. Also assume the veterans on that same campus had little tolerance for the brats, the mommy's boys (and girls), the deferment clinging whiners. These types of human chemistry can add up to the cultural implosions of the time and often did. This social environment alone can create certain obvious contentious moments on and around campuses and some moments not so obvious.

At a midsize state college in Illinois, returning Domestic Nam veterans seemed to naturally gravitate together in athletics but also in the town's "private" clubs like the VFW, away from the college bar scenes. The veterans of one normally quiet university of about eight thousand students typically went about their academic business but, given the chance, would make expressions of strength and perspectives, such as in intramural football games. A veteran's team against a fraternity was a sight to behold. It was a guarantee that the first play from scrimmage would transition from blocking and body heaving into fights all up and down what was a proverbial line of scrimmage to the frats but was a combat base perimeter line of skirmish to the vets.

Organized campus veterans also could take great comfort knowing that in the late '60s and early '70s, sooner or later, a campus antiwar demonstration would come forth for the pounding. Campus word for the event would spread, promoting a candle-burning prayer-like circle, demonizing and diminishing anything to do with the Domestic Nam, including those dumb or sick enough to participate, and in so doing create a fake embellishment of their own crafty wisdom for avoiding the draft. The events were kind of an anti-patriotism shield for the normal students, self-dressed and molded for the gullible and disingenuous part of a student body. As promotion of the scheduled/impromptu protest event drifted through campus to draw more numbers of students to their demonstrations, emotions of their own self-superiority would be spread unselectively. Such word of mouth event promotion by its nature cannot be controlled and thus would eventually reach the attention of the veterans' groups, always willing to participate, proactive, so to speak.

An antiwar gathering promotion to assemble at 8:00 p.m.-ish, meant that Nam veterans would gather at the closest bar to that location about 6:00 p.m.-ish, allowing a couple hours to prepare adequately and join the protest about 9:00 p.m.-ish or whenever preparation had peaked and the hidden hate clinging to a veteran's viral soul needed releasing. Thirty or more "prepared" veterans joining a war protest of hundreds of unprepared students in full-swing war protest are not a fair confrontation. Ooooh, the good ole days of college fun for the veterans in the late '60s, early '70s! The only downside to the whole exercise seemed to be that the ass-kickings were so thorough that it could be a whole year before another war protest was organized by someone not on campus for the last war protest. Rumor had it that a Wilson Street boy or two might have been involved in one or two of the veteran groups but the actual facts remain undocumented.

Consider the following passage:

> *The run-up to the war is particularly significant because it also laid the shaky foundation for the derelict occupation that followed, and that constitutes the major subject of books documenting the processes employed, or in some cases not employed. While the Administration and it's conference tables of Wise Men bear much of the responsibility for the mishandling of the occupation in early years, blame also must rest with leadership of the U.S. military, who didn't realistically prepare the U.S. Army for the challenges it faced and then wasted years by using counter-productive shifting tactics that were employed in unprofessional ignorance of the basic tenets of counter-insurgency warfare.*

Does this statement somewhat adequately describe or apply to the Domestic Nam? For sure it does, but the passage was written in 2006 to describe Iraq and Afghanistan with no reference to Nam intended.

Consequently, fellow Americans can assume as I do: *We are doing it again!*

Chapter 3

The Twenty-Seventh Marines with PFC Burke at Go Noi

"America's plaques and memorials display the profiles
of war's elite Medal of Honor recipients; know
one of them, his times and his journey."

America's Vietnam warring experience is truly a saga, never to be completely told, reasonably understood, or accurately recalled with any particular conclusive satisfaction for anyone. Perhaps these potential theoretic finalities of the Nam experience are not even important anymore as the issues are, and always will be, the height of individual subjective interpretation with a dwindling faction of America's population who may or may not even concern themselves with such historic issues. We may think the accuracies of event recall are important to understand, so leadership in government will avoid making such mistakes and similarly atrocious decision making again, but too late! The US government leadership, hand in hand with military and industrial leadership, is making the same atrocious commitments in lives and hard asset costs today in Afghanistan, predictably, to eventually experience the same cause/effect end results as in the Nam more than forty years prior and thoroughly studied. The commitments are now institutionalized.

A truthful scramble for any fragments of logical, face-saving strategies and politicizing in order to withdraw from the current Afghan fiasco with a semblance of global approval, slowly and painfully becomes the bottom line goal for the current crop of political cowards. Contemporary US leadership is in a modern game of musical chairs, to see who can sit, exit, and hide in their chambers, when the chips fall to an Afghanish unplanned and unpredictable conclusion. Musical chairs are a very difficult exercise to perform with one's head in the sand or up something; the visions are so impaired. More than likely, American concerns and reactions will rope-a-dope in time to drift into and out of politicized "rules of engagement" until an enemy initiative creates an opportunity to throw up hands and declare the opportunity to do the Texas two-step, side-step, or back-step out, while declaring some sort of benevolent task has been completed for the good of something forever undefined. It is all a façade, of course, while the regional enemies persist in their wickedness as strong as ever on their own turf become strategically smarter than ever, better armed than ever by rival bystanders, and gather that great sense of personal Allah-fed blessed greatness from sending the Americans home only three decades after the Russian tails were clipped and also sent packing. Sound, look, quack familiarly, just like the Nam? America's Afghanistan fiasco will conclude only when the chains of graft, payoffs, and institutional embezzlement conclude, and when the country's vast opium trade flow chart is more satisfactorily defined.

Yes, we did it again (are doing it again), as if in a self-righteous need to cleanse something for someone somewhere in an ongoing basis, for sixteenth-century socio-structures who have no idea they need "saving," or if they did, what being "saved" would look or feel like. Few in these current times even remember why we were in Vietnam in the first place, let alone why the mid-'60s escalations. Nor will a general, future US population remember why we were in Afghanistan. Something to do with something called 9/11, future generations may suspect.

Certainly none among the last two generations even concern themselves with the Nam logic, or lack thereof, other than a fleeting visit to "The Wall" in DC, if even that: What is that "Wall"? Why is it there? It represents something!

Accordingly, America must have a whole new generation of young adults who already can't really profess an understanding or logic of a military/economic/industrial presence in Afghanistan—a Nam-like, directionless, deadly effort still underway with no real signs of accomplishment in-country or domestically. Without a draft, and thus imminent military service of some sort for the nation's youth, America's youth may these days stay detached from foreign warring issues their entire lives, unconcerned, uneducated, oblivious to the trickle-down causes and affects deeper down in our country's core issues.

These types of warring, Vietnam and Afghanistan, are fought by the individual soldier as deadly and dirty as desperately and grossly as any other conflicts. However, the actions and logic of the original cause and justification become so fleeting and unaccountable that it is impossible to recall such regional wars with any comfort of understanding the ways, means, or what the hell was trying to be accomplished. (We have no more chance of defeating terrorism in Afghanistan than we do flawlessly implementing Obamacare. In both cases, it doesn't matter to those of political powering.) In fact, the overall actions of fundamentally trying to save ancient populations (who have no want, need, or cognizance of being saved) facilitate a hidden concept of putting a nation's own existence in a position to lose, lose big. Thus, within the battlefield and door-to-door village struggles, the fighting, the lying, and the fraud, the big picture of justification, or a winning strategy becomes impossible to even communicate, let alone execute in a shifting field of regularly reinvented strategic military concepts. But nonetheless, America does it. Well, perhaps not "America" per se, but American leadership commits the assets and invents the jibber-jabber of justifications. They go on and do it as if they can't help themselves. You know, the folks that will never do the fighting, never live in the muck, never hear the weapons womp or rat-tat-tat in a dark landscape, never see or feel the tracers racing to their contact targets, or never experience the human and family rehab that can never be completed.

In the end, the big stories of these less worthy wars cannot ever really be told. Even yet today, you see the occasional Nam documentary, perhaps from McNamara, that fumbles to apologize, legitimize and explain with some excuse-ridden fake pontification of what and the hell it was that he and the displaced leadership club were trying to do, which is a tricky business that is hard to accomplish without some self-inflicted treasonous style assimilations. Inevitably the fading, fumbling Nam explanations conclude open-endedly, just as the war itself concluded with no useful US macro-direction or national conscious settling.

The Domestic Nam experience, operationally, was nearly a decade of awards, medals, honors, and promotions for generals and staff, while sending thousands and thousands of young ground troops into meat grinders, most senselessly and in knee-jerk reactions to fleeting, always uncertain military strategizing. The May '68 Go Noi

Island mission was ordered by Major General Donn J. Robertson, First Marine Division Commander, awarded the Distinguished Service Medal for his Nam leadership, (among a whole chest-full of other medals) for a mission that was so ill-conceived that it had no chance of creating a positive result, yet cost the lives of hundreds of marines in an isolated mini-Tet effort. General Robertson, based in fortified, stabilized Da Nang at the time, ordered the Seventh Marines, and the ad hoc ill-trained reorganized Twenty-Seventh Marines, into an NVA/Viet Cong stronghold where every strategic and terrain card was stacked heavily against the brave Marines selected for that bootless fight.

The fact that the big collective, deprecating, hair ball Nam story is mired in collective haze and thus cannot sufficiently be told does not mean there are not individual stories to be told and recalled and numerous honors to be bestowed and recorded within the efforts of heroic individuals. In fact, the entire Domestic Nam war *was* about the individual and the individual stories from their experiences are overwhelming, overloaded with America's effort and goodness.

Vietnam, like Afghanistan today, became a war of, about, and with individuals. Leadership in pressed uniforms occasionally waded ashore for a quick look-see, but the boys on the ground were the guts and the backbone, the action makers and breakers. Vietnam became a war of, and about individuals, within a mix of dynamic, simultaneous great weird flows of social issues in the United States crashing against warring issues on the ground in Nam. The realities at first were as oil and water, not seriously mingling to compatible coexistent direction, intent, or usefulness. By the defining year, October '67—October '68, the two macro-realities had mingled (social chaos and war realities), were mingling more, and becoming inseparable. Certainly, the Domestic Nam was an iconic simultaneous struggle between the worst of conditions on the ground and almost the worst conditions in America. (Recognizably conditions certainly not as individually or collectively dreadful as Revolutionary and Civil War events, but those events were clear in definition, result, upside, risk/reward, and unified. Nam was none of those nor is Afghanistan.)

Soldiering and warring is a fascinating human endeavor once you can wipe away the tragedies. There is no pattern of human social order, mentality, behavior, or background that can accurately predict, in a life and death battle, who will step up with the heroic effort of the moment, or who won't. The real heroes, the Medal of Honor types, are not necessarily the big boys, the fast ones, or the smart guys or a combination of such. Heroes, America's lifesavers, come from the most unlikely strains of makeup, whether poor, typically unpopular and sometimes downtrodden, or just average folks like fence builders, car salesmen, pharmacists, etc. who will later return to the streets to continue being average folks on their outside. Somehow, some marines or warriors of any uniform find the moment and fortitude to step up to a battle's calling. Probably without overthinking, these rare individuals meet battle's life and death moments within the nature of their particular presence in those moments, spectacular once recalled, but reactionary and duty-bound to the boy in the fight. When the heavily decorated Major General Donn Robertson ordered marines into the stark Go Noi Island assault, he ordered Private First Class Robert C. Burke into that fight, days before, May 16-17, 1968. By May 18, Burke was dead, although General Robertson did not know it, comprehend it, know Burke, nor perhaps did he concern himself with the minor reality of the details or actual occasion of the loss. There were too many marines dead in that battle and too little time for a command-mode Robertson to be concerned with names or backgrounds. Marines like Robert Burke, eighteen years young from a small Illinois town, die in battle routinely in those days as displaced strategizing, map reading, weapons analyzing officers plan the next action or reaction. Likely, to Robertson, grunting and dying is what the Burke's, or more broadly generalized, PFCs are for.

In the Nam, once away from the desks and charts with pointers labeling hill heights and hot LZs, it was the individual soldier like Burke that carried the burden, felt the wins and losses, carried the day or lost the day, sweated in 110 degrees of Go Noi lowland hot, and carried the weaponry and ammunition loads against trained enemy's deeply hidden fortified positions. It was the individual Burke(s), plopped in a war zone of multiple means of killing fields that either conquered the fight of the day and night or lost in his effort for an uncertain, unexplainable theoretic assaulting cause (theorized by General Robertson and Staff). And as The Nam progressed (in time only, not in recognizable winning), the causes, reasons, goals, and actual field directions became less and less clear and less and less productive to any kind of acceptable micro or macro result. Regardless, the soldier was still on the ground following the next order, scratching for the next way to survive, hoping he is there in his miserable mentally bunkered existence for some sort of reason to the good of something that only other people higher up claim to understand.

In the Nam, various concepts of reality became undeniable as the warring mounted, spread, mounted higher, continued, infected all human elements, and became more and more confused and misdirected through month after month after year. The most basic truth for the soldier in the fight was as follows: the soldier (squad or platoon) "only owned the ground they stood on, that day, at that moment, with those nights, or daily sun angles." Nor would they (US troops and strategies) ever own anything but that ground they could look down and touch, ever. That simple negative concept, in fact, summarizes the entire American war effort in the Nam and currently in the Middle East. In a decade of Nam intervention, the General Robertson's never had a workable strategy beyond "only owning the ground you stand on." The building of fire bases, landing zones, camps, bigger bases, landing strips, helicopter pads, perimeter lines, Agent Orange, whatever—it was all temporary for the moment of the war and issues at that instant, and probably for the statistics reported to justify the façade of progress so that propaganda, promotions, and funding might continue to flow most freely.

Generals from far away had a name for every base, mission, hill and plateau, but they never had a name for enough strength to hold such terrain assets and thus actually make a difference. It was all fleeting, nothing more permanent or substantial than the latest bivouac or recon team report. The weary, torn, nasty, bloody terrain was fought for, won or lost, but all eventually abandoned, given up for a new order coming down the chain for the taking of a different hill or valley to stop some sort of new advancing threat. (The movie *Hamburger Hill* would be the prime real example.) Some terrain abandoned over longer periods of time than others, but some abandoned, given back to the enemy, within days or weeks after being won in a fight that likely cost someone's life that reverberated to a family and touched a community back home on a Wilson Street. Thus is the nature of intervention style warring, which, in retrospect, is impossible to really get good at. No winning streak can be put together in such fleeting wars, the societies are too different. The details of living and thus defining what is victory are too ambiguous.

To the safe, pompously postured leadership (i.e., Robertson, McNamara, Johnson) much order giving became busy work, became tasks in response to some other task and strategy, to keep the war active and stirred up, somehow productive to an unmarked shifting goal and thus relative to aggregate US expenses, asset applications, and human balance sheets. To the national detriment, in this case of weak or greedy or self-righteous leadership, such warring begets more warring as long as the resources for the warring keep pouring into availability. Ultimately, the entire fiasco explodes beyond moral logic—and thus, leader's tails must be inserted between leader's legs and the politicians who never made the slightest degree of sacrifice for their warring, fade with their beloved generals into some state of belated anonymity, heading for a rhetorical cover while the Burkes and other families flail away at useless warring associated efforts of mind magic to find justifications—ever failing to achieve that elusive, impossible emotional closure goal. But the soldiers are still there, grounded, aware of the next bullet, insect bite, poke, infection, rocket womp, or fever.

In the Nam all of the stories are true. If that story were not true with that soldier, then the transportable stories were true with another soldier. Thus, the story of eighteen-year-old Medal of Honor winner Private First Class Burke, with the Twenty-Seventh Marines, in a place called Go Noi, is a story representative not only of the whole failed Nam effort, but a story of the heroic and patriotic individuals that fought and gave their lives. We believe they gave their lives for the collective "us"; the rest of us, who, with the graciousness of knowing such struggles, may be able to embrace heroism, dedication, service when we see such human traits go down around us or amidst our own wandering well-intended paths.

Private First Class Robert C. Burke received the Medal of Honor, for his heroism in Operation Allen Brook, directed by Major General Donn Robertson, in a remote jungle stink hole named Go Noi Island, attached to company I, of the Third Battalion, of an ad hoc Marine Unit, the Twenty-Seventh Marine Division. Just like Go Noi was not really an island, the Twenty-Seventh Marines were not a real Marine fighting force, by any realistic, traditional USMC standards.

The US Marines plan for Go Noi was ill-conceived. Blind to realities of the opposing elements and obstinate to the human asset risk, within elements so overwhelmingly against accomplishing anything positive, that to understand why Burke and the Twenty-Seventh were even there takes some history reviewing and storytelling.

Go Noi Island, Robert Burke's battleground, was not technically an island. The annual monsoons would flood the Ky Lam, Thu Bon, Ba Ben, and Chiem Son Rivers and isolate the ground area in the middle, each late winter and spring. The compact, multiterrain, harsh land in the middle was called Go Noi. (Ancient names of Nam places, have a gentle flavor of innocence before wars, and then have a bitter taste of "evil" in the midst of war—Go Noi, just sounds ugly. All the names began to sound uglier once fought for.) Thus, in the monsoon season and for a while after, flooding created the island land mass in the middle of the tangled rivers. Other times of the year, the area was just forty-plus square miles, river bound, bordering mountains from the south leading west, with the large city and strategic US base of Da Nang about twenty-five kilometers north. (We would call that distance several "clicks" north.) Liberty Bridge over the Ky Lam River connected An Hoa and Go Noi Island toward the strategic central I Corps city, Da Nang. Da Nang with a subculture ancient city at the core, Go Noi would be the impenetrable hellhole to the south.

The flat, lowland nature of the Go Noi coastal area (much like America's east coast region from Virginia to South Georgia called the "low country") not only created dreadful persistent heat and humidity, the area often created clear fields of fire for killing. The NVA Communists and the area's Viet Cong had controlled the area for years, perhaps decades, as a safe haven for NVA regulars infiltrating from the mountain ranges going west, connecting eventually to the historic Ho Chi Minh Trail, coming south from N. Vietnam, skirting into eastern Laos, and then coming further, directly east into the lowlands of South Vietnam. An enemy regular NVA military command infrastructure with the local populace commanding a strong, impenetrable Viet Cong orientation was in place, established, and in control of the area for years. Go Noi was such a communist stronghold that the many local hamlets were all well-fortified and had been connected with trenches and tunnels constructed and maintained by the local population for years. This was, characteristically, an important reality completely unsuspected by Robertson and his safe crackerjack staff. It was just too difficult to suspect or see trenches and tunnels from the O-Club!

Also unknown to US command in May 1968 was the overall strength of NVA regulars committed to the area of central I Corps from the Second NVA Division assigned to infiltrate the area post-Tet. Further, US command did not understand nor did they attempt to understand the highly resistant physical infrastructure of Go Noi controlled by a population at war for decades, containing three main force VC units, and thoroughly adept at war's infrastructure building and maintenance. Also active in Go Noi was the trained and supplied Thirty-Sixth Regiment of the 308th NVA Division, working in coordination with VC Battalions working through the eastern leading mountain stretches from the Ho Chi Minh trail toward and into the depths of Go Noi.

> *The average soldier in the Second and 308th NVA Divisions responsible for the area was twenty-nine years old, with fifteen years military experience; the average age of marines assigned to the* Twenty-Seventh *Division to soon be ordered into the Go Noi was 19.2 years, with less than one year experience in the military, and no experience in the ways of Nam warring or in harsh Go Noi-type terrain.*

In the Go Noi's center, flat areas were not farmed or landscaped into rice paddies, which was most of any Vietnam flatland, ten-foot high elephant grass ruled the land. The waving of growth of the elephant grass was only interrupted by the occasional tree line bordering minor creeks or leading to one of the major rivers, which was overflowing in the monsoon season (late winter months and spring) and dry the other times of the year, the fighting months. Go Noi was an ambush land, perfect for booby trapping and punji-sticking from fall-away dug holes, land that leads nowhere in the '60s warring, except toward sniper-convenient semicircles.

Most unique in these particular Go Noi area killing fields were remnants and stockpiles of supplies from the old Vietnamese National Railroad construction project. In the '20s and '30s, before Vietnam was divided, there was a national effort to build a railroad from Saigon to Hanoi. The railroad was to be a great national coastal undertaking, although as usual in Vietnam, the project was never to be completed to its northern destination. However, the railroad building did succeed to go as far as from Saigon to just south of Da Nang and thus into the thresholds of the Go Noi area, skirting mountain ranges to the west and soft unbuildable coastal areas to the east. Within that great nation-building effort, the Go Noi vicinity became the stockpile supply infrastructure center for railroad building material, such as great finished lumber deposits, finished and unfinished rail steel, and equipment. Consequently, by the era of US military intervention in democratizing South Nam, the Go Noi area had more fundamental bunker infrastructure building material than perhaps any soon to be warring geography on earth. Major General Robertson must have been unaware that every tunnel, bunker, hillside vantage, and tree line was communist reinforced with high-grade railroad building steel and railroad building material of all types, so strong that most US mortar, rocket and air ordnance would bounce or roll off. The communists had been building defensive and offensive attack infrastructure sights for so long that gun port vantage points had been long covered by the foliage of the area and slanted with the landscape so that bombs or artillery fire would deflect, doing no harm to a waiting machine gunner tucked inside his own killing vantage point.

Go Noi Island existed quietly in the shadows of the larger fighting, well-armed, and strongly/expertly fortified, a communist stronghold with mature troops and experienced leadership, but basically not in the daily war headlines until the early months of '68. When General Robertson served up I Company, Third Battalion, Twenty-Seventh Regiment, post-Tet, May 1968, Go Noi would heat up, then explode to become known as the "mini-Tet." Because of the severe fighting, quickly mounting KIAs and WIAs and discovering large, well-trained, and armed enemy numbers. The tactical situation at Go Noi although on a much more compact geographic scale was a micro Tet, only detectable by US command and troops I Corps assigned. On a killing scale, Go Noi was more deadly real than the namesake national Tet offensive launched just a few months earlier, dragging on painfully for months to Tet's last battle in Hue, just fifty or so clicks north of Da Nang, within the threshold of extremely violent northern I Corps.

The very first element of US fighting marines to enter Go Noi was I Company, Third Battalion, Twenty-Seventh Marines, a most unusual unit who would have a fearless PFC Burke as a point marine probing through the strange treacherous oven-like terrain. Go Noi was no normal battle-ready stronghold; the Twenty-Seventh Marines were no normal unit. In fact, the Twenty-Seventh was and for its history, always has been an ad hoc, impromptu unit. The Twenty-Seventh had been an inactive unit since being deactivated at Camp Pendleton, January 10, 1945, having returned from Pacific WWII action.

Since reactivating the Twenty-Seventh Marines, in reaction to significant Tet offensive troop losses, the unit and leadership were constantly being assigned, then reassigned, constantly changing, often robbed of developing human assets which were regularly trained and then reassigned to existing units already in the battle field being diminished from combat losses. As a result, the newly activated Twenty-Seventh Division could never truly gain its working legs, could not actually become a cohesive, trained fighting force with consistent command and reactionary troops able to adapt to the demands and changing conditions of "incoming" fields of enemy fire.

The Twenty-Seventh Marine Division, by 1968, had only a brief history. In all actuality, the Twenty-Seventh Marine Division was not a real marine division, meaning a cohesive, well-staffed, and led fighting unit, as we think of "Marine" Divisions as first to fight. Since its formation, January 1945, the Twenty-Seventh had been operational for just the next one year, then non-operational/ deactivated, January 1946 up to late '67.

The Twenty-Seventh Marine Division was first organized for the combat assignment of the invasion of Iwo Jima, approximately 750 miles south of Japan. Iwo Jima was held by Japanese troops, the string of islands vital to US control as a base for American fighter jets that would provide protection for B-29s, in preparation for the final bombing and then ground invasion of Japan and thus contribute strategically to end the war in the Pacific.

Formed January 10, 1945, by February 19 (more than five weeks) the marines of the Twenty-Seventh invaded Iwo Jima, and thus the story and brief history of the Twenty-Seventh had begun. These brave marines stormed ashore in the designated Iwo Jima areas of Red Beach 1 and 2. The regiments were initially assigned to the mission of helping to cut off and isolate Mount Suribachi from the rest of the island. As marines pushed inland, resistance by the dug-in, bunkered Japanese became more and more determined but eventually fell in bloody close combat to the advancing marines. Once Mount Suribachi was isolated, the regiments of the Twenty-Seventh were ordered to move north to join with other marine units in continuing the attack on main enemy defenses of the island. Rugged terrain, heavy enemy fire, fortified, lined with land mines, the island's enemy could likely hold advancing marines at a standstill for quite some time, detrimental to the overall strategy.

On March 16, Iwo Jima was declared secure, allowing for tolerable enemy spots of resistance in perimeter areas that continued for two months but were not strategic to a completed mission. The fighting was severe and took the lives of 566 marines killed and 1,703 wounded in the Twenty-Seventh Marines alone. Four marines from the Twenty-Seventh earned the Medal of Honor. (Remember those numbers as we go through Go Noi.)

By April, the Twenty-Seventh Marines had moved north to Okinawa and were standing down to regroup and prepare for the invasion of Japan, which, of course, did not happen with grunt marines, as Japan quickly but reluctantly surrendered after the world's first exhibition of atomic weaponry devastation. Thus, the pending invasion plans by US Marines was cancelled, sparing the lives of millions of Japanese and many thousands of US ground forces already assigned to the task of defeating Japan with ground forces and waiting for invasion orders from bases on Okinawa. On September 16, the Twenty-Seventh Marines sailed to Japan for occupation duty, their last planned assignment (until reactivated in 1966, the defining year of The Nam). Two months after reaching Japan's mainland and standing down, December 20, 1946, the Twenty-Seventh Marines were sent back to Camp Pendleton and deactivated January 10, 1947.

The Twenty-Seventh Marines became a large military file, with a commemorative flag in an office corner until a new calling arose twenty-two years later. In the meantime, a deactivated unit builds no tradition, creates no admirable standards for the next brave soldiers to strive for and live up to. The Twenty-Seventh Marines became a closet force for the future, to be geared up and thrown together from paper to personnel and weapons, if, and/or whenever needed. Fighting forces often live off tradition or at the least can be rallied from high "tradition" standards. Historic success in various fields of duty is commonly part of their meat.

The directionless, confused approach to US military intervention in the Nam (especially in the late '60s, around and after Tet) really never advanced beyond "reactionary" episodes of one sort or the other. For US political and military leadership, Nam would be a tactical guessing game for rotating commands, who would react and guess at one strategy one day or month and then, as if a lightbulb of ideas, glowed brighter than the light bulb from previous guesses, and command would order a new strategy with a snappy new fired-up name and mission. That awkward, losing blend of command and control never changed in the Domestic Nam. There were not enough restraining paws for the many NVA and Viet Cong mice, who owned the hamlets and tree lines and always owned the nights and who always knew that a simple strategy of "attrition" would eventually be enough to eliminate the gut of their uncommitted foreign enemy. (A situation exactly today's reality in Afghanistan.)

Consistent with "reacting" (to enemy initiatives) US high command, for the second time, began to activate the Twenty-Seventh Marines from Camp Pendleton in January 1966 as warring in Nam hit an escalated steady tempo. Almost immediately, the reforming division became a convenient pool of human resources to fill growing ground troop needs from KIAs and WIAs, wounded and missing, in the ongoing Nam fighting. Twenty-Seventh Marine commanders could no sooner train a fighting unit, than orders would arrive to lend parts of that unit to some other existing fighting command already on the ground losing troop numbers in The Nam. As a result, the Twenty-Seventh training operations were a revolving door and could never really form a fighting force battalion until November '66. Training was oriented to fighting in The Nam with a constant goal to combat readiness for revolving Twenty-Seventh troops. Because of the revolving door of troops and middle command officers, the goal of combat readiness was not declared complete for almost two years, near the end of '67. High turnover of officers and enlisted plagued the newly activated unit from the beginning, and thus, not until the dawn of '68 had the unit stabilized and could be aggressively judged an effective fighting force, prepared and good enough by fighting Marine Corps standards to travel into exotica SE Asia beaches, mountains and the lowlands in between. By early '68, the Twenty-Seventh Marines existed as perfected ad hoc, a piecemeal unit, verily held together, but politically expedient as a command reaction into a built-up and deployable force. Actual readiness was merely a subjective opinion that could stabilize political necessities if leadership simply did not look to close.

The January/February launched Tet offensive changed US command reacting to the demands of war that the North had been deeply committed to since '56 in troops, assets, and dollars. The US high command concept became a recommitment to rapidly building a fighting force in California to replace and/or add troops lost or depleted in Tet fighting. The Twenty-Seventh Marine Division, with a history of such emergency force building, was already reactivated, staffed, equipped, and theoretically ready to be shipped to the ongoing post-Tet fighting front, now dominating all parts of the Nam countryside. To staff a fighting force of such replacement intention, Marine Corps high command would continue to pull existing troops from anywhere and everywhere that they could, as long as they were post-boot camp and rifle-range trained. Consequently, marines from anywhere in the West Coast base areas would be inducted into the soon to be mobile fighting unit. Cooks, desk jockeys, motor pool mechanics and drivers, communication experts, gate guards, and any post-boot camp marine with a pulse was poured into the constantly reorganizing Twenty-Seventh unit as directed by President Johnson and General Westmoreland, skirting Joint Chiefs input.

Notified on February 12, 1968, of orders to Nam, the regiments of the Twenty-Seventh began to reform for their mission. Immediately, the new growing ranks of the Twenty-Seventh—including some combat experienced Vietnam trained enlisted and officers—were depleted as hundreds of marines were transferred out because of restrictions relating to sole survivor son limitations, time between tours, etc., all of which acted to regularly deplete the built, trained ranks of the Twenty-Seventh and thus again devastating their combat readiness capabilities. Understrength and largely in a perpetual state of disorganization, void of tradition from the beginning, the Twenty-Seventh was once again the bastard division, dangling in vulnerability. Again command for the Twenty-Seventh dug deep into any non-commissioned marine ranks for a new wave of replacements, taking every available infantry marine assigned to the Fifth Division as well as pulling in over four hundred marines from ranks only vaguely related to battle field demands. The Third Battalion (within the Twenty-Seventh) was the last battalion to be brought up to strength and would take the brunt of the noninfantrymen force. A typical squad of the Third Battalion would have one to three infantrymen and maybe one marine with combat experience per platoon, meaning the remaining ranks would include ten to twelve green, new, young, inexperienced, wide-eyed, gee-whiz kids—for sure, new chicks for the experienced NVA and Viet Cong in waiting.

President Johnson met personally with this wide-eyed, determined group at the Marine El Toro, California, air facility in Orange County as the Twenty-Seventh Marines prepared to become the Corps' first new force to fly into a combat zone post-Tet. This freshly organized group of marines, the newest Third Battalion, were put together with no consistent officer leadership and no training as a group and were immediately assigned to Operation Allen Brook at the Go Noi under the command of the Fifth Division, operationally led by Robertson based at the large equipped Da Nang air base. PFC Robert Burke, from Monticello, Illinois, a friend of the Wilson Street Boys, was in Company I (India), of this Third Battalion, Burke being one of the last assigned to the ad hoc Twenty-Seventh Marine unit from his mechanics motor pool unit at Camp Pendleton. The Third Battalion was the last to be formed but would be the first in the fight at Go Noi; I Company, Third Battalion, Twenty-Seventh Marines to have Burke on the point.

At the same time as this Third Battalion buildup of troops and equipment, by late April '68, through reconnaissance observations and limited ground engagements, a determination was made that the enemy had fed into the Go Noi, the equivalent of a new NVA Division, infiltrating and beginning to control areas just outside the normal mortar and rocket range currently patrolled and defended as an extension of Da Nang occupation by US Marines. In defensive response to the growing new threat, General Robertson decided to change his tactics for the defense of Da Nang. Up to this time, the defense had consisted of heavy patrols in the mortar/rocket belt, extending in a semicircle around southern and into western Da Nang areas. With the addition of troops from the Third Battalion, Twenty-Seventh, it was decided to fan farther with patrols and search and destroy missions that would reach deeper into the enemy controlled areas of Go Noi. Operations would be mobile, showing a stronger force, still as an attack preventive measure for Da Nang and the military assets stationed there.

Although eventually devastated with losses in and around the Go Noi, in theoretical defense of an attack on Da Nang and thus a preemptive defense of an attack which never happened, the three out of twenty-seven survivors returned to the United States in September and were given a parade of honor in San Diego. After Go Noi and related area combat, high command reacted again by sending the new unit home, having concluded that other fighting units had become so accustomed to robbing combat trained troops from the Twenty-Seventh, that providing fresh fighting marines to other units would now be the sole mission of the Twenty-Seventh, after their San Diego parade, of course. Calling the Twenty-Seventh home would be an alternative to increasing draft numbers in an atmosphere of Domestic Nam protest and general upheaval of antiwar sentiment from a growing number of America's general population, in other words, a political Band-Aid, of course, with a parade in lieu of a declining intensity for the Domestic Nam commitment delusion.

With that deployment of the Twenty-Seventh at Go Noi, the brief heroic story of the recipient of the Medal of Honor award, the nation's highest honor, Private First Class Burke began in The Nam. In the two-war brief history of the Twenty-Seventh, seven Medals of Honor would eventually be awarded, six for heroic actions in WWII at Iwo Jima, and one for the dreadful work in the Go Noi region of the Nam by Burke with I Company.

Events within any historic account do not behave and build to become "historically notable" in isolated time capsules, as all people and events are linked to a past of other people and events, always bringing us along in unpredictable cadences. The history of the Vietnamese National Railroad building brought Burke and I Company to a battle field they had not imagined was fortified with decades of superior bunker building material. Circumstantially, the Twenty-Seventh Marines were formed using rotating and inexperienced officer leadership and assigned to a general who would always be detached and would never know the people or the skill levels of the unit or the terrain to be fought within. The Go Noi had been long ago built and fashioned with tunnels, trenches, and ambush killing points, the occupants waiting patiently in their years of warring for a probing, invading force to swarm upon. The Twenty-Seventh had its history, as did Go Noi, as does the Burke family.

Burke is a traditional north European name of historic connotation. Most accounts of "Burke families" are thought to originate in Normandy (France), moving to England via Ireland, a common path for earlier European population shifting. Eventually, a deep Irish influence became the character of most Burke inhabited locations. "Burk" means "fort," and thus, Burkes were considered to live near and inhabit fortifications, in defense of those fortifications for themselves and other area clans. Burkes arose in more significant numbers in the twelfth century and became considered Anglo-Norman, a common mix for the always warring and evolving British Isles populations.

History reveals a number of famous Burkes; among them were Robert Burke, Stephen, Jane, and another Robert who landed on US Maryland shores as immigrants, all in the mid 1600s. A new wave of Burkes landed in Virginia in the early 1700s. Most immigrating Burkes were from Ireland, not England, perhaps in response to centuries-old English suppression within the British Isles, though Ireland itself had never been conquered by the Englanders beyond Northern Island. The name "Burgh" remains as the French naming derivative from Burke.

Burkes currently are most common in the Northeast, Illinois, California, and throughout Kentucky, which, in the heavy immigration years of the 1600s and 1700s, was the western extension of the boundaries of Virginia. Many early American immigrants reached Middle America via a route west through Virginia into Western Virginia, which stretched all the way to the Mississippi river at the time. Later, Kentucky would be the first named state after the American Revolution and the original colonies, having been carved loose as a separate Commonwealth from Virginia.

Currently, according to the latest national census, there are about 5,500 Burke families in the U.S., most immigrating 1851-1891, from Ireland. According to Civil War records, 3,207 Burkes fought in that war: 942 for the Confederates, 2,265 for the Union. Most US Burkes in the nineteenth century were split within three main occupations: laborers, farmers, and a large number recorded as housekeepers. Historically, Burkes appear to be common, determined, hardworking people with an extraordinary number serving in the Civil War and wars since.

By the mid-1800s, through labor and farming opportunity and Civil War assignments, many Burkes and optimistic searching post-Civil War Americans had relocated through Central Kentucky, toward the timbered Elizabethtown area in north central Kentucky, along the main trails just south of Louisville and north of Bowling Green. The heavily forested area being a well-known crossroads stopping place for many families, considering further Western movement, perhaps into the growing and available fertile farming lands of Indiana or Illinois. Amidst that movement west was Levi Burke, Civil War, Union-side veteran, farmer-to-be, optimistic Irish-bred with family in tow.

Levi and family never found their farm but worked with and around many western Kentucky productive farming communities. Post-Civil War mid-America was being settled rapidly, and thus, land plats and land ownership was the opportune business grab of the time. With many Civil War veterans like Levi Burke anxious to settle down, farmland was being rapidly divided, settled, and becoming legally platted and owned by a constantly western flowing America into and beyond the Kentucky area, and thus other labor demands arose connected to the farm settlements as is common in the expansion and enterprising build-up of free societies.

Levi soon found abundant opportunity in building the fences that would divide newly acquired farms and contain the growing number of livestock flowing into the area's farm operations, as well as working with surveying companies to bury corner posts defining newly divided and owned property boundaries. Soon, Levi Burke was known for his diligent hard work in this new line of demand, fence building, and corner post locating and setting. Slowly and consistently, Burke would move the family a little farther west, one stop and work opportunity at a time, through Kentucky until again settling in an area just south of Paducah, Kentucky, in a most fertile farming timbered lowland area near the confluence of the Ohio and Mississippi Rivers, just south and across the river from southernmost Illinois.

Levi and Emma added two children to their family. The two soon-to-be hardworking sons, Edwin and Tho, who would follow in Levi's fence building expertise footsteps and would eventually travel the extreme western Kentucky crop production areas working with farmers and surveyors on new land platting and fence building. By the turn of the twentieth century, both Edwin and Tho were considered experts of their own making in their unique trade of fence building and survey boundary marking. The Burke brothers were considered in some demand and of good decent reputation, hardworking, and fair to deal with.

Edwin, being the more adventurous and always most curious, would begin to work across the Ohio River into Southern Illinois with every opportunity requesting his skills, having constantly been aware of and curious about the rumors of rich Illinois land opportunities. Eventually, Edwin packed what possessions he had and moved across the Ohio River permanently to a location near what is currently Benton, Illinois, where he would settle, build fences, locate and place property marker posts, assist to define further settlement boundaries and continue to look for land to farm, a goal that would take the Burkes another two generations to fulfill in a time beyond Edwin's own forward vision. Edwin would also marry, raise a family of two daughters and one son, but die too early on a hillside job as a result of attempting to halt a field wagon led by runaway mules. Edwin did survive long enough that the son Caleb would learn the fundamentals of fence building and related laboring trades, allowing him to carry forward with the aged reputation of Burke family fence construction expertise, now approaching one hundred years in the technique making.

Caleb would never prosper in his own right as fence building and working Burkes before him, starting with Levi. Rural Southern Illinois family life in the 1920s and 1930s was always a struggle for Caleb and his new young wife with four wide-eyed growing children in a land between the forested Southern Illinois river country and the flat richly fertile lands a little further north that were calling him to the heartland of central Illinois. The dreams and visions of a farm homestead kept alive from generation to generation from Levi through Edwin, now residing in Caleb, never seemed to depart the core feelings of this strand of the Irish immigrant Burkes.

Caleb's oldest son, Walter, always seemed to be looking north even as a young child, asking questions of life in places that seemed faraway, as if in another country or certainly another state, places called Decatur or Bloomington, Springfield or Charleston where the Lincolns had temporarily settled on their migration west and north from the same Kentucky paths as the Burkes had been following. Past the Benton southern Illinois area, always leaning toward the central Illinois flatter darker lands, Walter was convinced at a very young age that these new lands would surely be easier to dig into for future fence posts than the muscled grappling required to work the clay-based shallow timber soils dominating the southern Illinois landscape. Passing travelers rumored that central Illinois contained vast rows of hedge trees that would provide abundant post material for fence building of all designs.

At the age of twelve, Walter began to question his meager mid-Southern Illinois surroundings, regularly feeling he would soon be his own master, create his own world of opportunity, some day, when the ambition would meet up and join with the opportunity. Walter Burke would not contain his ambition or his curiosity for very long and would move north with the help of a drifter he had met near the Wabash rail lines that reached out to connect Illinois' most southern point Cairo to unknown State of Illinois richest land acreage, stretching infinitely north. Just as in most 1600s and 1700s immigrant expectations and realities, Walter had no specific destination in mind other than toward what he had heard was honest work and abundant opportunity, hopefully with welcoming farmers and communities open to a hardworking, honest descendant of Irish bloodlines. At that time, such individual and family roaming and searching for life's steps up were still most common in America's transient and rural interior populations, still just a generation or two removed from Civil War issues.

In 1937, Walter could not wait to look around the next corner, or over the next prairie grassed ridge, into an imagination of the workings of new towns and friendly hardworking community populations. With a combination of hitchhiking and trainhopping, Walter stepped from the back of a stranger's delivery truck, alone, customarily broke, temporarily tired of overwhelming uncertainty for a thirteen-year-old, in a town of 620, Bement, Illinois, a location that would do for now. At least, the Bement rail connected toward Decatur, and the small three-block area downtown was bustling with the area's farm-related activity at the feed and hardware stores—all of it right in the heart of those rich soils so often described and dreamed of by Walter. Walter hopped from the bumpy wagon ride one block from an Abraham Lincoln historical marker, appreciated as a token gift of welcome, but chose to head the other direction just south of the tracks and was soon looking into the Ablinger Hardware front door, hat in hand, hoping to find any kind of "friendly" among the busy population of this exciting new town atmosphere, in a place simply named Bement, surrounded by deep black soils.

As is the history of American opportunity for able, willing workers of generally any honest skill set, Walter found work immediately from the Bement hardware store front porch, where he intended to be seen and see any potential farm employer going by. Work may be for the asking, particularly if the asker can be defiantly planted at the highway and railroad track crossroads where he perched with only a smile and the good natured approval of Mrs. Ablinger, the store owner. Good luck in looking for work is particularly productive, when a well-respected store proprietor herself, a human landmark of a community, is asking all store visitors and general street traffic that day if they needed any fences built, chickens or general livestock fed, or haying. By late afternoon, Walter was on his next bumpy uncertain wagon way with a local livestock farmer to build his first Bement fence and then latch on to any other work he might squeak from his first employer and community relationship, reminding Mrs. Ablinger to keep him in mind for other work that may appear as he'd be back when this job ended, reminding her that he was the hardest and most honest of young workers. Walter would eat and have a barn roof for that night, at least, and thus start a new, very young life, in Piatt County, Central Illinois. All this Burke building started by the hands-on farm land search begun by Levi in 1856 and likely similar other Burkes even before Levi, as historically Burkes stretched out and built through early Virginia into parts of an unknown, open, wild, growing America for over one hundred years.

There would be more minor Burke ventures, as progressive life with growing evolving families is supposed to be that way. Such blind adventuring was the unspoken deal people made with early America and the growing enterprise of the country's enthusiasm.

The true epic Medal of Honor Burke family venture into national heroic recognition would be thirty years beyond Walter's Bement translocation, across the globe's largest ocean into the teeth of a waiting Asian enemy. So be it. Fence builders have little suspicions beyond the vision of perfecting the job at hand and an end goal not yet proven at a time of embarkation and stepping forward for duties yet assigned.

The newly arrived, still growing, teenage Piatt County Burke, although persistently curious, Walter never had a real chance at formal education in the area rural schools but did earn a fast reputation for hard work and expertise with fence building and lumber and soils related work. Walter Burke found work where he could around

Bement, never lived in one place for very long but built a hand-to-mouth business with the proper tool sets by the time he was eighteen, with the help of one after another satisfied farmer-client referencing Burke and his expertise to others. By 1945, still very young, but on his own for six years already, Walter Burke slowly built a working reputation a click further north to the center of Piatt County into the Monticello farming community and market and thus would move his limited belongings those few clicks north on the connecting two lane blacktop, later given a county road number 10. With the winding Sangamon river ("sangamon" meaning "land of good hunting" in Illini Indian language) slicing through the middle of Piatt County Northeast to Southwest, fence building was even more in demand through flat tillable land and then into the thicker river lowland soils, timber and flood plains. In addition, a variety of side jobs were abundant in town and with local farmers, if times in fence building were seasonally slow. For Walter Burke, it was all about having your head up with a clean nose and strong, ready hands.

Burke knew this was a good place and likely always would be a good place as other trades and industries were also growing around the Monticello community, each increase in commercial and growth activity leading to more work available for the laboring sector. The next Burke family, adding to the traveled ancient Irish clan, would soon begin with Walter's eventual marriage and include four sons, three daughters, and later include five more half brothers and sisters. Seventh down and the fourth son in the original Walter clan was Robert C. Burke, born November 7, 1949 in Monticello's Kirby hospital, which had been fashioned by the prosperous community from an elegant private mansion into a working hospital, gifted to the community by one of Monticello's historically fortunate families.

No one knows too far into the future with any certainty. Life's generally unpredictable path is supposed to be unknown. Fundamentally and often in living, the more *unknowing*, the better. Dealing with unknowing requires personal preparation and skill building for the ambitious in order to keep the highs not too high and thus unmanageable and the lows not so low and not so desperate. Through Robert's brother Raymond, who was three years older, the Burkes would occasionally run with and be friends with the faster paced townie Wilson Street Boys, who set local youthful mind-sets along the same similar futuristic pace of "work hard, play smart" and keep looking forward.

Young boys in big work-oriented families of modest existing means look out, up, beyond, and commonly wonder the following:

Why not? What is over that next grassy ridge, beyond that over there, and what would it mean to me? (As had Levi, Edwin, and Walter in their transforming years.)

Where can I go and build my place? Where will I go? I must go, you know!

And thus, Robert C. grew largely under the radar of a larger community and area farming issues, waiting to eventually feel his own niche and place within a large family in Monticello and Piatt County or beyond. In a countryside lined with creeks and tree lines filled with rabbits, deer, pheasants, and quail, all seemingly connected by location and nature's gifts one way or another and tied loosely together adjacently in a prairie package by the Sangamon River's roaming ways, many adventurous boys took to the woods and river bottoms for general adventuring of all types and often for good hunting. Robert C. carried his own handy 20-gauge and Bowie knife into the tree lines by the time he was twelve, tracking deer, learning the feel of surroundings, the feel of a calm or a cold wind, understanding the value and care of weapons, and absorbing the skills of stillness and patience along his own Goose Creek. Robert learned the sounds of tree lines and the difference between movements from the winds and movements from the game being hunted, always with stillness to his calculated steps and pauses. By thirteen, Robert could see nature's difference between morning sun angles through the trees and foliage and the sun angles of the evening, skills invaluable while waiting with a one shot 20-gauge for pheasants to fly low from feeding in corn fields to the timbers underbrush for the nights nesting.

No one is certain now, nor will they ever be certain, what makes a "hero"—a military hero fighting for a bigger and often vague unknown cause other than a "duty" has been assumed. What is it in one person that builds the fortitude of heroism that generally escapes the characters of the next one thousand or ten thousand people behind them or around them in the heat and chaos of a battle at hand that will likely take many lives certainly including their own life? There is no single identifiable characteristic that lends to heroism, but instead an accumulated, disciplined, youthful build-up from being out in the mix of real life adventuring, intricately gaining a feel for the reactions required in a situation, embracing an internal Semper Fi perhaps born within, no one suspecting or knowing the internal assets of bravery and duty are there. Whatever it is that builds heroism, it quietly grew within Robert C., strengthening through youthful years, waiting for a direction and feeling of usefulness and value, no matter the challenge.

Robert C. was very young (always very young), lived young, and died young, and consistent with his youthfulness and adventuring, he always knew he would join the Marine Corps as soon as possible, which would be during late high school as soon as he turned eighteen. Always on the fringes of being what was thought of as a normal teenager, Robert C. hunted, helped his father and older brother Raymond build more and more area fence to restrain the county's livestock and define transacted and platted boundary lines, and saw little need for groupiness with too many high school chums. Robert's vision was the Marine Corps and the skills required to first survive boot camp and then become a real marine, uniformed, armed, assigned to a real operating unit. He prepared for just and only that, while tolerating the hallways and ringing class bells in some so-what high school years awaiting the blessed chit that comes legally with the historic marker of eighteen years of age.

Gung-ho, but naturally timid about the demands of boot camp, Robert C. landed in San Diego on January 1968, twenty days before the start of the Tet Offensive on the ground in the Domestic Nam. In the next five months, Robert C. would move rapidly toward his destiny as internal America continued with urban riots and campus temper tantrums, as the assassination of Martin Luther King stirring more riotous ambitions by a whole new angered black sector population, and as '68 election year turmoil would build to further societal explosions. The demands and requirements of Marine Corps boot camp, an exploding war turning larger and more violent daily, from which there would be no avoiding, and an America turning inside out, were what Robert and other young marines had in their mess kits to deal with.

Those entering boot camp, especially in the defining year of the Domestic Nam, needn't worry about being good enough, tough enough, or entrenched enough to survive. "You will survive," one way or another. Drill instructors produce fighting marines. That's what they live for, and that is all there is to it. Burke had been in the hills and creekbeds, armed and tracking game, listening to the sounds of the country's natural elements around him, sensing the landscape's movements apparent and subtle. He knew the feel, sounds, and smells "out there." Everything else was physical training, learning to keep your head up and mouth shut at all times. In a boot camp drilling platoon of 120 strangers, you make some friends, but not all that many, not as many as you would think. It is just too intense, requiring constant attention to the detail of the next day's mental and physical obstacle courses.

In three and a half months, Robert C. would inhale the demands of boot camp, graduate, and be assigned as a motor pool mechanic at Camp Pendleton, just north of San Diego County, dividing the populace areas of extreme Southern California from Orange County, a few clicks north and just south of the sprawling, heavily populated human chaos of Los Angeles. Promoted from private, to private first class, the mechanic's MOS in the Camp Pendleton motor pool was a

Corps' head fake; no one in those days, able, trained, from a modest background of a rural fence builder, would for very long escape the Domestic Nam nor would Robert C.

By late April, reforming the mothballed Twenty-Seventh Marines was in full priority from top command. I Company, Third Battalion, Twenty-Seventh Marines would be Robert's new fast-moving duty assignment, a fate unknown and impossible to contemplate. Fate, luck, short straw or long, we never know what blessings turn to curses, or then back to blessings. We never know on whose shoulder an angel will be instructed to sit or under what expertise or intention of command will the assigned course of duty be for the soldier with an angel, or angel-less.

How battlefield "hot" can a new assignment be?
With what support?
Why Go Noi Island, which meant nothing to
I/3/27 in April?

These are only a slight few of the questions that quickly pop in and out of a soldier's mind who is about to be staged, armed, shipped, launched into a battle's snarling fight for life first, and the war's greater goal second. A company (a military company normally being 100 to 225), Third Battalion, Twenty-Seventh Marines would load gear and brave minds, souls, and determination on a poised United Airlines transport jet at the safe, peaceful, and sunny airstrip at El Toro, California. They would take in the scenery of America, some for the last time, the grace of the distant mountain silhouettes, see the free moving safe vehicles on their merry way over the highway next to the airstrip, and nod with a shy greeting at the smiling stewardess up the United Airlines jet ramp who, behind her smile, would be feeling very deeply and would resist a motherly hug, for she knew each of these boys who she had the care of for the next twelve hours would be in their own new deadly fight before another week would pass.

The young soldier's intent but curious mind cannot quite put boarding a United Airlines flight together with what they have heard and known of the violence and intense demands of their destination, now just at the other end of only one more take off, then landing.

United Airlines?
How do these clean, smiling, neat people fit
into this suffocating mission?

Burke and Company would soon be cruising over the vast blue, constant rolling endless ocean waves, racing westerly, so far westerly no one could grasp the feel of the flight's progress. The mission's flight was as calming as any other "trip" for some, not so for others, like the guy across the narrow aisle of the plane who already looks nervous and stressed not knowing what meets his personal fate at his flight's conclusion. Burke was now beyond America's westernmost continental boundary, zooming in a jet to some strange place, where no one owned anything, trusted no one, with a hundred elements of the land and its people that can kill you, and want to. A Burke family tree where no one in three hundred years of American history had ever set foot west of the great Mississippi River now found Robert C. was beyond the West Coast, zooming to Southeast Asia of all mysterious places, more than four months from finishing classes and dropping out at the hometown high school.

Transoceanic United flights stop in Hawaii, where Burke's India Company would disembark during a too brief refueling stretch. Hawaii! Great-grandson, grandson, son of a fence builder, not yet a high school graduate stood in the Hawaiian sun, seeing what could be seen in a snapshot stand-alone, a pause for contemplation in a strange, strange journey; half behind, half ahead. Each marine's mind was working differently, looking at the same surreal Hawaiian sight, thinking differently of the image according to each vision of his own next levels. Things were okay so far with the flight, smiling stewardess, refueling, all while knowing the next leg of the half globe journey would likely create an opposite sensation. India Company mingled about a tarmac that is but a micro-pause in a vast undefined mission, glowing in a warm sun that would never be as welcoming again, ever. United, all too soon, was fueled, gang plank door waiting wide open as would be a cave entrance—bright as an Hawaiian sun outside, dark as a cave inside. It was the same door as was open in California, but this time, it looked smaller, darker on its inside, like a huge casket with wings and a crew that seemed automatically several clicks south of depressed, eyes down this time, not making eye or voice contact with any reboarding marines, fake, plastic-looking, painted-on smiles, this final boarding time. Everything on the marines' bodies—boots/belts/helmets/PFC pins—all were immediately heavier. No angels were in sight, felt, or even suspected this time.

Immediately, this post-Hawaii flight, unlike the US mainland flight to Hawaii concluded just an hour ago, is totally quiet inside, no order or spoken consensus necessary. Solemnity blanketed the fuselage, individually and collectively as if a dark hand had passed over the occupant's pervading silence and delivered its oppressively dark mood upon each passenger and crew. India Company soldiers, new to the company and to the mysterious assignment and new to each other, dug in deep emotionally, crawling within themselves, deeper than any time in their lives.

A six-hour flight! Six hours to Nam!
Then what?
What waits at the end of these latest six hours
of each life aboard?

Minds are 90 percent numb, soldiers only slightly aware of a passing stewardess or another soldier's body shift to another uncomfortable sitting wait. Time is not fair on this flight, each fifteen minutes seems like an hour. United chases west to stay ahead of a pursuing sun, jet engines in a constant numbing groan of engines working an engine way, the relentless sun, eventually catching the flight, creating mysterious eerie bounces of light from the silver wings flashing into the fuselage of young marines. Three hours to an ETA, and the sun would pass and now lead the way on a direct course to war for I Company, only one more stop planned.

A jetting day of anxious feelings left two real hours remaining for a Nam ETA, and this group of new Wilson Street Boys would be on the ground, starting their countdown, of which some would make, and many wouldn't. Such is the nature of war.

> *What is the mission, anyway?*
>
> *Why again are we even in Nam, now for years, with hundreds of thousands of troops and equipment that drains American assets?*
>
> *Who is rioting or assassinating who in the United States today, largely over a war now just two hours ahead—unless this United jet turns around? (Maybe the pilots lost something, and will turn around.)*
>
> *Why would someone shoot Dr. King?*

Do United troop transports ever turn around? Naw, no chance. Oh well, the thought was worth ten seconds of a never-ending flight to a reputed hell.

More sun bounces off the sturdy wings into the side windows, a sure sign of still flying westerly. No marine was moving, or talking, all are within themselves, within full personal inventory taking.

> *Are we ready?*
> *Am I ready?*
> *How will I react under fire?*
> *How bad can this be?*
> *I believe all the stories! All of them! Will I have my own stories? Of course!*

The hollow monotone voice from United warns of the impending landing, thirty stretched minutes from right now, as United with its numb cargo dips in elevation for a landing somewhere on the other side of the earth from the 220 homes of the uniformed bodies aboard. Right now, there is no rank, just individuals with their own faith, training, thoughts, regrets, or accomplishments and their individual slow thumping heart beats.

United cruises lower, at ten thousand feet. Ships dutifully patrolling the South China Sea can be seen from the window seats as real objects. Dead calm quiet inside the plane is deafening! Only the consistent sounds of the four jet engines numb the atmosphere as United instructs to prepare for landing.

> *I wonder where we land?*
> *What will this confused torn place look like?*
> *What will the people look like, and how is it known which are friend, or which will carry the concealed weapon to kill Americans?*
> *How long will it be from flight to a first in-the-fight mission?*
> *Tomorrow? When the sun rises one more time, will that start a deadly battle?*
> *Right there is the quiet shoreline of South Vietnam, right there, just below, a place I am ordered to care about, and be prepared to fight over, and defend with my life.*

Burke had never seen a shoreline from the air, pretty neat: "Don't look so bad-ass of a country!" A break in the steady waves slapping a long shoreline is marked by a mountain, Marble Mountain, and United cruises as if held by a greatest force suspended in air through the land break, descending past Marble Mountain, passing over large and small vessels in the bay below making their singular mysterious way on untold journeys and missions right in the middle of a war. The crank and grind of downward stretching landing gear breaks the interior silence and, almost as if on cue, sets the team of stewardess in motion up and down a quiet solemn aisle, filled with now speeding heartbeats on both sides. Curious India Company heads stretch to any side window for a glimpse of sight lending a clue to a new committed reality in a mysterious land and war.

United touches Southeast Asia with a skip, Domestic Nam land, as some smart-ass speaks about "can't wait for the bus going the other way." Start the soldier's tradition rotation count now, 365 and a "wake-up" is the official tour process, unless powers find "other extension duties as assigned." This United's controlled roll gently to a stop cannot be long enough, just keep taxiing, rolling right along. Never stop. But United does stop; they always stop on the Da Nang tarmac. Stopping was the deal United had made and the soldiers had also made. Everybody in the war had a deal. Besides, United needed the seats for the beat up, displaced, and courageous survivors of their own tours, who earned the right for that coveted return trip across the Pacific, going back east to a shifted American world that they would find difficult to understand, fit into, or comfortably assimilate with. That discomfort would be a surprise to them, an out-of-place feeling they had not thought about.

I Company had arrived in the historic infamous Nam; the day was May 4, 1968, and they were now in the war. Officially in the war! Put it in the scorebook. It has happened. All the speculation was over. The now annoying quiet turned to a controlled robotic bustling of green marine uniforms beginning to find their deadened legs to embark and see the land of their "duties as assigned." One at a time, the 220 marines of India Company met the sun and pressing heat of their new Domestic Nam at the United opening. They would, one at a time, individually emerge from the dark cave of the plane into the hot Southeast Asia reality. The land was in post-Tet chaos, everything was uncertain, overguarded and overcautionary, everything moving about seemed awkward, as if going in the wrong direction. Orders flew for the formation of new human lines to receive stored gear buried in the belly of United, and Company I's new grunts, boys from small towns and ghettos, scrambled to comply in as much bumping unison as could be expected.

New officers appeared, strangers. New orders flew around the ears, into helmets, and in the minds of the enlisted, as if the extent of reorganization time was the mere half-minute down the debark steps. Equipment unloaded and laying on the sizzling tarmac blacktop, United, once a friend, protecting the last of the lipsticked Caucasian women to be seen for a year, moved as rapidly away as possible as if to avoid the inevitable waiting confrontations, and in a hurry to wash United wings of the dirty, deadly, confusing work the planes were complicit to routinely perform.

Burke was "in-country," needing only a 365 days and a wake-up. Burke would get fourteen and then never a wake-up again but would get the journey that the heavens offer to blessed lives.

Besides frantic military clean up from one Tet and preparing for a possible other Tet, Dr. King had just been assassinated a month prior, and much of America's urban ghettoes were on fire. Bleeding societal unrest stirred within every vulnerable corner of America, affecting the entire population. Troops had an eye on the United States as well as a foot in-country. Nothing was certain anywhere for anything. Soon, Bobby would be assassinated, another demoralizing strike. First for the loss of his electric smile leading good intentions, but just as much signaling another moral Domestic Nam setback, from the loss of a potential leader who at least had a chance to figure this war out and seemed to be trying to do so. Everything of national character suddenly was awkward, back-assed, upside down-ish. Burke had "his" boots, on that ground with an M-60, ammo, a side arm, and some buddies latching onto his own personal Bowie-knife along the way—and with that, ten days later, he would helicopter into Go Noi with an ad hoc company of fellow Marines, a most serious deadly place.

Selected for the Go Noi mission, I Company, Third Battalion, Twenty-Seventh Marines, no battle experience, unadjusted to the suffocating Asian heat, against trained equipped hungry forces, and on the enemy's fortified ground, unknowingly followed orders as if through cattle shoots.

The Domestic Nam was in full awkward operating force at 110 degrees, hotter on a destined Da Nang tarmac. I Corps military genius, in full post-Tet reactionary mode, was about to throw 220 fresh, largely untrained marines into the hottest, most-cards-stacked-against quagmire of warring detail that could be imagined. That first day from Da Nang, I/3/27 was assigned to G/2/7 command, already "probing" Go Noi but not yet committed to a "fight and hold" ground battle.

Since the '30s, steel and timber bunker building stock piles from the Vietnamese National Railroad had been turned to tunnels and fortifications and now awaited an enemy, the sons and grandsons of American families like Burke. Who knew?

> *How do generations of family building on one continent meet on history's winding course on a totally different continent with decades of warring assets to confront that infrastructure in a war undefined, without direction, on a battlefield of guesstimations from a general not even in and amongst the effort who knows nothing of the troops he commits?*

It does happen, and there is military and civilian leadership who must deploy young heroes for the prosecution of the deadly work to be undertaken, theoretically disposed. The stage for day 1, I Company, in the Go Noi was set; all that history needed was Burke and I Company. Day 1 would be May 13 and was the initial move into the suffocating, crossfire trap of the Go Noi.

In the Go Noi:

Besides an impractical landscape of ten-foot high bamboo;

    With concealing defensible tree lines and dry creek bed depressions crisscrossing the area;
    And despite daily temperatures of at least 110 degrees or hotter;
    Overlooking 20 years of bunker and tunnel building with railroad infrastructure material;
    Ignoring Viet Cong dominated villages, crisscrossed and connected by tunnels and trenches, with bad guys all over the place trained in jungle and ambush warfare for generations;
    Overlooking the reality of new fresh well-armed NVA Divisions now armed with AK-47 assault rifles and a new warfare invention called RPG launchers;
    With excellent supply lines and seasoned command intent on their own domestic purposes.

Da Nang command overlooked other deadly realities as Burke and I/3/27 awaited their specific assignment for first boots on Go Noi land. From the beginning, the ad hoc I/3/27 was expendable. Formed rapidly with new units under new inexperienced commands, it was physically impossible to adjust in two weeks from the cool ocean breezes fanning Camp Pendleton and other California bases from which marines were reassigned to the suffocation of Go Noi's 110 degree lowlands. No one knew what equipment was actually needed for missions undefined. Ignoring the long standing fact that "Charlie owned the night," unfamiliar off-site command would expect this new Third Battalion to challenge and win night dominance. To complicate matters, A-6 intruders from the aircraft carrier *Enterprise* ordered to soften the Go Noi area with 500-pound bombs, experienced control short circuits, and fourteen bombs were dropped, unexploded into the islands interior sands to await rearming by NVA boobytrap artists and provide one more gruesome unwelcome for new US Marine ground-probing units, ordered from Da Nang to expand the area of ground truthing reconnaissance for the safety of Da Nang.

More cards could not have been stacked against Burke's India Company. Perhaps all the angels in Nam would not have helped, other than within the journey of the individual heavenly spirit soon to be. The main probing, enemy seeking, armed body of I Company, would have Burke, but who would Burke have? In the fight, among the demands of act and react unselfishly, within a commitment as marines are trained and bound. Faith of duty is composed individually in a grunt's gut. It is time to love your weapon, see movements, and sense the slightest landscape signals and shifts as if tracking game in a slanting ravine, in a light snow with a 20-gauge, with a talent for an understanding blending with stillness.

On May 13, Captain Ralph, commanding officer of I/3/27 and 220 marines, crossed a sun-sizzling tarmac with full weaponry, ammo, and sparse supplies to crawl aboard twelve waiting, idling Chinook CH-46 marine helicopters from the HMM-364 Purple Foxes. From lift-off, before the copters rising left turn, Burke could see a glimpse of the colorful Da Nang bay bordered by Marble Mountain and scattered with growing US warring assets of all kinds which he had just crossed over in his now long gone United. Burke could briefly see the magnitude of the American investment and asset commitment—big, huge, extensive, a city of weaponry and warring support systems, incomprehensible at first glimpse as if a stationary D-Day movie duplication. Burke was now part of it all.

The south line of the Go Noi included a cleared dirt nob, labeled Hill 148, its surface soon dusting up by the huge long blades of the CH-46 carrying I Company for the first time into the teeth of the war. Hill 148 was stark, bare clay soil, angry looking, and unforgiving, all to its own hellish-self, as I Company deployed to form a perimeter and then to begin digging defensive positions in the hard ground in 110-degree heat. Hill 148 was just a place to land Chinook aircraft, that's all—a barren dirt pile with no shade to more reasonably acclimate the new boys from California. I Company would only have access to the water they carried in, with no resupply planned.

Day 1 on Hill 148 was war's initial introduction for I Company. Only two KIAs and three WIAs from booby trap incidents complicated the Go Noi entrance for I Company but first casualties nonetheless as the slap in the face that training, staging, reorganizing was over. This is it!

Burke's squad dug into the north plateau of 148, a vantage with a clear view of the menacing Go Noi lowlands from which an occasional NVA line of troops could be seen hustling to points unknown. It is impossible to land twelve noisy large Chinooks anywhere in a war zone without arousing a huge range of the country-side inhabitants to notice and observe, especially those whose attentiveness is war-heightened. I Company's arrival would be no secret and taken as a signal that the Go Noi was no longer an overlooked, lost lowland to an expanding war. Dried, boiling hot, obvious amidst the enemy's presence, Burke and I Company were now part of the war. United flight and stewardess faded in thought as if it were a year ago and I Company had two first day KIAs to prove it. Two dead already without a shot fired. On foot, staring into a strange demonic violent land just 148 clicks down covered trails, Burke's squad dug in for whatever war's next move offered, then waited for the creeping darkness that Charlie depends on to be handed the night. Marines, in no particular formation, rested as best they could, armed with safeties off, having no real idea what awaited. An inexperienced command of one captain and one lieutenant waited nervously on the hill's highest knob with handheld radios for any new orders from Da Nang. Darkness would surround and capture Hill 148 dotted with new marines, and the night's flashes and booms of far away struggles kept tensions high in a constant reminder of their dangerous situation and purpose. The Domestic Nam never slept, never.

The first glimmers of May 14 showed in the lower rolling landscape behind Burke, toward the coast. As the Go Noi lowlands lingered in the early morning haze and shadows, I Company was ordered to move down 148 and enter Go Noi for the first time. Free from immediate enemy harassments or confrontations, I Company humped through the strange land all day, often observing enemy signs and sensing enemy movements. Background radio chatter gave a sense of attachment, back up, being a part of a larger meaningful effort. Temperatures in the bush lowlands were now 120 degrees. The enemy needn't make contact, didn't need to, the temperatures were doing their wearing-down work on the probing marines for the hidden enemy, now patient for thirty years. Again, there was no resupply of water, nor did there seem to be a plan for water resupply. Food C rations were already scarce by the second day. I/3/27 linked up with G/2/7, a unit more familiar with the Seventh Marines command, and both companies dug in for the May 14 night's strange unpredictable war offerings, now out of water in only two days. In the bush a defensible perimeter is always sparsely defined. Again, I Company and Burke dug in, again with Burke's squad on a point northwest to Go Noi's interior. Enemy mortars would consistently break the night silence but not close and seemed only to be teasers, warnings that the enemy was well aware of who and where the probing units waited.

Burke was now in the bush two days. On the whole, his tour was now 350-something and that wake-up. Hugging and humping his M-60 and as much ammo as he could carry, over uneven thick terrain in 120 degrees with limited water, the whole frickin' thing began to already appear cock-eyed, operationally awkward, uncoordinated. Even a private first class could sense and read the hazardous signals.

Who sends new troops into heavy lowlands in
120 degrees without some plan for resupply?

On May 15, day 3 of this mysterious mission in no man's land, the mission named Allen Brooke, the remaining 215 marines of I/3/27 swept lowland areas all day, always leaning right, to the north, toward Da Nang rather than west deeper into the Go Noi lands obviously occupied by numerous NVA and VC. Eventually, Burke and I Company reached the Liberty Bridge crossing the wide and shallow meandering Song Thu Bon River, which was the main and only major land connection in that area to Da Nang and civilization, Southeast Asia style. Long since totally depleted of water, having not yet had a major confrontation, I Company with two companies from the Seventh Marines withdrew in the late afternoon from the gasping depths of Go Noi, across the Liberty Bridge toward food and resupply, having only been out three days, having accomplished nothing other than the two KIAs. I Company again settled for the night north across the Liberty Bridge, technically out of the Go Noi but only on the well-travelled edge, a guarded bridge in between them and the NVA who observed the withdrawal with typical patience.

Liberty Bridge was well guarded as the main traffic way over the wide river lowlands for area hamlets and villagers to cross into neighboring villages or go further on the dusty elevated trails into Da Nang. I Company observed the strange civilian traffic on the Liberty Bridge as all local travelers were casually searched for weapons or material possibly connecting them to local VC efforts. Burke could see for the first time that it would be impossible to tell who was a friend and who would be the enemy. (The 1968 friend or foe would be exactly the same as 2012 Afghanistan, where US ground strategies are no more defined or successful in the telling and implementing.) Squat, round Mamasans, four and a half feet tall, appeared just as dangerous as the path traveling, head-turning young men who seemed always to be looking and hustling beyond their immediate destination and business at hand.

I Company bivouacked just north of the Liberty Bridge toward night's fall, their entire movement to date, in and back out of the Go Noi, in reality being only a head-fake, a distraction invented by command to strategically convince NVA reconnaissance observers that the marines had probed and now were departing the Go Noi. It was a busy work command strategy, which forty-five years later seems laughable in its naive judgment; a laughable strategy if it were not so prone to eventual deadly disaster once fully played out by the marines in the strategy.

Burke would water up and man up the night of May 15, his beloved M-60 always cleaned, his head always up, eyes moving, K-bar wiped clean, observing any movements on the Go Noi side of his bridge, waiting for the next rabbit twitch in the underbrush. Rest or sleep was fleeting, it was just too tense, and always the night flares and womps of rockets elsewhere marked the struggles of other marines in other deadly fights. Three days of sweat and Go Noi muck now weighed on each marine physically; mentally, most of the inexperienced marines were in an ozone, moving, reacting, but very slowed, like mechanical robots now with depleting batteries. Burke knew of and had a sixth sense feeling for the pauses of the hunts, but other marines from urban or suburban areas kept their draining emotional and physical tenseness about them, even while at ease. Bridge traffic stopped, a night's quiet prevailed, only interrupted by the occasional pop of a flare, the splash of something in the river, and that horrible "womp" signifying another Ho Chi Minh traveled rocket had been used somewhere for its destructive purpose.

As the calendar flipped at midnight, to May 16, new orders from some safer, cleaner distant radio arrived for I Company and Burke to move out into a dark night that felt hungry. Charlie would now, this time, surely be behind every shadow. Burke took a point, moved across the Liberty Bridge again, back into the Go Noi, one step at a time, internally waiting for a first glimmer of morning, but knowing that would take hours and hundreds more cautious steps. "Ruby," the M-60 now named and now considered his favorite gal, was at a blasting ready, all safeties off. I Company had been into Go Noi and back out once already. Everyone knew this entry was permanent, the real mission. Enemy contact was certain, although no one knew what the mission was, other than a blind wondering search and destroy for a waiting enemy. There would be a fight today, I Company marines would die today, perhaps each day following.

By this time in the Domestic Nam warring evolution, May '68, the US military had engaged air, ground, and artillery war college methods and assets for four years. Enemies had become familiar with one another. The decade's experienced, trained NVA command could generally predict the order of assault weaponry in most picked battles and how the weapons would be deployed, in what order and to what potential extent. US air power would frequently soften targeted areas with air power bombings and fighter jet strafing of various severity, often then followed by artillery as the swift, agile fighter bombers exited the battle scene, followed by new grunts in boots humping M-60s for cover fire and M-16s for the ground fight, weighted further with as many hand grenades as could be carried. (At the time of Tet, the NVA and VC would occasionally have the new RPG (rocket-propelled grenade) weaponry technology, but US and ARVN troops did not.)

By '68 enemy command had developed a strategy to neutralize ground grunts that would be advancing on the NVA's dug-in, camouflaged positions. NVA or VC troops were lying in wait to spring field-of-fire traps on search and destroy marines. The enemy held their tree line and sniper positions and held their fire, waiting for point marines (i.e., eighteen-year-old Burke) to close in cautiously, a measured step at a time, only to pass the front lines of waiting NVA well into what would be the next field of fire. By allowing the point marines to move in farther beyond the most likely field of fire, NVA command believed US commanding officers, always somewhere else unable to actually see the situation, would not order covering air and artillery fire into the front line of a battle which now included one or two "friendly" point squads. Unable to employ air power and artillery assets for fear of eliminating their own point teams, the battlefield advantage swung to the concealed, waiting NVA or VC. The strategy had been perfected and used successfully, over and over, whenever the terrain situation and enemy troop numbers allowed.

May 16, Burke's squad of I Company, was again on a point, tough duty, dangerous, practically blind from one guestimate of a vantage point on a rice paddy ridge to the next terrain milestone in a tree line or creek bed, still in and out of the ten-foot elephant grass, all weighted with the ever-present Asian, suffocating heat and lowland humidity. Traveling in single file, through unpredictable footing, I Company grouped up to reorganize and wait until dawn. Displaced command was convinced the surprise midnight troop movement back across the Liberty Bridge into the Go Noi for the second time would be a total surprise to NVA, who had observed I Company's departure from Go Noi the day before and would believe they were on the other side of Liberty Bridge of no immediate consequence to a fight. In fact, other than the pretend glow of having outmaneuvered enemy expectations, no real field advantage was apparent to anyone within the actual movement.

Regrouped, momentarily rested for the days searching and destroying, I/3/27 advanced again at daylight, on line toward the Southeast of the Go Noi into lands thick with enemy signs, to soon surprise a sparsely guarded NVA Regimental Headquarters. The confusion of the surprise confrontation created a running gun battle, scattering soldiers from both sides. Eventually, I Company Marines and Burke seemed to grab an upper hand as more and more NVA pockets of fire were routed or simply faded into various deep foliage directions. To the NVA, the area was familiar ground. The fight took its toll. I Company could see and smell the dead, could now understand the confusion and power of their own weaponry and the weaponry they would now face daily. The May 16 wake-up battle concluded with 160 NVA KIA and the capturing of tons of equipment and enemy weapons. Twenty-five Marines were killed, thirty-eight were wounded, two dead and more KIA were from I Company. It was the first big maneuvering fight for 3/27, requiring various squads of various companies to work together. Before noon,

Burke was combing the battlefield, looking for any clues that would make fighting sense to be aware of for the many upcoming battles, certain to be soon, maybe yet that very day, probably that very day.

The May 16 morning fight was officially not over until medical evacuations were complete, and there were many. Removing the dead and wounded somehow seemed separate from the fresh fight, more of a bailing hay type operation, than a glorious USMC victory for the archives.

Does the world know this is the way it is?
Hump, fight like hell, kill, or be killed, then
cleanup?

Resupplies were brought in on the arriving Hueys for the next "seek and destroy" mission, bodies extracted for the short return trip to the Da Nang based medical and personnel processing facilities. Captured enemy assets would be destroyed in another of the house-cleaning operations of post-battle before I Company could move out. From just after dawn to midmorning, battlefield chaos prevailed. At dawn, there were thirty-eight more marines alive, crouched with other marines, anticipating the deadly challenges in a deadly place. Three hours later, those thirty-eight were dead, body-bagged. In a week, their families would be notified of each flag-draped arrival, spent body, words spoken, plaques placed, explanations and accounts vaguely extended. The remaining revelations would be command reveling in having tricked the NVA into thinking they had withdrawn across the Liberty Bridge toward Da Nang, ignoring the depths of the many larger pictures.

Reorganize and move out. Burke and I Company again bending to the right in double file, advancing cautiously more straight south, again moving, reacting to orders, but with no real idea or feeling for a logic or goal to the mission. Burke's "Ruby" was now a darlin' worth taking care of, worth being sentimental about. In the morning of the May 16 battle, Burke blew through near six hundred rounds of ammo, he and his Ruby alone routing two pockets of NVA fire and now was sufficiently re-ammoed up in the reorg pause, adrenalin continuing at a peak level. Next! A new hunt immediately underway. The remainder of May 16, I Company probed and moved in and out of flatland positions twice before settling in just to the north of another ancient Go Noi hamlet, Le Bac.

On May 16, other Go Noi locations became busy with fire power from US troops that included other new companies from 3/27 and ARVN (South Vietnamese Regulars) units on the eastern side as two South Vietnam ranger battalions also coptered in, all while entrenched NVA prepared their battle lines in bunker and tunnel systems that had been ready for years to accept the advancing fight now at hand. The war, the mini-Tet, had come to the long waiting and fortified Go Noi. Go Noi was prepared to erupt as battle lines and warring assets drifted to positions were focused, and erupt it did on May 17.

India Company was now deep into the strange Go Noi terrain and everything that went with it, which changes from hamlet to dry creek bed to elephant grass around every corner, always with the NVA secured mountains to the south waiting and hovering over the vast steamy scene. Da Nang with command central, airstrips, and beer tents to the north was still just clicks across the Liberty Bridge that now seemed to have been bivouacked weeks ago in the past, sometime after the long ago United trip. Blazing hot all day, with a sizzling M-60 and new hot heavy ammo, sparse hot drinking water, hot boots and hot socks and just frickin grind down and smother you *hot*. Burke could taste the day's remaining steamy air as if that same air had just been expelled from some other drained soldier's effort. Charlie's night crept in and around beat-up I Company, and new medevacs were filled with fainted, heat-stroked marines humping sixty to eighty pounds of warring necessities, verily able to catch single breaths. There was no evening. It was just hot daytime to hot nighttime.

The night life of flares and light splashes from exploding rockets and mortars would soon hold the field's attention. Occasionally, US

Marine Corps phantom jets accelerating out of Da Nang air space with dual burning engine exhausts would roar among some heavenly undefined distance, and then cross above, on their destructive way to some dark shadow mission also probably undefined. Always with a mind on numbers—KIA numbers, WIA numbers, tons of supplies captured numbers. Command wanted numbers to feed to higher command, to feed to desks in Washington, where the numbers would be hedged and fed to a press room, who then waited for more numbers, which they would get on May 17. (Burke and India Company would have a number for them, the big number 1, right up from the middle finger, but they weren't asked.)

As grunt marines do, Burke (now eighteen going on twenty-eight) and I Company grunts gathered by squad, checked assets, and bitched to no one in particular. (That's why they are called "grunts.") Who knew what May 17 would bring, and most unsettling the grunts could see that their young lieutenant officers had no idea either about what they would meet up with. Da Nang command operated on theories and O-School book strategies, having no real feeling for humping through elephant grass at 120 degrees, to for sure eventually advance into a waiting line of enemy fire of some type or another. I Company held today's ground, then and only then, and would certainly move out again at dawn into a Go Noi now filling with every sort of Domestic Nam fighting and maneuvering unit that the war could conjure up and lead in the Go Noi direction.

Burke thought the whole situation felt so awkward, with a strange reality of a youthful hunter, knowing sometimes you get the rabbit, but also sometimes the rabbit gets you.

Squashed in the muck of Go Noi, city guys talked about the deli on the corner at home, babes, the local rec areas, and babes. Officers did a rah-rah but wouldn't answer any questions because they didn't have any answers. Da Nang command had not pulled the next day's orders from the hat yet. The air tasted like May 17 could be the day. Word and location of the morning fight had certainly created an NVA stir among command. No question now where I Company and the larger battalion numbers were and which direction they were searching to destroy. May 16 was in the books, tomorrow was all that mattered:

> *Watch the night, and wait.*
> *See if the stars contained a clue.*
> *Find an angel.*
> *Wait. Have Ruby wait, Ruby is a good, patient, trusty, waiter.*
> *Everybody would wait in the heat. The suppressing, relentless heat would wait alongside each individual grunt as an unwanted hawk burdens a potential prey.*
> *Charlie out there was waiting; Charlie's families in Hanoi were waiting.*
> *America waited, not knowing for what.*
> *The politicians waited; to be fed more precious numbers.*
> *This whole SNAFU burdened, Go Noi poised scene would wait, suspended, simmering in slow guarded breaths and heart beats, earth continuing a slow methodic rotation—until just before dawn which would signal a time to hurry, the waiting would be over.*

As expected, May 17 woke and stirred to blazing hot early from Charlie's night. The day would define lives, earn battle fought ground with the ultimate price, ground that would soon be given up, and in the end, prove nothing beyond KIA and WIA report number theorizing. By 3:00 a.m., Col. Tullis Woodham, 3/27 commanding officer, anticipating a May 17 major fight, had ordered four more new Da Nang companies from the Twenty-Seventh toward the enclosing grip of the Go Noi. Companies K, L, H, and S did the traditional predawn nervous but deliberate scramble for weapons, supplies, and angels for their entrance into the confined Go Noi area of the day's killing operations. These four new companies, vaguely familiar with anything in Nam or each other, were to immediately depart by truck convoy to Liberty Bridge, cross as rapidly as possible and then deploy boots in a spread pattern south toward the position of I Company, also operating under the always vague search and destroy label. Already within the island, other marines of the Seventh and Twenty-Seventh stirred before dawn and headed south with India Company in the lead, Burke in the lead of India, all with no defined objective beyond search and destroy, or at least none spoken of at the grunt level.

Burke always wanted to be at the point. He had no trust in the timid officers and less trust in city boys that made up way too much of the company boots. At point, Burke would be able to read the terrain, see the fields ahead, and adopt stillness when it felt like stillness was called for. He trusted his instincts and trusted Ruby even more. Point was as good a place as any for Burke, fear not suspected. Besides, no one else would step up for point, all perfectly willing, gladly willing, to follow the rabbit-hunting, fence-building, determination of the quiet, Irish-descended country boy from the fields, creeks, tree lines, and river bottoms of Illinois.

May 17 duplicated the morning of May 16 in the beginning: slow, hot, probing of everything still or moving, green or muddied, open or tree line shadowed. On point, Burke could judge the ground ahead, pick his openings, and hopscotch his calculated moves to a new point of observation. Tricky stuff, one hopscotch too many or too fast would leave he and his squad out too far alone. No doubt about what waited ahead, the unknowing part was "when." The place had to be filled with NVA, who by now knew India Company probing directions.

What the hell. Didn't matter. Didn't care. It is what it is. Ruby was now Burke's left arm, maybe the right arm too. What the hell, didn't matter.

The May 17, Southeast Asian sun now up, the land was illuminated in spectacular flashes of sun angles and shadow definition, almost in 3-D. To Burke, the breaks from sun to shadow were extremely distinct as if he could see into the deeper parts of the tree lines or dense jungle-like frontage a split segment at a time.

>*That had to be a hamlet, right over there, just beyond that gap.*
>
>*That gap must be the trail into the small isolated hamlet.*
>
>*Silence, move silently, let the sun and heat rule, I am nothing.*
>
>*Wait for a rabbit to twitch, light, agile, deft.*
>
>*Pick through the landscape to gain the next vantage point before moving.*
>
>*Hold the squad back, in position.*
>
>*See through the shadows, have Ruby close, safeties off. Safeties off!*
>
>*Motion the squad up behind.*
>
>*Wait just a little longer. Still. Patient.*
>
>*See what moves; maybe get a feel for how many.*
>
>*Surprise will win the moment.*

M-16 pops swept the surprised small group of NVA who scattered, chased by Burke's M-60 deeper thuds of fire. India Company's second wave now caught up and continued the quick rout of the isolated NVA unit. A good start for May 17, like calisthenics before a football game, not too much strain, not too much ammo spent, no friendly numbers to be reported for the desks down the line to Washington. Better yet, other than a few rifles hidden by the hamlet's mama-sons, no enemy asset tonnage to report to slow down the day. Having thought the morning won, three mortars from the retreating NVA returned by air to the occupied hamlet site, wounding four more I Company marines, as if a new token reminder that in the Nam, nothing is won, lost, or over, ever. The Go Noi, mini-Tet, is a soldiering process, not a morning hamlet fire fight with a lunch break. The NVA complicit Mamasans would be left behind, obviously to be complicit again at their first possible chance when called upon. (Not their fault, it's a simple choice. Comply with NVA demands or get shot.)

India Company, Burke, and Ruby would form up again and continue their southerly sweeping intentions, with an eye for the remainder of the enemy who had escaped from the hamlet early in the fight and must be moving ahead of them. Burke was well aware the hamlet fight was not over. The hamlet's deeper forested/jungle cover of foliage led back into elephant grass, the day's heat ever-pressing, weighting everything. Progress is always slow to an "unknown" next vantage point. Whenever the harsh terrain would allow a little better view and feel for the next observation point, Burke halted, and then, so did India.

Eventually, Burke and Ruby held tight to a slight rise on the edge of another field of elephant grass. Then, there was a dry creek bed that would demand pause, would require special strategic consideration and a sixth sense of what vague shadows and twitches might mean in the way of an enemy location! Burke's squad pulled up to join Burke and Ruby.

> *Must be about noon! High noon!*
>
> *Could an enemy unit be on the other side of the angled creek bed?*
>
> *Just look hard, look into those shadows and see if a rabbit twitches.*
>
> *Don't see anything obvious; see everything with an eagle's eye.*
>
> *Be the eagle.*
>
> *Patient.*
>
> *Just sit tight and let the mood of the tree line come to me.*
>
> *Look deeper.*
>
> *How would I be a part of that tree line?*

Surely there can't be snipers in those trees.
Surely there are snipers in those trees!
The creek bed circles the south end of the higher grass field.
Search and destroy sucks! Go Noi sucks!
To move, we have to deal with the creek bed.
No other way.

The rabbit hunter could tell the sandy bottom looked weak to a boot, would give, would slow down, and would move forward across to a higher berm, sufficient as a position to hold for another feel and look. Twenty yards of dry soft sandy creek bed, sixty feet, maybe fifty-five feet. Some shadows reached out, but not many, drop dead quiet now, amidst the simmering likely chaos that is any moment!

Hot! No-way-out hot!
Somehow, someway, somebody's got to test the field. Cross the dry creek divide.
Maybe Ruby is my angel, and I have just now realized it.
Why am I here?
No wonder the United stewardesses turned their heads after landing in Da Nang. Now I get it.
The bastards must know where we were likely headed, probing, this way, now wait for us, for me.
That tree line is where I would be, maybe deeper, in a click or two, but pretty much right about there.
From that point, you can see up and down the creek bed. That point is an open field of fire. If they are there, they will twitch, right there, at that point.
Probably not enough time for them to place snipers higher in the trees, unless they are monkeys. Are they monkeys too?

I can cross, but have to avoid that spot, pick out a place to drop if a rabbit moves, maybe there in that dip. That must be a feeder creek in the monsoon wet months.

I'll only be exposed twelve seconds. Just twelve, about twelve if I keep moving.

Are they there—locked and loaded? Able to cover the creek bed with fire in twelve seconds? Naw! Probably!

I think they are there! They have to be. There is no other open field of fire for killing.

Do they know we are here? Of course they do. It's their business to know.

The bastards knew we were moving south. They knew we had to finally come to this bend of a creek bed.

"Able squad up . . . Spread out . . . We'll move in three minutes . . . Land on both sides of the feeder creek opening right over there . . . Quick feet or the sand will hold you . . . Low . . . Step as quick as you can to avoid sinking . . . Get to the edge of the tree lines . . . Three squads cover from this berm . . . Wait five minutes, then cross . . . Quick . . . . A squad at a time from different areas . . . Able squad will cover from the other side . . . When we get across and hold, we'll move in deeper when everyone is across."

It's just a creek bed. Must be 1:00 p.m. by now.

No rabbits twitch yet. Maybe there are no rabbits.

The sky is as blue as a bright, lit Illinois mid-October fence building day.

Wonder where dad and Ray are working today?

Get me through the 356 and wake-up, and I'll build Piatt County full of fences.

"Let's move!"

Robert C. did what he knew he had to do. These are the moments that split between individual terror and individual courage. War is fighting, and fighting is killing! Discovered angels will ride with some to safety, ride with others toward their gracious "journey."

A scramble—with one eye to the tree line, the other to the creek draw—Burke and A squad thumped to their landings on the other side, the feeder creek swale dividing the squad.

Scramble up. Flat, weapons, sweat, Ruby, isolated, if there are bastard rabbits, Burke and A were now among them—brave marines on a mission, other duties as assigned, "on point" wasn't for wimps or politicians.

The rabbits had not twitched; maybe there were no rabbits to twitch. It smelled of Charlie, reeked of Charlie, shadows wanted to lean and move. Too many thick nests here and there just ten to fifteen feet above the ground.

Burke and A squad were now too far out in front to call in arty or air support if the place is crawling with Charlies.

The three waiting squads poised for the next crossing, cautiously stepped into the dry open creek bed, slightly confident that A's successful crossing meant predictable safety in their own crossing effort.

Burke didn't think so. Five yards and then ten, Separated but lined marine grunt targets—halfway across when *all hell broke loose.*

Above Burke, in the tree lines, suffocating fire with RPG support bore down on the creek bed, and the next squads of marines crossing, taking one marine after another to the ground. Smaller arms sniper fire of deadly higher advantage opened from the thick nests in the trees dropping more marines in the baited opening. New fire soon opened up at Burke and his squad. No air support or artillery would lend support in this close mix.

Marines up and down the creek bed fell, some killed, many wounded: suspended bloody, loud, boiling chaos in a deadly fight smoldering under the smell of burnt firepower. These are the unpredictable moments in military history where certain soldiers fade and certain others rise.

Burke could easily see what the situation was. He would see that his pinned down squad was hopelessly committed across a great Go Noi divide. Burke could see that marines in the open of the creek bed were doomed, would die, be picked apart if rescue was additionally too deadly. Some marines died instantly, dozens of others lie wounded. Lying wounded, in the open creek bed, perhaps as bait, split, hot, and bloody.

Semper Fi!

Burke and Ruby raked the tree line with rapid M-60 fire and then up ninety degrees to what might be sniper nest positions. Used shell casings were flying, and burnt powder mingled weightily with the hot air and burning eyes. No move seemed right, and no move seemed wrong. Move, you must! Angels!

Moving closer toward the middle of the fallen marines behind him in the creek bed, Burke fired, took a sting in the left thigh, fired shallow, and then deeper into the tree lines.

Burke created so much firepower, havoc, force, inspiration, that NVA assault fire began to follow his darting, firing movements, leaving new marines not in the initial fight to rescue many critically wounded from the creek bed. Burke and Ruby filled the scene with M-60 deadly, gutting, gasping violence beyond what any one marine could be expected to do. Robert C. was no longer Robert C. He and Ruby were a spiritual moving, firing, fearless indestructible honored force.

Within seconds, suppressing sniper fire was directed down at Burke's darting movements. Dug-in NVA pockets could now be identified, and Burke leveled their camouflage-covered locations with more M-60 violence, killing all three NVA in that bunker, the bastards, while more wounded marines could be removed from the creek bed and other marines could take more aggressive support positions.

Grabbing two M-16s along the way from fallen or frozen buddies, Burke moved on to attack another suspected NVA machine gun position with a barrage of hand grenades leading his way and suppressing automatic M-16 fire, also knocking that NVA position from the fight, killing three more enemy bastards in his way. Deep in the tree line foliage by now, Burke took another sting in the left shoulder, letting loose warm wet sticky feelings. Bastards!

Alone in the heavy forest, against the cover of a tree, Burke fired again through the higher tree lines to the nests, searching for more snipers. One fell and thudded to the ground ten yards in front of him. Bastard! Sixteen Marines had now been rescued from the open firing field of the dry sandy creek bed in the eight minutes of Burke's personal assaulting war. Robert C. and Ruby Angel moved a little deeper, now half hiding and only half looking for another enemy bastard to kill.

Robert C. was now the rabbit and took another sting to the lower right side of his neck.

Ruby was no longer an M-60, Ruby was too light now to be an M-60, was too light to be a weapon, was light like an angel would be.

Burke suddenly knew his own destiny, not yet fully knowing the many lives he had saved. Now nearly one hundred yards into and past the enemy's creek side tree lines, Burke took one more hit, through the side of the flak jacket. A deep hit.

Robert C. Burke, young fence builder, was now down, vision changing, greyer, sounds changing, more distant. It was finally not suppressing hot anymore. Hands from earth were a soft/rising cradle of firmness.

No longer looking up through the foliage, Burke looked down at the foliage. Robert C. could see the place he had just come from, down there in the dry creek bed where it all started.

Robert C. was looking down on the scramble of marines saving other wounded marine's lives who had initially been wounded and stranded from help in the creek bed.

Burke could grin. He could *feel* what he had accomplished with his life:

> *I think I was over there and then went to that low spot, then I'm not sure I recall. I wonder if the white picket fence that Raymond and I built in the front of the house is still white and straight? Dad must be proud I made it as a marine. Sisters too! I know Raymond is proud. I did my very best, my worn, tired, hot, thirsty best! Those wounded isolated marines saved from their fight on this day will remember. My 1/3/27 buddies will remember. Marines remember!*

A long awaited cool breeze covered Robert C. Coasting effortlessly higher the breeze was even cooler, more caressing and leading a certain way, heavenly.

> *Large wings of this beautiful new angel caress. Feels good. Safer. Safest. The place I was waiting for, a place anyone would want to be. Don't ever let me go. Keep me. I like it here. This is my best place ever.*
> *I will savor this wonderful place, blend with this place as one, without greed or wishes of a next other place, blessed by the Lord's comforting patience forever and ever.*

Da Nang-based Third Battalion radios had now reached the other companies who had been trucked out of the area from Da Nang in the early morning and had subsequently been ordered to return. They had been called back to Da Nang having not spent a shell. SNAFU!

Division command had belatedly reorganized the support procedure. The four companies returned to Da Nang, loaded off the trucks, geared up toward the hot tarmac, and boarded on waiting Chinooks, all silent, thirty-eight to a plane, now a bit turned around, totally uncertain as to what the duty-call really would be.

By noon, the four support companies had traveled fifty miles, across the Liberty Bridge into the southern Go Noi and then back again, standing down right where they had started at 3:00 a.m. All while I Company battled the bastards in the creek bed, Robert C. made his final journey with his angel and remaining marines waited for backup.

May 17, Burke had scattered the enemy into fragments. At least those he had not killed were scattered. For him, Go Noi and the Domestic Nam were over, having just begun less than a month earlier. Robert C. saved many lives and provided much inspiration. His heroic young body was recovered, returned to Monticello in the Illinois prairies where it rests today, and is recognized daily with namesake area parks and monuments as well as inside and outside the small community's Piatt County Court House. Robert C. Burke would later receive the Marine Corps and Nation's Congressional Medal of Honor (MOH), the only marine in the Domestic Nam, Twenty-Seventh Marines, to receive the nation's highest military honor.

No one really knows the actual number of lives he saved in the Go Noi, near the hamlet Le Nam, still blazing hot, still on the other side of the planet from Monticello, IL. Some estimate the heroic Robert C. Burke gave his young life to save at least sixteen fellow marines who had been disabled in the creek bed until his one-man assault cleared the way for others to rescue them. Others of the moment say it was more as they counted those already across the divide and those who had arrived and not yet committed. Many of those men live in absolute indebtedness today. You cannot teach Burke's sort of bravery and reaction nor can you train for such a rare elusive trait as actual in-the-face-of-the-enemy heroism. Thank God some are made with heroism bones, fiber and grit, enough to step up, display the force to divide commitment from fear, real duty from pretending duty.

Assigned from Godly directions, the "truly given" will always find angels as escorts on their final unselfish journeys.

Semper Fi!

Burke's gifts of courage and his passing to a personal journey saved lives, but other lives are always lost on the other side of the vast fighting ledger. The broader battle in Go Noi's southern dry creek bed continued, as battles do, oblivious to personal sacrifice. India CO Captain Ralph tried to call troops together in the tall elephant grass bordered by the berm. As the troops approached, Captain Ralph and his two immediate lieutenants, Cummings and Fiebelkorn, were also killed. Lieutenant Thompson took over, but troops were scattered. No one knew at this point who was alive, what the wounded numbers were, where friendly pockets of fire still operating could come from, nor if there were friendly pockets still locked and loaded that could function against an enemy's well-laid trap, always in a hit and run strategy.

Once again, support companies K and L were deployed, this time by helicopter, landed south of the ambush site, and assaulted toward the fight. Company L landed and moved east, then north to evade a large stream. Company K landed and forced north finding a small dam to cross the stream, crossed in single file, unmolested by enemy fire and moved toward the fight of the beleaguered India Company now minus Burke. Enemy opposition finally slowed K's assistance and rescue intentions, but both companies pressed the fight and eventually met up with the remaining I Marines as darkness settled in on the scene of the day's fight and destruction.

Burke's I Company had been virtually wiped out: twenty more KIA, sixty-eight WIA, 90 percent of the remaining/breathing/shocked of I Company mediated from heat exhaustion (numbers and percentages eerily and grossly similar to Twenty-Seventh Division losses on the original mission in 1945 at Iwo Jima). Company M would copter in the next morning as further support for a battle past. Word passed that command and control of the south portion of Allen Brook would pass that very evening, May 18, from 3/7 to 3/27, and thus shift direct command personnel once again. No remaining marine grunt could understand what-n'-the SNAFU that meant, nor did they care.

Robert C. Burke's spent body was recovered where he had finally fallen, at the base of the large tree one hundred yards into the tree line, Ruby pointing back to the fight. Wounded and walking marines of I/3/27 gathered to make sure Robert C. was properly taken care of. Medevac copters filled the air with sound and hope one after another as they landed and extracted waiting wounded and heatstroked marines for medical centers in Da Nang. Two of Burke's fellow enlisted, with the help of a Huey crew, graciously laid the body of the future Medal Of Honor recipient on the floor of the Huey, boarded with him and personally escorted Burke through the Da Nang KIA process, making certain everyone in the process understood what had happened, what and how many lives had been spared by the young marine who took point, destroyed two enemy machine gun strongholds, and knocked snipers from trees while the wounded in the creek bed were being saved.

Operation Allen Brook continued for a few more weeks, command shifted, troops coptered here and there with continued losses of life here and there, punctuated with accounts of purported field victories. Always more numbers for the chain of command in the aftermath. New NVA regulars, well-armed and in fresh uniforms, continued to arrive in the Go Noi from the western reaching mountain range that always appeared to have eyes observing the entire lower Go Noi fields of battle. KIAs and WIAs reporting processes were perfected by the desk jockeys and captured enemy tonnage estimates mounted for impressive numbers up the chain, real or suspected numbers, but numbers always reported as symbolic justification for more and more warring commitments to the Domestic Nam, as if the enemy would run out of young soldiers for the next fight. The Go Noi area was never held by US troops, the area could never have been held. Nothing in the whole damn country could be held, except for the ground being stood upon. Da Nang was never attacked, which was victory enough for the commanding up line, who invented the entire proactive protective concept leading to the Go Noi mini-Tet. Two months later, the Go Noi was abandoned back to its NVA/VC stronghold ways: hot, bunkered, more blood in the sandy soil than ever before, reputed to those of I/3/27, mostly forgotten by the world's others.

The Domestic Nam is the story of Burke and thousands of other individual stories that will never be told. There is no conclusive overall sense of summary because there is no result or summary that makes any sense, no matter how mentally stretched for logical answers we become. Nothing satisfactorily redeeming can be filtered, molded or exaggerated from the deadly, costly repute of the US military/political Nam commitment.

Bless Robert C.: Heroes come from the darndest places. This story is as true as best the story can be reconstructed. Doesn't matter. Believe all the stories because if it didn't happen to that humping grunt with his K-bar and Ruby-Angel, it happened to someone else, *all duties as assigned!*

Chapter 4

TET: From Hue through 881 to the Brewery

"The American public could pay to be misled."

The concept and storytelling for veterans and their families of *The Domestic Vietnam* had no more personal and social depth nor more relevance to America's decrepit quagmire of self-deprecation in the entire "defining year" than the two months beginning with the nationwide outburst of violence known as the Tet Offensive. Historically, an annual Vietnamese lunar New Year celebration, the events of Tet created the landscape and locked in the war's basic mega-premises for the entire remaining intervention of US military and political assets, which eventually narrowed options to a final *one way out.*

Tet was realistically and symbolically many things to everyone concerning themselves with the Domestic Nam, in-country and back in the world. Eventually, in the leadership process of placing American assets and lives in wars and deadly armed conflicts of various types, those in the decision-making mix must come face to face with the actions and decisions of the struggles they create and/ or indulge. Tet did that for America or to America, put the face to face that had been previously dodged right up front, unavoidable. Tet brought Nam home, brought the soldier's struggles home, and brought to all neighborhoods the awful, tragic, self-destructive reality of America's Nam commitment. By the time of Tet, America had been actively in and around Nam for five to six years, levels of commitment ramping up with each load of weaponry, financial aid, and political "buffoonery." Tet told America in direct deadly televised terms what our government had gotten for its blundering ideologies fed by taxing cash flows and draft-boards providing an endless human supply from Wilson Streets across America.

Beginning January 30, 1968, Communist forces (North Vietnamese Army regulars National Liberation Front/Viet Cong/ related Communist bandits) for the first time since defeating the French twenty years earlier at Dien Ben Phu in the north, implemented coordinated attacks throughout the entire country of South Vietnam, attacking and penetrating major and minor installations and assets of the South Vietnamese Army and those occupied by American's, including attacks on all forty-four provincial capitals of South Vietnam. Previous to the Tet Offensive, American propagandish developments with a collaborative half-active, half-alert press and four-prong institutional tunnel vision could head fake and two-step a scenario for progress and winning, although no one would ever actually go so far as to define "winning." Winning, like battlefield actions of many kinds, would eventually become an individual affair, one thing for one person, another thing for another person. For the common grunt, "winning" was surviving to the "wake up" and seeing home and family again. For the arms/weaponry dealer, "winning" was another trip to the bank and new armament and weaponry orders (they won regularly). For the supply officers or their commands, "winning" could be purely the movement of assets, some out the front door, some assets out the back door, into the black market. For the bandwagon war politician, winning was finding another way to fool constituents within a reelection cycle. There was no patriotic aggregate concept of winning, never was, didn't exist, never would be, and still isn't, even in retrospect. No one had the winning vision, or if they did, they did not have it for long or consistently enough to sell and implement such a vision. "Winning" was an elusive foggy ghost of uncontrollable circumstances, forming and fading away by a thousand unmanageable events of weekly unintended consequences.

The Tet Offensive shattered the false veil of comfort built by the instigators of US military logistics, motion, and action, who had assumed the confidence that goes with global powers. Tet proved that no place in South Vietnam was safe from enemy penetration, no place was off-limits to surprise attack, and no piece of Nam real estate was ever going to be securely held for very long toward the development of a Democratic South Vietnamese government and society competent or strong enough to manage an unsustainable democracy. Tet's avalanche of violence circled all of the Nam. Each camp perimeter and guard post was a target nightly or was properly assumed to soon be a target nightly. There would be no gimmies on convoys, no such thing as casual "milk runs" for the remainder of

'68 and on into uncertain futures as long as this Second Indochina war would last. More domestic Wilson Streets would have to push their boys forward, had to with the Tet-factor into it now, unalterably permeating the loose sand and bottomless soaked pits of Nam's human and ancient terrain depravities.

With Tet's face-to-face, gathering and then refashioning a third-world Asian population of unfamiliar deep-seeded cultures into the modern American image was beyond practical expectation. America had not advanced Vietnamese social structure or awareness nor established anything new or different or attractive that was buildable. Instead, America by '68 had been drawn backward into the methods, behavior, and reactions of the ancient third-world system it intended to modernize. Every soldier, pilot, Seabee, supply station, or artillery outpost was face to face with a new reality that, previous to Tet, did not exist for America's stated or unspoken hidden ambitions. To the stalwartly pompous White House suits and certain stars of the day and times, what actually happened in Tet, could not happen. US troops were big people, and Viet Cong were little people. US military had big guns and trucks and big air things, biggest in the world. VC were little people, had few or no trucks, and no air things at all. Big people and big powerful stuff normally womp on and crush little people with no stuff or at least that had been historically the case. (The more one breaks down the true elements of Nam [and Afghan] the more obvious becomes the eventual trends to concluding options.) Nam's little people knew what their Asian core beliefs were. American's had no Asian core beliefs, importing only out of place American core beliefs, which, of course, is impossible to make work to a satisfactory American-style conclusion.

Domestically, Tet's prolific battles proved that the war doubters, street opposition, and growing Nam anti-war protesting legions might just be kind of/somewhat correct about the uselessness and eventual demise and waste of the US warring commitment for a proxy-Nam war. The original deriving impetus for America's street or campus protesting action class might be illogically diverse and basically rather wrong-headed, certainly poorly stated, but the core focus of the protesting issues were valid enough to survive their own radical, generally unpopular and disorganized behavior. Tet added essential flammable gasoline, domestic napalm, and cold reality to the sizzling fuse of United States. Domestic war opposition displayed in growing numbers of organized and spontaneous war protesting and displays of outright general population rebellion of the blithering government policy concerning the Nam.

In late '67 and escalating through '68, domestic protesting actions mounted so quickly and seriously in cities and institutions that government's assumed tight society reign within the larger coast-to-coast general society, all the way down to thousands of Wilson Streets, could no longer ignore the ripping street movements pulling more and more otherwise detached parts of the civilian population into increasingly more bold and violent protesting actions. "Anti-Nam" became American society's popular subculture of choice for a lot of folks good and wimpish, like a magnet to the otherwise stand-by youthful energies without a previous position on the matter or a dog, or duck, in the fight. For many of a more conservative ilk, "Anti-Nam" merely rose as common happy hour or dinner conversation. Nonetheless, dissention toward Nam as a grand global SNAFU became the common opinions of simmering popularity racing through public consciousness, no longer to be denied or overlooked, which meant eventual series of societal boiling points. The reality of the fighting and dying, and the wasted American assets was only absent from the population's view from one evening newscast until the next evening newscast as Tet's affects tsunamied globally across all oceans.

Thinking back, American Domestic Nam opinion building could really have transpired in no other way. The obvious was the obvious, the duck started to quack, walk, and poop like a duck, no matter what blabbering think tank heads were barking with innocence, righteousness or insistence. Political ostrich heads buried in the sands of denial, while distracted with power, or worse yet distracted with avalanches of government cash flowing, could no longer buy public opinion. Tet shattered the façades of SOP (standard operating procedure) head fakes that had insulted the public's intelligence and common sense on Nam through early years of escalation.

Naturally, there was a four-prong institutional attempt of a response to Tet. Blustering politicians found a way to profess how the mass killing and chaos of Tet was a good thing—having drawn out more of the enemy than ever before and produced record numbers of enemy KIA, WIA, and tons of hard enemy warring assets captured in frontal confrontations with an enemy previously guerilla'd in the shadows, a rosy early evening analysis from 12,000 miles away. DC suits can get away with this kind of head fake crap because orders for retaliating boots on the ground go down, not up. The revised monumental warring struggle reshaped by Tet battles might even require a new senator and general to be photographed with their lopsy-dopsy walking off of a LST, newly positioned onto a safe Nam beach, with a "you've done it now" scowl, drenched to their knees in icky salt water.

DC's post-Tet confusion lay heavy, gooey, thick. Misguiding the new incensed public back into languished disinterest in Nam became the new mission of the Johnson war council of McNamara, Westmoreland, Taylor, and Company.

This Cronkite fellow is using daily fed actual accounts of bad stuff, troops stretchered from walls, and streets that are supposed to be secure, and once were. Hueys in a constant relay of US KIA and WIA emergencies to offshore medevac missions is upsetting the previously sleepy US population.

Where is the cord we pull to drop the curtain and regroup or the permanent top to keep the box closed before too much of the fooled public wises up to the four-prong waste, corruption, and futility and is unfooled afore the next fooling election? After

all, war is only one thing we do, not to be confused
with reelections.

Johnsonites could certainly retreat to that overtheorized "domino effect" leaned on, fictionalized, and promoted for so long. In reality, the dominoes had become a shifted theory. They were no longer Asian dominoes. The dominoes were us: industrial falling and knocking military, who fell and would knock political, who fell further to reach a population group here and there. The domino effect was right here. We (the American citizenry) were the dominoes. Individuals, East of California and West of New York, all space, towns, farms, we are to fall like plastic brainless dominoes in a line of motion, bumping the next guy into a fall, who bumps his cousin and neighbors, and others who fall, all in patriotic acquiescence to the '60s Nam intervention facade. And thus, in a panic of covering asses, within suits or under stars—in response to Tet—they did it. Ingenuity with desperation being the mother of necessity and invention in love and war, the Think-Tank Brethren created the ultimate institutional affront to the grunts and Wilson Street boys and families who struggled and became bent from deep within the more they knew of actual action accounts of in-country Nam atrocities.

Government and Hollywood propagated the ultimate contumely to families, troops, Wilson Street Boys, towns, and church groups, fueling with rocket fuel the growing aggressiveness of the increasingly organizing protesting network. Complete with marching music and the nation's premiere macho-super-actor-big guy of the era, John Wayne, the four-prongers threw together the most publicly insulting propaganda film that could ever be dreamed up and shamelessly drabble-dripped for public sucking. *The Green Berets*, the movie in 1968, bringing the Domestic Nam gibberish to a new insulting level and delivering it to neighborhood movie theatres in every unsuspecting corner of America. *The public could now pay to be misled!* Relying on public emotion and ignorance, Wayne would walk in the water to the white sand spooky threatening dangerous beach, instead of on the water. John Wayne would be really, really serious, grumpy-looking, no-nonsense expression leading his rascally kick-your-sorry-butt way. No more messing around now. John Wayne, complete with movie mogul entourage, were in-country, right there in Nam, joining the fray. Clean, bright actors would shoot clean, bright scenes of really, really tough movie guys doing freedom lover's tough work to secure, change, elevate a third-world rural anciently cultured population into our bright shining modern image of enterprise trade and social goodness, if Wayne and his momentum can just rid the countryside of black pajama'd, heavily armed, night stalking bad guys. To a returning veteran, or anyone with a public opinion coordinating pulse and mind, the movie was an anticomedic farce, an insult, another in your face message to an increasingly angered, teased America that what we want you to see is not bankable. *The Green Beret*/Wayne movie was obviously such a plastic, cartoonish misrepresentation of the true picture that it had the opposite affect than the national rallying cry planned by Wayne and the four-prongers, now joined by a friendly, budget watching Hollywood. (Four-Prong, just a reminder, is military, industrial, and politician, holding hands with backroom think tankers who could set megapremise and prod the whole business to an economic flow chart, overlooking national moralities.)

With the mockery of *The Green Berets* movie, instigators and directors reduced one of the military's premiere units, Green Berets, into a trickery circus stage show. The now engrained elements of the Domestic Nam opposition, the protestors, would become inflamed with the tomfoolery and PR pabulum of *The Green Berets* movie, with the result of fueling antiwar descent assets into higher, more violent levels of street frenzies. Everything about the movie *The Green Berets* was disingenuous. The movie amounted to no more than an aggregate effort of deception by princes of bullshit, all the while grunts and soldiers of all types have "orders" to be, and to do, in a nasty "otherworld," not acted or pretended or whitewashed. The real soldier's tasks were not choreographed fantasy, not synchronized screenplay, not camouflage smokescreening, not distraction-building of head fakes. Real soldiering wasn't for creating more public misdirection about Nam's thousands of issues of real doubt and confusion, the misspent application of the war strategy du jour or the ongoing wasteful application of America's financial base of the '60s. Nam was a dirty deadly business, the dirtiest business on the planet in '68, not to be whitewashed by John frickin' Wayne.

From the in-country grunt point of view:

> *You guys wanna "play Nam," get your fat asses over here! The point position is open! Head right down that trail at dusk, we'll see you in the morning, maybe!*

Tet provided a domestic news reality that for the first time in the Nam war could not be manipulated into stories of American intervention progress. Hundreds of thousands of Wilson Street boys had been committed in-country by the time of Tet. US military assets, along with gigantic unheard of wastes and shady dealings of all kinds had grown incredibly under the bravado of the dim-witted President Johnson and company. As more human assets and warring hardware mounted for Nam dispatch, industrial assets would keep pace with military. In a free press democracy, as human assets deploy, so must the public explanation and logic of their use. (Do we kind of miss a free, enterprising press?)

With hundreds of thousands of boots on the ground comes hundreds of thousands times ten, of families, home buddies, girlfriends and wives, past teachers and neighbors, store front owners who miss the boys once zooming by all week on bikes with ball gloves, bats, sporting all-American grins, all once stateside in every town on every corner that made up America. These good honest folks are the reliable, backbone, Domestic Corps of America, clinging to the evening news broadcasts for any fragments of accurate information about conditions in the Nam, laboring to draw some sort of a digestible temporary conclusion from the frustration of inconclusive newsy information, trying to match local rumor of one of the boys being in Hue or Da Nang or Go Noi, with any newsy TV mention of a day's battle of destruction and new KIA/WIA numbers. With Tet, troop, and battle reports, accounts and resulting numbers could no longer be whitewashed, Tet was Tet. Every camp, LZ, scrap clay dirt hill with a meaningless elevation ID number, distant perimeter line, or isolated helipad were assumed to be under attack, or soon would be. Remote field grunts or base camps no longer had to search and destroy; the war had come to them, up and down every pocket and trail, ravine, riverbed, tree line, and rice paddy dike of the entire country. Everything changed while the Domestic Corps of America tried to "believe," tried to maintain trust in leadership, tried to deny that the true falling into a pile of spent dominoes were actually us. Nam became face-to-face. One face was the ugly truth of waste and violence in Nam, the other face was the US public. Those two sides would stay face-to-face for six more years. For all practical purposes in the faces of veterans and many others of the times, the face to face remains yet today, more than forty-five years later.

> *February 16, '68*
> *Hey Dad, Mom, Sis, Gma & Gpa*
> *I don't really know what to write home about, I'm mostly OK. We are generally spent, well into it now, here in what they call the top of I Corps. You may have heard about a thing they are calling Tet, the broad name given to the surge of violence I understand is all over the Nam. With 287 and a wake-up, I'm obviously here for the full Tet experience. Tet has changed it all, everything is up for grabs. We fly from an hour before dawn in support of the battle or demand of the moment. Constant resupplies needed for isolated field units, bodies coming out bagged or medivac'd for the lucky*

ones. I quit looking at the faces. The command bunker on the landing pad is constantly passing orders from somewhere, 2, 4, 6 or more birds at a time lock and load then disappear into a mission. We are in a constant whirling of copter blades, blowing sand and dirt, birds in and out in a frenzy to get to a location where ground Marine's lives depend on our arrival. I mostly hang on, tied in, lots to shoot at from the side gunner's door once the sun comes up, coming into an LZ we blast anything that looks slanted, sleep now is in 20 minute flops but I've gotten used to that, the trouble will eventually be getting un-used to it.

No rest at night as we all lock and load and slither into some Quang Tri perimeter mud hole to wait for Charlie's night to start. I keep as many hand grenades with me as I can carry. Throwing arm never been stronger. Teamed up with a flight crew marine, we can carry weapons and two crates of grenades, 100. Nights are long out there in the hole, flares lighting the sky, then drifting up and down the line, then new flares, all night. We have now been hit with something from Charlie every night, about 20 nights in a row. With the Quang Tri River on the north, that side is the place to be, until it's not the place to be. Marine tanks roar in now and then and blow the hell out of whatever they feel needs blowing the hell out of. Those things are bad; I love the sound of them before they even arrive, love the sight of them, might want to live in one of them when I get back to the world. The guys on the tanks never look at you, never have a smile or thumbs up, I can't help but wonder what planet they trained on.

Twice we have had "Puff" overhead with three 50 cals on each side making Swiss cheese of the other side of the QT river. Puff is named for "Puff the Magic Dragon," fires about two jillion rounds a second, with tracers each 10 rounds—what a show. The other side of the river bulges toward our perimeter lines on the north, where we caught a waiting NVA battalion two nights ago. Marine tanks rolled up just before dark, and about midnight Puff engines started circling and filling that side of the river with red flying tracers, we all opened up on the Bulge. KIA count late the next day was over 600, you might not see that slaughter in the news. But, I don't think it makes any difference, they'll just send 600 more.

Rumor is that they are pulling everyone (enlisted) from our present copter duties for a couple days, head down highway 1 a few clicks to a place called Hue; they say an ancient Nam city. Army Air Cav is supposed to arrive and fill in for us here with the copter missions. OK with me, get the hell out-a here. Hue can't be as blown up as this place, can it?

Can time move any slower? Nights are like on some sort of delayed stop light signal, only in the darkest dark. We wait, still, intense, try not to see things that aren't things to see, listen thru the heavy stench of air for any movement—frozen to a position, poised—then 30 more seconds or 2 more minutes pass. Uggghhhh! Like pulling teeth to get morning pink in the sky to the east. I think I liked being hit with fastballs better. I'll write from Hue if we can, have no idea how that's gonna go but they've been fightin' down that-a-way for a few weeks now,

maybe we are a mop up. Hope someone smarter
than me knows what the hell we are doing here.
Keep my stuff dry—I even miss doing chores.
Rollie

P.S. I wrote Darlene afore Christmas, but haven't
heard.

By mid-March '68, from the multitude of changing conditions in-country, the longer range warring situation of US assets could be more accurately determined considering the true results, reactions and consequences of the Tet Offensive. Presuming there were those who "wanted" an accurate determination. Even the Battle of Hue, which captured the world's attention as a final drawn-out symbolic Tet-Standoff, had dwindled by mid-March into a complicated deadly final wall to wall fight among neighborhoods, alleys and Hue's stagnant waterways, killing the last trapped VC-rats hunkered down in the Citadel. Media that were brave enough, no longer had to prioritize what to cover in I Corps. Hue was it. Like the only game in town to access, it had all the elements of news, a movie, compelling historic accounts, symbolism, young marines, all in a strange heavy fog of monsoon overcast and lit sizzling powders, with an occasional squalid VC cat or island dog darting to its new hideout for temporary safety. Hue had one more human element of its own, a smell unlike any other, as if the whole place sat on a deep steaming dump. But it wasn't a garbage smell or a fired ammo smell. It was a haunting smell as if once given into it would become held within, a human-bound species of clinging virus, a mist of hanging unseen evil in a windless low-country, with the daily death to match.

Hue was the center of I Corps. There were bigger Nam installations holding more human and mechanized warring assets, but none more symbolic to the ancient country population or political history. Hue was an ancient capital in the centuries of a united Vietnam, reaching backward for hundreds of years, changed little from one regime to the next. French colonialism and then American intervention diminished Hue's internal majesty, but hundreds of years of history do not long diminish an Asian culture's engrained truths.

Hue was a location midway strategic for South Vietnamese command and US command to mix strategies and firepower implementation. Highway 1 connected Hue north to Quang Tri a few clicks south of the DMZ, which was really the threshold of the DMZ. South from Hue, Highway 1 could carry ammo and troops to the larger bases at Phu Bai, and then connect with the largest US I Corps base at Da Nang if need be, which could feed assets west into the more mountainous fighting of a whole different style, tactically unique.

Hue was also a strategic logistic network for the hard war assets that it takes for continuous fighting and killing. The Perfume River (named for its gut wrenching stench), which divided the ancient Citadel in the center of Hue, from the city's south sector, had a verily detectable stagnant flow from the center of the city's business, straight east several clicks to the South China Sea. Deep enough, the Perfume was ostensibly the only accessible port for I Corps, other than the huge port at Da Nang much further south. Navy supply ships could unload at sea, with smaller motorized boats making their way into the mouth of the Perfume almost to Hue, supplying the interior with enough war tools to blow things up to various destructive heights in many different ways, and provide normal troop necessities all the way to Highway 1 for further disbursement.

Besides a normal peasant population of neighborhoods and the ancient walled Citadel on the north side of the Perfume, Hue contained substantial airfield assets at Tac Loc Airfield on the south and housed a significant South Vietnamese Army Mang Ca command compound. Hue was a center for everything I Corps that required coordination between ARVN and US combined offenses, defenses, or more likely just guesstimations of the most numerous dangerous or vulnerable gray areas of preparation or battle. Previous to Tet, Hue was also largely off the daily battle radar, as was Go Noi, until it wasn't off the battle radar. Hue was so off the radar that it became underdefended, overlooked as a priority of defenses against communist bad guy attack dominoes, even though it was a provincial capital of some significance.

In fact, in early '68, Hue was not just underdefended, the city and strategic locations were completely unprepared when, on January 31, '68, twelve thousand NVA and NLF well positioned and supplied enemy soldiers stormed through the south side of Hue attacking every significant location asset and covering neighborhoods with determined enemy troops securing for their next advantage every strategic killing location. ARVN and US Military lines, sentry stations, and other assets fell like defenseless straws or mini-dominoes one to the next. Within one day the enemy controlled or isolated its priorities of positions at Mang Ca, the airfield and in the center of Hue just across the Perfume into the ancient, walled, historic Citadel. Although isolated battles would seesaw for days at the airfield and within the city, the overall vulnerability of Hue, and I Corps had been exposed and pounded by determined Gooks from multiple unit designs. After one day, the enemy controlled nearly all of Hue, with all of its new rubble, the general population darting out of sight like two-legged prairie gophers. ARVN and American defenses of the Mang Ca headquarters compound and the airfield never were overwhelmed and fully taken by the enemy, but it took fierce defenses to save the shrunken good-guy assets and neutralize their usefulness to assist in the ongoing defenses of the larger city.

Within one day of Tet attacks into Hue, the Viet Cong were, for the first time in their new offensive war, able to raise their red background/gold star flag over the Citadel tower in a major I Corps, South Vietnamese strategic city—an awesome, in your face statement of victory and the enemy's determination. ARVN reinforcements of the First Battalion and Fourth Battalion of the Third Regiment failed to enter the city on the southeast and the First retreated to gather at the coastal outpost of Ba Long just a few clicks east down the Perfume. The First Battalion would renew an effort toward Hue, debark from their truck convoy, and load upon motorized civilian river junks to advance up the Perfume waterway as far into Hue as they could before enemy mortars and snipers closed all river traffic and ramps. The First Battalion finally reached a Citadel offensive position after two days of advancing nearly six miles. The Fourth Battalion did not reach a battle useful position for several more days. Hue had exploded into the hands of the enemy! The unorganized, reactionary ARVN, now on their confused heels, finally reaching the Citadel to be greeted by the red flag with gold star. Determined trained enemy snipers, who had patiently awaited the ARVN-led arrival, were enthusiastic at their deadly work, ripping the new arriving ARVN into scattering shreds of death before their general retreat to anything safer for a regrouping moment.

As the surprise attacks occurred, NVA were storming Hue with chaos and renewed statements of Ho Chi-Tet unification. Early defense of the city of Hue was largely a South Vietnamese affair. No one of any significant command influence imagined the fighting started would continue for a month, or be near the last of the Tet initiated attacks to find an unleveled, uneasy bloody bottom. To the South Vietnamese command and the distant US political watch dogs, the situation at Hue was at first just a fleeting phase of disbelief, soon transpiring to the in-your-face feeling of I got "gotcha'd," on a declining fast-paced trend, far beyond logical, actionable, predictable belief.

The first marines into Hue were the First Battalion, First Marine Division, just a day after the initial surprise attack and mass insurgency that swamped Hue's neighborhoods and overran into the historic ancient Citadel. Coming into the teeth of battles from the southern suburbs 1/1 was met with significant well placed NVA sniper chaos, tucked away invisibly within the city's ragged wall to wall inconsistent neighborhood landscapes. Increased sniper fire forced marines of 1/1 to dismount convoy mobility far south of their intentions and create a priority of advancing by clearing the way house to house on both sides of the main road in. In a full day of bloody fighting the Marines finally made their way to the MACV command compound where they met up with US senior advisors to the First ARVN Division and could, for the first time only partially understand the extent of the attack of Hue and what they would be up against to regain and clear, dirty, deadly areas, a fighting marine, man job which would have to be done. Unbeknownst to US command, an estimated twelve thousand enemy had targeted and advanced to all strategic points of the city and dug in by the next day, committed to fight to their death for their causes. For the time being, the Citadel was lost to total NVA control. For the first time in Nam, marines would face extensive WWII-style house to house, wall-to-wall city fighting, an untrained endeavor for the new generation, totally uncommon to the guerilla warfare that had defined the war to that period.

Days of sniper-ridden, mine-setting, brutal-hit and run house-to-house fighting would begin for the marines of 1/1. It would be two weeks and a couple clicks before some reinforcement marines from Quang Tri and various outposts would make their way to Hue to lock and load within the battle's grinds of fighting to advance forward positions and then bring up the rear. Battles in all parts of the city would rage like six different wars pumping weapons and destruction at various paces of killing, advancing and landscape ruination, peasant population silently disappearing to safety any way possible.

Each day added a new level of burn, smoke, blood, and killing to the isolated events of Hue, ten thousand miles from the nearest US city. A so-called proxy conflict of some sort to stop something more extraordinary in the global communist threat from advancing even further to something else in the global communist threat even worse, or so the DC suits told Americans. With the burn, smoke, blood, and killing comes the smell of Hue, the heavy stench that lays across all things and attaches to every moving or still object. A stench that becomes heaviest with night's darkness as things lay down in an ancient city no longer lit with anything except tracers, flares, or wars other inventive destructive devices. Then, the air only slightly stirs when a far off pink signal of dawn arises as a subconscious first signal for the day's new fighting, and then the occasional cracks of renewed small arms fire and screaming orders begin to replace the early morning's new attention to the old stench. Marines could maneuver to miss the sniper fire, and the moving glimpses of not yet trapped NVA darting from a pressed position to a new soon to be pressed position, moving farther and farther into the city ahead of determined marine firepower relentlessly trailing them for the kill. But no one, night or day, hunted or hunting, could overlook that hanging heavy smell. It was the smell of the battle of Hue, growing heavier, heaviest, and no one could tell exactly what it was, why it was there, why the nauseating smell was increasingly stronger—a devil's floating message, an aromatic ball and chain clinging to lives in action, soaking into visions, impressions, eyeballs, and earholes. The smell would have a taste that couldn't be spit out.

The fatigue of the marines' daily grind would blend and mold with the heavy smell of Hue, all overlapping in the early morning slightly drifting fog of a new day. Everything about Hue's first morning lightness rotted guts, then nerves. In the new day, as if scripted, a single marine would dart forward a click from a covered position, as if released by some unseen signal. Then another darting marine click of a movement and another into the residue of the heavy morning fog of humid stench, always toward a new fight. The cover of the early hanging fog spent itself on advancing marines until the pop-pop of enemy fire signaled a stop to the advancing, and set the day's walled battle lines to slower moves, or no moves until night slowed, then straightened out the momentum of each side. From that point, the marine's day would be about cover and city inches, and about sniper angles and vantage points, forward, sideways, up and around, quick moves and pass the springloaded full-metal jackets. The wet fog that had mixed with worn muddied ground, made the surface of each move on a surface of clinging paste that held annoyingly tight to the boot's step. Early in the day, each marine was confronted with the same ole, same ole, "the homie-Gook bastards that tried to kill me yesterday . . . will try to kill me today."

By the morning of February 1, the fourth day of Tet in Hue, marines were in position to provide some counterattack pressure from MACV. The ARVN division recorded some success as did marines, but both units eventually retreated to regroup, rearm, and count any blessings drifting through lapses of concentration. A new heroic marine unit effort recaptured Tay Lac Airfield with minor losses and the loss of one tank knocked out by enemy 57 mm. recoilless rifle fire. No good guy progress in a counterattack would be made toward the Citadel in the early going. Angels worked at their illusive pace. Monsoon weather was marginal, with a shifting two-hundred- to five-hundred-foot ceiling for flying the CH-46 trooplifts into the ongoing fight toward the Citadel. Eventually, about 1400 hours on February 1, part of the Fourth Battalion, Second ARVN Regiment were able to arrive on CH-46 Sea Knight helicopters from MAG-36 Purple Foxes, reassigned from the Dong Ha south DMZ line defenses. Arriving to a Hue improvised LZ under mortar fire, the new ARVN troops were immediately pinned down, silent and motionless until night fall. An hour after ARVN troops coptered in, F/2/Fifth Marines helicoptered into southern Hue to retake MACV Microwave Troop communications center that had been surrounded by VC forces and was the main communications center for the Hue area, the DMZ, and the new heightened battles exploding at Khe Sanh to the west, too many clicks away to be an influence on Hue's hammering. One half mile southeast of the MACV compound the US Army Signal Corps, Thirty-Seventh Signal Battalion communications site came under heavy attack and was ordered as the next priority for marines of the Fifth to recapture and secure. They never made it. The Signal Corps, taking heavy losses in wait for help, was blasted to uselessness and then booby-trapped.

Late that same night, February 1, the US Army's First Air Cavalry ordered two new battalions into an air assault west of Hue, with orders to attack and move southeast into the city, closing future enemy supply lines that were likely still open. On February 2 new troops from the army's Twelfth Cavalry, Second Battalion coptered four miles northwest of the city, with orders to push to the center of the city, while marines to the south were making some useful headway, by battle standards, bringing in further reinforcements and killing firepower. By late February 2, some advancing successes were felt toward Hue University and winning back relief for the MACV communications center. Although the NVA had dropped the large railroad bridge over the Perfume River, the bridge across the Phu Cam Canal was untouched and became the concentration of Fifth Marine advancement and first crossing to focus on recapture of the Citadel, plus some general payback that would come their way. More marines of the Fifth crossed the An Cuu Bridge over the canal, with a bad ass, fully armed new US Rough Rider convoy to soon follow. Battle lines for the longer battle at Hue had thus begun to be drawn as Marines now fitting into the new challenges of Hue dug in to renew attacks for each following day. By the end of the fourth day, there was no area of the city untouched by battle and there was no way out for the committed NVA and VC units entrenched in Hue's various neighborhoods especially for those occupying the Citadel. The NVA and VC of Hue had arranged their own Nam-style Alamo. Everyone understood Hue and its ancient Citadel would be a fight to many deaths. Thus, Hue's immediate future would be determined one sniper shot and return fire at a time; one wall gained at a time; one sniper eliminated at a time; while Marine and ARVN commands evaluated, and additional friendly assets were deployed from somewhere else and arrived for the fight at Hue. One thing was clear, no easy route, orderly or disorderly, of the enemy solution was practical to plan or expect within a make belief time expectation from a command bunker.

For more than 3 weeks, heavy street fighting dominated ground efforts and any news stories home that escaped Hue. Little by little Marines of the First and Fifth, with coordinated ARVN and Army support drove enemy resistance out of Hue, one dreadful wall dogfight and neighborhood block at a time. No U.S. forces had urban, close-quarters training, except for those to whom it came naturally from a youthful hit and run rural or urban past, Wilson Street style. The lingering monsoon season made it impossible to employ air support tactics to lead advancing ground efforts. In addition, the "Rules of Engagement" syndrome saw first implementation in a killing field when Marine command from out there somewhere, gave orders not to bomb or shell the inner city destroying historic structures, a policy creating temporary ground war malfeasance, confusion and anger, ultimately overlooked because of the intensity of the eventual fighting required. Enemy resistance for weeks was intense, from hundreds of sniper attacks from inside buildings, from spider holes and makeshift machine gun bunkers. At night VC booby traps were set, even under dead bodies, in the paths of the most likely advances of the next morning's fighting by Marines now growing gung-ho-committed, and eating nails for breakfast seeing their mission clearly, uncompromised.

Eventually the city's fighting boiled down to the Citadel and the Imperial Palace inside its now torn, pocked and tattered ancient walls. The historic Citadel became a true Asian '60s version Alamo, except this time the Americans were on the outside, gathering forces, stacking arms, eyeing the target with hunger and revenge from sniper losses. Clearing skies eventually allowed USAF A-4 Skyhawks to drop some bombs and napalm on the Citadel, historic or not. Doomed NVA and VC units, originally part of the infiltrating Tet attack, would become the trapped and hunted, doomed to a fate they could only expect. Unspoken determination of the First Marines, supported now by the Fifth Marines, had become focused fighting beasts with a bite into the enemy's ass, relentless in the hold, chomping further toward the head.

A far-away domestic US population watched each day's Hue fighting and advances on their evening news, as the futility and mounting losses of the entire Nam proxy endeavor became blatantly obvious to the awakening public. The Citadel was retaken, but not for a long, hard month, as the Imperial Palace in the center was entered by marines on February 29, very early in the Defining Year 1968. The NVA flag over the Citadel, which had flown for a month, finally came down as surviving NVA found hidden unseeable paths out of Hue any way they could in a scramble for their own lives and their NVA-Ho-style commitment to regroup and fight again, as long as it takes.

In the small space between the clamor and destruction of warring in Hue, and the standing down, marines glared into exhausted space, amidst lingering waves of war's remnants. Hue could have been the nastiest of all, although degrees of nasty warring seem useless to contemplate. Hue's smell would latch hard to each soldier's countdown and wake-up, and into dates and years far beyond for many. Eighty percent of Hue was destroyed. Communist forces lost were around 5,133 dead in the city itself, and another three thousand more were estimated to have been killed outside the city. Big KIA/WIA stuff for the government tweekers to tweek-on and broadcast selectively on days when war news might not need blasting.

Ultimately, the Battle of Hue had to be considered and promoted as a US and friendlies overall stirring victory. Two-thirds of the original twelve thousand enemy troops committed to Hue's insurgency and Tet contribution died, thus would not be recycled for future killing incursions. Hue was destroyed, in order to save it, but would eventually be abandoned from American troop concerns as all South Vietnam assets were fleeting and expendable. "Commitment" to holding a hard-fought-for position, was a matter of continually shifting compromises, configured someplace else.

Many believe Hue was the beginning of the end for American public opinion support. Evening news film footage could not be sufficiently whitewashed, not denied to the concerned, curious, regularly tuned-in living rooms. Political at-a-boys could not rev up much flag waving or rah-rah support in the face of a long month of TV broadcasted Tet battles, especially those from Hue. With the

Battle of Hue, the Tet Offensive, long planned and well implemented by North Vietnamese Command, had its undeniable reunification exclamation points. In many, many ways, the relentless, heavy, wreaking, humid stench of Hue stretched thousands of miles across the Pacific into millions of Wilson Street homes in small and large American towns everywhere. Still does!

> *Mid-March, 1968*
> *Dear Mom, Dad, Sis, Gpa & Gma,*
> *Everybody knocking off from warring early today, like an unspoken truce I guess, more than likely just low on ammo, saving what's left for any night action that might come our way. Doesn't matter why, just less killin' things flyin' around in the air is a gooder day. Compared to the constant house to house, wall to wall, constant small arms fire, there is a sense of everything shifting here in Hue. We can spend two days not moving, behind the same wall, seeing our "spot," and then a rush to a new position as if that next area has been freshly given-up and abandoned by a retreating Charlie. War's musical walls! Seems like progress, but we just see the tiny part of the battle right before the eyes of our worn unit, and that skimpy view is always from behind some wall or street intersection we are supposed to scramble across at some signal. Have no idea what the real big picture is, hope somebody knows. Every now and then you hear some rumor of what a beautiful historic city Hue is, but I don't dare look up long enough to sight-see anything.*
> *Marines here are beat-up, tired, numb, mad; not to mention the dead and wounded. Can't believe I thought Hue would be lighter duty than Quang Tri. We can't see the infamous inner city Citadel yet,*

but they say that is now where the battle is—all the bangs, cracks, womps and bloohies, rising smoke, shouts, orders, come from that direction. 1st Marines are up there, been up there the whole fight they say. My guess is that the 1st Marines are so pissed, they will stay up there, in the lead and take the Citadel themselves having earned the right, avenge losses. We hear the 5th has joined, once they got a good hold, they won't let go either. Everything we do is to guard their rear, pass the ammo, always with an eye for snipers. Word is, just leave the 1st and 5th alone, they are really pissed, not to be denied, every gook in there will die. Yesterday about 100 ROKs went by toward the front, meanest looking people on the face of the earth. No enemy leaves alive once the ROKs are in the fight. Prisoners don't happen.

Occasionally we see and help the poor remaining villagers. Families come from deep hiding holes as we secure each different neighborhood area. Blank stares, all starving, they have no idea which way to go or what to do. Poor bastards may as well be standing in their own graveyards. We all realize they will eventually be left here, in the rubble, and the smell. They try to give us their youngest.

The big news is new orders. Apparently our unit pulls back in two days, leaving Hue to the ROKs, 1st and 5th Marines, and whoever shows up in final support of this burnt-out smoking crater of a city. According to rumors we'll be back in Quang Tri to mount up and fly support for Marines at a place called Khe Sanh. Remote, Northwest, not far from Laos. Be glad to crawl in a Huey again, where the air moves and we can see the war in a bigger picture, hopefully have a clue about what is going on. Not sure what the rush to Khe Sanh means, but it has to be better than Hue. Leaving could be tricky, probably not like walking off a ball field, still lots of snipers trying to make a living.

The smell of Hue struck us 3 miles before we got here, the whole stagnant area is a heavy wicked smell, smoke from fired guns or grenades hardly moves, hanging on every street intersection and alley in the mornings, then mingling with all the other burnt human smells through the day, the only way we can describe it is the heavy smell of evil, or death. We have known there is something more specific to the gagging smells, turns out it is—According to more rumor, the enemy are burning their dead, and of course we are here to help them get that way—the smell that has gagged us all, that hangs so depressingly heavy, the smell is burning blood and flesh. I fear it will linger within all of us for quite some time; I can taste it, the inner-otherworld of bad dreaming I suspect. Surely we will meet with real air soon enough on the way out, if the world still has real air.

I've been in Hue 12 days; it seems like 3 months, not much of a dent on the way to a wake-up. Still sleeping 20 minutes at a time, the kind of sleep where you can hear, smell, hold tight to an M-16, within a helmet that never comes off. The constant helmet is a head-heavy feeling that may also linger for some time to come. I may run around for years thinking how light and free my new head is. All of this, the smell, heavy helmet, green cans of dehydrated compressed meat loaf look-alike day after day, the passing dead and wounded; all of it is sticky, un-washable, suffocating.

Off to Khe Sanh, only Marines up that way, maybe not so blown up.

Rollie

P.S. Nothing from Darlene yet, but then not sure how any mail would find me.

On the way out of Hue for marines reassigned to various new I Corps crisis of mixed dying and wounding methodology, the used units could not help but wonder whether the whole Nam cause was "horseshit" or "bullshit." Horseshit being the lighter brand American intervention insanity. Bullshit would be of a more serious nationalized misjudgment nature, the "institutional" class of insanity, perhaps militarism with someone's financial gain hidden within. A grunt can imagine the Joint Chiefs daily briefing, starts with defining topics of a horsheshit nature, versus those projects with a bullshit nature. Horseshit, being the surface issues, would arise first to the table on the outline of discussion and consensus seeking. Bullshit being deferred until midday, or the next day, as real bullshit takes time for points of fact and concepts to rationalize into action and implementation, none of which is stationary enough in Nam to put to a Joint Chief's decisive consensus in short periods of bullshit discussion. By the time a bullshit item is tabled for discussion, there is a new version of the old bullshit that they couldn't quite get to, making the original description or the ensuing discussions, nothing but a bunch of chickenshit.

Horseshit or bullshit, to the marine grunt, is all in the same pot, but the exit from Hue is real. Ten times the fatigue than on the way in, loaded with stench, the creeping slow-motioned crawl out is like moving through thick sludge grasping to hold each stepping boot. "Getting out" looks different in the streets, now wrecked and bombed to smaller particles of a city that was bleak on the way in, but not so broken. The only real encouraging sign is that the sounds of battle slowly seem further behind than twenty steps ago. Out of

Hue remains covered in the humid hanging fog and stench of the Battle of Hue. Fifteenish days in Hue, the marine only focuses on what is right directly, smack dab in front and close around him. Now moving slowly, directly, on a street, things seem wider, more open, more sniperable, except the snipers are supposed be back there in the rest of the fighting, with the potential exception of that asshole that is in his own unique sniper world, out freelancing. A sludge-held-boot step at a time, things aren't as dangerous but are just as cautious and more curious as to what we just did or didn't do.

In compressed, measured stop and go moves "out," marines see South Vietnamese civilian officials, full colonels disguised in civilian clothing, ARVN soldiers, professors from Hue's university, society ladies clinging to supply thieves, all hiding in or peeking from various US-fed supply centers, seeking protection from passing marines going forward or backing out. Boot heavy marines recognize this supply side cadre of Nam officialdom formed into a cadre of looting enterprise, leaving the stricken street population to their own starving. Officialdom or peasantry, all are stricken within the battle's tangle of uncertainty and daily flow of violence, "depravation" the realistic human certainty. None of the onlookers would befriend or smile to a passing marine in a token expression of "thanks" or slight friendliness nor would they condemn the Communist insurgents. Now at war for thirty straight years, and periodically for centuries, there is no reason to believe these passing marines from America's Wilson Street will be the last army to move about their city. In X years, others will trudge and sludge the same pre or post battle routs, with other generations of half-dead civilians watching and looting— new snipers with killing weapons of the future will do their aim and launch work as designed. It won't change. Fight your way in, save a few spots, blow some things up, drape some enemy bodies on some useless rolling barb wire, and move on, all while Command out there somewhere draws up a new battle on a new map in some place called Khe Sanh that will also soon mean nothing, except to the marines and their families who fight and die there.

The grandest signs of life's ingenuity and Hue survival instincts are the returned appearance of the wily Island Dogs along the road sides, sticking their invincible heads from neighborhood cracks and openings, watching passing marines with their own sense of standing down and getting back to their energetic scavenging of Hue streets, alleys, back doors, and neighborhoods. Poor, dirty, torn, shrunken Hue families, stand silently behind walls in their generational order, holding or leaning on one another, staring at the passing marines, too worn to offer babies or daughters for some sort of relocation to safety back in a world they have no idea about and can't even imagine. Obviously, anywhere but here, in Hue, is thought to be a better place on earth. The way out finally has lighter air, air the marines can actually see through, air that is not so heavy of the Perfume/Citadel smoldering stench of the final battle's backlash. There is finally a hazy but clearing vision as if the trudging exiting grunt is coming from a covered tunnel into a new awakened world lit by heaven's graces or perhaps fresh awaiting angels. Clinging ground sludge gives way to firmer ground and eventually a dust-up from a boot step. Clinging stench gives way to the smell of new sparkling sunlight as if the marine is rising through clouds so high the sun breaks out to regain respect, to light the way out of the killing tunnel this precious one time.

An easier, quicker way out would be to just attach each of the worn marines to black country crows and have them airlifted out, nothing sneaks up on, or catches black country crows off-guard. Marine brass probably hasn't configured the black-crow strategy into a logistical plan yet, only the country boys know those tricks.

How many lines of conquering or conquered soldiers have limped and staggered out of Hue in the last thousand years?

How many will do so in the next thousand years?

The First and Fifth will no doubt capture the Citadel, and the ROKs will have their way with the captured enemy gooks. So what? Charlie will regroup, reweapon, reeverything, and we'll see them all again, do it all over again in some other fog and stench next month, then next year until the futility and losses rev up the protests into an undeniable frenzy domestically. The roads and paths out of each battle will always be pounded to a hard surface, sludgy mudish in the monsoon season, blowing dust trails the other nine months, except when they aren't. Mamasans and Papasans of the surrounding countryside, followed by generations of family peasantry will always travel back and forth to Hue delivering meager foodstuffs, tradable goods, minor farm produce and hidden weapons. It is what they do. It is what life is in the Nam, when the civilized armies finally go home.

So many lessons in Nam, just in Hue alone. Surely, lessons that will linger in a national conscience, acting as some sort of future warning to safeguard America's interests or at least separate real interests from false, made-up, tricky concepts of national interests. Hue needed to be regained, so our marines regained the place. Never mind the place was destroyed in its saving, the peasants left behind to struggles of old or, at best, struggles of only a slight difference from the old. The clinging sludge of just the exit, combined with the stench of battles fought will take years to wash off, about as long as it will take politicians and generals to forget the hard fought lessons they may have never learned. Maybe it isn't even the battles themselves. Maybe it is just industrial R&D and manufacturing, creating new weaponry that needs testing and perfecting by new batches of Wilson Street Boys. Test enough weapons and maybe someday unmanned flying things can hover and float through battle's air all dropping laser guided stuff to blow up stuff we used to crawl toward and blow up by tossing a little round bomb like a baseball. Once we trudge and duck and dart to the outskirts of Hue's areas of declining interests, maybe the warring stories will complete themselves, and marines forty years from now will fight and die for causes that are real, instead of proxy, maybe not.

In the final days of the Battle of Hue, surviving, mobile NLF/ VC/NVA would retreat from Hue as best they could, also finding their own trails to the countryside. Those NVA not trapped in an Alamo-like last stand in the Citadel moved out in small groups under darkness, with their deadly work not finished. Weaponry not totally expended, enemy troops as quickly as possible moved to Hue area countryside hamlets on paths to retreating and set up again, to mortar and rocket-womp backward killing and wounding more marines following paths out to new assignments. Brief but deadly battles greeted departure as they had entry, three long weeks prior. Only when all the unused enemy firepower was used did enemy troops finally disappear into surrounding rice paddy, bamboo and elephant grass ghost lands via well-organized tunnels, paths, and rehearsed getaways. US command responded to the retreating attacks with SOP. They ordinanced up and bombed the hell out of the countryside. Hamlets and surviving populations they had just fought and often died to protect, on the brink of their own survival, were eventually destroyed along with inner Hue. If wars and battles are run by spiritual evil devils, they completed their Hue work at the exit, making complete the Indochina-Alamo.

After the Tet, Battle of Hue, it took six years before that red flag and gold star would fly again over the bombarded Citadel. But we were there at Tet, standing ground, following orders. Ordered to defend and retake the damn useless, stench-filled place, and we did. Then, as always, it is "other duties as assigned," another booming Semper Fi to which there is no denial. Focus, breath again, move out, wait for a letter from home, Darlene's letter, or anyone from the old neighborhood or back patio. See if one letter catches up to a moving unit on the other side of the planet, in a place called I Corps, for the time being. Hoping when the front is full of Charlies, the rear is still full of America.

Marines stayed in Hue to close the Citadel deal, others moved on. Nam had many constantly arising needs to move on to. Moving on has intervals of grind, when a grunt marine sludge's forward looking for the moment where they are "through it," really "through it." Sniperless clear air with a full sun, dry socks, and a blessed revitalized sense of "indeed I have." I have fought the fight. After each layer of war, there is the moment of personal inventory of bumped, bruised, swollen, and torn parts, and the attitude check, alone, while surrounded by fellow marines also checking their body inventories and angels, if they are yet aware of angels. On with it, 231 and a wake-up. Get good at it!

The Citadel at Hue was South Vietnam's midcountry symbol of centuries past history and the spiritual cultures engrained in the lives of the countryside population. The Hue Citadel was the symbol of unified Nam, historically and spiritually. The city of Hue and its mystic ancient Citadel, locked in the midst of crossing rivers, stood with a gracious but defiant statement of the country's deep self-enclosed quiet ancient history that has not altered or shifted in core internal or outward Asian expression since before the discovery of America. It still does embody that expression in an Asian mystical sense sustained by many generations!

March/April, '68, the stoic Citadel took on a whole different mood, in-country and to the world. The worn, dark, streaking plaster of hammered walls became an eerily similar replica of America's Alamo, fought over, fought within, and fought for, up, and around battered sides. In the end, just like America's Alamo, those within were defeated, crushed by numbers of opposition and the superior warring assets of those sieging its eventual penetrable confines. America's Wilson Street Boys fought toward the walls of the Citadel, yard fence by yard fence, cobbled home by dirt street. Skin and bones Island Dogs kept hidden, stray cats used better judgment and would starve rather than to scavenge for scraps in the open battlefield. Herds of wondering fowl found the stagnant non-flow of the Perfume River a better habitat than their usual safe Hue backyards of caretaker peasants. In the Battle of Hue, nothing was untouched until in the end, thirty bloody days from the overwhelming VC/NLF attacking commitment strategy, the historic city was in shambles with the population turned to transit refugees or Asian-style ghetto hideaways or killed in every killing way thinkable.

A young marine on the tail-end force of exterminating the communist enemy forces was greeted with sights unthought of by America's Wilson Street standards. The remnants of the brutal confrontation in the end were too destructively graphic in remaining human debris for the evening news. From the filth and shot up rubble of Hue's neighborhoods to the Citadel were cratered dirt roads and war's burnt and burning remains, pushed aside by probing marine units and clearing machines. Those Americans who actually made it to a Citadel entrance would cross the few stone and dirt bridges still intact, connecting the Citadel side to the south neighborhoods of grouped huts and hamlet structures all strafed, pocked with small arms fire, blackened with burnt trails of what had happened. Barbed wire lined each semblance of open space in mean tangled warnings of unforgettable menace, most prevalent inside the river's dividing boundaries.

The strung rolls of barbed wire served another purpose at the conclusion of the Battle of Hue. Among America's Wilson Street Boys who won all the rights from that long iconic battle, from the rural streets and youth bike gangs, who knew instinctively sturdy rolls of American made barbed wire would be perfect as a display for enemy dead bodies? Marines would not "go there" but did not have to. The pop-pop, smoke and fire, danger and bravery, and womps of a ground war had receded into another extraordinary month of Nam history. On the barbed wire would be the results, the ravages of battle, ROKs conclusive battle trophies. The defeated, slain, nearly stripped or totally stripped, disfigured and bloody, dead NLF, or VC, were displayed—crotches cut out, removed, and flung into the adjacent Perfume River just very few feet away for the feeding of the carp. Parts of the defeated were fed to the frickin' carp as a conqueror's victorious expression to the carp, hungry Asian carp—the only real winners of the entire Battle of Hue.

In Hue, early '68, after the main body of Tet, and afore Go Noi, we took the damn place back for the South Vietnamese government of the times. Then, as always, we packed up, counted and reported KIA and MIA, stacked captured enemy weapons and assets, pablumized the late arriving press with heroic accounts, and moved on to the next fuss up on Hill 432 or Hill 387 or fire base/LZ dummkopf or a deadly Hill 881 at Khe Sanh. America, in its proxy/domino concepts, only owned the ground we stood on, a reality never really gotten used to, certainly never admitted. (Sound like Afghan?)

New orders from energetic command recalculations arriving via communication jabbering radios were always quick to change a temporary outlook on the ground and with air support. No time and grunt assets wasted, new lieutenants arrived ahead of, or with, the new orders, and the same ole grunts grunted, one battle deeper into their countdown and wake-up, found a smoke, asked no questions about buddies, counted their angels if they got the "angel thing" going for themselves, cleaned their precious weapons, counted ammo, tightened belts, looked over the brain-housing metal pot, breathed, and knocked the last clinging sludge from the jungle boots which had officially turned into a part of their senescing human bodies.

These battles don't end on the battlefield, not in those days, or in these days. In the Domestic Nam, there was the spin, the PR effort to embrace public opinion concerning publicized battles, such as the faraway place called Hue. In the thriving PR tradition, grand enemy KIA numbers were reported, four-prongers thus making the case for the sacrificial justification and loss of our own US assets, lives, and hardware. "Five thousand enemy soldiers killed" supported new banners of command's boasting successes, especially in relation to Tet, as if reporting enemy losses would deplete the likelihood of ongoing battles or somehow bolster one side and deplete another side. Nothing could have been further from the Nam truth. NVA's General Giap and Ho's disciples of revolutionary leaders entered Tet and Hue with admittedly expendable NLF/VC troop assets. Large losses were of no surprise, no concern, nor tactically were large human losses on their side going to be depleting for future attack strategies. No matter the numbers of NLF and VC lost, no matter how high the KIA's sored, Giap, and Ho-boys considered them expendable, lost to the worthiest historical cause ever, the uniting of their country. All the KIA domestic reporting actually meant was that fighting would now elevate with the broad, aggregate, structured use of a more experienced, more trained deployment of North Vietnam Army "regulars."

The Domestic Nam was always about multiple crisscrossing of fighting and vengeance building for more fighting. The war itself resembled the mixed-up patterns and turns of the hundreds of lowland rivers that confused the area's dark Asian landscape that had been awakened for these fifty years of the latest war. Lowlands draped by upland mountains, which were always a reminder of new battles with entirely different troop and support requirements, different surprises from the enemy's generations of warring practices on their familiar land. For every placement and explosion of warring assets on the ground and in the air of Nam, their seemed an equally devastating event on the ground and in the airwaves at home on the streets of America. Once, familiar homey streets that had become a body part for rambunctious youth would slowly become farther and farther away from the in-country Nam focus of the committed soldier moving from one battle to the next, learning to only see and concern themselves with a narrow focus from the next set of orders.

In the meantime, Rollie had escaped Hue, would be up the road to Quang Tri, mount up, lock and load air stuff, and meet new exciting friends and enemy firepower around the low rolling mountains of Khe Sanh, within another iconic battle that started ten days before Tet and lasted until June. Khe Sanh would be another exclamation mark for the Proxy War and live forever in Nam's tailspin.

Khe Sanh was Westmoreland & Co. at their most Profuse. The extreme NW I Corps battle at Khe Sanh roared upon Domestic and family televisions and public consciousness with a media nuclear exclamation to the degenerating events surrounding the Tet Offensive and the entire Domestic Nam fiasco. In the hindsight of Khe Sanh, America would ask, "What and the heck were we thinking?" But at the time, Khe Sanh was dreadfully real, especially for the marines in town for the mixer that had to be dealt with. With Westmoreland's dream of attrition strategy, Khe Sanh was like putting the bait in the water on a three-pound test line and finding a twelve-foot shark.

Twenty five years before Tet, the French, still suspended in their Asian colonial adventure, established a "fort" of their own in what became extreme Northwest South Vietnam after the country was divided. At the time of the French fort building, at a small insignificant village called Khe Sanh, 1938-ish, Vietnam had not been divided at the DMZ by the ideology and persistence of a communist leaning North regime based in Hanoi, and the eventual democracy seeking symbolic profile of the South regime of Diem influence, based in Saigon (now Ho Chi Minh City). French fort building was SOP for the dug-in Asian-integrating intentions of the French, clinging to one hundred years of quasi-industrial, colonial-based Vietnam occupation. Eventually abandoned, post-Dien Bien Phu (or "dinbinphoo" as a dim-witted President Johnson referred), Khe Sanh was left to its ancient small village ancestral habits, in a rolling landscape just clicks from Laos, and a few less clicks from the southwestern edge of the DMZ.

For all practical purposes, Khe Sanh was another of a thousand small peasant hamlets, generally left to their own agrarian survival Buddhist roots for unknowable, unmeasured times past. The French fort building fuss-up was a temporary local phenomenon for curious peasants tending to small patches of subsistence crop production with their tamed water buffalo and screeching packs of free roaming animal husbandry gigs. Khe Sanh was a foothill closed society, on the edge of mountains and harmless Montagnard populations who had learned to live just a little further west, in a geographically well-protected Laotian border terrain. A few clicks further west of the Laotian border with then South Vietnam was the Mekong River, dividing Laos from Thailand, constantly feeding the entire region in its flowing south, eventually from Thailand through Cambodia, supplying the far South Vietnam delta region with whatever could be made to float. The entire area was conventionally called Indochina, an area warring long before America created a dreamed up a proxy— domino falling war room flow chart, warring enthusiastically through America's Nam experience and is still in unsettled warring depravities.

Two years prior to Tet (starting January '68), America's supreme military commanders fabricated a strategery for the broader Khe Sanh area. Although a village in itself, Khe Sanh would become a "region" to include the ancient village and a new US constructed fortified area a click away, centralized to a short airstrip. (Very much like the small base at Quang Tri was not actually in the city of Quang Tri, but just a click outside.) By 1968, the broader American Khe Sanh outpost was expanded to include the areas of the mortaring and rocket belt surrounding what would be the central airstrip, firebase, and command center. Once established, the broader Khe Sanh American militarized area could have been as much as ten miles out from the center of the airstrip activity, twenty miles from extreme western LZ outpost to extreme eastern LZ outpost, the same distances north to south, in rolling, unfamiliar hills, not adjacent to a supply route or source of water, terrific bunker mentality planning. Indigenous roaming water buffalo drew up better plans. Occupied solely by marines, the geographic separation and scarcity of Khe Sanh related mini-LZs and firebases would be practically impossible to support logistically. All of which would seem War College 101, if it were not for the detached command SNAFU's of Nam and creeping hidden military/industrial influences.

From Khe Sanh, theoretically, US reconnaissance could monitor enemy troop movements along the Laotian border, moving north to south along the infamous Ho Chi Minh trail, dispersing troops and weaponry to VC Units as ordered into the South Vietnamese hamlets and countryside terrain intricacies all up and down the undefined western border of the unofficial, unsettled country. Occasionally, the moving human chain assets could be temporarily disrupted by probing marine ground units, artillery, or marine phantom aircraft on bombing or napalm flaming missions. Troops or fixed assets of war weaponry supplied by Russians and Chinese carried by foot or prodded animal, fed the war machines of the communists north to south as routinely as the Santa Fe railroad carried goods from America's west coast ocean ports to domestic Midwest markets. Jungle canopies hid moving NLF assets for one side and covered US tracks for the other side. A newly assigned significant marine troop presence at Khe Sanh was designed to be the relatively removed business center for all things of north Ho Chi Minh trail, forward and backward, up and down Indochina. Supported by air from Phu Bai or Quang Tri, Khe Sanh prior to Tet was SOP in design, a good idea, as long as the good idea commanding 'ole boys didn't have to actually be there figuring up those good ideas, and then implementing. Theoretically, logistics control would be as usual inside the rocket belt at Khe Sanh central, with dug-in marines occupying the rocket belt. The plan draws up and balances nicely in a displaced covered map room with a fresh water cooler in the corner. What's not to war along with?

Nothing remained constant in the "defining year" in the Domestic Nam. Things, locations, bodies that were routine in duties became extra scrutinized for usable American in-country assets performing all duties as assigned into Tet. Khe Sanh's real position, fate, and historic reputation was being carefully dissected by NVA General Giap in Hanoi, creating an action plan of his own that would create US command defensive survival reaction. The action and reaction of Khe Sanh would rapidly merge in front of more cameras of an awakened media and Wilson Street societies, among street protestors now becoming professionals in their own right to become one more unavoidable national symbolic frustration at best, a national military embarrassment at worse.

On an isolated Hill 881, over nine clicks from the Khe Sanh Command Operations center, Lance Corporal Blevin Slyhope dutifully and with grunt determination kept his post along with marines from every US background and national heritage possible to circumstantially integrate into a working unit. Two platoons (approximately 220 marines) counted night ops, field rations, and full canteens on a daily basis, all sharing the unpredictable fate of their 881 duties as assigned, existing one hour and one sun angle at a time. So far, from political and military strategists, Slyhope and buddy foxhole grunts could not even imagine why'n the be-Jesus they are on this bare-ass dirt pile of a hill, looking west for a glimpse of tonight's disruption, isolated, detached, with only their Semper Fis and M-16s, most not suspecting an angel's assistance, guidance, or whereabouts. No explanations or strategic ops planning would hopscotch along the lines of Hill 881 beyond the normal dug-in nature of defensive preparations for dusk and then the night's surprises. Anything was a surprise on 881, even nothing. Lance Corporals are not in the loop of command strategery, never have been, never will be. In fact, within Nam who knew what, when and where the loop was. "Loops" changed, depending on blame and claim to KIAs and WIAs. Some place on that hill was a commanding lieutenant who held just as much dark speculation about the ground they held as his troops who were depending on him for a laundry list of war college leadership skills, with a take-charge and follow-me outward personality. Little did Slyhope and his lieutenant suspect that the real detail planning for Khe Sanh, the rocket belt and Hill 881, with all duties as assigned, had been completed up north by Giap, the guy on the other team, supply-less reaction by US command pending. Slyhope wondered if in the war college 101 they discussed if it was better to be an "act" or a "react," perhaps too deep for the lance corporal level.

Planning in DC for Khe Sanh's most likely action contingencies Westmoreland style would instantly follow Giap's initiative, even before Tet would kick up an avalanche of bad guy infiltrating violence, leapfrogging down the entire South Vietnamese nation. If Slyhope had known the content of upper command's characters, he and platoon buddies could have saved more green cans of dehydrated meat loaf than they ordinarily would have. They could have lined up a few more canteens of invaluable potable water, a commodity they would become desperate to behold in just a few more short days. They could have absconded with a few more metal jackets of M-16 assets and laid in some wired clays and grenades and prompted distant "arty" buddies to do the same. They could have refreshed terrain coordinates to the west, and as far as they could see to the north, maybe they could have looked back better and clearer at the ten thousand eyes looking at them, studying the terrain detail of 881.

As Lance Corporal Slyhope made a home of his hard dirt perimeter vantage point, in a three-foot hole often filled with three inches of monsoon, counting 207 and a wake-up, NVA supreme field commander General Giap (the same General Giap that had commanded the communist victory twenty-five years prior against the French at Dien Bien Phu [dinbinphoo to the dimwitted President Johnson]), built NVA assets for the NW South Vietnam version of the launch of Tet, planning Khe Sanh as an early strategic launched explosion pad for renewed warring across the entire country.

Ten days prior to the national explosion of Tet, Giap ordered forty thousand North Vietnamese troops, coordinating with NLF (National Liberation Front), into the Khe Sanh area loaded down with weaponry that had been on and around the Ho Chi Minh trail, NW South Vietnam for literally years, awaiting the destructive use that their Chinese and Russian manufacturers intended. At the end of '67, a total of three thousand five hundred US Marines were at central Khe Sanh airstrip and command and occupying multiple pinpoint isolated LZ/firebase outposts of rocket belt defenses. Giap himself would relocate out of Hanoi's command center to within eighteen clicks of Khe Sanh, just amidst the western jungled DMZ belt, hidden with a command center in the higher elevation foothills. From this strategically selected point, Giap would initiate persistent, coordinated, multiple weaponry attacks on Khe Sanh Marines.

Ten days prior to the national alerts of massive enemy preparations and deadly trends of a Tet, Khe Sanh exploded with numerous NVA, Giap directed, attacks. US intelligence was quickly reactionary, forced to a war room flow chart of interpretation and response. The chaos, threat, and counter-action strategery lay before Westmoreland, who quickly checked his dry ammo, and in full military/industrial tradition, "reacted" (without consulting Hill 881 and Blevin, it is safe to say).

Latently, Westmoreland faced his troop and asset deployment challenge of the war and his commanding lifetime. Khe Sanh instantly appeared to be a pivotal, merging moment of the war, especially recognizing Tet had not yet occurred and generally was only vaguely suspected as a theoretic possibility by various inconsistent "intelligence" sources and would not arise to its massive conflict reality for ten more days. Westmoreland first saw the early fresh multifaceted attacks on the Khe Sanh outposts as a defining moment, just as Dien Bien Phu (or dinbinphoo as the dimwitted President Johnson bellowed), had been pivotal for Giap fighting colonialist French ambitions twenty-five years prior. Westmoreland would soon be challenged whether to interpret the elevated actions at Khe Sanh as a diversionary tactic or a main force, conquering, decisive enemy effort.

In fact, the actual intent at Khe Sanh from Giap-command and the highest commands of the entire North is still arguable. In the face of Tet, a mere ten days away, was the North Vietnamese warring action strategy of Khe Sanh the build-up to Tet or were the Giap strategies meant as a diversion designed to draw important I Corps Marine assets to that region, away from the more populated coastal cities, and thus allow a greater chance of success with planned and pending Tet incursions such as in Hue? Or was Khe Sanh planned as a Class A target, to be overrun and occupied, destroying deployed marine units in that area who had already been hung to dry, self-isolated and cutoff, and thus, Khe Sanh would become the second Dien Ben Phu, pivoting the war in many ways to favor the North's ambitions?

That very war college command dilemma and exercise still floats vacantly about the echelons of intellectual warring, among those who concern themselves with such historical conjecture of Nam recollection, attempting forever to find the correct round pegs for the correct round holes. Only here, in the exploratory open-minded confines of *The Domestic Vietnam* is the actual answer. Having completed years of serious contemplation, over vast amounts of cold beer, around flickering seasonal firepits, safe in the inner elements of a contemporary post-Tet, post-marine, post-being about to be blown-up, can we profess true focused speculation toward a defining Giap strategy for Khe Sanh.

To get to the answer, one simply has to ask the core question. How would I do it? If I were Giap, and the bad guys? How would I win Khe Sanh, while lending support elsewhere? Having the experience at Dien Bien Phu (we know what dimwit called it), I would coordinate the same effort (as Giap), troop numbers, terrain displacement, weapon logistics, and build a familiar potential scenario to be predictable. Then, my inner Giap would recognize the "differences" in the lines of battle to be prosecuted around Khe Sanh. Differences which were mainly US air and general arty weaponry power—big, mean, fast, squash, and blowup Charlie undeniable differences. Therefore, Giap Plan A would create the diversion tactic scenario, pouring in as many resources as possible to create the illusion of preparing to overrun the Khe Sanh main camp, replicating the proud moments of Dien Ben Phu. If this overrun attack strategy appeared to be a certain victory, Giap could proceed to overrun Khe Sanh, but this was not required for success. If the Plan A strategy could not guarantee a monumental NVA victory, Plan B would be to pound the hell out of Khe Sanh and the inner rocket belt, implement Tet-like contingencies and be happy with the "diversion strategy" while NLF and VC were preparing to charge through the streets of Hue and another forty-three provincial capital cities on January 31, as the US press extolled the bravery and inevitability of Slyhope and fellow Khe Sanh Marines directly and daily, to living rooms and Domestic Nam apparatus all across America's sea to shining sea. Thus, Giap would be simultaneously affecting the internal American PR war.

Westmoreland himself bit and fabricated one more deprecating impression from the Giap strategy. Frustrated for years with the fleeting, hit-and-run, terrorist-style non-battle line fighting of the Communists, Westmoreland longed for any quasi face-to-face large unit battle and ground war that would lend a direction and decisiveness to the Indochina war at a particular time and battle scheme. (Lance Corporal Slyhope had no such face-to-face military longing from his hillside foxhole.) Westmoreland needed a flag waver, a drum beater, a halftime show, a battlefield explosion creating a victorious patriotic display of power superiority, unquestionable ferocious military superiority, even if the facts surrounding such a confrontation would have to be twisted into dangling, fleeting, mostly vague strategies and end results.

Westmoreland first responded to the reality of new Khe Sanh targeted attacks and massive enemy numbers surrounding the main camp and outposts by ordering massive amounts of weaponry and support assets into the main LZ and command center to be stockpiled for his own personal "Gettysburg" with Giap and the NVA. A supply side military/industrial gold mine, Westmoreland filled Khe Sanh "central" base as if it were a modern day industrial park of ammo and gun support things, most supplies and ordnance arriving by a constant relay of Phu Bai or Da Nang dispatched C-130s. A truly massive supply of weaponry and blowing up things it was. Westmoreland also ordered more marines into the area, doubling the size of the marine forces assigned to the defense of Khe Sanh but would still be hugely outnumbered by hill and valley hidden NVA almost 8 to 1. Right before Tet, Westmoreland had rushed valuable troop and weapon assets to this far off, remote foothill post, just as Giap had predicted he would do, pulling those assets from use elsewhere, back-ordering more assets. All elements of the battle of Khe Sanh would prepare for its television premiere!

Personalities matter in war's commanders, and Westmoreland had his own. Referred to as a corporate executive in uniform (fitting to a tee military/industrial institutional personality qualifications),

Westy's core strategy, which was realistically a pipe dream requiring serious disregard of strategic fact, was "attrition," as in "attracting," in this case "attracting the enemy." Westy believed if he could just attract large opposing armies to face each other in a modern day Asian multi-terrain style Gettysburg "stand-off," within which America's fighting and weaponry superiority would prevail, leading the war in a direction of some sort of more rapid successful outcome, as in actually winning something, perhaps for at least the moment, then a quick flag-waving rah-rah.

Giap's concentration of NLF, backed by NVA regulars at Khe Sanh, was viewed by Westy as his long awaited attrition hope and opportunity. Supporting the long standing Westmoreland massive battle line premise, he militarily and industrially led the influence of the confrontation, spending orders to increase overall in-country Nam troop numbers from 16,000 in 1964 to 535,000 at the peak in 1968. Westy had opened the Wilson Street pipelines, nourished by his constant, highly publicized positive assessments of US military successes and prospects of more successes. Resolve and determination blind wishes would steer Westy's war to his dreamed of benevolent, global superiority ends. Give me enough-armed, confident Rollie's and Blevin's, and we will hold hills; tame and reshape mountains, corral moving rivers, and streams; and halt the winds and rains of communist dominoes falling on helpless peasant populations.

> *"Blevin, get your ass out there on Hill 881 and dig the hell in, hang on, have faith, and bless the sacrifices you're about to endure. That is why you exist, and By-God we love you for it."*

In fact, Westmoreland was so "attrition principled," more troops would be planned for the expansion of the war into more of Indochina, into Cambodia and Laos—a notion impractical to implement because of rising "no longer overlooked" protests in the lands between such faraway places as California and Jersey.

Blevin thought he could actually see into Laos from 881, right out "there" somewhere just a few clicks away. To Blevin, Laos appeared to not need expanding into, not by his boots anyway.

Tet eventually outmaneuvered all of Westmoreland's pronouncements of positive indicators for winning the war through fictitious attrition or in any other theorized circumstance. Westy had no Tet refocus. In the end, he would have no legitimate claims to conquering fame or defensive fame, although he would rise stoutly to accept Nam accolades. Khe Sanh would be bombarded for over a month. Blevin's world would laser focus to precise area foothill movements and counter terrain movements, real and/or imagined, eventually amidst a lack of rations, water, and ammo. Westmoreland could get thousands of tons of weaponry to Khe Sanh, but no one could get potable water to Blevin on Hill 881.

Now let's ask the question: What happened to the vast mountains of warring supplies that was constantly flying in to Khe Sanh's main US command center by C-130s; the explosives and ammo of all types that US industrial supply lines had carried and nurtured from west coast ports; carried all across the Pacific by gigantic navy ships with cavernous bellies, unloaded to landing vessels manned by a slightly different type of boy from Wilson Street; boated into docks and Perfume waterways; forklifted to C-130s and swan-dived by brave pilot crews after brave pilot crews into a vulnerable shortened airstrip in the middle of Gook country right in the bull's-eye of the North's leading General Giap staring down daily at Khe Sanh central?

What happened to all that millions and millions of dollars worth and millions more dollars worth, costing millions more dollars worth of logistic expertise and explosive/booming planning?

What happened to that ordnance and weaponry that would fight Westmoreland's war of attrition to a decisive positive for America warring direction?

What the hell ever happened to all of the weaponry in a world of Nam SNAFU? As if consciously making the decision: If we don't have a gigantic SNAFU for the moment, let's create one!

Well, war shocks! Turned out, all that hundreds of missions of C-130s dropping in and out and all those big ole American fork lifts carrying big ole pallets of stuff got kind of noticed by Giap's own recon intelligence guys. Yep, turns out the Gooks had a few thinkers themselves, right out there with Gook binoculars, up close in Gook land and Gook radios transferring their own versions of intelligence back to Gook commanders. They probably learned that "observation and report back to command" stuff twenty-five years ago at Dien Bien Phu (or dinbinphoo as the dimwitted President Johnson referred).

So just as us vision-less war gamers would do playing war in backyards or at Allerton, cagey-accurate Gook hillside mortar tripods and rocket launchers zeroed in with exact coordinates and bombed the hell out of the airstrip area, bunkers and all, right where all of the US weaponry was housed. Khe Sanh ammo dumps and logistic centers at the airstrip blew up for a full eighteen hours, exploding and counter exploding tons of "paid for" industrial manufacturing and handling expertise, into a massive display of Gook gotcha again!

Blevin could see and "feel" the sickening sounds of his exploding resupply hopes from all the way out there on 881. He knew what it meant to him and his two dug-in platoons. They all knew what it meant. Back somewhere, Westy probably knew what it meant also. War is hell, killin' and breakin' things, except within the supply-side manufacturing. It was not the industrialists' fault that Westy couldn't manage the assets more productively once in-country.

All Khe Sanh *numbers would eventually* explode. But everything else in the Domestic Nam, the war and the stories and the knuckle-dragging fighting was with real individuals from individual lives and real neighborhoods from back in the world. After Tet had transformed the war to a new unknown feelingless direction for command, Westy went home to terrific heroics and adulation, replaced in June by

General Abrams. Westy left Blevin right there in his foxhole on 881, who by March would be off 881, into a repair mode before a new mix of orders would spend him to another hot I Corps world. In true military/industrial nature, Westy graciously accepted a promotion to Chief of Staff of the entire United States Army and held that attritionless post for four years into '72, a time when the Domestic Nam was still SNAFU-ing at a precipitous, unsustainable rate.

Westy left an incredible number of attrition numbers behind, in typical CEO style. Concerning Khe Sanh, US directive air and artillery firepower, Westmoreland spent ammo assets in record amounts unheard of in previous warring on this planet. Soon, the Khe Sanh bombarding effort itself initiated a motto of "be generous," a motto that then was a prevailing command "battle cry."

Khe Sanh precious KIA/MIA numbers were never really determined. How do you roam the thick jungled foothills looking for bodies in a Tet craze of mobility? At the end of the Khe Sanh campaign, enemy body count guesstimations stood at 1,602. Westy and staff immediately termed that count false, adding their own numbers in a rounding manner good enough for enemy dead, estimating ten thousand to fifteen thousand. Now that's more like it.

Westy and Staff initial US Marine numbers were 205 KIA, 1,668 WIA, but admitted that those numbers conveniently only included casualties at the main combat base and certain surrounding select hill positions. US KIA numbers were later revised to 476, but that also did not include relief operations and wider spread operations immediately after the siege, certainly part of the entire Khe Sanh troop experience. Finally, Khe Sanh US forces and friendlies combined KIA were approximately one thousand and the WIAs were four thousand five hundred. Ouch! (So much for Westy's "attrition" model that sounded good until the war started.)

The Khe Sanh base camp artillery battalion fired 158,891 outgoing rounds at any suspected NVA locations.

The seventh Air Force fighter bombers flew 9,691 sorties, dropping 14,223 tons of bombs and rockets around Khe Sanh.

Marine aircraft pitched in for 7,078 sorties and 17,015 tons of ordnance, mainly from Phu Bai.

Navy aviators flew 5,337 sorties and dropped 7,491 tons of ordnance from various bases including from aircraft carriers floating about the South China Sea.

(All this is just at Khe Sanh, for the one-month Giap-led siege, if it was a distraction strategy it sure distracted.)

Air Force B-52s (the biggest boys that darken the sky on a flyover) flew 2,548 sorties, often from Okinawa, unleashing a staggering 59,542 tons of munitions, just around Khe Sanh, the equivalent of a 1.3 kiloton nuclear device, every bombing-beautiful NW South Vietnam day. If you love the sounds and smells of exploding weaponry day and night, that was the place to be.

Estimating enemy forces to be around forty thousand, US aircraft and artillery expended over five tons of munitions per NVA soldier. Wow, now that's military/industrial coordination at its best. No wonder Westy was promoted. What's the sales commission on that sort of order fulfillment?

Let's just guesstimate a little. Estimate your average 500-lb. bomb to cost .50 cents per pound to manufacture $250 per bomb. Double that figure for shipping and handling, ocean logistics, bomber fuel to deliver, etc. That's $1 per lb. or $500 per bomb to put to good booming use. The $2,000 per ton × 5 tons per bad guy is equal to $10,000 × 40,000 bad guys is equal to $400 million just to bomb "attrition" areas around Khe Sanh for thirty days. Total cost of Khe Sanh, in addition to American KIA/WIA lives, would be one hundred times that figure or $40 billion well spent domino dollars. These figures are guestimates as best as I can guestimate. But I guestimate they are not far off and, if anything, are way low.

This was a US taxpayer's proxy fiscal nightmare. From one cost segment, within one conflict, in a countrywide Tet that is one segment of a ten-year commitment, the expenditures resulting from and heaped upon the Domestic Nam concept put enormous pressure on the US economy contributors and would have easily broken the accounts of any other world intruder. That money to support theories of proxy warring and domino falling is the essence of military/industrial expansionism and execution, in the full flavor of late '60s LBJ political posturing.

All this begs multiple conclusions of layman logic, one of which is this: How close are we to those sacrifices and costs in the Middle East in the last ten years? (If one were a bit of a cynic of national policy, one could surmise our general American youth population of the '60s was a Hessian-like relationship to national government, as

Hessian-like relationships were to the British government in the era of 1776.)

What must all of that rolling hillside Khe Sanh explosiveness have looked like from Blevin's isolated half dirt/half mud outpost foxhole on Hill 881 early February 1968? The ground itself would shake for a month, teeth rattling explosiveness would drill shell shockingly down a Blevin neurologic system head to neck, neck to spine, spine to the heels in crusted jittering boots, bomb struck, "shell shocked." On the west perimeter of 881, four foxholes in from the terrain break, staggering amounts of "friendly" bombing masses filling dark or lit skies, dusk or dawn, all over out there and around the lost world of Blevin at 881. Underbrush and slightly waving Nam things, mixing with dark shadowy perimeter lines just off a Blevin foxhole ground truth. Imaginations slide and slink out and then back inside a mind, amidst shadowy nights and relentless exhausted early morning hours lit by constant rattling, rapid explosions, and secondary backfire explosions. Flared illumination, then a crack and another crack of small arms fire just to keep the air mixed with killing things.

US bombing assets so prolific, Blevin could not tell an incoming enemy rocket launched from Gook land, from a marine Phantom fighter jet strafe and bomb drop. No one on 881 could determine who was blasting who or when a blast with their foxhole coordinates would be "incoming." From Hill 881, there might be more dangerous unintended consequences overlooked at the far away command bunker, *X* location, than there were intended consequences employed. To Blevin, in a world of countdown limbo, life was now not just the ground he stood on, but a world of earth shaking Khe Sanh blast-to-blast brain and gut-shaking ground, below the ground, within more ground scattering routinely in the air then falling all around him in hard little ground chunks.

Sleep? How? Resupply? Dream! How? Think?
Faith? Hope?

Stay focused! Stay down! Stay alive!

Water? Ammo? Dry stuff?

Click and tap an M-16 metal jacket to the helmet, keep ammo tight, see into "out there," feel "out there," do not light a fag. Tighten the eye level another click. Ignore the obvious; look into it. It is moving shadows we are concerned with, then a bright flash, a tracer racing to a target.

Light travels in unpredictable shadowy time, Gooks move at the "boom" flash, one to two seconds per low advancing dash or crawl as that light fades quickly into dark, plenty of time to scope.

See deeper into the nighttime owned by the Gooks, tree line details wiggle with bomb blast reflections/concussions. See around dirt corners and over dirt humps. Watch claymore wire lines, everything earthly constantly flickering and darting by the night's destructive sporadic illuminations.

Don't drink or eat. Resupply may not exist. The "world" may not exist. Countdown 204, -03, -02 may not exist, way too far off to even provide a microsecond of survival world-image inspiration. What, how much, is a reach of faith from 881? Name this weapon. It is like others, but this one is yours, your comfort, your companion, and your angel.

Each sunrise is a night survived. I think I'm getting used to this, and that can't be a good thing either. Once a part of this violence and terror, earth and hole, how does it ever wash away and leave the person alone? Or does it ever?

How again did we get here? In a dirt hole, on the other side of the planet?

Westy's grand attrition strategy at Khe Sanh became a grand SNAFU.

> *"Winning"? Are you kidding? Win what? This frickin jungle view dirt hill on a meaningless lost "Indochina" edge? Westy? Come on, man? Really?*
>
> *Indochina itself isn't even a place to win, just a global stretched hot jungle something, a clustered group of global somethings, kind of connected, kind of not. Do they not know it is worthless?*

Khe Sanh's second phase slowly evolved and passed, after realities pinched-off speculation that Khe Sanh was in fact a Dien Bien Phu type siege of a new era. The only Khe Sanh main airstrip serving resupply had been blown to landscaping "smithereens." A second phase of resupply planning would depend on new air assets, readying up Hueys and Chinooks from Quang Tri, now the closest air asset LZ free to operate post ricky tick, squadrons of Marine Air Group 36 scrambling to the task, focused on Khe Sanh. Rollie Cahill would arrive in Quang Tri from Hue, reassigned from his wall-hugging and passing the ammo up to the Hue fighting front. Rollie would mount up at least twice a day, for as long as it took, copter-bird air squadrons with a full focus on Khe Sanh assets in and out. Rollie's new life rushed back to a war from four thousand or eight thousand feet, then to a hot landing, tethered in to a side door, .50-cal ready, top view stuff, pigeon sitting stuff, then a fight.

Most everything about the early years of fighting for Americans in this second Indochina war, "merged" at Khe Sanh:

> *The French were a distant conquered memory. The second Indochina war was now an American war, the South Vietnamese somewhere in the background marching in circles, the two theories of French colonialism and occupation having merged*

with America's proxy war occupation of flimsy, vaguely committed ideology.

For American soldiers, faith and service merged with shaky hope into uncertain, blurred, directionless visions.

Millions of tons of US warring assets merged in the air and on the ground with millions of tons of Russian and Chinese manufactured warring assets, filling Khe Sanh's violent air. An early "globalization" reality, at a time when "globalization" was not yet an actionable concept!

NVA country-uniting command theory met US proxy and domino theory, and both would merge at Khe Sanh into a long siege mentality of who would blink first from displaced upper commands, while foxholes filled with the boys of Wilson Street focused and waited, under thunderous poundings, dirt raining as they waited.

Wilson Street moms and dads would take bigger more frequent steps to merge with rowdy long hair unorganized street protestors in some cause of national unification that would rattle political offices and begin to wake America's sidelined quasi-attentive media late to the war's realities.

Bombs merged with foxholes.

Marines merged with angels.

Moms, wives, and girlfriends merged with evening news broadcasts within the comfort and merging of one another.

Ammo cartridges merged with M-16s.

Blood merged with Asia's winds and loose soils.

Nam's guerilla military history merged in conflict to Westy's dreams of his wishful attrition battle.

*Let this squeaky corporate McNamara fellow
merge with Hill 881 and Blevin's world, bring some
DC suits along with him to share the merging proxy
invention sensations!*

Among the Wilson Streets of the North Carolina Inner Banks region, the Cahills trudged about daily business, holding strong to a domestic faith that Rollie Cahill was trained, determined, on the right side of his God, with a dose of ancient Scottish Luck that guided without touch from spirits of an elusive Scottish specialized angel. Their Domestic Nam was real, every hour, of every day into every night, sharing the countdown and wake-up strategy fundamentals they had learned as well. Accounting numbers meant less and less to Mr. Cahill in his auditing world. House work was more mindless motion than cleaning intent of the day for Mrs. Cahill. Headlines only fed anxieties and sleepless jitters of helplessness to a desperate family cause, not of their making, only of their burdensome hesitant, forced embracing.

In St. Louis, the brewery workers kept a concerned eye on Mr. Slyhope through their shared daily motions of Nam viewing and careful mention, not fully understanding what a President Johnson and his applauded cronies were actually trying to do to either country. Company and union picnics had introduced the entire workplace community to the energies and serious eyes of son Blevin and select others serving from neighborhoods farther out and apart. One worker to another kept a focus on evening news from Khe Sanh, each day strung out, for the ninety seconds of news from I Corps and hopefully a better more meaningful mention from dug-in Khe Sanh. But in reality, the news and the prospects only got worse, more desperate, more helpless on a daily basis. Everyone shared the desperation and futility. If daily news itself didn't drag spirits down, the dark assaulting moods of personal compassions would.

Everybody in North Carolina or in St. Louis, in the Quang Tri air or on 881 knew with certainty that more and more marines would die, were dying, daily, probably hourly, perhaps by the minute. Mystic dutiful angels, uncertain in numbers, impossible to count, could not save them all. Those marines had been committed to a fight to the death concept of "attrition," which necessarily meant human investment in the form of young lives, America's best lives of the generation, just one gigantic click beyond the returned lives of WWII's patriotically determined. Divide the square footage at 881, by the number of foxholes, times marines per hole—times incoming Gook fire power and at the brewery or the accounting office, any one could factor their own concept of survivability. At least, that'd be the KIA/WIA calculator method. Of course, those most realistic would have to factor in dehydration, small arms, snakes, disease, blood pressure, and mental brain explosions from shell shocking concussions to get to a bottom line of survival optimism per square foot.

By day twenty-six, sometime in mid-February '68, Blevin had become a moving, fast, blending, reactionary part of the 881 landscape. Fear had been replaced by training, inner character, instinct, intrepidity, and a weightless angel. Sunrise had become an inspiration, not a challenge. Gooks were beatable, predictable in the tree lines, shootable, not dancing unfocused night shadows of imagination or wondering fleeting dreams. Blasts, zings, womps, and hot metal were things of inconvenience, as routine and manageable as a hot stove at a camp ground. Marines get used to the darndest things!

Most nights were the same: listen, stay awake, focus, lock and load, hand grenades as the best precious deadly beloved ornaments of daily living. Love your hand grenades and be generous with their purpose. By day twenty-six, you could talk to hand grenades, talk about their mission and worth, talk to them about their potential distance and flight angle, unending respect, talk about their friendly feel, where they came from, how they could—would—fly to a target, maybe roll about, sometimes they would answer, good grenades also recognizing duties as assigned.

A good bunch of hand grenades would be hard to replace in the World. So will this heavy helmet, and a new pair of socks and boots would be nice though—that's what I'll tell Mom, first thing. She'd be off to Menacher's general store in a flash for clean white stretchy feelin' good socks, dry.

Blevin had it, the touch of 881 at Tet. He had the rhythm of the whole messy deal, the focus. He got it—knew exactly what decades of marines before him breathed and measured heartbeats by, a silent lonely thump at a time.

Don't need no stinking orders. I get it. Kill them that's trying to kill me. Then take as many others as my ammo can reach, then kill more of them. M-16 is my first Indochina war, grenades my second Indochina war, then me. I get it!

I should know the names of the marine buddies in the next holes but have forgotten. They probably moved around anyway, but I know that landscape. I've studied, practically tasted each bump, watched all the shifting shadows at dawn, dusk, noticed if there is a slightest change, registered the shadow angles and depth of the jungles darkness at certain passing times of the day. I'll know any change. I know every square inch, starting to like it, we like what we know.

I know hand grenades, better than I know a supper fork.

When I get back home, I'm gettin' my own dog, to look at 'n' squeeze his sloppy wet face."

How useful will I be in the world? Can you be useful dead?

By day twenty-eight, up in northwest DMZ Charlie-land, Giap had gone back north, left a bunch of orders to more junior NVA officers to harass, destroy, spend all stockpiled ammo, blast as many incoming main landing strip resupply copters as possible, and overrun a couple perimeter hills killing all dug-in marines, occupy the hills, and then disappear, scoochy dow-dow to new Gookvilles farther down the trail. Create chaos, create headlines in US papers and on US evening broadcasts that will compel the population to a unified rage against their own government.

Hills, like 881, the highest and furthest out, would lend the best Gook vantage points for final Khe Sanh main camp mortars and rockets, and thus were to be over-run. 881 was the most obvious highest target, and would make the most impressive victory statement, the west perimeter of 881 being the most vulnerable. NLF around 881 were expendable, so were the VC. 881 had been harassed plenty but not the focus of a ground attack by multiple scampering waves of AK-47 armed pit-cong.

The assault of 881 began in a late afternoon, stagnant heavy heat, with steady incoming mortar patterns that would echo into early darkness. Early evening was hungry. Moving fog waves heaved the air around in different kinds of moonbeam shades, circles, and angles with unpredictable moving flows of misty cover creating a surreal sense of ground movements where there was no such thing.

Mr. and Mrs. Slyhope and St. Louis brewery workers, their Scottish heritage neighborhood with connecting streets and store fronts, went through their day leaning toward one another in faith and foresight, hanging for one of those rare times to their collective unspoken patriotic allegiance. Empty-suited politicians, trained military leaders, and busy-handed industrialists had all done their work with diligence all had fed the beast and were far enough into the Domestic sand to ignore shocks and become deaf to the unique chatter of AK-47s and the yells of a rushing, advancing thousand Gook enemy. On the evening news, the first report February 18 would be from an isolated outpost on a faraway scathed dirt bump,

Hill 881, guarding a western edge of a distant place called Khe Sanh, as a ducking nervous face and microphone doo-hinky brought America's living rooms up to speed on Blevin's daily and nightly view of his world.

Foxhole spirits were merging in the air and on the ground with another of Nam's closing sunsets, which could just as logically have been on Mars. Locking and loading, deep emotions spiritually merged with low helmet covered eyes focused out, west, down trails into the waiting-suspended Charlie-land. A sudden coolness signaled change. These things don't start all at once. Good battles that are intended to last a bit, pace themselves to more slowly ignite and chew on the inner emotions of "prebattle," pulling a grunt's senses and abilities one way or another to and from an unknown outcome soon to be delivered, giving "fear" its best chance to grab any timid minds that would be a part of the fight. There is no temperature, there is no atmosphere, there is scarcely air to breath, but there are marines who have become a part of the 881 landscape, backs to a wall not of their making but to their ends.

Blevin took some closies in the air, up and around as early night's bad guy metal sizzled in unpredictable shrapnel-crossing directions.

This must be IT, *the night, but then, every night felt like it must be* IT, *until it wasn't it, sometime around an exhausting dawn. Then, the next night would be* it!

I don't give a damn. It don't matter. About time. I'm ready, twenty-seven clips, eighty baseballs, and two views—one mine, the other off a bit, firmly holding, almost caressing from my shoulder, kind of looking further out, further in the bush, and sometimes to the heavens.

Glimpses from flares, made broader low hanging jungle cover move, but it might just be the falling flare angles. Silence from the jungle tree line side, I don't give a damn! Let's get with it and get off this hill. Tonight's as good as any other night, better, best. I understand me now. I finally make sense to me.

A few early dark hours later, just mortars and rockets, no biggie, we get that with dehydrated plastic tasting supper from the green cans. Small arms zingers pop-popped all over the place, in all directions; Who's that at? No matter, just part of the 881 neighborhood!

Puff illumination and .50-cals showed up with marines in the fuselage business end. How'd that happen? Is that a good sign or a bad sign. They wouldn't send Puff to us unless they knew something, something big. Holy b-jesus, maybe this "is it." That's OK. It's time.

Shortly after, or before, in timeless suspended prebattle limbo—mass high-pitched mostly human yells converged in yelling unison up hill, and downhill, ground moved in individual pockets of bunches of darting helmets and feet. Puff opened up, tracer displays as if from another planet, looking down at this planet. We love Puff, tracer power like no other in the world. You have to be "right here" to "get" the world of Puff.

The Cahill's had gone to bed on the East Coast to lay in silent stares to a dim-lit ceiling with growing shadows accentuated by the slow moving ceiling fan giving a sense of human motion where there was no motion. In St. Louis, Slyhopes finishing nervous evening house chores sat in the small fenced urban back yard, squeezing off a final cig, the evening news having left them and America in an 881 state of angered frustration, personal self-inflicting shock at a next level. Mrs. Slyhope trembled, her inner message and breathing deep, her mind far, far off in a foxhole of her own wrangled imagination—

on a hill she never knew existed, never thought she would care to know. Nam was Nam, but the heavy tearing drag of Domestic Nam was not for wimps either.

Tomorrow would come for both families, for all of America, and everyone would go dutifully to work, then spend all the exhausting emotions all over again, from the morning paper headlines to the evening news leads, no upside or progress even possible. Now it was not about winning anything. It was about the depths of losses and the names attached and losing patriotic faith that we were no longer in competent leadership hands.

Hill 881 would physically bend and transform through the night of February 18 into final hit and run skirmishes of February 19. Cut and thrashed, grenade blast and kill, marine-up and fight like hell, fighting faceless deadly movements of a persistent moving tan uniformed faceless other body intent on the death of all marines in their path.

Blevin would not fall until an early morning slash to the thigh from some killing piece made long ago and far away by some half-enslaved Chinese factory peasant. A few short clicks before the first real light of that day, Blevin, ignoring the searing pain, carefully moved so slightly, low, to appraise other perimeter fox holes. Looking backward toward the still partially intact command bunkers, he heard and felt a bonk to his helmet from a last departing, stray zinger from some smart-ass Gook who could just not leave their night's assaulting work alone. As Blevin lay that early morning in the low, ground-hugging, simmering smoke, vaguely sensing movements around him, he felt for his canteen and leaned toward the dawning sun certain to grow larger in the sky, not soon enough. It was then that he thought he saw his translucent, endearing, light blue and gray angel reaching next to his M-16 for his soul.

Soon, shouting orders from somewhere took the place of the night's pops and womps, shouts this time from friendlies.

Mr. Slyhope started his routine, a thoughtless eight-block morning walk to work, a walk he could now do with his eyes closed, oblivious to his actual familiar stationary neighborhood surroundings. Mrs. Slyhope waited for her husband's departure from home before nervous exhaustion controlled her moves, felt her way to the downstairs bathroom, and then threw up the night's held-back bile into a hazy toilet bowl. Mrs. Slyhope slumped to the toilet's cramped side, experimenting with small desperate breaths, one exhausted breath at a calculated time, then again, planning each contiguous breathing motion as if herself wounded by the long-reaching shrapnel of the Domestic Nam Hill 881 night. The convergent evening news still ten hours off, through another long bottomless pit of a day. "I want to blame someone!" Mean, hateful thoughts of a nice lady, her own precious Blevin countdown and wake-up lost in time and now total uncertainty. Suddenly, she thought to herself, maybe my son will never come home. He may never get off that thing they call 881. She thought maybe 180-ish in a countdown. Checking for sure would eat up ten minutes of her directionless floating day.

On the Slyhope's living room coffee table was the morning's *St. Louis Post-Dispatch*. Bold front page headlines screamed through the house and down the streets, across sidewalks and into alleyways before crashing across storefronts and merging with coffee shop talk:

MARINES AT KHE SANH HANG ON

KHE SANH, South Vietnam (AP)—Rolling hills occupied by Marines around the small NW South Vietnamese village of Khe Sanh continued to receive WWII level bombing and destruction for another day and night. Surrounded by an estimated 40,000 enemy ground troops or more, and artillery. . . . Early reports of high casualties on both sides . . . Hill 881 took the brunt of overnight enemy small arms and artillery . . . relentless in . . . a siege that has no end in sight for the U.S. Marines caught . . . Mrs. Slyhope—

thoughts and emotions unleashed, gushing, crushing emotionally:

How will all of us ever get off these faraway useless hills?

What will happen to Hill 881 when America wins? Will the US build a post office on it so Asians from Laos can mail happy cards to low-country Asians on the other side toward a desolate coast?

Or maybe US command in the spirit of Vietnamization will build them a Fair Grounds, with concession stands of rice cakes and blue gill heads?

What is it for that is standard operating procedure in a twentieth century, this Asian Proxy War concept, once a useless far away dirt hill, is defended with lives of our Wilson Street Boys?

Then what?

Knowing tomorrow's *Post-Dispatch* will include numbers of KIA/WIA for all of the coffee tables in town, to prep the automated morning walk to the brewery and set off the toilet hug of moms throwing up to the death of other mom's sons, knowing what goes around comes around in Domestic Nam living.

Are there families left that pick up such pieces?

Warren is not alone at the brewery. All the families from thousands of Wilson Streets are like this, all kinds of morning bile and evening suppressions, silent final cigs in dark backyards, couples not knowing what to say to each other that makes any difference or any sense to the tragedies in limbo. It is America's inner emotional venturing, America's Domestic Nam, fed by decisions and circumstances, born of concepts from different kinds of Pentagon/ Capitol bunkered hallways and tunnels filled with suits and uniforms that we will never see and probably never understand, shifting and trading places from bricked bunker to brick bunker, so fast that a finger cannot be laid on a decision's source or evolving logic. An entire global leading nation asked to suspend itself with unquestioned faith and national allegiance in the towns, countryside, cities, and suburbs, that a national cause or necessity creates reactions worth dying for. What cause? What cause is being served?

Blevin's downhill wounded challenge was to get to main camp, central command Khe Sanh, at the main airstrip, for medical help and the big medevac to serious med camps and a few gulps of water. Finding a full clip or two wouldn't hurt anything either. By February 19, Blevin had defended his frontal western facing piece of 881 for near a month, the vision of which is now permanent, would always be permanent. What was left of him and his soul was depleted, spent. Angels had worked all night, close-in, visions unimpaired, unmoved, also right there in the morning, settled, right next to the warm M-16. Not bending, never leaving.

At Quang Tri, all elements of MAG-36 were roused off perimeter lines to a flight-ready, up and out to the tarmac near 2:00 a.m. Sixteen Hueys prepped, fueled, and fired, to be loaded and idling by 3:30, ETD 4:10. Rollie Cahill took the right door behind Major Parsons, lock and load, hook in, another game day, helmet chatter intense this early morning among the high-pitched sounds of awakened, revving copter engines—Khe Sanh this and Khe Sanh that—on their way.

Mission design: relieve Khe Sanh in any way possible. It's hot, been hot all night. There will be lots of dead and wounded. Sixteen Purple Foxes with sixteen trained crews lifted gently from a dark Quang Tri steel sheeted tarmac, leaned forward in unison, air-gracefully forward, noses slightly down, pivoting and leaning in as if attached to one another at two hundred feet, leveling toward the NW. Khe Sanh ETA just prefirst light, 4:50-ish, lock and load all air and personal weapons, including 45s strapped tight. Tet goes on, in your teeth, gut, and hands. Pilots and crews in dark morning flight silence, intent to the cracks and chatter over helmet radios, tense to orders to shift from QT ground command communication to Khe Sanh ground command communication predinky dow.

Major Parsons lead Huey, third squadron known as The Outfielders, 4:45, two thousand feet—scattered cloud cover, slightly clearing, headset chatter:

> *4:45 a.m. "All right, Outfielders, heads-up, New orders, we have a plan. We'll skirt Khe Sanh main camp to the south, relieve Marines on a Hill 881—a few clicks out to the West—we are looking for Yellow flares, just before first light—Yellow Flares, report any sightings. Starboard looks out and back. Mark incoming tracers return all ground fire immediately."*
>
> *4:48 a.m. "Weapons to ready, lock—we need a Yellow Flare, will drop fast. Gooks have coordinates on main LZ; we'll find a side clearing. Need a Yellow Flare!"*
>
> *5:05 a.m. "Yellow Flares two o'clock, elevation 1,200 up. Lock and load. If this was easy, they'd send the army. Bull up! Double hand full of ass!"*
>
> *5:08 a.m. "ETA two minutes. We'll go in hard. Anything outside the perimeter and moving—kill it. Be generous! Return all tracer fire."*
>
> *5:10 a.m. "Assholes and elbows Outfielders! Crews out with ammo crates, we'll be in and out all day—take 16s and a belt. If you get left, don't worry, we'll be back every two-three hours. Load wounded first, God and Squeezes back in the world love Outfielders."*
>
> *5:12 a.m. "Sergeant Rollie, find the CO and get a read, catch your young ass next trip. Go go go! Have a great day, everybody!"*

Rollie's Huey jump and scamper met with rushing stretchers of wounded marines emerging from 881 from behind lines of scattered sandbags, dirt, and dust kicked up by powerful welcome blades. Six Outfielders back in the air in three-ish minutes, twenty-four wounded, strapped in, door gunners looking for incoming tracers, the gentle lift, airborne-pivot and nose down, air-lean back to the Southeast signaling a successful Outfielder first mission for the day to Khe Sanh. No marine left behind! Out of Khe Sanh air, shift to Phu Bai air command chatter, blank eyes on top of bloody bodies stare up from bloody Huey bottoms—silent as heavenly journeys can get. Two thousand feet, OK visibility through scattered broken landscape clouds or mist suspended for the departure, 1,500 feet and a quickened leaning pace forward. Major Parsons, confident, cool, focused: "Phu Bai air traffic ETA forty minutes, clear the way for medics and stretcher transfer."

Major Parsons and the five other Outfielder birds would life-save their spent human cargo to the hands of new Phu Bai marines, some with lipstick, and wish them the best, then lift slow and pivot to refuel. Another Khe Sanh mission before noon planned by someone in command some place, radioed pending. Unlock, ammo up, it's early.

Blevin's stretcher would have been number 25. A near-miss, the story of his grunting 881 life lately. Another few hours on 881 seemed doable, would have to be. Bleeding seemed to have stopped. Pain was now just numbness. Thirsty was normal anyway, M-16 angel handy.

Rollie rushed by, searching for the CO, if there was a CO. Maybe there wasn't today. Maybe the CO was some sergeant somewhere who didn't even know he was now the new CO. Or maybe the CO had just been airlifted out.

By noon, the twentieth, it was time to take 881 inventory, then lock and load for late afternoon routine mortars and rocket actions. No sign of Parsons and the Outfielders. Rollie soon found that the CO Lieutenant Comstock was alive but would be the last to know anything going on off the Hill in the way of returning Hueys. The

220 Marines on 881 were now 162, WIA's lifted out, KIA's resting silently, bodybagged and parked in a row, identities lost for now. Their war was over!

Rollie had to help cover gaps in the line on the West side. Blevin, soon discovering that lying in the dirt on a stretcher out in the open had a serious nighttime downside, gathered his strength, thirsty body, and weapons, crutched his way back to a site he knew by the square inch, where a new guy named Rollie was waiting.

There are certain people, marines, who, upon first sight, you can tell you will go to war with. Same in all life, really, as in Tet-life on 881. Blevin had transitioned his mind-set to support a new zone of survival made as comfortable as possible. Blevin schooled Rollie on the landscape, what he was looking at, likely movements, mortar patterns, dusk, then the last evening trails of the sun's shadows, secondary flares, and the power, art, and personal affection of hand grenades.

Rollie's first thoughts were how good he had it, back there a few days ago, behind the shattering walls of Hue.

One Tet night in a hole on the West slope of Hill 881, clicks off Khe Sanh's main camp, is literally worth gold in expedited buddy-building. A NC auditor's son and the son of a St. Louis brewery laborer stroked their good fortune, nursed Blevin's drying/closing wounds, sharpened their sight, game-faced-up, and embraced all other duties as assigned for the night ahead—both understanding and accepting to be front and center at first light for Major Parsons and the Outfielders' return. The night of the twentieth, from the West side of 881, was a walk in the park compared to the assaulted previous night before: light mortar fire, fleeting flares, and just enough incoming tracers to make the night an attentive war.

Blevin and Rollie would join the weak and wounded at center camp at another 881 dawn while the dead and bagged remained calm and quiet in their zipped cocoons, spirits long gone to higher spirit missions. At the first sight of Major Parsons leading the Outfielders, Blevin and Rollie made sure Rollie was easily spotted, drawing Parsons to their landing site. Blevin stretchered up and out, for his flight to Phu Bai. Rollie hooked in, began to report 881 CO comments:

> *Get all marines off this Hill, shrinking perimeter cover to the center, dead and wounded all out on next wave, 1100 hours. Last wave 1400 hours, all fighting marines transported to Khe Sanh main camp. 881 abandoned!*

That section of the "rocket belt" no longer important as a part of the larger Khe Sanh defenses.

Cahills and Slyhopes, frozen in a Domestic Nam suspense one thousand miles apart from one another, unacquainted, through another evening news broadcast, and another petrifying report from Khe Sanh, to include a final report from 881. TV reports don't include names. Neighborhoods and coworkers, shopkeepers, and intersection friends dropping concerns at each interval of conversation or chance meeting was the heavy mood. America on an edge—six thousand marines in a frickin Gook month-long "siege" in no man's land, spitting, coughing morning toilet bile from more mothers and zombie walks for fathers, friends, and families.

What is a "proxy war" anyway? "Proxy war" is a vague bureaucratic name, so subjectively obscure that it cannot be defined or questioned of detail for purpose or direction. A term that is supposed to be so gray in notion, it exists in singular limbo, unquestioned by those who would be doing the questioning, because they have "live skin in the game."

Blevin saw the lipsticks and big brown caring eyes of the nurses at Phu Bai: soft, unmatted, clean rolling waving hair, and relaxed with the stretcher's motion of transfer to the belly of a large CH-54. Finally loosening his tight grip on his M-16, he laid back the steel helmet so often pressing just above his tense eye level and gave in to it all—inhaling the comfort of angel's gliding around, pressing, concerned about him. The flight of his life, surely to be like that flight with the end-game future wake-up, hurrying but not rushing, he and bound others to a safer place, at least for a while. Giant, magic air CH-54 blades blasting the massive copter and mix of passengers forward in a tight airborne unit, all leaning in unison to the angles of flight, then over a coast line, lifting up like a strong pull from the heavens, into clouds so thick and high, easily described as a whole different spiritual journey, the cyclical tensions of evening 881 darkness, the fight, then the sunrise, finally being lost in the distances, at least for a moment.

Then pop! Like springing up. They were all above it, above the war, carried into a new world only the lipsticks were used to, a world the marines did not know still existed, one they had not even imagined or suspected, held in the trained flying hands of American pilots up in their cockpit. Pilots saving real people who Blevin would never see or know! The thick carpet of enormous soft rolling cotton covered everything down just at the 54s bottom edge and out as far forward or back as eyes could reach, a clear delineation, blue sky resting on pure gently rolling white cloud carpeting, high, way high, a moving capsule of wounded marines and soft angels held tightly together. So heavenly stationary and thick was the cloud carpet that it seemed as if wounded, or well, could all step out of the copter side opening and stand upon the crystal white solid looking clouds untouched by the chaos below. Attached lipsticks of the journey never left marine's sides, a special corps of them, unafraid, confident, transferring their confidence with just the slightest touch of bare skin and gentle hands— big dark brown luscious eyes and their slender delicate fingers poked for marines attention, lightly pressed, and pointed, while securing, without actually embracing all the wounded marines now willingly helpless in this new journey, given in to the miracle and the dream of all that had graciously befallen them this war day.

Lipsticks and angels:

> *Look, Slyhope, bring out your soul. Don't miss*
> *this heavenly white carpet of God's welcome for your*

behalf. Your journey today is our daily savior and mission in life, taking young marines to safety and embracing care on our ship of healing. This moment will stay with you forever, and so will we. You don't need your angel, not right now. Let your angel rest. We are here instead. Lots of new angels just for you, walking—touching—alive and concerned, deep felt, extending love that you will get well, recover from your wounds, and we will not leave you, ever. For once, we enter your healing heart, it is our gift forever.

The CH-54 landed on the floating Red Cross ship's waiting deck, way too soon.

Hi Mom/Dad

How is our home, the neighborhood, St. Louis, the Cardinals, the work of the brewery? Sorry I haven't written, the library is often closed. Breathing is what I mainly try to accomplish.

4 days ago I got out of Khe Sanh, off Hill 881 on a big beautiful copter. I'm OK, I'm in a place full of Angels, disguised as Red Cross nurses, on a big ship, floating somewhere in the South China Sea—don't care where. I intend to marry at least 4 of them, so clean up the place and make room— they have saved my life, then my mind, and I think maybe my heart.

You may know more about Nam and Khe Sanh than I actually know, if the war is being reported. I know a foxhole, on a faraway hill, and the red mud at its bottom, and I still see every square inch of the downside slope, probably will see it the rest of my sober life. Probably reach out now and then to see if it is real, or finally gone. Everything hit the fan Feb. 19; I may or may not describe it later, for sure not now. I do know my pitching arm is mid-season, as I threw enough hand grenades to blow up East St. Louis—may have been better used there—not sure anything blown up in Nam does any good for anybody for very long, saving the moment is generally good enough for a hand grenade and is all we really expect.

We are all wounded here; dazed quiet Marines come and go, following orders and their skills to places they are not expected to easily survive. We don't talk much about the war in general on this Red Cross ship, mostly about home, but there is an overwhelming unstated sense that we are losing. Tet seems to have merged Asia's most evil forces against our intentions, if we ever had intentions. We just don't know, seems any line defended with lives, is soon then given up.

I suspect you have been worried; news must leave more loose ends and questions than provide answers. Just like here. Don't be worried, wounds are healing, I drank water for 3 days, now not strong but gaining on it, I'll get there, weighed 142 when I got here. My big worry is my 180-something and a wake-up. That's too much time for them to send me home for these wounds. But, I have 4 holes in me, and if that is 4 Purple Hearts, then I dee-dee to Hello St. Louie. If they count that as 1 Purple Heart, I'm afraid it's back on the bull in the bush. If that's the case, at least I'm smarter now.

I know now that I will make it home sooner or later—these lipsticks tell me so, know it too. They are the loveliest creatures on earth. One is from St.

Louis, Westown-ish, Paula. Says she's here because she has to be, and will be here as long as she has to be. OK with me.

I'll write again, before they kick me off this wonderful peaceful white ship—let's hope its United east, not CH-54 back to I Corps. Do not remove my baseball cards, my stuff—I will need it all to get new feet on the ground. All the battles now are one at a time, individual, focused. You should see these copter jockeys, nervy. Met a great guy from NC named Rollie; war's hottest spots seem to follow him around. He got me off 881, made sure I got to Phu Bai to the hands of the lipsticks. That boy's gonna have some stories someday.

Luv Y'all. Thanks. Let's hang in there, my hand reaches home to you, Blev

By March 27, Blevin, with his purple heart salute, said goodbye to Paula and a troupe of other lipstick angels who had all stolen a piece of his heart. He then dutifully joined his new unit forming in Phu Bai, with orders north in relief of marines at Con Thien. Two new platoons formed, introduced to one another and organized into agile squads with unfamiliar squad leaders of lower enlisted rank, to relieve shell-shocked marines of the Third who had been dug into Con Thien hillside points since they relieved other marines in January, who relieved other marines the last half of '67. The new platoons of Third Battalion, Fourth Marines would Chinook into Con Thien within the week, after fresh weapons and ammo had been counted, distributed, locked tight, new socks handed out like special Christmas gifts, and the spiritual-style fleeting angels had a chance to return and pick their mates for a new challenging assignment.

Everyone was part of a new company, building new history with a conglomeration of Wilson Street Boys who had no chance to actually know one another, nor would they ever know one another, except for the docs. Everyone meets and knows the docs. Con Thien had a history known through I Corps. The place guarded the middle south and some east of the DMZ, nothing between it and the edge of enemy hell where constant reinforcements of NVA were assumed. Blevin had written home about his new orders before he understood what the name Con Thien meant. He wished he hadn't, just a useless new worry for Mom, Dad, and the street to the brewery.

The Tet Offensive was nothing new, of no importance, not noticed at Con Thien, or generally elsewhere along the DMZ where the violence of war never paused. Tet was crushing, but generally, the same crushing as September or October or any other '67 Con Thien month. At 158 meters high, it would be a low vantage, not good, squat compared to 881 of Khe Sanh fame. Con Thien had two nicknames among marines: "The Hill of The Angels," referring to the constant KIA actuals or "The Meat Grinder," self-explanatory.

Closest to the DMZ, Con Thien was covered with area NVA, constantly probing and pressuring, fussing up the air with small arms and the usual mortars and rockets. The original intent of the vulnerable Con Thien firebase was just like that of Khe Sanh. That is, to act as a stop gap south line from DMZ Gook activity heading further south unimpeded but also as a force to place and monitor sensors inside the DMZ, in an effort to guestimate Gook troop movements, one direction or another. In actuality, Con Thien was the same old flat red clay dirt top of a far away, isolated hill target, as were many other numbered hilltops. Foxholes filled with water throughout the monsoon and needing bailed out two to three times per day, sticky red mud that can reach up for passing boots and the same "sitting duck" feeling as so many other places at the outpost "fronts." NVA probes every night, always a sniper threat, tons and tons of incoming rocket and mortar fire were blasting Con Thien relentlessly. Constant crashing, sizzling sounds in the air left no time for day dreaming! Each unit of marines rotating off the 158 passes the story of September 25, 1967, when the hill and its Wilson Street Boys took over 1,200 enemy rounds (plus small arms assaults) in that one day—two rounds per minute, for twenty-four hours. And thus, Nam's version of "Nam Shell-Shocked" made Con Thien I Corps infamous, the honor being eventually picked up by the darting in and out visiting press of the moment.

A little more than a dozen to fifteen clicks from the coast, Con Thien could hold tight day to day because of supporting navy guns—big guns—boomin' mothers that preannounced their arrival with a screaming sizzle-sound for the DMZ and just north. Daily air ordnance accoutrements filling the Con Thien atmosphere included phantom jet flyovers and bomb runs from Phu Bai. Phantoms with their unseen, unidentified, forever appreciated marine pilots executing their Phantom jet air rodeos spontaneously, pouncing, aerobatic, fearless killing war bravado, forever admired. Phantoms strafing DMZ south border elements with napalm were a favorite Con Thien 158 view. B-52s launched from out there and up some hundreds of hundreds of clicks scattered thousand-pound bombs generously according to spotters somewhere else in the war, who hoped they were correct about their guidance info. Con Thien and north into the DMZ was a war machine proving ground for weaponry and support weaponry logistics. Except it was no experiment, no test for accuracy or explosiveness, or killing's efficiencies. These bombing destructions were to relieve and hopefully spare the lives of Con Thien Marines unlucky enough to draw that 158 straw. Con Thien had it all, had the whole war composite directory of a winningless standoff and had one more thing.

In a war with little or no definitive lines, no definitive fronts or rears, only protected circles, and moving war things, Con Thien was along an actual line to its somewhat sister firebase Dong Ha just west some clicks, the only theorized command "line" in Indochina at the time. The man-made theoretical line was the south line of the DMZ, perhaps the only static line in the whole more than ten years of killing fuss-up proxy war and domino thing. A "line"! *Don't you cross this line!* This was the north I Corps neighborhood rule and marines of the Third Division and rotating other divisions were there to guard the fictitious, invisible "line" of supreme command importance.

"Lines" have to be managed, advantaged by high command and then the highest command, or what would be their use? Why would we need a line in the middle of nowhere, if it were not to be managed? The line is needed because it is "static" because it is there, in your face. Such a line cannot be ignored. What good is a war line, if the birds and stars and war chiefs anointed, don't apply some special strategic brilliance to the defense or offense of the line?

Somewhere, secluded safely in a deep cavernous bunkered brain hole, "command" led by Defense Secretary McNamara, "they" decided and ordered that Con Thien's portion of the line be defined by bulldozing to bare soil the south edge and two kilometers further south to the edge of 158. "I shit you not!" Undocumented, but not a stretch of vision to suggest those same heavy armored earth moving dozers are still half buried in the bottoms around the "line" by red wet clay but may be largely exposed upwards of the clay as the cycle of defoliation soon advanced from ground crawling earth pushers to airborne Agent Orange deliveries. The war against DMZ south border defoliation was so intense and recognized in-country and Domestic, that the effort soon became known as the McNamara Line, born into the war's realities in some sort of experiment of bulldozing and herbicide infecting that portion of the world. Con Thien Marines could see the attention given to their vulnerable position as orange trails drifted from floating propped cargo dispensaries. "Orange" drifted and drifted merrily in swirls from inland sea breezing air now filtering through varying hill elevations into earth's DMZ crevices. Applications delivered by a week of dozens of flights to ensure good foliage control kill and a clear clean defoliated McNamara Line to see beyond and defend from 158. The deadly, drifting, toxic foliage killing stuff was manufactured and delivered, following the same half globe supply and logistic sequences as was your average household '60s five hundred pounder. (Again, I shit you not! In retrospect, it seems insane. Follow the Agent Orange money trail.)

Late '67 and early '68 were still quite early in America's execution of an Indochina proxy war theory. Domestic military and civilian leadership were still manipulating theories and concepts of massive weapon application and tightening the domestic countrywide net to assure constant flows from draft boards for thousands more Wilson Street Boys.

Meanwhile, one more new discouraging revelation arrived at Con Thien. Marines were pasted to the most remote, faraway, nothing-land foxholes ever dug and occupied by proxy humans. Enemy rockets and mortars again pounded the 158 battered hilltop on the distant edge of that *otherworld* among isolated other battered hill tops making up a Nam version of archipelago-firebases. Three marines in their mud hole on the far north edge heard the familiar singing incoming whistle-scream of another rocket, screaming closer and closer as if guided with singular screaming detonation angered intent. Trained "rocket ears" learn the unique tone of rockets precrash screaming announcements. An eerie rocket-song, closing space rapidly, this time followed by a "thud," not the usual violent, dirt blasting rocket "Womp," that terrorizes and slashes all surroundings. This time, it was a powerful thud. A collision with earth but no blasting "Rocket-Womp." Grimy, cautious foxholed marines with a pause and deep breath would eventually, nerves tangled—barely controlled, peer up, over a slick muddy foxhole edge, and out to the direction of the heavy thud, unfamiliar with "thudding" rockets.

There it laid, a twelve-foot long rocket, potentially a dud, unexploded, bad guy rocket limbo-land of a thud as a dud. Time passes very slowly when a rocket dud lies close-by on the ground, close to your own foxhole, violating your choices of other nearby space options, complicating a chaotic war, an enemy dud rocket between you and the normal war you had just become used to. Nearby duds grab full attention. Occupy all focus and time, time that could be used for other good mind-exploding chaos and struggles. Unexploded rocket staring one direction, like a stationary steel quietly resting cobra; Marines staring back, in low mumbled conference of the uncertainty of dudly rocket technology detail, as if even raising a voice or lighting a cig might antagonize the steel-finned thing. An hour passed, the sun moved through its warming multi-sun angles of an Asian day, while the rocket lie still, somehow paralyzed by its own non-booming intentions. Mud dried on the top of boots, the whole micro-climate half trapped in a potential bomb timing device, the other half harmless in hopes the newly arrived rocket actually would be the one in a rocket million forever a dud and give up its womp-op to dudly rocketville. A dud of all duds, the dudliest ever! But there it was, real as dirt, not easy to approach or negotiate for marines who would like to eventually experience their beloved wake-up plan. A classic standoff of man and mechanism, nothing in War Book 101 staging training exercise to guide this standoff encounter in the easiest three steps to check out your dud rocket, lying next to your foxhole. Is there a private in the hole? Anyone whose only value to the entire military complex is the lowest of dirt level crawls with a wrench to ping the side of a dud?

Lance Corporal Duneadin finally, after over two hours of observation, slipped up and over, out of the foxhole's relatively safe confines, crawled under ground kind of close to the rocket, then closer, then back to the hole, with only a slightly better idea what is to be dealt with. 45 caliber pistol, an aim and shot to the body of the monster cobra, a ricochet with a ping and zing off to other red clay somewhere up or down the hill. Test one! Three cracks from the M-16, pings and zings again, with the motionless cobra rocket staring back. Still weighty uncertainty held the not so cautious moments, still marines, still rocket patiently hissing back at the hole, playing a Nam rocket version of opossum. A precious hand grenade rolled to the enemy rockets side, successfully exploded, with no rocket counter explosion to answer the marine's quest for a direction to the dilemma.

It had to be a dud. It is a dud. Surely, it is a dud! Lance Corporal Duneadin up and again out over the edge of the safe Con Thien hole, helmet first, shoulders tucked into unusual smallness, covered with all three-hole flak jackets, scoochy-along low crawl to the cobra beast, then closer to a straight-on good look, just Dunny and cobra-rocket thing in their Con Thien low-lying face off. The rocket had no clicking pulse about it, its nose firmly dented—pushed in from contact with 158.

> *How can this thing be here with me, with us?*
> *What was its journey like to kill and then not kill, not even detonate to kill?*
> *How disappointed the bomb-maker would be to know his rocket was a dud, didn't kill anything, like a motionless dead child uselessly born to no future?*
> *How about the coolie-peasant-Gook that carried it five hundred miles to the hidden launcher and then got no kill from it, not even a big booming, bloohy womp?*

Duneadin looked into the rocket's sleek, stream-lined nature, perfectly proportioned guiding fins, and then the scribbles and strangest funny looking writing along the side of the cobra—writing not Chinese, writing that looked Russian, he thought. It was Russian!

And thus, for the first time, from a Lance Corporal Duneadin and two marines in the foxhole on the north slope of Con Thien 158, the world would learn that the Russians were officially in the Vietnam Proxy War, confirmation certain. Russians also had their proxy war, now kind of a global proxy war for testing new rockets, RPG's, Daisy Busters, M-16s and AK-47s, for new kinds of, and endless other bomb stuff. A modern proxy festival of merging new weaponry at Con Thien! For the marines, all over I Corps the war would now be NVA, NLF, Viet Cong, Chinese, and our old WWII friends, the Russians. Dominoes that fell long ago are in refall back the other falling direction, with new Dominoes to join the falling and clunking process, with numerous new style American Domestic Dominoes uncertain in their falling orders or angles.

Con Thien was the same good ole blown-to-hell Con Thien. Blevin, with two new platoons of obedient teammate Outfielders had a Chinook flight scheduled to arrive in Con Thien, late in the early morning of March 26, 1968, smack middle of the shifting "defining year."

No new Nam warring mission worth its aggressive effort and orders starts around noon, after a happy lunch crowd. All such missions have a top to bottom order sequence of actions to rouse into motion about two uncomfortable tense dark confusing hours before first light, as if morning's earliest moments might mean sneaking up on something, gaining a moment's advantage in a war of constant alertness. Blevin's new company to be formed, armed, supplied would be Company Z.

Lordy, that doesn't sound good, thought the experienced Blevin, second squad leader in A-squad. *Which sounds even worse, A to Z.*

Hurried from Phu Bai hooches, Z Company waited on the cool dark tarmac as the night's last pair of marine phantoms launched to save a life or take one, filling the air with occasional roaring burning power noises shaking everything in the dark area, blazing red hot contrails rising and banking, then disappearing into their early morning mission's in a matter of dark, heavy flight technology seconds. What mission could they be zooming toward, from what orders? Another one of thousands of bombing missions, the ground guys ready up for their unknown parts of more missions daily.

Sun's early pinkish announcement expected any moment off to the east. A sun that would rise too fast into the day's duties as assigned, M-16s packed tight into the body, 45 tight, old lucky helmet down to the top of the eyes again, but lighter, rather weightless over a hydrated body for now, twenty-four new metal jackets of ammo, precious hand grenades, and one folded invaluable lucky white card signed by twenty-seven lipsticks, some lips pressed red to each of the four sides. Cautiously, the distant morning pink in the east synchronized with the arrival of the heavy, powerful fury of slashing rhythmic helicopter blades dominate the position, kind of like a long harsh-looking needle shows up in a dentist's hands. Ever so slightly lightened sky, the poised mindless waiting, quiet marines could first feel the big birds hover, the turbulence, slightly see the side opening and waiting motionless crew, and with one more click of the sun's rise, staged marines could see the familiar grinning Purple Foxes on the bird's tails. Major Parsons landed his lead bird and the Outfielders followed. Those guys are always exact.

And just like that, life for the 220-ish waiting marines of Z Company changed back, back to the uncontrollable tempo of Nam warring, back to a treacherous feel of hourly uncertainty, uncontrolled, mood soon confirmed by lifting Chinooks leaning north, slanting forward in unison, 8 birds, 120 marines, at dawn, in a frickin' proxy war, that had now been joined by Russian rocketry. Two trips, Phu Bai to Con Thien and back again. Twice up and back would have all 220 of a scarcely manned reinforcement relief Z Company landed and scattered to their red clay dug-in holes of peering defense of something, potentially some buddy-building and squad-building on the way, but more than likely, just a check of gear, rations, water, and ammo, lastly checking guts and individual relationships with faith. Lean north and air-whiz along, held within a breezy deadly quiet ride, door-gunners glued for any spontaneous tracer trail to respond to, or any vaguely moving out of place target, slightly exposed. Just deepest inner thoughts and the winds from invisible blades, beating to their own theme of war's changing rhythms. Blank nineteen- or twenty-year-old young faces, sullen, hard eyes covered to the edges with dark camouflaged helmets, occasional radio chatter escapes the crews head gear, from hidden invisible voices, another Nam sunrise, heading to a hill called the Meat Grinder. Z Company being the new "meat."

Phu Bai to Con Thien is a good distance apart north to south, but south to north into a morning fight, it goes quick as a bull ride. Con Thien was an infamous marine hellhole of its own dimension, in a straight line SE to NW with Quang Tri, Dong Ha being near the middle of that line. This created a triangle with Khe Sanh mucho clicks west, and then, the same number of clicks back to the east from Khe Sanh to Quang Tri. All the same neighborhood, the same wet mud, cloud cover then boiling sun. The same intense populated Gook pressure in a microtheater of war understood nowhere else on the planet. Con Thien was a war place constantly blown to shit from hidden waves of all things north I Corps violent. An experienced marine does not fly into any LZ, firebase, or countryside without noticing one thing upon final ground approach: How many wounded and bagged marines are waiting to be lifted back out on the turnaround? Con Thien had more than their share of returning marines had more than their share for ten months now, so much more that the dreadful body bag return duty had practically become just another strange Nam routine, like returning emptied coke bottles to the neighborhood small grocer. Coptering into the Meat Grinder was no small deal, with limited longevity as each successful landing and exit seemed to diminish future odds, if there was a future to diminish. Time could run out on any entry.

Blevin Slyhope and A Company knew the next routine also. At the drop from a low hover, out fast and group, stick together by squad, platoon CO to the command bunker for location orders, learn the new view, take in all things 158, and look at living bodies and weapons, never faces. And so, Blevin's new assignment began as the Purple Foxes lifted and leaned south, returning dead and wounded to a place of trust and respect, to a ship for wounded, a home country for the bagged, but first these spent copter warriors had to visit Phu Bai where journeys continue next phases. Drop the wounded to lipsticks, lower the dark-green bags of heroes to waiting transport arms, where the dark-green zipped bags are sorted, labeled from dog tags, then grouped with others arriving daily from all over I Corps for their last flight, the big last flight back east. Purple Foxes to load a new platoon of Con Thien bound Wilson Street Boys assigned to Z and get back in the air to lift and lean north again, most ricky tick. The Purple Foxes would be lower this second trip north, more zoom-zoom in the slight lean forward, there would be a higher sun thus more stray smart-ass Gooks with an AK pot-shot to gain smarter clear aim at the midhigh, sunnier flying altitudes. Copters low, zoom-zooming, offers only a flash of a target, high stuff, once the sun is up and working, attracts crosshairs. Second Company delivered to Con Thien/158, Purple Foxes wasted no time in pickups, a lift and lean back SE to Quang Tri for new orders, positive their work for the day would not be finished. It was never finished. Even when it was finished, it wasn't finished.

At Con Thien, Blevin received notice of his new 158 stature. He was to fight and slog his soon to be dehydrated, thirsty C-rationed way through Con Thien life as a corporal, how promotional, now the lowest of NCO's, a $28 a month pay hike.

Everything was lower for Blevin at Con Thien. From 881, Hill 158 was an unfamiliar strange angle to the renewed war look, a squat angle that would take study, a little getting used to. The foxholes were lower, sandbagged retaining lines were lower, the CO's bunker was lower—tree lines out there looked back from a lower pitch, right up to that bare strip stretching both directions, the lowest McNamara Line.

> *Why did McNamara need a line? His line was stripped devilishly ugly, stark, bleak, menacing, making a mean place look even meaner.*
>
> *Mom would never want a "Slyhope Line." She wouldn't stand for such a thing; she'd clean it up right away.*
>
> *Does someone think Gooks can't just pound rocket stuff right over a dark, dirty, orange line?*

March 28, 1968 morning *St. Louis Post-Dispatch* clunked on the front steps at first sun as usual from the dependable delivery boy speeding past on the way to his next war news clunking delivery. The war rolled to an angled, teetering St. Louis stop on the edge of the short stoop. More Nam news-grabbin' headlines, to then grab minds and emotions, as Nam news had grabbed daily:

CON THIEN BECOMES MARINES NEW KHE SANH

> Con Thien, South Vietnam—For I Corps Marines, the newest standoff is at another little known location at the south edge of the DMZ called Con Thien. Fresh reinforcement Marines arrived from the Fourth Marines, Z Company, choppered in . . . Under terrific ground and bombardment pressure for months, at Con Thien there is nothing new in rampant assaults of the Tet Offensive.

Warren Slyhope laid the paper down quickly, as if the thing were contaminating the day's purpose. At Mr. Slyhopes routine departure for the brewery, Mrs. Slyhope only hurriedly scanned the morning news reading just a headline. A mother's deepest instinct and passion to touch and blend soulfully to things not real, emotions forever unseen and innocuous to others in an excluded world gathered about her, pressed her inward, to a deepest unfamiliar inner self, slumping to the closest chair with tucked shoulders as if the chair itself could embrace and hold her nerve tangled body's inner thoughts still for a quiet moment's hesitation.

On March 29, she knew this Con Thien reality was too much, that she and the family would be defeated, that Con Thien would be all, the last stop. She knew, with a mother's instinct, Blevin's personal proxy war would end at Con Thien. The notion crawled about her like a blood leech looking for the right place to hold fast and penetrate her body for the blood-letting work to take hold. Khe Sanh was barely survivable for them all, now Con Thien. Two dying target bait bumps of useless red clay hills would finally be one too many. Guided remotely by nothing but unseen strings of persistent spirits,

Mrs. Slyhope floated about the house with nervous fake intent, without any real meaning beyond a comfort of busyness, seeking a day's direction, Domestic Nam rushing over her and holding her progress as a tight emotional hostage.

This early morning beginning to another hazed-day led her up to Blevin's room, now full of regret and lost hopes. As she suspected would happen, he was there. The room "was" Blevin! The room would be their son until someday, way out in a faraway future life; the room would also fade to a more useful, less regretful future and purpose. Shrunken, dejected, lost in jagged thoughts, she sat hopelessly on the edge of the forever vacant bed of a son lost at his prime. Mrs. Slyhope pushed back the teasing notion that her gloomy thoughts were untrue, just silly, just self-defeating, and prepared to refine the same gloomy thoughts nonetheless, prayed for strength. She tried to understand how this happens, the actual steps, one to the next, then to another step in a path not retrievable once stepped out upon. Steps to death, permanent, despicable steps that hundreds of thousands of others in America are also helplessly stepping within.

> *What was so important that required throwing a nation's net over thousands and thousands of Wilson Street Boys and extracting them from free lives deserved, forever to be unlived?*
>
> *What was so important that a miracle of creation can be so easily stepped on and squashed by our own American jackals of leaderless powers, publicly pronouncing this pompous aberration of war upon us all, then professing the war effort is in some continuous idiotic circle pretending to save the world from Communism? Where is there any logic to it?*
>
> *When the final word of Blevin would finally arrive by some blank-faced, chin to chest source, Mrs. Slyhope knew she would have to be fully prepared, staunch, brave, bravest, because Warren will not be,*

and without her strength the entire home would crumble. Then what?

What would the worldly goodness of this home, swirl and decline into?

Warren will bull-up, before he collapses, and when he does collapse. Then what?

For What?

Five days on 158 and Blevin had met and accepted his new lower otherworld but did not really understand it or blend with Con T 158. He'd been lucky to do that once, at 881, not easy to do. It takes confidence, and he had none now. A strange feeling covered his subconscious, that those beautiful lipstick angels just passed, might be his last angels. Although all marine orders are to rotate eventually when a turn is up, 158 seemed too spooky, unreal, as if layered with dark veiled multiple layers of presumptive daily causalities and dying, wilder musical chairs of destruction, or musical foxholes, dodging incoming. There was no familiar foxhole downhill scene to absorb or feel into a logical plan of surviving this time, to assimilate with, as Blevin had adopted at 881. Everything felt low at all points, and then lower, bottomless, as if low was not the lowest and never would be, that there would always be a new level of low at Con Thien.

April 2, 1968, the forever dependable sun clicking up in its steady dutiful morning rise brought the thumping rhythmic air sounds of approaching new Hueys, with new water and dehydrated cans of stuff marines have to eat to stay awake, alive and free of the hunger enemy. Ground marines love Hueys and crews, the sight of door gunners in the darkened openings is the marines daily hope of a someday dee-dee out.

Living in a routine of one mission after another, the loading hustle of early morning dark tarmacs and pink sunrises as guides, Huey jockeys learn to athletically ride within the air they skip and glide through, always a lifeline for the ground marines. Blevin drank in the sounds of the Hueys approach from the east and two clicks slightly south where Quang Tri was supposed to still be, looking for the Hueys in the distance, loving the idle moment of Huey thought, searching for and finding that small dark air spot that becomes larger with the whipping blades bringing birds in closer to a 158 actual sighting, then full view, especially this April 2 moment. Another 158 night had passed, not a small thing in this violent Asian world. The morning light arrived to moderate last night's occasional rocket and mortar blasts, merely harassing ground fire, at last, darkness giving in to a new sun and one more war day.

The comparatively calm morning of 158, unusual quiet thoughts, crashed open instantly, broken by a new sizzling, singing air sound of unknown weaponry coming from the bad guy's side. Not a plane, not the usual airborne rocket whistle sound. An unusual powerful air sound this Con Thien war morning, again from up north, across McNamara's ugly line—across the fake DMZ. Perhaps such a new larger high-pitch singing weapon-sounding alarm could come from way, way up there, way up in Charlie-land, the sound of a missile? The missile sound bounced and then seemed to echo through the rolling hills around Con T. The sound bounced among the low hills, slightly to the southeast, if you listened close enough. Missiles? At Con Thien? Awwwwee man!

Blevin stood up, leaned forward to a balanced perch on the edge of the slimy dirt foxhole rim and immediately kind of realized the *possible* missile sound was now a *real* missile sound, echoing east, headed toward his Huey, probably another Purple Fox Huey. He realized he hadn't seen Rollie since Khe Sanh days followed by the Phu Bai drop to the lovely lipsticks to take him away from it all for a while.

Rollie, look out, big rocket-missile screaming thing your way! Heads-up!

Charlie-Missile sound, distant, faint then not faint, and circling, Huey boys now a clear growing dark image reaching closer, just one this morning, only one Huey in the morning run to Con T?

*Could the missile be the SAM (surface-to-air
missile) rumored to now be a part of this war?*

Singing missile sounds merging with womping blade sounds,
and quickly, magically air acrobatic like, the SAM was behind the
Huey, closing, trailing the Huey's hot exhaust. More big powerful
air sounds in the sky, Con Thien's theatre of air-thing sounds, a
special morning of air-things zooming over and around 158. The
Huey was the rabbit in this life and death early morning, SAM the
beast—a Huey drop and awkward lean/roll in elevation, followed
by a SAM drop and bend, new big-ass jet sound approaching from
somewhere. Today was a different war. The war was all up there, up
where our lifeline is, in the Huey/Phantom world. Fast air now, dip
and layout, and dip and fast toward 158, too fast for a Huey's good
guidance tastes, slow to a SAM, both cat and mouse air dancing,
motions slowish to a big-ass jet sound now booming clear to any 158
ear—booming sound wave shocks to the ground peering up foxholed
young marines, now turned spectators.

*Gooks now have SAM's? Frickin' Chinese! Or
was it the Russians again?*

The powerful zoom-zoom jet sound blasts in magically toward
158, just off the tail of the Huey so precisely and fast it seemed an
animated illusion. A phantom illusion, a Phu Bai Marine phantom
jet morning air acrobat maneuver, just as the Huey pulls a nose up as
if a reins on a galloping horse, for a quick descent to 158. Phantom
air brakes halted the sonic booming, the usual jet trail marking
a clear way, drawing SAM sensors to the new hotter target as the
Outfielder's Huey pounces to 158 in a controlled crash, long blades
slightly skipping over red clay.

The SAM can play with the Phantom in skies above Blevin's
foxhole, above Con Thien, just a couple clicks off What's-His-Name's
Line, and then the Phantom plays with the SAM. Captain Jupe flew

his Phantoms for a living now was one with the seat and controls with any phantom fighter jet, on any run. Radio chatter had drawn him from the homebound ETA that morning, diverted him to find a lone Huey in a race for life with a SAM. Jupe remained engaged, slow and steady for his phantom, circled up, SAM followed, then around the west side of Con T, SAM followed, a rare free morning air show for ground marines—then back to the east side, north a bit, foxholed eyes enjoying the show until the SAM ran out of SAM rocketing stuff and slumped its missile nose to a harmless descending journey back toward the land from which its first sound had originally arrived. Cockpit Jupe grinned, did a wing waving fly over to the waving-back ground marines, some standing openly above their foxholes now, others just waving arms, helmets, and up-thumbs from below ground while the-Jupester banked south and disappeared. Jupe would approach Phu Bai air in about twelve minutes.

> *SAMs! They got SAMs! The warring part of the planets early version of the smart bomb. Now another way to get blown up at Con Thien and I Corps!*

Nam was the weapons testing center of the world for future warring generations, Con Thien one of the labs!

Plenty of ground marines raced to help and unload the control crashed Huey and greet the teeth jarred crew with smiles and handshakes. Huey pilot's cockpit heads hanging motionless in denerving relief, slowly smiled toward one another. The crew unloading the morning's crated reason for a mission, slapping helmets, looking for the familiar stretchers for the low, more tame usually predictable ride back off the 158. Room for four, let's get 'em loaded, docs and lipsticks waiting.

Jupe radioed back to the 158 CO through Q Tri signal corps: "Call me if you need me. I got all day. You marines are what I live for!"

Blevin sensed the war had now moved beyond the reasonable logic or functionality of any lost foxhole and harassing ground fire. Russian rockets, SAMS, it all seemed bigger than a month ago, lower into the ground, but strangely higher in a sky with new killing stuff. Another day on 158, the day still new, probably seventy or so more days to go before some other poor bastard Hueys-in up here for his replacement shell-shock torcher longevity treatment.

Excited, urgent radio chatter, April 2, all day, excited chatter, endless radio fuss-ups of warnings and orders of all kinds.

Marines scramble, all over 158, in hunts for new better positions.

A day that got tighter and hungrier with each passing click of the sun.

The "lowest" surreal day, time crawling low, evening mortar and rocket activity when it wasn't even evening yet, only late afternoon on that April 2.

April 2 pressed on, way too hungry of a day now, in the life of anything at 158!

CO up and down the sparse lines of dug-in young marines shouting false encouragement, but at least, he was there, all remaining ammo passed to reaching foxholes.

Blevin grabbing as many hand grenades as he could, arm good, a refocus with a slight grin now and then thoughts of lipsticks gave some thought-freedom. Blevin knew this act, 881 fresh in his mind.

Dusk small arms fire usually starts a pot-shot and tracer at a time. On 158, you could hear the small arms bullet sizzles, close, but a few feet up from low positions. *"Here we go, frickin Nam!"* Maybe Puff is around, or some tank buddies, although we haven't seen any tanks at Con T at all. Maybe we can howdy up a tank, radio a tank convoy in the area to drop on by before the night's tripping, like right now. Copters long gone, tucked away from "this" night. They will monitor distant radio chatter, prep up in the pre-dawn early morning for a run.

The 450-ish leatherneck '60s jarheads on a low hill, and April 2 brought the whole war in, around 158 and then brought it on. Dusk blending to darkness elevated the booms and crashes—as if the two typically unrelated realities were on some sort of balanced rhythmic weighing device. As darkness creeps in one side lowers, causing more incoming violent booms lifting the opposite side up, enemy arty adding to incoming mortars and rockets.

> *Shoot anything down. Lower than your 158*
> *foxhole, or moving out there, and keep firing.*
> *Be generous tonight, leave nothing unexpended,*
> *pitching arm up, strong, strongest.*

April 3, Rollie Cahill and crews from seven other Purple Fox birds, reported to a familiar dark Quang Tri tarmac at 0300, fueling, ammo, three extra docs found somewhere, quietly tucked aboard with their vital med bags. *Mission: Con Thien!*

> *Get up there and on the ground at first light,*
> *ammo out, land in two's on all sides, 50 cals out, be*
> *generous.*
> *We will resupply, lend ground fire, take*
> *wounded first, return for bags.*

Quang Tri radio chatter kept Purple Fox command informed from Con T all night, hot, superhot even by Con Thien standards.

The "Meat Grinder"!
"Strap in, lock and load, kill anything moving on the ground on the way in: radio locations of moving gooks: phantoms behind us will clean up."
"Do not dinky-dow off the bird, won't be down long."
"If ya get off for a stretcher, throw it on and follow your throw."
"We can do more good on supply runs and extracting wounded than we can staying in the fight."

Still, warmed, Nam morning air moving through the bird took Asia's atmosphere into the mission. Blades thump-thumped northward, whizzing through warm air too quickly. There it was, the bald 158 knob, slight darting movement by the scrambling marines: "The Hill of the Angels." Rollie saw nothing to blast the hell out of with his 50 on the way in, finger tight on a familiar trigger, itchy, plenty of golden rounds to share with Charlie. A dip and slant and then level on the northeast corner small flat spot. Ammo crates out first, drop it all along a line, marines will get what they need. A busting mishandled stretcher dumped a wounded marine on the way to his scramble for a precious Huey ride out, off the hill, and Rollie leaped to help the staggered wounded marine previously stretchered, after a quick heads-up yell to his pilot.

Rollie was on the ground, and he didn't want to be on the ground at Con Thien, never intended to be on Con Thien ground, nobody wanted to be on Con Thien ground.

Then, there he was, up forward . . . A glance back, Rollie could see the cockpit eyes, see the helmeted pilot face, clearly see concern of the face. Rollie stopped, dropped to his knees.

What is that, that marine right there?
It looks like Blevin!
Blevin from Khe Sanh?

A quick wave-push downward from Rollie to the pilot, meant "wait on me," and Rollie dashed closer to the sitting marine, just ten yards away, completely out in the open, alone, helmet down over dazed eyes, smoking a cigarette, totally still, except for hand to mouth and white puffs floating slowly up under the helmet.

"Blevin," as Rollie ran to him. Blevin looked blankly up, recognizing nothing in particular as if on a park bench overlooking a serene lazy coastline or slowly flowing river.

"*Blevin, get up, come on, I'll get you to the bird,*" but Blevin would not move to help himself this time, only a blank hopeless stare back. Rollie looked closer, deeper from eyes, then lower. Blevin "could not move," could not even reveal a leaning body motion. Blevin had no legs. There were no boots at the bottom, where wet used marine jungle boots are supposed to be, only bloody tangled hanging bottoms of muscles and bone below the knees, slightly exposed, dangling from what remained of tattered green cloth once a part of a marine's combat uniform.

One more, quick downward motion to the pilot, and Rollie threw Blevin over a shoulder for the heavy sprint to their waiting Huey, suspended in idling blades and mix of dust for the time of the Rollie and Blevin carry and run. A crash of the two helmeted heads first leap and landing of the two bodies of distant buddies on the hard metal Huey floor and a gentle Huey lift, pivot forward to the SE, off the wretched hill. Semper Fi!

A combat Huey, with three stretchers, holding wounded, dying Marines. Rollie holding Blevin's head and silent expressionless eyes. Blevin looked up, with his last slight grin from this dying Marine of Con Thien, after his Khe Sanh, after his quiet St. Louis neighborhood where dad walks to work without moving, and mom just waits. Blevin would not see his beloved lipsticks on this trip. He would only see

Rollie's face looking down at him before he closed his worn, battered eyes to embrace a final dream, cradled within the thick full white carpet of peaceful clouds that marked his awaited journey away from his final battle and final departure off of "The Hill of the Angels," out of Domestic Nam, captured by the war's ceaseless demands. April 3, 1968 was as far as he could go in this life. Final, as far as he could carry the heavy weight asked of him, not yet twenty years old—never to marry Paula or see any of the lipsticks again, ever.

Blevin Slyhope, young marine from a St. Louis neighborhood, completed his Proxy War concept, another fallen domino, knocking other dominoes to their own falling, clear across the Pacific, over a California coast, over interior plains States, back into his St. Louis neighborhood of origination. Dream of it, make or mix Blevin and Wilson Street Dreams of it. Dance with the boy's dreams until they are too heavy to be danced with or are spinning out of control too fast to catch and hold in the dance of final journeys. Then release those dreams, follow them later at a different time, when a new dream has arrived. That's all you can do, all Mrs. Slyhope will be able to do, all any of us could do.

The 1,419 marines who died at Con Thien and 9,265 were wounded before command ordered the Third Marine Division to stand down and abandon the area and Hill 158. They took with them an estimated 7,563 dead North Vietnamese, captured another 168, all of which would be immediately replaced from up north, from Giap Streets or some such streets, and sent south for more human wave mission to unite their split country.

The McNamara Line can still be seen from spatial high-resolution imagery, vegetation and soils altered forever but nothing else can be seen, except somewhere in a cemetery near the brewery in St. Louis on the other side of the world just off the constantly flowing Mississippi River. You can see a tombstone marking Blevin Slyhope, Corporal USMC, and see the same name again marked on a black depressed wall in DC where Blevin is remembered with over fifty eight thousand others. His is the name of a deeply loved, precious son of Mrs. Slyhope who by April 20 had cautiously joined the momentum of local antiwar neighborhood activists. Warren Slyhope spent twenty more years at the brewery, retired with no notice, walked home one more time, and grieved nonstop, while drinking himself angrily to death in the small back yard rather deliberately, having digested and attached himself to his personal virus of grief forever. Holding the grief tightly, he would never share it with even his dearest wife and Blevin mother in pure selfish Domestic Nam psychologically infected fashion. Neither of the Slyhopes ever met a politician from whom the slightest expression of regards or understanding would come. They were told by blah-blah talking TV heads, flags in a fake background, that such Blevin-like eventualities were all in a line of patriotic duty, blah-blah freedom fighting, or blah-blah liberties of this or blah-blah that.

The Slyhopes never met Rollie, any of the lipsticks or anyone who had been on 881 or 158 or anywhere else in Nam. Nam was largely a haunting illusion in a world that would remain separate and silent forever. Unspoken of! Not understood, perhaps for eternity, by those committed on the ground or domestically. The only way to approach an understanding of Nam would be to actually accept the unacceptable, which was still unthought of in those times, still in the post-WWII patriotic mind-set. The Slyhope's could only quit taking the *Post-Dispatch* and then quit a lot of other minor things in their lives. Token efforts to adjust something that made no sense could never find a final adjustment to relieve their loss of an only son.

Rollie flew all day April 3 after releasing Blevin, settled exhausted on a constantly busy Phu Bai tarmac with the crew of seven other Purple Foxes, regretting the loss of his best friend he would never really know. That night, Rollie with his new sergeant stripe, borrowed a MAG-36 jeep and went alone to the pitch-dark takeoff end of the long runway servicing his friendly and mighty Phantoms. From that runway end, he could sit alone in the dark, alone with his jeep, watching, feeling the powerful roar of dual jet takeoffs one after a warring other, seeing the bright orange burning glow of jet trails disappearing into night's dark missions, double jet takeoffs by brave pilots within their own fast moving, isolated confident world, only attached to the earth by a chattering nameless, faceless radio signal. At that time, in that moment, at the end of that far off remote runway, Rollie was as close to the war as he could be, at least for that night.

The next day, April 4, the "Domestic Nam" blasted backward to all five hundred thousand Nam troops that Johnson's machine had committed to the proxy war, back across the entire Pacific, past the Nam coast, over the big bases, firebases, LZs, into foxholes or bush patrols, with a whole new type of war to be added to the regular types of war, as if marking some sort of pinnacle of Domestic self-inflicted American style turmoil. Reports filtered to, through, and around troops as common rumor that Dr. Martin Luther King had been assassinated by some white guy, a bullet on a balcony, a balcony in the South. Great! Just hunky! Add that to your Nam platters and generous servings of things to irritate and war about. Within hours, rumor became fact, confirmed.

What and the hell is going on back there? Well, at least Bobby is running for president to replace the dimwitted domestic shell-shocked Johnson. Can't help it! *Life in the Nam is . . . life in The Nam!* Can't do nothin' about balconies and dimwits or Bobby. Here we just fight on, always looking, always aware, believing the stories, and believing in angels. It's what we do here, must do here in The Nam.

Chapter 5

Nam Cryseez—Dawn to Dusk

"For a new marine, arriving in-country, the thought that
Nam is now the *real world* and home is the *otherworld* is a
spooky, startling mental virus of suspended thinking."

American troops living on an in-country continuous edge, counted down to their wake-up, fought the fronts and the perimeters, fought the tree lines and hot LZs, and fought all of the deadly booby-trap elements, insects, heat, connecting tunnels, and trenches. Heavy heat and oppressive humidity rotting what it could reach of skin, boots, attitudes, confidence, and outlooks while warping everything else. Morning sun marked one more notch on the countdown. Dusk readied soldiers for Charlie's night and a chance for the next morning sun. Every direction was the next direction to be taken or charged or flown circles around. Nothing was fixed or certain or if it seemed certain it did not seem that way long enough to actually gain a focus or spirit for that certain challenge. Every story was believable because nothing was steady, explained, going reasonably into nor coming from a consistent direction or method logically intended or perceived by those entering or inventing the directions. Living the front or rear of a "cause for the day," Nam life for marines was a wonder world of unknowns, not just in-country, but also from back in the world created by stringing rumors of fragments of macro-American issues together with the soldier's individual thoughts of home, friends, parents, future jobs, or the training for future careers, and certainly daydreams or night fantasies of girl friends or frolicking with homeboy sports buddies. In '67 to '68, there was an extended connection of national grief, mystic, elastic in feeling, America to Nam, then constantly back and forth.

When a young soldier is in the States, training to a fighting and dying task, then staging for Nam in-country issues only imagined and not yet seen, thoughts of Nam are of an "otherworld," a strange unexplained place, with unexplainable people that have to be seen to be believed, and even then seeing, would always be far from understanding. Slowly, transitionally, as a soldier physically and mentally moves through the "go to Nam" process, arrives in-country, and settles into it all, biting off and digesting pieces at a time, accepting an individual fate of position, what was known to be the embodiment of that person, meaning all of that left behind in that past life, becomes the "otherworld." The "otherworld" is no longer Nam. Nam is the reality. "Home," with familiar comforts, is now the "otherworld." This is not an easy mental transition for a nineteen-year-old to grasp and hold as a reality, with any sort of reasoning confidence or sense of actual purpose or place. The thought that Nam is now the "realworld" and home is the "otherworld" is star-gazing spooky, startling, surreal, a mental virus of suspended thinking, all new to a young soldier. This transition of worlds changing places in a period of forty-eight hours is pretty quickly assimilated and then processed into a logical reality of a rapid, low-rank, transitioning USMC or army life. This is particularly true when the new "otherworld," the one now at home, seems to be turning itself upside down with its own directionless '60s rampant trendsetting, meaning the actual footing of both ends of the soldier's world is full of an unknown too violent shiftiness. Yet soldiers follow orders, and fight on, for pride of service, love of country, and individual unexplainable "faith" that is essential to cling to.

For the Nam soldier, there are even heavier thoughts, the heaviest thoughts of all: the thoughts of death, how death might occur, from where death will arrive, how death will arrive. These death thoughts are a part of the business of the war, not to be avoided, as much a part of the whole mess as is breathing daily life. Thoughts of impending death, on some stinking red clay hill off somewhere in a vast Asian shadowy darkness, occupy the unoccupied moments. A hill that is certain to be abandoned, whether the brave fighting US troops blending with its elements die on the hill or successfully defend the hill, is not the place to spend a life's last blessed regards to himself, country, or loved ones, no matter the depth of pride of service. These are tough thoughts to reconcile for a nineteen-year-old in a new "otherworld" changing in a literal flash. In Con Thien, a soldier is met with the nickname The Meat grinder or The Hill of the Angels. At Phu Bai, a soldier soon discovers the nickname is The Graveyard. For US soldiers entering Nam, initially, the strange Asian setting is the "otherworld" to be quickly learned, hopefully transitioned to "real world" as the soldiers come to know they have another journey that lies ahead, a foot or sand hill at a time.

Once in Nam, a "final journey" is the goal, of which there are two types. One type of journey is home to relative continuous warm friendly daylight, opportunity, and expressions of security, to a future that needs building once Nam has passed and given up an inner hold and is shed from weighting down emotions and influencing behavior and relationship decisions. That journey will be when the soldier becomes free of the obligation to follow orders from some unattached far away crackling radio voice, too high in rank to smell a ground conflict.

The other "journey" is *the* journey. This is the journey over fifty-eight thousand Americans from thousands of Wilson Streets felt and made when lifted above and away from Nam by souls and spirits, unseen angels showing the way with God's gentle reaching hand to a heavenly sanctuary forever free of all future "otherworlds." That journey is the respite of Nam's chaos and weighty atmosphere of compounding human made evils. Making that "final journey" is the individual's own personal experience. That journey is heaven's layer over all other experiences as a personal inventory of life's summary of events and relationships no matter the length of time on earth as a human part of real miracles of living. There is no reason to fear such a journey, it may likely be the best, most enlightened journey of all, perhaps too quick to come, but we do not generally control the timing of our final journey, especially in a nation's "otherworld" of wasteful wars. Once at the threshold of that final journey, peering toward the possibility, it matters not the circumstance leading to that special journey's beginning, war or no war, lost forgotten hill or no hill. The point is only the journey's threshold. That's all, the spiritual point crossed in deep personal acceptance of the journey's beginning. Journey's timing is unstoppable, indifferent to life's expectations. In Nam, tomorrow, there will be more body bags, and scrambling stretchers looking for lipsticked angels. In Nam, it is a twenty-four-hour, never-ending cycle that has no place to go, cannot go another place or break the repetitive patterns, until enough is enough, a distinction not controllable by any soldier or by "command" echelons. In Nam, there are too many armies, too much weaponry, too few visions of progress, and no visions of how to gain a concept of what progress might actually be, when enough is enough. Or how much progress is enough progress to step down and off the cycles of political ambitions that pull and string such destructive forces together.

Then, in a world of how much is too much amidst the Domestic Nam rising and falling chaos came April 4, 1968, and the assassination of Martin Luther King. Now, after Memphis and King, the US Wilson Street Boys from thousands of cities and rural towns could just go ahead and have a great reason to fight and frag one another.

The Nam unrest, post King assassination, was not particularly just racial, although there was plenty of that. Civil and domestic unrest signaled by the King event, was just more trans-continental grief to heap on top of the negative attitude and consciousness of many of the marines and other soldiers trying to slog their way through a year of war that made no sense in the first place. If the greater Nam were a greater business plan, within the operating business of America, the King assassination in April '68, the Defining Year would have been the undeniable message of "stop." Just stop the entire flimsy, fake business. Everyone just stand still so we can see what we have and don't have, and if what we are doing in this business of America is just, worthy, and within the core values of a midtwentieth-century global democracy of humanly respectful leadership. Just stop this whole damn downward spiral mess of killing our own people and country, not to mention bankrupting our nation. Step back to take a look at what simply is right and what is not right. That boisterous message from the King assassination raced away to obfuscation at the very levels that the message should have registered. The message, however, did not race away in some of the various trenches of Nam living and fighting. Each Domestic tsunami coated another layer of uncertainty with doubt on the Nam soldier, already committed to his eyeballs, life, and limb exposed.

A previously tamed domestic social structure, reaching into early '68, with a nation in elevating urban and campus rioting, bleeding internally from lack of direction or leadership in anything to do with Nam or our own American streets, the domestic situation became dreadfully close to "the inmates runnin' the asylum." Suddenly, the unorganized, defiant antiwar demonstrators (no matter the individual reasons) shifted from just demonstrating to actual "hating." Now the lowly and unauthorized had hate legs and higher hating voices from which to whip-up increasingly more attention to their "anti-establishment" hating cause. The smug "establishment" seemed to more increasingly deserve the degenerative attention. Nam's Tet, with resulting constant evening newsfeeds, had shown America's lack of progress to the world as well as a lack of control in managing the war at home to any productive ends. Any future ongoing warring or domestic progress appeared unlikely, although no one would yet identify what "progress" would actually look like, meaning actual progress to a productive conclusion could never be recognizable and thus could not be strategized or acted upon. (Desperately close to Afghan 2014, today, right now.)

Progress had become KIA/MIA reporting, and there was plenty of that as if on a weekly quota from that flimsy business plan that no one was in charge of. But anyone could see through that PR and lack of a real strategy façade, and in '68, they did see through some of the four-prong military/industrial façade, having been further awakened to the general national futility by the King assassination anti-event. America's mounting "public" unrest was not the only unrest. Hidden in the kitchens, backyards, and garages across the country lives within millions of America's core families had been put on hold, or stopped, as a general population watched and waited for their Wilson Street Boys to prosecute and return from a suspicious, vague warring commitment.

King would leave his final unintentional mark of leadership influence in a strange, unpredictable, assassinated understatement. Ever-present racial tensions, because of the ultimate racial event of a century, became an indelible impression for many US Black Nam soldiers, a lit fuse, perhaps rightfully so to some degree. Racial attitudes, not to be confused with racism, are an inherent American right. America, at least partially grew up with "race" as a subconscious population issue, spoken or unspoken.

We fought the great war to free America from skin color dominance, and by golly we can feel racial when we want to, turn racism off—then turn racism on again, for as long as it takes, no limits.

Previous to King's American loss, racial issues among Nam troops were largely latent in and among ordinary troop populations, mostly left to personal internal attitudes from a person's own youthful lack of maturing.

In Nam, given the option, black troops hung mostly with black troops, and white troops hung mostly with white troops, just like neighborhoods back in the World, pretty normal standards. The only real difference seemed to be that when whites and blacks did become friends, they became good friends, deep in their friendships far beyond any skin color lines, sort of a feeling of "teammates," except war teammates are way beyond sports teammates. Before April 4, there was not much commonly outward racial anger or threats about any racial divisiveness, except of course for the 1 percent of crazies who spend all day looking for trouble wherever it can be found or "manufactured" if the trouble is not naturally occurring. There was just too much other stuff to hate, not time to hate the copter crew member or the guy in the next hole down the perimeter line because he was black, white, or brown, poor or even lazy; hating "stupid" was different and had no color lines. There was simply not the time or the energy for racism efforts of any kind in I Corps Nam.

Common natural elements supersede racism in many Nam ways. Racial anxieties pass in concern once the low-country Asian heat exceeds 102 degrees. There is no racism in a shared foxhole along a perimeter line, especially when the field of fire darkens into the night's dancing shadows with sporadic lighting from flares launched by somebody, somewhere, signaling an attack is either likely or already on the way. In the Domestic Nam, here and there, April 4 changed a good deal of that, especially in the bigger camps at the rear with the gear. As news of the assassination of MLK flamed and flare popped through camps, crews, platoons, and remote firebases, bad attitudes looking for an outlet were more often on a pivot to worse attitudes. Hate priorities sharpened and shifted, traditional frustrations of all kinds had a reason to rise to action. Watching your back, or your buddy's back, became a little different kind of twenty-four-hour SOP.

The new anger wasn't so much that troops of different races, who previously had coexisted, would suddenly hate one another. The atmosphere was more of a general overwhelming feeling that America's domestic decline had caught up with and joined the deadly chaos of Nam and thus needed a reaction to that assassination action. The "reaction" was not readily emotionally processed by young armed soldiers on the other side of the world, perhaps with an engrained categorical racial itch to scratch in the first place.

Individual reactions to the MLK assassination were different for everyone, but for some were reason enough for a hating priority, first for the black reaction of troops, but secondly as the whites reacted to the black reaction. Officers had no "book" on racism control in Nam, let alone in reaction to such bizarre home-front waves of anti-everything that would undoubtedly affect troop attitudes and actions.

Where was the Officers School class of instruction on a useless war with no direction, nor a goal—while America exploded racially and morally,

while draining the national treasury? How does that
training book read?

In a daily existence on the boundless battlefield, with plenty of hating to pick from, all of a sudden racial hating was a raised priority only adding to compounding misjudgments of daily Nam challenges.

It was almost like "Oh, Gee. We all forgot that we are supposed to also be racists, fighting this stupid war had distracted us." The anger and resentment were instant. It was like blacks returned to the lessons and anxieties of black neighborhoods where you don't trust or blend with whitey, except for uncomfortable situations where you must, all in a micro-population of isolated, armed-to-the-teeth war mongering.

For the weary, leery white crop of counting down to a wake-up youth, most from rural strictly white society backgrounds, there was an instant atmosphere of the return of the dreadful Domestic racism that commonly hangs like a heavy, dark, antagonizing cloud over America's main business of human prosperity building. With the sudden death of MLK, under the most blatant racially dividing conditions, no one even had time to fuss up a good reason for a new Nam variety of hate. For a week or more, hating the night owned by the VC was an irrelevant meaningless hate venture. Hating the chicken-shit messages from obscure, displaced command radios was no longer on the chart of hating. Hating a jammed M-16 or sizzle and womp of an enemy rocket was just a part of a day, not a hate plateau.

King, dead?
By a white guy?
In the South?
Will we not ever learn?
Can we not proceed further up a societal chain
of a sort of maturity that lends to actual progress?

Is America no longer the hope, the global example of statesmanship and multicultural nation building?

Troops, families, and neighborhoods committed, armed, over their individual thin red lines; fighting for what again—while America self-destructs in a racially separating domestic sewer?

Do we conclude the tour and wake-up and fly the big pond back the other way, so that we can officially war with ourselves? War with the guy I just shared a foxhole with because we changed locations?

How ridiculous must America look to our enemies?

From the camps, firebases, landing strips to the bigger I Corps bases like Da Nang, Phu Bai, and Chu Lai, word of the useless loss of MLK was a new lit sizzling fuse. Suddenly (once again for most all of the troops), the reality of a useless war with useless losses and useless politicians directing useless/faceless yes officers was the ball and chain never to be shed in favor of good warring implementation that simply can kill an enemy and blow his things up. With immense personal sacrifice played out daily on a life and death stage on and after April 4 in the Defining Year, the Domestic Nam was in your face perhaps more than ever.

"Carry this baggage too" young soldier, a new message of compounding difficult circumstance, compliments of an American society separated by ever-widening social gaps. The times and conditions, just post Tet, made it seem as if the assassination of MLK was a strange punishing extension of the Tet Offensive, as if the slight calming that had just occurred needed another violent fussing up in case a few nerves and stress levels have become untangled from their constant nervy, gut-wrenching, blood-boiling tension.

The insinuation to the beat-up grunts and the daredevil heli-jockeys, or the isolated hill-top artillery womp-master, the bottom line from the warring gods was, you have sweat unspent, energies unapplied, having moments of unchallenged semblances of sanity, take this little bit of unexpected Domestic MLK demise and just fit it in right there where you once had nothing to worry about for ten to fifteen minutes a day. Pick up more weight and uncertainty to haul up the next hill or over the next tree lined berm through rice paddy dikes and open creek beds. Add this to the no-sense and un-sense and illogic-sense of your mission. Then drop it all on the wake-up as there is no more domestic space for bad attitudes or reactionary warring back in the US of A. The population at home is already full of bad attitudes and hate. Come home if you must but leave the Nam baggage in The Nam. "We will barely tolerate you in the first place, and we certainly don't want your negative opinionated baggage."

Licking Tet wounds with a scramble of strategic reaction to a new war that Tet defined was unmistakably the future of America's military Nam struggle. Commanding officers, militarized politicians, and their circle of rank climbing yes men, had no collective or progressive mid-'68 response on the ground. The public reaction for public consumption was numbers: KIA numbers, WIA numbers, enemy tonnage of captured weaponry numbers, or bombing tonnage dropped numbers, with a film clip here and there of a nameless skull with a helmet professing some sort of US victory or accomplishment from the capture of a useless hamlet, and the relocation of twenty Mamasans with their hungry dirty children for something called Vietnamization while their straw hut burned behind their trail of tears out of a hamlet that may have been their family's home for hundreds of years, communists or no communists, dominoes, and proxy warring aside. A firefight, skirmish, or booby-trap, then tally and report the losses, airlift medevac someone, check that on a list, and move on.

Post-Tet burned through the US consciousness, shaking multiple levels of morality and strategic commitment. Post-Tet was the unwinnable signal, starting an infinite steady moving clock that would never have a limit, but only a destined uncertain end to be arrived at some time in an unpredictable future. The clock would get there, marking an end, when it got there.

Only the clock would know the limits of "enough" and the clock wasn't telling. Post-Tet was the unmistakable indicator of the iconic uselessness of the Domestic Nam. Just a few short months prior, US financial commitment was at the fullest extent ever imagined as Johnson gathered his economic and human marbles to scatter wherever the warring whim of the day led him. Then, the MLK assassination burned awareness of the fake leadership's bottomless situation into the minds of the troops, on the racial surface and deeply into their already flimsy individual commitments. Two months later, Bobby would be assassinated in an underground LA hotel kitchen on an alternate route to his post-acceptance exit of political victory in the California primary by some other phantom, faceless crazy on some additional unnamed cover-up mission of Domestic self-destruction. The Domestic Nam was in full gear. Conflict roaring on both sides of the Pacific, America's public grief exposed, embracing half of a globe in the confusion, infecting the rest of the globe in unseen, unpredictable ways while the namesake Wilson Street Boys and hundreds of thousands of others from thousands of other Wilson Streets plowed through another day of armed forces foreign conflict duty. Are you kidding me? But Nam was still early to America, which was already a decade deep to a Vietnamese philosophy of some elusive sort, politically revved up now and then by a new name for the war or a new political vision of rationalization.

Previous to April '68, the growing military base at Phu Bai was generally a base of marines and was the largest US military base north of Da Nang, closer to the DMZ than the big and growing bases at Da Nang and Chu Lai, also within I Corps designation. Marines operated out of Phu Bai with military and quasi-military strategies including fixed wing fighter jet capability, large helicopter installations with Chinook-power, Huey, and later, the new Cobra flying war machines, and the ever-present, mysterious fixed prop, shiny silver planes of the Air America fleet, which were Nam's mysterious version of commercial air traffic, eventually proven to be an in-country operative instrument of the deeply embedded fully operational CIA. Phu Bai command coordinated air and ground activities all over designated I Corps, but mainly north and west, toward the DMZ and beyond into lost lands like Khe Sanh, dealing with determined N. Vietnamese army movements in and around the entire I Corps geography, processing young humans, weaponry, communications, big squishy dangerous G-2 (Intelligence) and G-4 (Logistics) stuff.

Phu Bai was a collection of military camps within a Military Base City. All of warring's necessities for I Corps passed through Phu Bai, eventually to include everything from forklifts to aviation parts, from an occasional Caucasian nurse to various O-Club niceties. Supply officers and NCOs doubled as scavenger conduits to anyone with an influence or tradable commodity. The expanded, large, growing base was a scavenger's paradise on the low-end and an enterprising civilization within a rocket's range on the high end. At Phu Bai, parts of bases were barbed wired within parts of bigger barbed wire parts, as if a barbed wire salesman someplace back in the States had done a terrific job within his vision of barbed wiring the whole damn country into compartments of duties and fleeting security. Phu Bai was a major military city compared to the camps, firebases, and LZs farther north or west in the mountains, where VC owned all the ground that Marines were not standing on.

Phantom jet units at Phu Bai flew out and then later landed, constantly at night—bright orange burning tail jets flared just above the dark airstrip at take-offs, two at a time, launching into the dark skies of Nam's alive violent nights, dedicated to one attack mission after another as two more powerful machines lined up aside one another in their turn to launch, for another night run of blind bombing, pilots translating rhythmic monotone air traffic orders and just hoping something of some consequence was being damaged in exchange for their night-flying, adrenaline-pumping, within enemy anti-aircraft exposure.

Squadrons of marine helicopter units huddled within and around their aircraft work horses at night, within sandbagged walls and corner-stacked fifty-five-gallon oil drums filled with sand, also protecting the fueled armed flying machines within. Among the Phu Bai Chinook and Huey units was the famous HMM-364, Purple Foxes, part of the First Marine Air Division from Mira Mar, California who gathered great offensive and lifesaving acclaim throughout I Corps, particularly for their fearless life-saving offensive and defensive Tet and post-Tet operations. Within the 364 on that April 4 was Rollie Cahill, huddled amongst the machines and oil drum walls waiting for early morning predawn next mission orders as word of the assassination of King spread from barracks, to perimeter line, to NCO and O'clubs, as if the information and reactions were flowing water seeking a natural level of undefinable depths in and around the populated razor tense camps.

Rollie sat that night with his mind exposed. Rollie was exposed to his own shifting fate, out of Hue, Khe Sanh, off of Con Thien for the moment, exposed to the creeping feelings of a lost, shredded buddy he never truly knew. Slyhope's unknowing St. Louis parents would be suspended in their own time, waiting, not knowing of Blevin's whereabouts, and then emotionally suspended in an even deeper human daze as some dutiful suited courier delivered Blevin-news, the finality, closing chapter of news about their son. After a couple more days, as the body traveled, there would come an end to the accounts of that boy's life unlived, that dream lost forever. Rollie knew better than to make friends or relinquish any feelings that are better left within and swore it would not happen again.

From now on, it will just be faces and shirt pocket names, sometime with a rank, mostly not. That's the plan. Believe all stories, own the ground you stand on, and don't worry about the other

*ground. Friends and Nam don't work. All a good
plan, right? Work it!*

Just prior to April 4, internally within the bunkers, sandbags, and barbed wire of the actual Phu Bai base, the daily pulse and ground scenery was changing, becoming altered with thousands of attitudes and different moving uniforms. As the war grew more vigorous and angry via the nervousness and increased weaponry of the Tet offensive, military commanders changed their I Corps troop placement profiles. The northern I Corps illusionary concepts of military "front lines" facing the always probing, hiding NVA enemy moved north, and therefore, so did marines on the ground. Tet displayed the vulnerability of fighting grounds and facilities in the entire country of South Vietnam but especially north of Phu Bai. Thus, slightly armed camps of marines increased their population with soldiers and orders of a more aggressive and determined "stand your ground, search and destroy" nature. All, of course, being symbols of military leadership shooting from the hip toward any strategy that could conclude to be aggressively victorious or provide a position to become victorious or at the very least profess strategies to claim an elusive vision of a state of progress within some brilliant war college synopsis. As marine troops moved north a platoon or squadron at a time, Army Air First Cavalry units moved in behind them in places like Phu Bai. The same type mobile units portrayed in the terrific movie *Once We Were Soldiers*. Suddenly, inside the base parameters on the ground in Phu Bai were the yellow and black First Cav patches on uniforms and helicopter snouts, mixing the new assigned army units, with the established, salty I Corps Marine fighting forces, who had some vague notion of claim to that ground they were standing on.

Marines at Phu Bai, marines who had secured and protected and fought from the camp, around the area, and had befriended the local villagers for quite some time, now were working with what they considered the fumbling, bumbling and less fearsome, less organized army, draftees. "Commoners/I Corps Rookies" as far as I Corps Nam battle experiences were concerned, or so the more battle hardened I Corps Marines felt. Of course, in reality, they were no less eager, and no less prepared to carry on the warring duty than were the marines. But that didn't matter; in the Domestic Nam, you found your rivalries and fights wherever you could, especially in those rare grouchy moments when hardened, reactionary marines had nothing new to hate. The resented nature of the beast was for marines to clear a way, with First Air Cav troops stepping in to resecure the already secured Phu Bai area, layered and compartmentalized with good ole American western style barbed wire. Gradually, without intention or notoriety, Phu Bai was building a powder keg within the American troop population: armed youthful soldiers/King assassination-racial tensions/marines vs. army newbies. What could go wrong?

Other demonic-driven, totally unnecessary changes were also becoming a reality at Phu Bai in early '68, thanks to more genius of the ranks above regularly deciding fates from as far away as they could staff desks. Previous to March '68, there were no on-base clubs with alcohol, no entertainment outpost of any kind that far north in the proxy war, into the I Corps' dimension of the Domestic Nam. Suddenly, the distant powers, blending supply side with blind side, busily arranging things for others, had ordered the organizing and building of "field Clubs" attempting to provide a little on base R&R for the Wilson Street Boys just in from the greasy, bloody, exhausting fight of the day. Social clubs, as in impromptu places to gather and drink alcohol where there had been no such facility or activity before. Nor was the need for a Club spoken of among the enlisted ranks, in a frickin' active war zone. Charlie had no clubs. Charlie had rice, hard rice, water, with hunger and strength, fueled by a dull ideology good enough to create marathon movements.

In Phu Bai, an Officer's Club grew tent poles and dark-green canvas from one sandy ridge at the south central edge of the Phu Bai base. Then, just a short baseball throw down the dirt, mud road, then dusty road, then mud road again, from the officers club a Sergeant's Club arrived in a smaller tent, and finally the granddaddy of them all—the Enlisted Club. In the middle of the Phu Bai military camp of hundreds of millions of dollars' worth of war assets, the huge dark-green tents went up from the dusty, sandy, normally useless landscape officially "circus-fying" the camp and the war, with an out of place "four rings" for partying, grunt style—right there, mid-I Corps. Gook intelligence observers from surrounding rolling hills must have been impressed with the Americanization process. Pound the ground at fleeing black pajamed Gooks with scattered 50-caliber machine gun fire, trip a wire, throw a grenade, then get back ricky tick to base and go have a "happy hour" cold one. Prosecution of a confused war, modernized, Americanized, distractionized.

Inside the circus tents, much to the surprised pleasures of everyone enlisted, old oil barrels connected by plywood tops became a good enough bar. Then, the wobbly, cheap bar stools from somewhere, tables from somewhere else, with more barrels to sit around the out-of-place bare wood tables. Whap-bam, the enlisted of Phu Bai had their very own beer drinkin' bar. Or kind of a bar, sort of, a good enough bar for eighteen-, nineteen-, twenty-year-old elbows and rambling Nam stories, Domestic home stories, grunting, complaining and bitching stories, and cold or hot cheap beer to service their eighteen-, nineteen-, twenty-year-old and up tastes, fears, tensions, prejudices, or anxieties. Much of the youthful enlisted Phu Bai troop population had little to no training in proper beer drinking under any circumstances. Stepping from 100-degree dust days from fields of fire, into a darkened tent, to nickel Nam beers, as if at the end of a "workday," was a strange sensation. Even worse, or better (depending on your personal consumptive outlook), the enlisted club didn't always actually have nickel beers to sell to their captive clientele. Somehow, from some place, occasionally, a truck full of hundreds of cases of hot beer would show up to the enlisted club or two trucks full of hundreds more cases of hot beer, if things were really clicking on up the supply chain and too many hands didn't get involved between the original supply and the low priority field grunt destination of Phu Bai. The green flag of the enlisted club would be raised high, word would spread, and foot soldiers footed their dusty duties as assigned, pied-piper ways to the club's waving signal, weapons checked at the tent flap by MP's, Wild West style.

In Nam, planning for tomorrow was an unsuspected artful talent; tomorrow may not actually arrive, and tomorrow had no guarantee. In addition, no respectable enlisted marine grunt gathers a few buddies and mosies on over to a frickin' Nam enlisted club for a cold "one" on that rare day when the green flag goes up without an honorable goal: If a truck load of beer had arrived, always Ballantine (at the time the worst beer on the planet), the enlisted ranks consumed a truck load of beer. If two trucks of beer arrived, causing the green flag to rise in glorious camp-wide announcement, then two trucks of beer were consumed. "Last call" was simply the splash of the last beer out of the last truck, anything less would put the club manager in desperate unexplainable straights. In Nam, you shut off the flow once started, at enormous bodily risk.

Post-Tet, early April '68, troops of all kinds in I Corps passed through Phu Bai. New guys heading north, hard bastards who had already been north, slinking back into Phu Bai to catch a breath, check weapons, rearm, and see if there was a green flag that they had heard about. Air crews always tense from a mission just finished or one that could be called up at any moment, ranged sharp-eyed all about Phu Bai. The lowest of the hardest grunts had been in Nam for months or some for almost their year tour of duty, rested in platoon-size groups of 100 or 120, depending on how severely their platoon had been hit and decimated from the latest search and destroy missions. Some fresh troops, clean-looking new troops were always within the moving parts of Phu Bai, their newness easily identified by the Nam regulars. Phu Bai had every type of passing group, with every type of attitude to go with their passing countdown.

No one knew what the hell we were in Nam
trying to do and why for. Or who and the hell was
running this thing and for what end.

*The real troops, the ones on the ground, free of
the domestic illusions, knew that Nam could never
be "occupied." What was there to occupy?*

Everything in Nam moved, constantly shifted, all soldiers could really do is occupy, hold, and defend the ground that they stood on, that day, at that time. One assignment, justified as complete by a faceless command at the far end of a displaced radio transmission, then troops moved to the next hill or ridge, or into a new flight pattern, to pick a fight with whatever was there to assume the other fighting side. The ground they had just won was then given up at their next assignment and reverted back to its unoccupied vulnerable existence, exactly the way it was before the marines or army had been ordered to secure it.

Race relations in the United States in '67-'68 were the worst since the major 1928 floods in the lower Mississippi River that sent tens of thousands of work searching, freedom seeking, and frustrated blacks north. Numerous major US cities (Newark, Baltimore, Memphis, Detroit, etc.) were being burned from the revolting ghettos out, as domestic blacks found self-destruction of US cities a last choice way to express their interpretation of being held back as black, down as ground, or worse in their minds. Driving additional anger for the black communities came from being fed distortions of inflammatory conditions by those of their own kind, who were beginning to make race relations a more aggressive US industry for selfish and political party interests.

Domestically, late '60s racial tensions mirrored the overall social and political quagmire of Nam. Inconceivable violence and disruption was occurring at home while no one (white or black, enlisted, officer, or politician) really knew what would develop from the results of the heavily prosecuted Tet Offensive or when the American media would finally wake-up and report war issues that were previously either overlooked or intentionally ignored in favor of political positions and favors. It was known that United States and South

Vietnamese troops, together, killed a bunch of the Gook-Enemy all over South Vietnam, but we also now knew that the NVA regulars and PAVN, NLF, and Viet Cong and bad guy XYZ, with plenty of logistical support in weaponry, could sustain attacks any place, any time, likely with local village population support from North I Corps to the Delta. In the midst of all these new realities, tensions were chattering away in troop's confused, frustrated war-functioning brains. Army and marines thrown together, some genius supply-side officer or politician, dining who knows where, thousands of miles toward the moon, decided it was a good time to build and supply a BAR with alcohol, in two green circus tents, in a camp as far north in I Corps as Phu Bai. Domestically and at Phu Bai, the dynamite fuse was out, matches found, and the lighting was imminent. It would just take a little more time to ka-boom, at the first major perceived excuse for extraordinary, reactionary, impulsive action.

> *Why would any command think it is appropriate, or beneficial, to import massive quantities of alcohol into this war zone, at this time, into these places, for these troops? What possible good could come from that sort of decision?* (You'll figure it out.)

Simply put, Nam had evolved to become not about building democracies for the third world less advanced peoples nor about saving the globe from advancing Communism or any such illusionary national gestures. Nam had become about military/industrial partnerships and money then more money then more and more money until someone said, *"Whoa, Nelly, wee'z runnin' out of them other people's money!"*

Money takes "deals," any kind of a deal—arms sales deals, importing equipment deals, tent deals, forklift deals, helicopters, runways, etc. Deals—any deals. The more "deals" the more exchanges of money, and thus, the more opportunity for skimming, graft and organized criminal enterprising in the name of a flag, any flag. Deals to manufacture and deliver chemicals, like Agent Orange. Deals with "Wrap Arounds," creating unseen and unsaid stimulus, to encourage the ranks and methods toward more and more "deals." Rampant deals that would have no boundaries, dimwit Johnson carpet bombing deals, Westmoreland's attrition deals, McNamara's "Line" deals.

The Pentagon and Congress were like mall kiosks, making deals with those who could pay the gate fee admission to be in the mall and move around to see whose hands were out to shake into a "deal." Sweet jobs if you can get 'em!

("Deals" may be what keeps US military/political command from rolling up and packing the tents in Afghan and from totally removing ourselves from Iraq. The roving kiosk operators of war can't bring themselves to close up the deals, or at least, they can't give up the deals until some other massive unaccountable replacement arises for new disguisable deals. Why else would we build a $40 million Khan Bani Saad Correctional Facility in Iraq, at the cost of American taxpayers, to now sit in rubble, never opened, and never to be opened? A deal! Why else would a Defense Department pay a Vienna, Virginia Subcontractor $900 for a control switch valued at $7.05? Deals! Wars mean lots and lots of military/industrial/political deals. Deals for noble hidden, strategic causes, too important and complicated for citizens to concern themselves with—deals! We need wars so that more and more "deals" can feed the perpetually hungry deal-machines and stay in good, fluid deal-making operating systems.)

Stories about the "Third Game" frequently explain why unintended consequences create unintended directions that change lives. Troops can eventually blend with the orders they are given, into the war they are sent to. The "otherworld" of a faraway war becomes the real world for troops on the ground with a new rhythm and soul. Anything outside of that dangerous existence becomes the Third Game and will only get in the way, operationally or mentally, slowing reactions or commitment, squashing the concentrations of very young extended minds in the midst of hot ops.

On the night of April 4, twelve thousand miles around the world from Memphis, with word of the King assassination, Phu Bai exploded. The motel balcony sniper-style murder lit the fuses of America and lit the fuses of individual and small groups of troops who were always left to their own reactions to actions, always sharing Domestic grief. The green flag at the new Phu Bai grand beer tents for the enlisted had gone up late that hot Nam day, and hungry, thirsty, itching dirty troops from all corners of camp headed to the enlisted club at first opportunity to empty a truckload of anything cold, even Ballantine. The club was crowded with marines/army, rural Southerners and urban-ghetto northerners, blacks and whites, and Rollie, with some copter jockeys, who, for some reason, chose the enlisted club that night instead of the Sergeant's Club where they would normally relax in a slightly more civilized style of war's beer slugging.

There was only one reason for the riot that night: The Domestic Nam!

The whole mess, fueled by a couple truckloads of America's nastiest beer in ugly red and gold cans, at about 10:00 p.m. Nam time (if there was a Nam time), turned into a belated, no-win, nasty-ass civil war beer tent brawl. Americans had finally done it, finally created the atmosphere for troops to forget about snipers, forget traps, tunnels and pits, and forget about perimeter probing crawly Gook guys. That night, in honor of Martin Luther King, blessed by rivers of Ballantine, you could fight anything that moved in front of you, friend or foe. Some troops caught in the chaos had not even yet heard of King's assassination and thus had no clue of a building anger as Ballantine empties piled higher and higher through the dirty, hot compressed evening. Fights from inside the tents spread outside, up and around the dirt streets. Some fights spread into the wooden barracks and then wherever the Ballantine's led them.

Rollie had no axe to grind, nor did his crew and thus shoulder to shoulder backed away as best as they could. But others gave no regard for a reason. The brawling mess took no reason, just hate and frustration pouring out cause it needed pouring out. The brawling mess was just a chance to unload some of war's baggage that had collected, and unload they did. Sober, or with Ballantine's, the sight and place was an unruly, unreasoned dangerous mess. Drunk and mad at the world, other or real, in-country or domestic, the fights were simply a different kind of exploding Nam.

For a Nam while, it seemed there would be no end, no way to pull troops apart and take a reasonable chance at a momentary truce. Then, MPs with German shepherd dogs arrived about the time the enlisted club manager could finally get the bar closed, coolers locked up, and a manager dash back behind store room doors. Within an hour of street and tent fighting, enough time had passed where only the toughest bastards at Phu Bai were still squaring off to crowds of circled supporters. With an occasional blind side bashing and new fights erupting on the fringes of the crowds, ugly scenes persisted. Rollie's crew stayed together, showing that anyone intending to throw a punch or wield a knife at one would be throwing a punch at all, a strategy that worked.

Sights of Nam were always unpredictable, unbelievable, always in a transition from some killing action to relatively safe shady places to sit and figure out your day or your next move or what may be right side up or upside down back in the world. But few sights would be remembered as action packed and attention grabbing as a dozen German shepherd MP-trained dogs turned loose on a brawling crowd to break things up. Most Nam troops weren't even aware there was a German shepherd within a thousand miles of Phu Bai, but the animals were there that night. Where they came from, or went to, was always a mystery, with a hanging threat that they could reappear if needed by the MPs. All Rollie and his troops knew was that when the dogs were gone, they were just gone. No one cared why, how, or to where. Hearts could slow their beat. Who gave a damn where the dogs went to, not right here was good enough and all anyone needed to know. Even the toughest of fighting guys can't put on a good fight with a German shepherd headed his way. Instant sobriety spread over the camp like a layer of deep resolute inner prayer. What the hell are we doing—originates with twelve German shepherds running loose—them things gots an attitude! Just turn 'em loose in Charlie-land, and we'll all sit back and get this war over. Rollie had never seen anything like it, never would again, thank goodness.

The night of April 4 was now a strangely different kind of American-made chaos, not only in Memphis and across America into living room televisions and car radios, but the Domestic Nam had struck again, into Phu Bai and many other vulnerable US minds and bases where news would reach unsuspecting troops assigned to war duty in a priority first place. Rollie's orders and the orders for the Purple Fox Outfielders were to get to Quang Tri. The dark isolated helicopter pad would be the night's barrier against the fighting craziness and threats from within Domestic Phu Bai. Quang Tri, back to the war we knew, back to the basics of fly all day, search a shadowy perimeter all night, none of this useless brawling. Hopefully! Surely!

The business of copter flights north to Quang Tri would start with the high hissing sounds of Huey jets firing to life an hour before first light, followed after a short pause of regular Nam stuff, by long blades beginning to thump against the lingering morning still humid air, held in Asia's darkness. Pilots and crews speaking softly and calmly in the early morning, prechaos conversations, checking vital signs, weapons and attitudes, trying to ignore beer tent and depressing street fights that just drug things down another click or two, a decline that didn't even seem possible twenty-four hours ago.

If not too fearful or anxious about the day's missions, early, early morning on the tarmac is the best time to be on a dark warming Asian airstrip, climbing into trusty solid-sounding copters. Once you got used to the war, early morning on the tarmac was kind of homey-comfortable, in a strange way. For those crewmen within nervy control, moments, and things on the early morning tarmac make a little sense, and deep comfortable breaths can be reassuring. Morning preflights are routine, all in a business process that you can see and touch, and be sure that the things you are sitting on, or in, are real, and that your crew is your crew, and they are also committed to the mission you will soon be within. A unified synchronized sharp focus takes over and leads America's morning progress as crews and pilots with an unspoken mutual commitment go through familiar routines, mechanically, as if there is another whole person directing operations, but there isn't that person. The motions have become professionalized instinct. One step at a time, up and in, hook up lifelines, helmet, radio chatter from a controller who may as well be as far away as the moon, signals from outer space, pilot response, lock and load. *Thump, thump, thump,* blade thumps becoming more rapid against the previously still heavy air, announcing the previously silent new day and first adrenaline-driven mission.

In predawn Nam, on a tarmac flickering with small red and yellow pre-flight copter-dash lights shining through side doors and cockpits from all angles, like out of place strobes in a dance hall, adrenaline flows heavier and heavier. Adrenaline instinctively increases in unison with the faster spinning, thumping blades, an unseen dance between the machine and the humans inside. Sometimes, the growing mission confidence also straps angels in with the pilots and crews, if you got 'em, all keeping in sync with the screeching, singing firing up of engine jets and rotor blades busier against the air. It's a small part of the war that actually feels good and confident, and can last about twenty goosebumpy minutes into the lift and lean of the mission start.

> *King's dead, but I'm not. Not gonna be either, not today, even if America itself died a little with King.*
>
> *Feel good today, this day. Feel light and strong, perfect vision and reactions, down to 161 and a wake-up. Keep it together, let the rest be distracted. Bastards won't get me today.*

Quang Tri is too small, people too tight, no time or attitude for King fighting, not there. Lift this puppy, then lean north with the seven other Outfielders, an impressive warring, trained gang of our own, a slit of early morning pink and orange over east between the low clouds and the South China Sea just over my right shoulder.

161, a wake-up, and I'm over that coast for good, the coast I can just barely see in this morning elevation liftoff, or imagine I can see, leaving Phu Bai down there for a while. Just gotta get past Quang Tri one more time, then maybe back to Phu Bai for some milk runs and poker games.

No more enlisted club. Don't need it. Too crazy. No more Ballantine, ever. And no more German shepherds, really—for sure never ever.

Rollie and seven other Purple Foxes slipped into Quang Tri low from the east flat scrub lands stretching to the coast after the short low run north past and around Hue to the east. Hue still stinking from Tet street battles and citadel bodies now melting daily in the sun's heat and along the Perfume. It was April 5, and the Domestic Nam fighting from the King assassination was just beginning in the outer camps that were always a day behind with news and reactions.

There would be no crazed German shepherd chomping machines in Quang Tri, but there was a new guy. His name was Emmerson, Sergeant Terry Emmerson. He would say he was from Norfolk, Virginia, and then the University of Virginia where he became disgusted with ordinary life, and apparently, impulsively joined the Marine Corps. At least, that would be his story. He would be disgusted with "ordinary life," disgusted with fundamental stuff, or ordinary anything. There was nothing "ordinary" about him nor would there ever be. Emmerson vibrated with electric-toxic, super charged quiet cerebral, restrained violence, the poised, clenched type of violence that sends out vibes, warning of extreme cautiousness dealing with this guy.

Rollie, now a sergeant himself, first encountered Emmerson after touching down at Quang Tri from his strung out low formation of the eight Outfielders. Squaring away copter gear and moving toward the edges of the tarmac, to rally up and catch a short- or long-term plan, there Emmerson was. When Rollie first saw him, Emmerson was alone, standing arms folded at the edge of the tarmac now mostly lit from the rising sun. Emmerson's dark black hair framed a beady unresponsive pair of dark roaming eyes, over a hawkish no-nonsense nose that gave incredible accent to his stationary lean face and bold six-foot one-inch presence: Nam personified, an inexplicable piece of human Nam accent. As Rollie and crews moved with gear in that direction, Emmerson patiently watched, with his intense observation sending a strange signal that he was going to be a new part of Quang Tri life for a while.

Nam was full of surprises. Not surprises like in the World, at a surprise party or with a new car or slick hot-babe date kind of surprise. In the World, surprises jump out now and then once a month or weekly and are mostly harmless fleeting moments that fade quickly in search of the next feel good search for a new surprise. Nam surprises were different, could fill a day, one after another. Just walking one hundred yards off the tarmac to a sandbagged command bunker can draw stray mortar or the urgency to help with a passing stretcher on a preflight way to a waiting lipstick. In fact, learning about the surprises was part of it all, part of the survival deal. In Nam, along with the genuine frequent surprises, were the people and spontaneous events to make them happen. Nam human traffic came in all shapes and sizes, all colors, from all parts of America's stretched out geographies, social structures and economies—all thrown together in places like Quang Tri, Con Thien, lost hill tops like 881, mountains and river lowlands, sometimes in the air, other times in the bush, and always on the way from one surprise to the next. Armed, hot, mad, itchy and thirsty, mostly a trigger-happy world of surprises not really knowing who or where a next friendly or enemy surprise was.

Emmerson was a strange, strange instant surprise that needed no introduction as a surprise. Just standing there doing nothing but looking casual, like the last thing he wanted, was to surprise anything. "Characters" in Nam came from nowhere, with no explanations and would likely leave just as mysteriously on the way to someplace else to be a strange, come-from-nowhere surprise. Emmerson had the look of one of those special imposters. He dressed as a marine but with the added weight of a mixed-up inner soul that floated above the daily drudgeries of a war others had to deal and struggle with moment by moment.

Human nature, regardless of rank and duty, divided troops from one another in a natural progression of relationships. Some troops carried fear and desperation on the outside of their dark-green unis and within their nervous bloodstreams. They were to be left alone in their own groups, in their own misfiring ways, except in special circumstances. Fear and desperation begets more desperation in a losing negative cause, where a guy's last "numbers-up" rise from nowhere often.

Some quicker, more agile troops could run between rain drops, aloof to what might or might not happen next, their survival was purely a numbers game.

Other troops just didn't give a damn, about anything. They may as well be cards in a deck to be spent when the time comes in a next deal or a deal tomorrow when the deck has shrunk. To these type troops, an effort to put oneself in a position to *win* was a concept not suspected. Sometimes, it worked out for them; sometimes it didn't, which strangely enough was the summation of their total plan. Fate and reality rested in hands other than their own.

With angels and faith, if you were gonna ride a lucky Nam horse toward a finish line, in a countdown, ride with guys like Emmerson. You could tell instantly! Written all over Emmerson's determined body was there "ain't nothin' gonna" slow him down in a

Virginia-bound countdown, and thus Rollie, now wise from I Corps life, headed straight to him for an introduction and a brief review of what was going on back at Quang Tri while he and the Outfielders were all the way from Con Thien to Phu Bai street fights. Besides, Emmerson was practically the only sign of life on the tarmac sideline that morning, most unusual.

Emmerson had been in Quang Tri one day, just enough time to look around, check the river on the northwest boundary, check the bunker lines and the road in, past a flimsy guard gate with focused young marines pointing weapons east to Highway 1 just half a click. He gathered a quick feel and perspective on where things were, including troop bunks, tents, and perimeter line foxholes and the airbase small ammo dump. Then, he heard about a near fatal prenight crash landing of an Air Force fighter jet that had been shot up and did a controlled crash landing right there at Quang Tri. The pilot managing a controlled crashing because they needed more runway than a copter pad with C-130s now and then had for a Nam style F-4 out of Da Nang. The F-4 pilot, a captain, had survived, according to Emmerson. Emmerson had showed up an hour after the incident, landing with some passing copter crew who were probably glad to unload him, then they immediately took off. To Rollie, there was no good reason for Emmerson to be there, but there he was!

One other strange Nam thing had happened just before the time Emmerson showed up in Quang Tri. A squad size unit of twelve, in a bad-ass Marine Reconnaissance team had showed up, rolled in from the western badlands, from across the river, and taken over a small strategic vacant spot in the middle of the small base, right up tight to a tarmac corner. Twelve of them in total, two were handcuffed and had been placed in a temporary instant brig at the tarmac edge. The handcuffed marines were placed in a steel container with an open front and a sand front porch, as if a makeshift jail. Rumor soon spread that the two handcuffed marines had been captured by American Recon friendlies for the second time—that the two had gone rogue since December, four months ago, when they broke away from another Recon team patrolling westerly into Laos along the Ho Chi Minh trail, dropped in by silver Air America props. According to Emmerson, more and more appearing to be an official source on everything, the two of them solely instigated and implemented multiple hit-and-run operations all up and down the notorious trail, blasting Gook caravans, stealing weaponry, and blowing up more Gooks from up north heading south, basically completely terrorizing enemy stuff that US general command had avoided or could not seem to organize. The "traditional" war didn't interest these two guys. Perhaps it was not actively violent or productive enough. Apparently, from their perspective, the war was overmanaged, with 90 percent of in-country troops moving gear in some compound logistic facility, operational rear.

Emmerson seemed to know all about it, while he observed the temporary holding cell from a distance, just like he had observed Rollie and crews landing and walking off the tarmac in his direction that early morning. More immediate issues gripping Quang Tri for the moment had to be dealt with immediately. The Americanized virus of King Assassin-fighting had also reached Quang Tri, in news of Phu Bai street fighting turned to riots, advancing to stories of fraggin' incidents, made-up or real. The small camp expected a rough fighting racial night of some sort, either within the perimeter or from the post-Tet outside lines in Gook-country. Emmerson mumbled to Rollie he would not let stupid worthless fights happen. Whatever that meant. Rollie wondered if his luck could be any worse.

Turned out the two rogue Recon boys were a couple of overgrown, overmuscled, hay-seed yea-hoos from Arkansas, Fletcher and Steube. Busted in rank so many times they were perpetual privates and perpetually pissed at everything. Fletcher was built as thick as an Arkansas grain bin, Steube leaner, taller, meaner looking. Both of them had deep Nam style anger and rage written all over them, carrying bad-ass "nasty" in place of any angel as a third unseen partner in their spontaneous roving to kill bad-guy improvised missions. Along with everything else at Quang Tri, (Emmerson, Recon devils) a chaos tension different from Phu Bai had built-up inside the perimeter. Unpredictable opposing influences had gathered in their aggravating million-to-one Nam way of doing so, poised to a Nam surprise, waiting to surprise the whole Quang Tri camp.

If Marine Corps Commandant soldier-makers had ever constructed two marines more violent and aggressive appearing than Fletcher and Steube, those human products had been kept isolated as specimens to study, not released, ever. Trapped in their temporary cage cell, the two wreaked of anger, death, and calculating destruction. With a glance, you knew, they were in Nam to die and would keep killing until they met their goal. No one would even approach them for a comment, let alone an introduction, dare not hand one a canteen. Emmerson simply checked once in a while to see if they were still there. The two recon marines, captives in a captive camp of a captive domino war, squatted Nam-style like the Gooks they tracked and killed as much of a part of the rugged landscape as the burning sun and blowing sand around them. Neither looked up, hardly moved, truly caged, cagey animals. Both captives squatted, quiet, aware, not wasting energy in a premature effort of reacting to their pause of a captive situation. Handcuffed, isolated, Fletcher and Steube still gave a weird outward impression, that time and everything Nam was on their side.

Fletcher and Stuebe had no "otherworld," no homes, no countdown, let alone a concern for a wakeup. They lived their own private "Third Game," a world not to be understood by any others. Their lives had committed to the jungles a few clicks west, a border with Laos, any other border did not exist. The world was borderless to them. For whatever reason, or events, fleeting elements drove them to that violent mentality into those mountains as deep as they could blend, the real world left out of their plans. Officers, structure, and orders left out at some point in their Nam world. Their "Third Game" was easy. They'd kill as many Asian enemies as they could get close to before dying themselves in their singular cause. Simple plan, except they had this little temporary incarceration thing to deal with, again. This was the second time they had been captured by Americans for being "too violent" in the establishment's proxy war, where violence is good, to a point, and there was no red line of what exactly "too violent" was. A soldier trained and put in a fight, all violenced up, at some point was supposed to put some violence away, then keep other stuff violent. A soldier's individual Nam red line!

Rollie and the Purple Fox Outfielders soon learned, also from Emmerson, that the Air Force F-4 pilot had been shot up on a fast low attack mission to drive back NVA at a firebase 448 to the Southwest several clicks. With Da Nang too far to make a shot-up run, the coast also a click too far, Captain Trigger, made an air race scamper, fighter plane dash style, for the short strip at Quang Tri where he would at least have a chance to crash land with friendlies around, cut engines to drop and float in, touched, heavy metal braked, and backfired before crashing off the north end of the short runway into the safety sand berm piled as high as a Seabee end-loader could stretch. All went as well as expected in a threatening run for the roses of life, at least for a while. Trigger emerged practically unscathed from the awkward skid of a barely controlled crash landing, took an aircraft inventory, radioed some bunker-buddy somewhere, gathered a breath and a 45-caliber side arm, and checked out his new surroundings as tarmac regulars of QT came running to see if he was human and to see the first and only Air Force Fighter Jet to ever land on a remote runt hideout helicopter strip like Q T. Trigger simply pronounced, "No hill for a climber," pretty much all in a Nam/F-4 day of "believe all the stories." He swaggered on through camp regulars as if on his way for an ice cream, with an outward attitude of almost enjoying the landing challenge. Government Air Force plane or no plane, Captain Trigger's priority would be to catch a ride out, most ricky tick if he could, off to his next County Fair Air Show.

Night's darkness swirled in with broken low scattered clouds, and more word of the Phu Bai fights, riots, and dogs from hell reached through the ranks of the small remote base and airstrip of Quang

Tri. The million to one composition of nervous circumstances were mounting, again:

> *Emmerson came in from nowhere, also apparently on a strange Nam breeze, as no one could actually recall having him aboard.*
>
> *Captain Trigger roared in on an F-4 jet from another planet.*
>
> *Fletcher and Steube were "American POW's," held by and around American soldiers, who observed their bravery and determination with fearful admiration and wondered why the whole US command was not like them.*
>
> *The Outfielders had landed at the tail-end of a mission that started over a week ago up in Con Thien saving some marines, losing others on a long lost hill to be abandoned when it would be determined enough had occurred, all while the general camp population had fought through lingering Tet perimeter probes and attacks and were weary and tense for the unknown "next" of the Nam.*
>
> *The whole multi-layered scene now peppered with more unexplainable Domestic Nam news of a King assassination and hometown riots burning over forty cities across the "US Otherworld."*

Twenty-three African American marines loudly began to roam Quang Tri's dirt street-ways, four or five to a group, showing their stuff, making sure everyone was aware that a racist Southern bastard had shot and killed King, who was now their revered hero, and that they were no longer willing to be held in the grip of America's class war where some squeaky cracker general sends black boys off to fight a proxy war.

The crap in Domestic Nam just never stopped in the Defining Year. Fighting a hit and miss guerilla war against faceless enemies was enough of a winless reality. Then, always without notice, the Domestic snuck into the minds and angers, first like hot knives to the guts and then like balls and chains, or handcuffs.

This particular ensuing explosive outburst would potentially be small, more personal than at Phu Bai. As the Quang Tri dusk turned to early dark, marines settling into their places feeling strangely alert, some soldiering price was again going to be paid by some unsuspecting dupe just trying to do a job and survive. Louder noises from the camp's east end raised anxieties. These noises were away from the tarmac, coming from where the twenty-three blacks of Quang Tri frequently gathered in small groups in and out of their two-tent conclave that should have never been allowed, a small black neighborhood unto its own. Men separate and divided in their personal Domestic Nam war, just like any other mixed race small US civilian community, except there was nothing civilian about Quang Tri.

Rollie and the Outfielders settled into their ten-man tents, just west of the two tents where the blacks were.

Pilots gathered at the CO's bunker and map room at the far Southwest corner of camp, so far away from the enlisted that unless in the air, one never even knew the pilots were a part of camp life.

Fletcher and Steube squatted, peered left, then right, then down, powerfully silent in their inner planning and inner ticking.

Trigger would just wait the one night out before being picked up by the Air Force CH-54 flying city to be spiffed back to Da Nang for new F-4 digs. In the meantime, he'd mosey on out to his lost forever, past familiar partner F-4 machine for one last checklist and affectionate, thankful pat on the wing.

Five loud, black marines strode through camp showing attitude stuff, threatening, and eventually out on to the stark, empty tarmac, not particularly going anywhere, just moving with a strange Nam energy because the energy had to be dealt with, and the domestic anger had to be dealt with. That's when the trouble seeking group saw Trigger, down there, alone at the crash site, checking fuel lines, kicking landing gear, clicking things off for a second time. No one had a chance to know Trigger; he was just dumped in Nam on a way through proxy-war-life, just like everybody else on the Quang Tri scene or in America, for that matter. No one knew if Trigger had a family or what state he was from, where he went to school, or what baseball team he followed. No one even ever knew his first name, not even Emmerson knew anything about Trigger, other than with that out of place plane stuck in the sand at the end of a small landing site which may as well have been at the end of Trigger's world. Quang Tri knew he made a helluva gutsy landing, and Emmerson apparently saw no need of resource management attention to a pilot who made a magic landing and could obviously take care of himself, generally. Trigger was merely a passing war implement, just like everyone else, a twentieth century late '60s flying Hessian. If asked, the guys at Quang Tri later thought that Trigger was about thirty-two years old, but no one ever knew. No one even knew if he was married, if he had a family.

A slight fuss-up of distant voices from the landing pads drew a little attention at the Outfielders tents, but not much. A few Outfielders noticed the five threatening, wandering black marines when they first swaggered by, cock sure of their intimidating, unfriendly impressions, and noticed them again post-haste, back across the sand and road to the edge of the tarmac for that one post-King night. But no one heard a shot or a loud cry for help or anything that seemed a fight or like anger from a confrontation. Everyone's attention was poised to the long night ahead; if just one night could pass without fights and disruption, Quang Tri would have a chance to settle in, get back to the more controlled violence of general warring as usual. That evening, Rollie wouldn't even be in the tent, too restricting, too visionless. He knew better. He knew fraggin' could and does happen. For a salty marine, on these nights, stay with your weapon and angel, stay outside, pay attention. Notice everything.

The small roving mobilized sentry of camp MPs found Trigger's dead body lying bloody under his F-4 on their first round of night-checks of all things tarmac. Beaten and dead from multiple knife wounds in the torso, perhaps the most useless American death of the whole Nam proxy deal. Senseless, pure evil destruction and the trail was back to the two tents where Quang Tri's self-deployed blacks had gathered and were humping their stuff to the tunes of a far off, irrelevant Detroit. The camp fuse had been lit. MPs had no choice and eagerly gathered their very small numbers to follow the obvious.

It wasn't for Trigger that the lines became drawn that night, nobody knew who Trigger was. He almost seemed unreal, like a ghost visiting with an unsaid message, then disappearing, snatched away, like some sort of symbol of something good and brave to be shown, then dashed away and destroyed, because that's what Nam is for, destroying things, good and brave, or bad.

Once again, the real faceless instigator was the constant anger in Nam, often imported from stateside, the constant buildup of frustration to fight whatever seemed to need fighting, day by day, with no weekends or holidays to pause in perspective or even pause to breath a few times free from some alarm going off. There was no baseball World Series to unofficially mark a passing of a season, no college football weekends, no fishing trips to trout streams, and no family weddings or reunions. It was always just the next damn fight. With the mobility of Nam's inventive helicopter corps, the next fight could be found anywhere. Troops no longer had to march and position themselves for days or weeks to get to a next fight. Huey's had you and your buddies in the next fight, in any direction, on any day, at the whim of any order barking radio from some far off bunkered Officer studying a map and processing reported rumors of enemy movements. The next fight was as close as the next need for a KIA/WIA report to feed a restless PR machine whose main job had become fending off the anti-war movement by justifying the insanity of Nam.

A few more of the Quang Tri black troops swaggered out and around their tents, armed, and then a fight broke out with a few

Outfielders outside their tents, Outfielders too savvy to sit in a tent unaware of outside motions and threats. Punches and threats, more lines drawn, and Detroit rhythm and blues got louder at the camp's edge as if to supply more false inspiration to some evil atmosphere, a long night of unpredictable self-destruction ahead. Rollie soon realized Phu Bai had followed him here, just like Khe Sanh had followed him to Con Thien.

> *Getting to be a bad habit flying into new battles all the time, must find a way to shake that whole collective nature. Odds could get short, run out. Pretty soon, the rabbit is you.*

A few lines formed among the whites looking back at the lines of the blacks about their tents, whose eyes were formed together as one glare, looking at the white's tents—a thick slightly lit greasy air in between. The staring standoff controlling the moment, and the slow awkward clicks of time crawled like a lit fuse. Without an outside influence of any unexpected nature, this was the standoff, waiting for a first shot or first frag or first challenge, first anything.

Time stood still. Silence held the camp. Tents, lines, clouds, appearing stars held the evening, only broken by the sound of a faint click. Then, another hardly recognizable click. Then another barely noticeable click. Click, click, click, the sound of safeties being clicked off weapons.

Emmerson came up the middle on the white's side, appearing from the now dark tarmac in the far background. He was alone. He measured the whole scene, paused, and walked slowly halfway across the short open space toward the gathered blacks, head down, long arms dangling as if useless to a cause, all things on both sides came to a deeper dead silence, passing clouds stopped. No one moved as the face-off paralyzed Quang Tri for that moment, on that day, in that proxy war, among those two groups of Americans. A few of the blacks sported false-looking grins, streetfight dares, hate pouring out and around where there was no hate just three days ago when King was alive on the other side of the planet. Threatening black grins aside, Emmerson was in charge of the moment, in charge of the whole camp right then, in charge of his Third Game. Emmerson stared the blacks all the way back into an uneasy silence of fake courage caught off guard with his out of place, unexpected bold presence:

> *You boys hang loose, right there, gather up your rocks and sticks—jabber up all the courage you can. I'll be right back and we'll dance to that Detroit jumbo. Give a couple minutes, be right back. You hear me? I'll be right back, be right there with ya! You won't have to wait long.*

Sheepishly grinning blacks, caught off guard, uncertain, encouraged by pack numbers, silently grinned to Emmerson's back as his suspicious stature disappeared back toward camp's darkness, into the direction from which he had just arrived, toward where the edge of the tarmac used to be.

Sometimes, it is better for power to be more suspected than known. Men of vision and strength are few. Their depth of goodness depends on the men of hunger and strength to follow signals that are not always clearly before them to follow. Sometimes, the signals are instinct; sometimes, spiritual and angelically unexplainable, must be felt, not reasoned, especially in a Third Game, when it gets to the human trenches of a proxy war that always operates on instinct and guts, not reason or logic.

No one had a clue what would happen next, except of course for Emmerson. The whole scene became tensely frozen in a strange limbo of building forces and strange hope of a calm solution for some or a fighting face off for the few others. Like the force of a strange magnet, most everyone now suddenly knew there was a way out of the night's chaos and stupidity. Not one marine understood the flow they were within. They couldn't understand. No one knew

Emmerson well enough to understand, and no one would ever know Nam well enough.

Ten minutes was an eternity with lines still drawn as opposing forces, too much time to keep checking weapons. There were no more clicks; everything was already clicked. The enemy was no longer within the guerilla war. Now it was a streetfight. So be it!

Would Emmerson really return, or was he just back there in the dark watching, a strange sergeant-dude, no authority over anything, only command over it all. He's probably back there in the dark flow-charting and figuring the percentages of likely scenarios, versus the likelihood of various small arms firing angles.

White marines gathered weapons and held lines, black isolated marines bulled-up around their two tents and leaned on sandbagged walls as if on front porches to pick off an opposing drive-by. Not an officer in sight, nor was one expected.

Quiet uneven jabber on the white side sporadically silenced. Past the bunkers and tents, on the tarmac side of the road, came three dark shadows, a good aggressive pace about them as if going to a fight, weaponry silhouettes and shadows hanging from shoulders and long powerful arms. Still mostly in the shadows, merging into the middle of the drawn white's line was a mass of muscle and hate named Fletcher, stoic Emmerson in the middle and, lanky arms waving for a fight, Steube on the other flank of the moving violent missionaries, night-shiny with aggressive prefight tension and sweat, lit with evil practiced prefight grins. The three human grim reapers practically bounced to the center of the night's tensions.

Emmerson gathered up the white side to leave strict orders:

We'll move across the open, take those marines into their tents and put this whole useless mess to bed for the night. Lock and load, you hear one shot, or a fight, level the place—these two bastards are walking dead on their way to brig hell anyway. I'll take care of myself!

Emmerson, Fletcher, and Steube moved out into the open space between the lines of Americans, moved across the space, right up to the sandbagged walls around the two tents into the middle of the waiting, now quiet blacks, caught totally off guard, and the mixed group went inside the two tents, Detroit's best rhythm and blues wasted sounds immediately off.

Silence! More silence! Ten, twelve, fifteen, now twenty minutes of silence in a steady pressing evening darkness, when a couple tent flaps flew back, signaling some sort of potential progress. Emmerson emerged, still loaded with weaponry, backed across the open space, and told the tense white troops the night was all over, stand down, stay put, stay alert, but stay put, click safeties on.

This was Domestic Nam, heavy, heavy tense Domestic Nam on a violent perch, prepared to violently leap at a slightest next click or uncertain quick reaction. Human baggage, more surprise baggage for troops to carry. Baggage impossible to unload at the wake-up and journey east to the World for those who survived skirmishes, firefights, night attacks, and surprises. Nam was piling it on.

Emmerson disappeared toward the tarmac and command bunkers. Rollie hopped up and out, over his sandbagged fortress, caught up to Emmerson's angered side, now in a quickened cadence stride to any direction that would put his mysterious influence away from the confrontation for the moment. The enlisted camp took a simultaneous deep breath. MPs guarded Trigger's wasted body. Emmerson and Rollie leaned back on a pair of sand filled fifty-five-gallon oil drums on the edge of the tarmac, under the South Vietnamese skies of scattered rolling cloud cover, decorated with twinkling stars between the clouds heaven's bigger stars now beginning to show to the night's business. Rollie soon remembered and, at the same time, noticed the empty holding cell of the two nasty asses from Arkansas, Fletcher and Steube. Everyone seemed to forget they were with Emmerson across the drawn lines into the black's tents.

> *Rollie: Sergeant Emm, what'd you do with those two crazy sonsabitches from Arkansas?*

Emmerson's ever present sly hawkish side glance, never committing to a face:

> *Sergeant Emm: Well, I didn't have much to work with, you may have noticed I was gonna be outnumbered. As soon as they saw Fletcher and Steube, I think they figured they were the ones outnumbered. So I made a quick trade. I traded two bad ass mules from Arkansas for a little peace and quiet tonight. After the mess cleared up a bit, Fletch said they'd just stay and guard things up good for the night. I thought it might come to that, so I cleared it with the Recon First Louie. Had to clear it or he wouldn't unlock 'em, couldn't get 'em out, then I'd be that outnumbered thing.*
>
> *Rollie: Emm, they're prisoners, headed for a trial and the brig for sure.*
>
> *Sergeant Emm: Exactly! Oh, I'll go get 'em in the morning. Things'll be calmer then. Besides, the Recon First Louie said without that baggage, they'd just move on out, right yet tonight, probably gone already, got recon'n to do. It was just a trade to him. A real war goin' on out there, ya know, hard to remember sometime with all the in-fighting crap. Recon is important, doesn't have time for, not built for prisoner keepin'. Just seemed like a big win*

for everybody. I knew that black marine bunch over there wanted nothing to do with Fletch and Steube—who would—you should have seen their eyes and expressions when we were walking up to 'em. I knew right away the thing was over.

On the morning of April 6, Trigger was a lost passing ghost of some unexplainable vision, choppered out on the CH-54 he had ordered up for himself before he knew his final journey, or time, like ordering your own funeral to begin. No one ever knew what his first name was or if he had a family. Blacks buddied back up with the whites they generally liked in the first place. Everyone in the entire Quang Tri camp acted like they had never heard of, seen, or talked about two guys from Arkansas named Fletcher and Steube who had plum disappeared in the night and were probably halfway back up into the hills and already near their own personal war target of favorite choice, the Ho Chi Minh Trail. Emmerson leaned on the command bunker, still observing it all, all to himself, within himself, all tidy with his own thoughts and plans.

Nam! Believe all the stories!

The Nam/Proxy/Domino war from Quang Tri didn't change much through April or early May. Outfielders mounted up, usually in the dark early mornings. When they weren't actually mounting up, they hung on the pad, with their birds and each other, waiting for mount-up orders from the next radio jabbers and emerging pilots from a command bunker with a mount-up pace to their steps. Everybody else in the camp made it possible for birds to launch when the launch was ordered. By Tet standards, things became normal and quiet. A few mortars and rockets now and then kept marines diving behind sandbag walls and into bunkers. Good ole red flaring tracers through the front door and down Main Street stirred things up now and then. Idle marines created stupid games and fantasies as idle soldiers of all types tend to do. Dimly lit poker games became a necessity for the naturally social, didn't matter to some who won or who lost, nothing to spend piasters on anyway. The exception to that were the hard core poker savvy, within whom winning was a point of priority and personal pride. Those guys cared who won or lost and generally cleaned the enlisted camp on a regular payday-oriented schedule and were almost respected for their skills to do so.

All kinds and sorts of characters flew in and out of Quang Tri's tight air space, stopped for a while or didn't, including Emmerson, who, when in camp, would go see Rollie so they could sit in the dark of a night tarmac. Always night restless, leaning on Huey runners, Emmerson would talk about reorganizing the Marine Corps logistic standard of operations for battalion relocations or about specific numbers of troop deployments into strategic bottle necks of enemy threats or about the unique blind ostriches in Congress pretending to run things for some subjective good of some subjective cause but more than likely just lining their own pockets with war's unwatched and intractable wrap-arounds. Emmerson would mention Laos. The best way to get there and back, to take a look, was with Air America cowboys. Rollie was twenty years old, twenty, trying to embrace his ever shifting wide, wide world.

Occasionally, the two would speculate about the possibility of Fletcher and Steube still being alive, walking through the main gate, right down Quang Tri's Main Street, with Uncle Ho's head on a bamboo pole. Or placing bets on how many Gook KIA's occurred in their transplanted Arkansas trails of their own personal war, KIAs that would never be heard about or suspected, except for within the remote suspended families across the DMZ, north to the China border.

"Ya think those two destruction war machines are still alive?"

"Would command send more recon missions to find and bring them back, again?"

"It's a war. Why can't we just let them be? They seem to get it!"

"There must be two Arkansas families that have no idea that (think) Fletch and Steube are in some tight unit, following strict orders. Moms, dads, sisters, grandmas, probably waiting for a word. They have to live. The movie would be too good for them not to live and tell their story and show the deep human feelings that drove the story to such bizarre behaviors."

"Can you imagine those two guys back in the World? No, they have to die here! The World couldn't possibly get it!"

Emmerson seemed to report each day to a small half leaning shack by the tarmac, concerning himself mostly with some sort of lost supply chain, and then he'd fly out and disappear again for a few days. But generally, a cot in a hot damp bunker had his name on it for a while. Now friends with all the whites and the blacks, Emmerson carried a strange sort of celebrity around with him. He concerned himself with all passing grunt units who held up and fed for a day at Quang Tri, as if any information was valuable to process in some major plan of action unassociated with anything in normal Marine Corps channels. Every passing trivial piece of info was of interest to Emmerson. Other camp marines never tried to know or understand him. They just nodded and observed, extending some sort of vague nod of appreciation for keeping everyone from killing each other on April 6.

Quang Tri enlisted, displaced humans as they felt and were, also appreciated Emmerson's maneuvers to arrange for the escape of the good ole boys from Arkansas. Through Emmerson, everything had a link, all was good, or good enough, or as good as it gets for Quang Tri, post Tet, twelve thousand miles around the frickin' earth. When the small things were touchable and understandable, it was temporarily good enough. Quang Tri's veteran marines rotated out; they all came to see Emmerson as they departed, if he were around. New marines into Quang Tri got the story and stayed a distance from Emmerson. They didn't have to stay a distance. Emmerson was friendly enough, but he let the mystique live unaltered with the new guys.

Rollie's deal with HMM-364 was simple. He would volunteer to go north to the Quang Tri, stuck out vulnerable outpost near DMZ hell, and in return, having spent his time and term, could be replaced by some other brainless, fearless Schmuck headed to I Corps "war-ocracies." Rollie would then return to Phu Bai, which now would be almost like returning to some new kind of civilization, like the "World" compared to Quang Tri life. In fact, considering Khe Sanh and Con Thien, Quang Tri is to Phu Bai as Phu Bai is to Louisville, Kentucky, quantum leaps of civilization, minus babes or lipsticks of any kind. Emmerson said he was headed to Phu Bai as well. He could now be mysterious someplace else, in a bigger camp, where mysterious would not be so noticed. Late May, rather than ask, Rollie informed S-4, he'd catch an Outfielder ride to Phu Bai, find a sergeant's hooch and report soon. Emmerson simply disappeared one morning as usual. A strange Virginian fellow, the kind of guy you go to war with or you want across the table in an eight-man game of poker with six strangers.

Phu Bai was a step up in the world by any Marine Corps SE Asia War standards. Everything but white women hustled about the dusty tent, wooden barracks, and jeep-filled place. Phu Bai had a PX, in a big green tent, with American soap and toothpaste for trade, more water buffaloes for a splash and shave, big long open mess halls in big green tents, with cooks, hundreds of outhouses, offices in big green tents with typewriters, and even a concrete basketball court with a couple balls and bench weights alongside, as if those Phu Bai boys needed extra ways to exercise. In another big green tent was a medical clinic you could just walk right into, without an airlift medevac through small arms ground fire. There were tables and chairs, decks of cards, and the bars, in big green tents were still there, an O Club, a Top Sergeants Club, and a Sergeants Club, and the lowest rank Enlisted Club. Sometimes they had drinks; sometimes they didn't. If you actually ran one of the clubs, were the army's proprietor, you were a very popular human being, very popular indeed, the world-at-your-fingertips kind of popular. Tops ran the clubs. Connected Tops!

Bars with alcohol at Phu Bai, post Tet, late May-ish, represented the kind of distanced command decision that creates another type of unforeseen Third Game and can instigate all kinds of unintended secondary consequential forces into motion. The new Phu Bai enlisted bar, regrouped after the fights and riots of April 4, and in some brilliant supply officer/politician—military/industrial minds was still apparently intended to provide a little alcoholic spinmeistering to the worn troops of the camp, to the stupid surrogates in the fight, and to the more common base support rummies who twisted in the wind with any order coming down an uncertain pike-way. One unintended consequence was that, previous to the Phu Bai enlisted BAR and sergeant's tented bar, troops had absolutely no place to spend any money, which would arrive monthly from the US Treasury as good ole American style paychecks. (Explain the concept of "payday" to a Vietnamese peasant some time.)

Paychecks are another domestic reality. They make sense in the World, but paychecks on a dirtbag base with not a single US product in sight to purchase or an American female to entertain create only an illusory suspected connection based on memory and a dim view of war's realities that has no factual connection to economics. Nevertheless, paydays rolled around, had a place on the slow-moving calendars, and actually occurred just like in the movies. Dirt worn troops lined up outside a tent, slowly processed to their turn to the front of the payday line, then an about-face and reappeared in the sun with a handful of something to count for the moment.

Most troops had some sort of personal cash flow element from their paychecks, even though many sent most, or all, of their paycheck money home. Single guys—who represented 90 percent of the troop population because married guys were regularly draft deferred—had no balance between payday, judgment, and vision of a future. But you could convert US paychecks to Vietnamese currency, "piasters," and thus create a personal illusion of good ole US-style commerce within a weird unofficial subeconomy. When you have troops of all shapes, sizes, colors, educations, and backgrounds, with a little money in their pocket they have to find a use for it of some sort, just to keep the process Americanized.

At Phu Bai on payday, for many enlisted, the use of their money took on two forms, the Ballantine beer tent Club or maverick-style poker games. (The beer tents were easier to find than the poker games.) Every two weeks at the time of payday poker games would organize. The most prolific of those games was often the gathering at the S-4 Logistics office at Phu Bai, which is where Rollie Cahill would land after his rotation from Quang Tri. S-4 poker hosts would clear the normal war office material in late afternoon of payday for the night's poker tournament event, ever networked and popular in enlisted circles. Games would shuffle up about dusk. Someone inventively would always have some new decks of cards and those not on some US essential war mission, in the air or on the ground or out in the bush, could try their poker playing luck among "friendlies."

Other than the marine green uniforms and insignias of rank, the whole picture could have just as easily been the Wild West. The payday poker games were collections of United States enlisted from anywhere and everywhere, all backgrounds, some knowing the game of poker a little, some just curious, and then of course the silent, see-everything sharks of the game who had likely long ago, pre-Nam, honed the finest of poker's skill-sets as well as the table conversation to go along with the actual skills of card selection, card handling, and most importantly, betting strategies. Many others new to the game and believing poker game winning and losing has mostly to do with "luck" also could not wait to participate in the manly arts of deals, bets, raises, bluffs, and victoriously scraping pot winnings to their side of the makeshift table. Each pay period attracted thirty-five to forty enlisted around the S-4 highly reputed regular games. By 6:00

p.m., games would be forming with cock-sure guppies and sharks circling for the action, six to eight players per table, often five or more tables, and the mostly sober games would begin. Generally, five or seven card stud, sometimes high-low split pots, in the early going kept the games simple so the guppies weren't overchallenged to try their payday luck and potentially retire too early before "all-in" with their paychecks.

If you were attached to one of the units at Phu Bai, or were stationed at a rocket belt firebase, or further away at Quang Tri, and you were a good-to-excellent poker player, you wanted to chopper back to Phu Bai for at least the first night of payday card-sharking, when the easiest pickings wondered into the games for their lessons first and payday spanking second. Most soldiers would play until they were broke or actually owed some slight IOUs from a hand they just couldn't fold, IOUs that would never be called, and then, they would drop out into the night and scuffle off wondering what just happened. By late evening, the number of soldier-gamblers would be about sixteen to twenty, down from an original fortyish players, the rest having departed so-what broke, often surprisingly proud of their token mechanical efforts, generally just one-card flop away from a winning breakthrough and change of luck to an imagined streak of upside. Just unlucky that night, that's all. Play became more vigorous deep into the night, as another eight to twelve middle profile players perfected different ways of losing, became broke, and shuffled bad-luck-faced frowns back to their hooch and tents, trying to figure out the bottom line business of card lessons just extended, swearing to a better performance next payday.

A second night, now post payday, is where a player wanted to be. By then, everyone remaining at the table was a solid winner, easily in hundreds, some perhaps with a thousand or two of winnings if they had the right first night table, the lucky table populated with the most guppies. Everyone still in the games the second night had shared the pay checks of those compelled to take the chance to learn the games the first night, and now long gone.

On the third night, post payday, those still playing were now entirely spending, or betting other people's money and the games became gutsier, wild, bluff-ridden, stone-cold mechanical serious, most sober, and the card table language elevated. Not mad serious as in tempers, but professional money-making mad serious, as final players had a real chance to make enough to buy a home in the United States, if tastes weren't too high. Any player who survived to be in the third night's poker gaming would likely be winning a few thousand. The games took hours, each evening, in a winner-take-all, balls-to-the-wall focused intensity.

What war? Enemy incoming, mortar or rocket attacks causing camp lighting blackouts signaled by screaming camp sirens—no problem, you simply take the entire card table and chairs out into the dirt street and finished the hand by the light of flares illuminating other folks all dutied up in the war that night and hopefully defending the camp. Deal with the next flare, bet in the middle of flares lighting the night with quick calls or quicker folds, and determine a winner by more flares.

Not enough incoming—no flares? Hands off until the sound of incoming rockets echo away, gone in the distance, and the war is over for a while. The flares are put away by the flare boys, another siren to put the camp lights back on, and tables are moved back inside—all seamlessly routine as a fire drill at your local grade school. Players expected such interruptions as a part of I Corps warring inconveniences and the games went on. It was Phu Bai's underworld. There may have been other Phu Bai underworlds, but this underworld was one well-run poker playing operation. Halfway around the planet, there's not a better feeling than walking into the poker game the first night and having thirty or more card-sick buddies give you a respectable nod of poker playing "howdy." No one seemed to pay any attention to the games except those who played and lost, those who wanted to play next time, and the sharks that always played, and almost always were there in the third night. Always the same guys who couldn't wait to see who would wonder in, new and curious about something to do on payday, like "gym rats" at home who attract the "shooters" and other "gym rats."

The new bar at Phu Bai virtually ruined or certainly damaged all of that payday poker playing constructive rivalry. Suddenly, soldiers had a different place to throw away their pay checks, and they did. First night payday poker games that would normally draw forty players, on six to eight tables, suddenly started with sixteen or eighteen on three tables. In retrospect, the goody officers/politicians who would never set a clean foot in a dirty Nam had no idea of the unintended consequence of their new two-tent enlisted Phu-bar. The enlisted bar alone would cost the good poker players of Phu Bai thousands in winnings, as all the truly untrained poker players, the real losers of the bunch, the guppies, would now go slosh beer until they could hardly walk, instead of playing poker and disbursing their pay to the truly hard at work talented poker pros. Phu Bai poker games were a just, redistribution of revenue til the bars came along. The sudden competition for honest paycheck-taking was like breaking up a synchronized quasi-subsociety all slicked down with war's accoutrements.

The winners knew what they were doing, played and won as they had always played to win, and prospered. What was right was right. The losers were actually doing the same thing they had always done, World or in Nam—losing. Get minor paychecks, blow the money on something, and survive in Nam while waiting for the next minor paycheck. The only difference now was that, in the process of blowing their paychecks in a first-class, well-run, synchronized rocket attack adaptable poker contest, the fun loving guppies were acquiring enormous drunk-ocity, preparing for the enormous dawn headache, all in a quite active War Zone. In addition, the enlisted bars experienced some sort of punch-out fights about every night. No one ever got punched or cold-cocked at the S-4 poker tables. Which makes more sense? The entire base was actually much better off before the bars, but leave it to the officers, untrained in I Corps warring and poker games, and the politicians to screw up the common sense and natural tendencies of American field-ingenuity and organizational skills, poker playing style.

> *Somehow, somewhere up the ranks, those in charge and pulling the strings knew pouring container loads of beer and alcohol into the war zone was, in the end, not good for the soldiers or the war. The supply side wraparounds on the business end must have just been too juicy to apply common sense over kick-back greed.*

Poker games on payday have been traditional soldier activities since the early fifteenth century, or so the "come-play with us" rumor insists: a proud tradition, a right of remote soldiering in the caverns and confines and corners of "Otherworlds." In fact, the better I Corps players failing to find ways by helicopter back to a main base on payday would gather one, two, or three other marines wherever the urge and cards struck, across a cot, along some sandbags, or in a candled bunker, just to keep the guppies happy. Nam's stories are often of such creative, phenomenal salesmanship and teller ambitiousness that it is hard to actually decide what was fact, although what was fact, in the end, really didn't matter.

Rollie Cahill, now a sergeant, fit into Phu Bai life like a knife to its sheath. Mostly out of the air, days in Phu Bai had a semblance of a civilized work day routine, except unlike jobs back in the World, the war did not take weekends off nor did the days have much of a clock. Rollie's youthful background had honed his physical skills and his poker skills, having at a very young age become a poker playing regular among the much older kids with whom he was a traveling teammate in American Legion baseball games all over North Carolina and the mid-Atlantic. In fact, Rollie could describe his moment of his poker playing breakthrough in a basement in his home town. At thirteen years old, Rollie normally played poker with townies seventeen or eighteen or older. Losing tobacco walking money for a few weeks in a row during the summer of '60, Rollie hit a stride that would carry him through poker-Nam. He never forgot the day or the moment and could clearly describe the sensation:

I'd played poker with these same older guys, day after day, pretty much each late afternoon and evening, after I got out of the fields from weeding tobacco or soybean fields, baling hay, or some other menial physically draining local farm job. It was always the same basement, Mullvain's on Market Street, the same guys, all older, smarter, more poker poised. Back in those days, in that summer 1960, I was the guppy. But I learned. I looked through the game just like I had learned to do on the baseball field—look through the game, past the obvious— see inside the moves and strategies. Know where the ball is going to be. I kept losing hard earned tobacco walking money, which seemed a shame, but losing wasn't the real issue—learning the game was the real issue. Youthful early losing was simply the fee!

Then one day, it happened. I swear it happened like a special hand of a poker angel had laid a precious soft awakening touch to my sensitive needy shoulder. Five other guys were at the relatively quiet game that day, and the cards were dealt, seven-card stud: two down, one up started the game. I had two Jacks in the hole, one was one-eyed and a ten, which with two, we called twenty miles, but I only had one when that game started with those first three dealt cards. I saw everyone's bodies lay back or elbows up. I saw all the eyes, sniffs, eye rolls, scratches, and blinks. I saw it all, one opposing player at a time. Some scavenger betting kept me in the game, riding my two Jacks for the moment, but always loving twenty miles.

A second up-card deal, and all the players settled into their hands a little further, my next card was a Jack, now I'm loaded—but it's hidden—two Jacks in the hole, and it was early. I looked at every face, some bodies leaned more into the table and their hands, some sat back with superior bluffing style postures of those who know something no one else in the world knows. A couple guys had straights and flushes beginning to show, and table betting raised substantially, with all players "in."

The fifth card rolled athletically off the dealer's deck with the appropriate side language about players' sisters in relation to a queen up, eighters from Decatur, and ducks with box cars, jabber galore, to distract the guppy-prone. I sat cool as a cotton mouth in a creek bed, content with the power of my hidden Jacks, and believing in twenty mile, watching the opposing flow. Betting, raises—raise you back, jabber-jabber, blah-blah. Some players squeezing cards until the turnip blood would run, some in card holding reverence.

And then it happened. It truly, apostolically happened—perhaps my first grandiose life revelation, maybe a signal that there are true angels, and other revelations in my future, and only thirteen years old, my poker angel put up a soft precious signal to my eager inner ear, and whispered.

You know what every player at the table has in their poker hands. Your lessons have been well earned. Take their money! It is now your turn, to take their money. (Great angel that day!)

And I did know [what every other player had in their hand]. I knew all the faces and all the body language and all the cheap meaningless jabber, and I knew the money scattered over the table—I knew who could afford to be there in that hand and who couldn't. And I knew my three Jacks were in good shape, a little help appreciated, but three Jacks were worth the betting, and worth the hold I would have on that game, that moment, with those older guys. Bottom line, I knew I would win that hand, with a great, growing pot, the kind of pot that can make the whole day, and I had the minds of every other player in my back pocket.

Card 6, again straight up, increased the betting action, but it didn't matter, cause I knew what everybody had in their hands. I knew the good players couldn't beat three Jacks, let alone some minor help, and I knew the guy to my left, and the one across the table were goin' on hope, bluff and table stakes. But I was young, hadn't been the winner much, today they call it "had no (poker) respect," so my hanging around that day, with game, with that hand, seemed inconsequential to my opponents. I was invisible before my opponent's eyes.

Seventh card down, I squeezed, and hit my precious twenty mile. Three Jacks/ twenty mile: Hello, full-boat! As they say, the rest is history. I got my degree that day, the type of degree that makes money. I won the rest of that day, knew what each player had almost every hand. I could see inside, through the game, feel the whole game atmosphere at my young fingertips.

I played for the next six years, always with the older guys and more of them, bigger games, up in ratty apartments over the town's businesses of hardware, insurance, and drug stores, in the small county seat of a town square. We played deep in basements or on local farms, in old chicken houses converted to poker rooms and beer bars, gun racks all over the walls. Later with cars and dates, Fridays you dumped the date early and headed to someone's basement or back room for poker games. I went to all of them, collected the town's money as quietly as possible—had new players figured before they sat down—guppy oriented. I hit an inside straight once, in a dump apartment over the square, which beat a big town bully named Buck out of a hand he thought he had some inherent right to win—and survived, barely.

That poker playing talent served in more ways than one in the Nam. Domestic Nam training started early, at home, domestically, and can come in many forms.

No matter the comforts of Phu Bai, Rollie couldn't get Quang Tri off his mind, Tet, the other pre-Emmerson actions that kept Marines fighting at night, in the air each day. Now salty, a sergeant, obviously with some sort of angel, Rollie would often tell the Phu Bau rummies about life at Quang Tri.

During Tet, Quang Tri came under attack nightly. Estimates are, from start to near finish, which was when area warriors turned all their attention to the Battle of Hue, twelve miles down the road, Quang Tri was attacked twenty-eight nights in a row. One hungry evening, midway in the gauntlet, with the help of Puff the Magic Dragon, over six hundred NVA were dead on the north and western perimeter of Quang Tri where they had massed for an attack. A battalion-size of NVA troops were discovered earlier in the day in the bulge toward the perimeter line, created by the bend east of the Quang Tri river that stuck the river out closest toward the camp's western defense perimeter. The NVA had drifted into the area in smaller groups, holding tight in deep bush for orders to attack that night. Once discovered, then confirmed, the defending line marines notified the line CO, who called their aerial buddy Puff, and four bad-ass tanks into the upcoming fight most certainly to be that evening. That minor battle of the river bulge, with unbelievable fire power, saved the Quang Tri base and its troops in the major battle of Tet for Quang Tri. The view from Rollie's foxhole was powerful and spectacular. Made a person real proud to be on the east and south side of the river that night!

Quang Tri had been mostly attacked by NVA rockets, which scream into a location to land their destruction with an enormous, unique sounding *womp*. Enemy "rockets" don't create a *bang* or a *sssskew-blewie* like mortars do. Just a giant, massive, muscular, blood curdling, vibrating, strange *womp* sound. A surprisingly unique, powerful sound at detonation, rockets were something like ten or twenty times more powerful than a mortar. Rockets were launched from a greater distance, and thus, for those who were the intended target, if alert enough, you get a couple seconds of screaming warning *szzzzzzzz* before you are *womp*-ed. The Gooks seemed to have a good supply of the rockets all the time, almost everywhere in I Corps. Some opposing military/industrial bunch of rocket builders must have been real busy some place up the road in China. For a bunch of sway-back, rice-humpin' Gook field hands, they never seemed to run out of sophisticated rocketry.

Scrambling to bunkers, from *womps* or mortars, almost every early nightfall before the line probes would start, and then again later into the night's deeper darkness, marines of Quang Tri created a scrambling science on methods to enter their closest bunker. Some dove in, some slid in as if to home plate, and some actually stayed high and often took a gash to the head by the steel armor that supported the sandbag roofs. But once in, with a light, it's a great place to start a little poker game. I mean everyone is there, ain't goin' anywhere until the Gooks quit trying to blow the place up, so a card game made a lot of sense. Light up and deal!

At this point, it is sometimes difficult for the pampered, cozy civilian back in the World to understand and appreciate the creative nature of some marines who have been shot at for six to ten months, still alive and have gathered a routine-ness about their war ways of survival, and about the various methods the enemy will employ to try to kill them come evening. Adrenaline rush is one thing with some mangy rocketeer launching eight-foot rockets from some slope of a hill. *Womp!* Twenty-five yards away, dirt and sand blowing through your bunker area, two hundred new holes in your already half-shredded tent, so what. A dirthole bunker, *womps*, poker game, cigarettes, what else can we do to make this more exciting or competitive? I mean otherwise, you just lay crouched in the dirt hole, listening for rockets, and waiting until one actually *womps* on the top of your bunker, for the lights out trip home in a dark-green zipper bag.

In a popular Outfielder's bunker location of great womp-protection nightly use, the latrines were about seventy yards away, out the bunker, low between a couple tents surrounded by sandbag walls, over the killing field road and shoot through the latrine door like crossing a goal line . . . do your business, pants back together for the return seventy-yard dash run and into the homeboy bunker with a headfirst slide and slap of the imaginary home plate, a couple high fives from buddies gauging the extent of wartime lapsed. All this is to be accomplished before the next *womp* blows the hell out of everything in your area or game over. With a flashlight and a second hand on a watch, the whole exercise can be a whole lot more fun than a poker game or a "routine head-run" *womp*. But something was missing for these feisty marines, who didn't need anything in that war zone as precise as a second hand on a watch. The whole developing contest was soon renamed as the WOMP'n-Dump, more of a fun signature project. The idea was to light a cigarette, while waiting for a rocket to explode trying to kill you and your buddies who were usually the Huey flight crews. With a crashing *womp*, and then at the precise end of shrapnel ripping apart everything around the bunker, the smoking competitor of the moment lays the lit cigarette out on a level surface and takes off to the latrine, running low and hard, hitting the earth indentions and slight rises with spring loaded knee-flex athleticism. A good run could have you at and into the latrine in six to seven seconds, winded a little but in the three-holed wooden box, safe from nothing. Only number twos qualified for the WOMP'n-Dump token trophy at night, so grunts and moans in seconds, up with the trousers and back through the rocket and mortar gauntlet with a headfirst slide down the open chute of the bunker to comparative field-of-fire safety, and earned adulation from your fellow marines. (Every WOMP'n-Dump was a good WOMP'n-Dump, no matter the actual time or ash.) At first sight inside the bunker, with the headfirst slide, the cigarette ash was measured and the amount of ash collected on its end recorded and honored. Corporal Fisher, left gunner on bird 8, often won, with an average ash collection in the 1/4 to 3/8 inch range, a phenomenal WOMP'n-Dump feat. To this day, we expect that Corporal Fisher's WOMP'n-Dump records still stand and thus always will stand—an unsung testimonial to warring commitment and general patriotism to a team cause. It wasn't long until WOMP'n-Dumps became more fun and enduring than the cot-side poker games. Within the battles of Tet, everyone at the isolated, edge of the Quang Tri base would know, around payday, you would either have a great poker game or adrenal pouring WOMP'n-Dump races, with any kind of aerial bombardments. And that's what the war and the Tet offensive occasionally came to in that small base.

About halfway through Tet, the WOMP'n-Dump races were altered to require the racer to complete the tricky event, while carrying his loaded M-16, slightly increasing the degree of difficulty. Consequently if ground troops were invading, the competitor could actually start camp defensive measures. Just logical! The requirement slightly lengthened some of the ashes but actually required more athleticism, and in general, everyone felt better about the event, now having some camp defense element to it. Soon, the real nasty Tet war moved from Quang Tri down the road to the famous battle of Hue, which of course ended the WOMP'n-Dump event. The event just never seemed to catch on in other small camps. To this day, I don't think it has been revived, although similar gamesmanship arose in late June at Phu Bai, under attack, competitive field-of-fire Salty Dog deliveries during mortar attacks became popular. Phu Bai was more civilized.

(Some experienced WOMP'n-Dump guy from Quang Tri regularly won the Salty Dog delivery events. When you "got it," you "got it.")

I Corps battles and wars came in all kinds of shapes and sizes, from Dong Ha adjacent to the DMZ, to the more urban battles in places like Hue and Da Nang. I Corps was like Forest Gump's box of chocolates, you never knew what you were going to get, unless you were Sergeant Rollie Cahill, and it was going to be payday. Then, you knew you could have a good chance to find a poker game. Poker games gave soldiers that once in a while "unusual" chance to look forward to a side show to the war and the Domestic issues that always seem to swirl rumor-style in and out of troop's vulnerable minds. Some inexperienced players seemed to play poker and lose, just to be a part of that kind of a "So what, it's fun with my buddies" atmosphere. At least some players felt that way; those were the bottom feeders in the game, then they were broke and bye-bye after the first night. They were always there, and even if a regular bottom feeder lost all his money regularly, new bottom feeders would show up, not believing or not understanding the strength of the elite players. Never educated on poker, they seemed to think luck of the draw was a big deal, same kind of guys that probably go through life thinking things are always happening around them, to them by strange circumstance or just bad luck.

To Rollie, the Domestic Nam tour of duty was beginning to all string together in his mind affecting his actions, sometimes making him more casual about things that should have been considered more intense. Time passed strangely in Nam. On one hand, it seemed an eternity since landing on the shores in the strange country, seemed like another far off time and place that didn't really have a normal time element to it or have him in the picture. It was someone else that did that, landed there, moved up and around, flew, scampered, lost contacts, and made new ones. Countdown to the wake-up was plodding through the days, must be toward 125 or maybe 130, all in a surreal world where everything moves but nothing gets anywhere. Battles fought, won or lost, and then the base, LZ or hilltop abandoned. All the while, more and more troops and war's equipment poured into the country and into big bases like Phu Bai. More tents popped up, and better mess kits, the drinking clubs, and more basketballs. (Now, who ya think is sitting some place in a clean uniform and cozy office and is responsible for getting more basketballs to a concrete court in Phu Bai?) The longer you stayed in the war, the less sense it made.

More and more Phantoms and their trained, focused pilots roared off the Phu Bai runway at night, off to missions designed by the other human phantoms, the radio officer phantoms keyed up to reports and maps and SOP's, in a number's game of missions and bomb tonnage noises, fake and real. New, reportedly higher tech attack helicopters showed up called Cobras. The work-horse Hueys that sent and retrieved troops all over I Corps would be more selectively used, with the new Cobras and a special-looking kind of clean pilot now in-country and Cobra-trained. The Cobras, they're just for killin' things, not for delivering or picking things up, had rocket launchers on each side and .50-caliber firing power in the front bottom of the cockpit area, controlled by pilot's buttons, not crew members. In fact, the things had no crews per se, just the two pilots, one sitting behind the other instead of side by side like in the Hueys. The pilot's position was the big deal and was the essence of the newness of Cobra design and future fame. Cobras could be narrow, slits of flying air machine weaponry with more mobility and provide less pilot target practice for the Gooks on the ground and the now more frequent SAMs that were rumored to be persistent in pilot killing speed and angles. The Cobra-thing made some sense, but then again, not really. Hueys could deliver and pickup, which means they could and would save lives. Cobras were another way to deliver fire power, with bigger guns and with the one pilot behind the other—ground marines cared, but not really. Besides, when the Cobras showed up, there were only a very few, and they mostly sat, always getting ready to just about be ready. But they were sure signs of the military/industrial world being well and hard at work with new stuff for the Domestic Nam.

For Rollie, a few letters from home trickled in, and he sent a few back to the World, being as vague as he could. Did no good to try to explain anything! Explaining things would just sound stupid because nothing made any sense to try to explain. In Phu Bai, through the S-4 office, it was a little war here, and little war there. Do a job, keep your head down and mouth shut, and count. Appreciate these days not in Quang Tri or Khe Sanh or Con Thien. Just count one, then another one, twenty-four hours at a time, then one more, always looking around, always a hip .45 and an M-16, always listening, always staying away from the enlisted Club trap.

Emmerson was in and out of Phu Bai and would always check in to S-4 to see Rollie. Never spoken, but both understood they were friends or as close to "friends" as Nam would allow. Emmerson was the one exception to Rollie's "plan," they were the only friends each had, or would have, or kind of need. By now, Rollie had been in country long enough to look inside the war, inside the camp, just like inside the minds and eyes at a poker table back home a few years ago and notice things that previously were just parts of various sceneries. He was noticing things to be a part of things, not with a focus of a winning kind of "noticing things." This winning meant surviving the chaos.

One thing Rollie began to notice was that whenever Emmerson showed up, there seemed to be one of the Air America silver propped passenger planes parked near the control center on the airstrip. Air America was said to be a part of the CIA, who were also said to be the people that were partially running the war, and not just in Nam, Laos also, all the way through Thailand, and had been for years, many years, like since 1954 from Laos, but also before that, as in Burma since 1940 where the unit started and was known as the AVG— American Volunteer Group. Emmerson commonly moved around Nam I Corps on Air America, as Rollie would learn later, but for the time, the whole Emmerson/Air America circumstance just added to the mystique. Emmerson seemed to have a bit of business about his visits, but mostly when in Phu Bai, looking up Rollie, Emmerson seemed relaxed, between unspoken-of things, catching a breath. The ultimate observer of all things war, he radiated a vast knowledge of the whole deal, in-country Nam and Domestic, and seemed to sense vague surrounding pressures before anyone else would notice. Always armed, fascinating, bigger than the lives and minds around him, he was usually a little beat up but never wounded, just worn more and more, never actually explaining where he came from, had been, or was headed next. If he spoke of things nonwar, it was always about his precious Virginia that he was determined to see again, but regularly curious about other places in the States that he had never seen, like Oregon.

At the time, Rollie didn't know much about Air America. Later as his countdown to the wake-up dropped and rolled into two-digit land, Rollie would run into Air America more and more, and pay attention more and more to their comings and goings, and especially to the expressions of the pilots. He would hop Air America flights from remote airstrips on various logistical ID or collection missions. At Phu Bai, that early April, it didn't seem the time to put the Air America story together in his mind, but there they were, bigger than Bald Eagles. Air America and Emmerson would always find useful work to do for somebody's war.

Emmerson pounced through the front flap of S-4 in late May, on a hot war day, acknowledged no one but Rollie and told him to grab his weapons and let's git. No one ever questioned Emmerson. Out the front to the idling jeep, Emmerson did a quasi-violent, dusty, rapid U-turn and headed back toward the far south end of Phu Bai, past the command center and air control, past an idling Air America prop passenger plane that was shutting down from some sort of a mission, pilots lumbering out of a high cockpit to the ground where Phu Bai camp officers obediently waited. Rollie hanging on to the tilted windshield trusting the quick mission but not the actual drive while Emmerson drove intensely past it all, quickly, hurriedly, but not rushed, in partial control. That day, Phu Bai air was full of depressing heat and the ever-present dust whirlwinds looking for a place and chance to annoy anyone in the whirlwind path.

Emmerson left the edge of the main base, without a word to Rollie. No word as to why Rollie had been picked up or where they were going with such purpose and intent, silent, just the two of them in a Phu Bai mental swirl zone intent on landing. Near the midsouth end of the camp and airstrip, amongst the flowing dust and dirt, was the MPs camp and headquarters, lined within its own confines with its own barbed wire and armed gate. Frag-proofing precautions were a big deal to these guys. MPs nodded to Emmerson like they'd known him all their lives as he dropped gears, slowed and passed through the MP front gate. Rollie still a clutching clueless about the mission and need for such determined urgency. Never mind, it's Emmerson! Emmerson is always urgent!

Emmerson brought the jeep to a quasi-controlled skidding stop, within it all, but in no particular place, kind of hidden in the open amidst the scurry of routine MP busyness.

"Look," he said, chin dropped to his chest.

"I'll be frickin' all Jesused-up, just *look!*" repeated Emmerson.

Rollie looked, could see the obvious hustling of MPs and their striped jeeps and white or silver helmets, in and out of MP places.

Emmerson barked, with low vulgarity as if spitting a nasty piece of country, "*Look.*" And Rollie looked deeper into the unusual scene where most Phu Bai folks never visited, realizing there was a point to the mission, probably a whopper of a point. "The Nam. Look into the Nam." This means nothing is ever what it appears to be in Nam, Emmerson's low vulgarity most insistent. Direct ordering, without looking up.

Rollie's trained eyes and mind looked inside the scene, knowing Emmerson had not pulled such a stunt to this intense extent for lack of filling idle time. And sure enough, there it was: blending with the whole scene of moving bodies, dust, and equipment, two slumped bodies up close to the MP headquarters, tethered to a water buffalo.

"Ah'll be damned!" Fletcher and Steube, all captured up again, jailed in the open, must have been just brought in and handed over to the MPs, probably by that nasty-looking Recon-looking, killin'-looking group over there, layin' out all warred up and haggard from weight of the bush.

Rollie couldn't believe his eyes, those Arkansas good ole boys had been out of mind since April 5 and Quang Tri. There they were, big as life, alive, all hunched over quiet, playing opossum once again, drinking in their captive surroundings already, and looking dumb and weakened to anyone not familiar with them.

Lowest jeep gear, Emmerson circled the scene at a distance from Fletch and Steube, and road up closer, making sure the Command

MP Tent was between the jeep and Fletcher and Steube with their firm hold on the MPs water buffalo. Yet unseen by the two entrepreneur warriors, Emmerson leaped from behind the cheap steering wheel and cozied up to two Recon teamies, most likely to be the lowest in command. Rollie held tight, still with a grip on the dash from the wild ride. Apparently introducing himself, Emmerson brought the two Recon Marines to their feet into some sort of awkward unofficial semblance of an "attention" and half salute. After a brief exchange of comments and Nam regards, Emmerson returned to Rollie in the jeep, angrily slithered into the driver's seat with no wasted motion and took his deep, get ready for action, breath that Rollie had seen before.

> Emmerson: *"Them boys has been out on "Ho's Trail," Recon Info and orders to track down our buddies if they heard word of their nastiness and got a location read. Trapped 'em into a rendezvous in some clan mountain village just off the Laotian border, with orders to get them to Phu Bai this time, with a firm locked grip, no chances."*
>
> *"These recon guys don't even know their names, where they are from. Don't know nothin' about them except they are rogue and their lieutenant has orders to bring 'em in if they can find 'em—dead or alive they said. Can you believe, dead or alive?"*
>
> *"We'll watch, see who's runnin' things. Looks like this time the Corps really wants 'em bad, must of done some serious Gook killin' that someone's having trouble explaining, probably didn't spend enough time trying to determine the good guys from the bad."*
>
> *"Damn, I ain't got time for this."*
>
> *"Recon boys said our buddies been raising hell, but figured they was out of food and ammo. Would*

have to show up some place sooner or later to get all laid low, rested and regrouped. Said they knew it was them, when they ran across a small hamlet with a bunch of hanging black pajamas, ears gone. Said our boys now and then moved with some ROKs, kinda of gone rogue also."

"You ready for this, Bud? We gotta bust 'em one more time—after this they're really on their own. I can't be running all over I Corps keeping these guys out of the brig."

"Let's give it a day, maybe two, you fuss-up some S-4 run somewhere, I'll round up a couple parachutes and talk to the Air America jockeys. If we can get 'em out of this mess, we'll dump 'em in the middle of Indo China, where they can't do nothin but kill folks, bust things up and hide good—maybe the next time their captured I'll be in Virginia, and it won't be my problem. We'll airmail in a drop so far out, the war'll be over, and they'll have their own growed up Gook families by the time anyone finds 'em again."

"I swear, got missions all stacked up, one in Da Nang, and run into Fletch and Steube. Man, I love those guys!"

With that shoot-from-the-hip non-plan, Emmerson and Rollie moved to the open between the Arkansas Ruffians and the razor wired lines that closed off the MP Camp to the rest of Phu Bai and the rest of Nam. Making sure to be seen, they moved slowly toward the handcuffed ugly pair of the two biggest scoundrels in Indo China, never making eye contact. Fletch and Steube, animal instincts always sharply aware of every slight piece of their surroundings, especially anything out of place, stayed naturally motionless, heads down, eyes up through the top of their eyelids, dirt and hair covered by nasty crumpled bush hats down to the eye's tops. At ten yards, Steube nodded once to nothing and no one, paused, and nodded again, and with that, Emmerson knew the two-man fighting machine understood something new was in their lives, and so he and Rollie could veer off toward their jeep. That's all the plan that was needed at that point. The new "Third Game" was on!

Emmerson collected all the elements of this weird war scene and began to work on plan detail. Wasn't the highest priority plan he had but was the most fun and perhaps the most needed. It took a Phu Bai base the size of Norfolk and three thousand in the rear with the gear noodles to support a bunch of battalions in and out of fire fights that in the end meant nothing. Seemed reasonable he and Rollie could get the Arkansas Rebels back in the fight with a better ratio of support assets to enemy KIA.

Rollie fussed up some logistical reason to visit the MP Camp daily. Looking for vital equipment that would make MP lives easier made the welcome mat roll out as his jeep hit the MP front gate on a regular familiarizing basis. Emmerson stayed ghostly, showing up here and there, now and again hanging out at whatever Air America flight was in and out and would check with Rollie at S-4 or at chance and planned meetings on the roads, back or forth, one way or another, on a daily basis.

Emmerson could count on Fletch and Steube being most content to not be going anywhere, right there in the middle of MP-land, like old folks stuck in a nursing home for the time being. They did get moved to a makeshift cell, outdoors, but with a canvas tie-down cover, as they squatted Gook style in their new shade, looked at the world through eager, caged eyelids, counted things, noticed where jeeps were parked and left, and waited, gaining a sense of how the MP compound functioned, and who might be a weak link or when an unguarded moment in routine movements might become predictable.

A couple days, then a couple more days, and pretty soon a week, and the late Phu Bai May days turned to post-Tet early June, '68. The daily report to Emmerson from Rollie's MP-land visits was always the same; no one in command knows what to do with them, which to Emmerson was perfect. By June 3, Rollie was free to move about with his S-4 news and logistic concerns. Free to move in and out of MP-land all on the MPs logistical processing behalf, move about, and casually ask, "What's up with the two guys in the cage?"

Who knows how minds like Emmerson's work, but suddenly, the whole thing magically fit together. First of all, if no one knows what to do with them, they must be shopping ideas up and down ranks, in and out of country, all over the place. And if they are shopping ideas, potential orders and processes all over the place, then no one really knows who's in charge. Better yet, no one wants to be in charge, and even better than better yet, maybe someone should step up to be in charge. There is only downside to being an officer in charge of this cluster-bunk. There's no upside for an officer to stick his neck out to punish two yea-hoo guys from Arkansas, doing what the rest of Nam is trying to do, but not as efficiently. Perfect, again.

Time to step out in the open, take charge:

"Rollie, I'll pick you up at S-4 when the other guys in the office close up for the day. Tomorrow, we'll come out past the MPs to the south end of the runway and watch some Phantoms take off to blow the hell out of something. You get some parachutes, small arms and ammo, C rations in back-packs, good long knives, a few canteens of water organized in one run and grab bundle. Oh, throw in some matches and cigs and a couple Band-Aids. And a trenching tool!"

"I'll go get an Air America jockey and see how their missions line up, see if one of them can disappear west for an hour in a faulty flight plan that has some crossed orders. Most of those AA pilots owe me a trick or two."

"They ain't seen me down there in MP land in over a week, and they're used to seeing you now, so you're the ticket in."

On June 4, Rollie had all the equipment at the Air America staging site next to the silver two-prop plane that always posed like a local, everyday prop moving ordinary passengers around on some sort of shuttle milk run or ordinary goodwill PR tour. He then went to the MP compound, faked some sort of business process important to MP life, and passed by the alert prisoners, dropping a crunched paper that was sure to blow inside the bars, and did. The note simply said, "4:00 a.m., hard rice." Troop and air movements had many slang names, milk runs, rice runs, see 'n lipsticks, etc. "Hard rice" was hard Nam, hard slang for armed and hot dangerous—"hot action."

Emmerson talked to the chummy Air America pilots, who by '68 were likely four-time reup war volunteers, hot to any action, made any action hot just by being in the action. Emmerson made sure they'd throw the equipment in, told them to rev engines at 4:30 a.m. and sit tight. He forgot to tell them who their VIPs would be but made sure the pilots knew it would be a short run off their normal course, and they'd have orders handed to them at boarding, another flight that never existed, scarcely briefing the pilots on their VIP load:

These guys are special, special forces, top secret—once aboard, get in the air, most ricky tick, we're gonna chute 'em west just before light, I'll be along.

Pitch-dark, long before Phu Bai stirred for another hot miserable day of supply counting and radio jabbering, Emmerson and Rollie climbed in their jeep with orders from Colonel Stafford, Okinawa, to retrieve Private Fletcher and Private Steube, and fly them handcuffed out on Air America, under the watchful eye of heavily armed Sergeant

Emmerson, special envoy to First Marines. They should be flown to Da Nang, where Emmerson will be met by a larger group of Marine MPs, as ordered in from Okinawa, all real official, real organized, real bullshit.

Armed with Emmerson's extraordinary self-made stature and Rollie's familiar gate face and practiced look of no-nonsense business-like authority, the two imposters easily passed through the front gate at MP-land and pulled in front of MP Headquarters, which was right next to Fletch and Steube. At 4:15, all four sets of eyes met, the team was poised, synced, follow the signals, take orders quickly, then give orders, quickly, no wasted motions.

Emmerson didn't even want the handcuffs off, just wanted the keys. The prisoners were to stay handcuffed until Okinawa MPs took over in Da Nang, a serious prisoner keeping precaution. Orders passed, then the new MP caretakers could do as they pleased. Everyone was glad for the two dangerous Arkansas murdering derelicts to be gone, out of Phu Bai MP responsibility, on the way out of country.

Bleary eyed early morning traffic at the MP Headquarters was nothing. Orders were orders, and Emmerson trailed the MP third in charge to unlock the cage and put the bad-ass Arkie mules in the jeep. The sooner to the airstrip, the better, so the offer for additional escort security was declined, and out the MP front gate that happy, smiling foursome went, slicker'n water buffalo snot. Halfway to the strip, which was just six minutes away, Emmerson did lean back with a friendly greeting: *You bastards, I ain't doin' this again after this one!*

Air America props droned and purred amidst the dark morning, the only sound on the strip, early that June 5, but not the only sound to be heard in the Domestic Nam that day. Another crashing/bashing/ depressing sound would soon start its Domestic Nam news tsunami way across the Pacific, east to west. Rollie briefed the Arkies on what was in the supply bundles, with no response, only nods of grateful understanding. Thirty seconds at the strip, out of the jeep, into the humming, idling Air America prop with faceless pilots poised in the cockpit, and Emmerson with, Fletcher and Steube, could begin to smile a little and take off the handcuffs.

Y'all be dropped from ten thousand feet, right before sun light hits the west side of the range, get the chutes on. Sorry, it can't be lower. These guys don't want to attract fire. Here's your side arms! Have to kill some Gooks and round-up some AK's and ammo. Rations for five days, one trenching tool to bury everything you don't want to carry, like the chutes if you don't want them.

Here's the hand-cuffs back and key, you may run into an unruly date. In the pit, they say you got twenty-four minutes to drop time. Good to go? Semper Fi.

Props droned in a pivotal tarmac revved dash and lift of RPMs. Early morning prop and blade drone sounds are special, special solid, more powerful than at other times in a warring day when everyone listening is distracted with other war stuff. No wind yet or small arms nervousness to distract from the muscular sound of America's props bringing the day alive. Kind of like the special feel of early morning napalm petroleum fireballs on an open stretch of trail or mountainside, maybe not.

Fletcher and Steube spent about four words each, thanking Emmerson, then about six more telling him to thank Rollie. Nice, guys! Fifteen minutes!

The three sat in Nam peer honored silence, confident, intense from their work that early Nam get-away morning. Ten minutes!

Air America had no flight crews. No one could stand to fly with these cowboy reup volunteers. Silence except for the dual drone of the engine props against the early morning air leading into another warm damp morning in the Nam, this time stretching the western unmarked borders first thing in the new day. Five minutes: now well into Laos.

Nothing to say, just concentration toward the task at hand, precise actions! Three minutes: The AA pilot from the left seat surveys his passengers, all equals in warring talent. Awkwardly, hand over hand, AA left seat pilot moves his way to the side door behind his empty pilot seat, motioned Fletcher and Steube to their feet, then to the open door.

One minute! As Emmerson watched the two Arkies with strange admiration! The pilot checked and made sure the two rogue, killing machine marines knew which chute string to pull, two nods to signify jump-training was over.

Fletcher nodded back at Emmerson and then disappeared through the open door into the barely lit morning. Steube, quickly looked, flashed a strange "I'm loose again" grin and followed Fletcher's descending flight path. The plane instantly banked north into a tight loop, Emmerson checked to catch a glimpse of two white spots immediately disappearing into the dense jungle floor, then swore he'd be done with these guys this time. The scores were all even and then some.

But would he? Would he really be done with 'em?

Makes ya talk to yourself sometimes:

Where'd they say they was from? Searcy! Yep, Searcy, Arkansas! In forty years, the government may stop lookin' for 'em, and I'll stop into Searcy and see if they made it. Bet so! Bet they'll be sittin' pretty on a green park bench, next to the town's fountain and some war memorial, right down town under some big ole Searcy shade tree, next to a court house, sittin' big as field cotton, lookin' over all the passin' skirts mosey'n up and down the Searcy sidewalks main streets.

Two roughest bastards I ever saw, ever wanna see!

Emmerson laid back for the rest of his morning Air America flight, which droned back around and a few clicks south to Da Nang. He'd hang out a couple days in Da Nang, check on stuff, pick up tidbits of war news, check in with Air America guys in the know, check on more stuff, maybe follow a rumor or two, and then hitch a ride at the helipad back up to Phu Bai. Rollie had mentioned some sort of new S-4 orders he expected and could use some help with, back toward Hue, maybe out to some navy supply ships, blue water stuff. Seems some new forklifts, maybe eight, got lost in the transit of war stuff from blue water to in-country. Emmerson thought maybe he'd go along, make sure Rollie stayed out of trouble, check out Hue, had heard it was a helluva fight up there couple months ago.

Turned out Emmerson didn't need to go back to Phu Bai to hook up with Rollie. Rollie walked right down the middle of the Da Nang air and fleet support base late on June 7 and saw Emmerson holding up a sandbag wall with his left shoulder, outside some sort of MACV Headquarters center. Buddied up—again—they shared a big belated success Howdy for the work with Fletch and Steube and a whispered confidential check to see if they made their debarkation schedule OK. Rollie reported that no one in MP-land at Phu Bai even mentioned the Arkies were gone. "Orders is orders, especially from Okinawa!" And that was worth a huge Da Nang buddy-plan laugh.

It was the day before payday, at a much bigger base. Probably swimming with Guppies!

The comparatively soft afternoon gave Emmerson a chance to tell Rollie a good deal more about Air America. Rollie was all ears! Rollie had seen them more and more, looked through the Nam to sense their whole deal was some sort of special ops. Kind of like American women, to be seen and appreciated—never understood—but Emmerson tried:

Air America originated pre-WWII, as American Volunteer Group (AVG), part of the

Chinese Air Force, worked mostly out of Burma, with Navy and Marine Corps pilots. No one ever much heard of the American Volunteer Group cause it ain't much of a catchy handle, and weren't really supposed to exist. They were known across Indo China and later in the States as The Flying Tigers. The main mission at first was to help defend China against Japanese forces, kind of as private military contractors. Their work was desperate, took a special kind of volunteer, plus the shark faced fighter jets made it all real special and struck fear to an enemy.

Even way back then, we were fighting communist advances. The Russians were supplying Mao's Communists with air power, and we were working for Chiang Kai-shek. Just all one big Asian on-going "hard rice" hair-ball. For all the legal reasons FDR started some sort of Chinese Defense cash and carry provision, clear back in 1939 which kind of got the supply chain rolling, soon to be filled with one hundred of WWII most famous P-40 pilots for the AVG. With such a black operation, pilots had to resign commissions and sign on as volunteers for a new Central Aircraft Mfr. Co. (CAMCO). Eventually, the sixty navy and marine pilots were joined by forty from the army and ten more flight instructors. The AVG had its first combat December '41, when aircraft intercepted Japanese bombers from airfields at Hanoi and downed three of them. What we see today as Air America has a deep and wide history in Indochina, fight'n things from Hanoi even back then.

After WWII, about 1950, AVG was officially purchased by the CIA, Special Activities Division, which would supply and support US covert

*operations in Southeast Asia, along with flying assets
came a corps of experienced, skilled combat pilots
who, with not much else to do, wanted in the fight.
They used to call 'em, CAT, Civil Air Transport.
At that point, the Flying Tigers shark teeth faded
for covert reasons. That's what you see flying around
Nam and Indochina today, the new Air America,
like a local civilian airline, but a lot of the same salty
pilots. That's why they're so damn fearless. Besides,
they've been runnin' Indochina for so long they don't
have real homes. The actual company headquarters
is right in the middle of DC, 1725 K Street, a short
walk from Congress.*

*After '59 into '62 CAT provided direct and
indirect support for CIA Operations, mostly in
Laos. After '62, the covert operations were in
Vietnam, and more passengers looking for Air
America planes became common. They did all
kinds of things, insert and extract US personnel,
logistical support, transport refugees, pick up and
dropped bales, just whatever was needed, and
there was always something, always with civilian
markings. Everybody flying and running things was
actually military personnel forced to resign military
commissions and then transferred into CAT and Air
America.*

*Air America flies civilians, diplomats, spies,
commandos, sabotage teams, doctors, war casualties,
drug enforcement officers, drugs, and VIPs. They
even work in urbanization policies and widespread
application of that nasty Agent Orange stuff. They
allegedly transport a good deal of opium and heroin
on behalf of Hmong leader Vang Pao, while pretty
much everyone looks the other way. But what the*

heck, they take big risks and get very little pay. Sometimes, it's easy for a small bale to get thrown aboard, then thrown off again. Best friends in Nam are Air American. Orders or no, these guys will go out of their way to take a mission and get you where you need to be, or better yet, get you out.

These guys carry a lot of weight too. When they have a mission and need aircraft, the Air Force and Army jump to loan the aircraft, mission unknown, not even asked about. They are never stuck or down long. One phone call and they have what they need. Now they even have guys on the ground that move ahead of the missions and needs and let 'em know what might be next. That's why we got Fletch and Steube out so slick and easy.

Rollie sat in awed silence:

Rollie: Emm, how'd you get to know so much about AVG and Air America, Burma and Flying Tigers and what they do here in Nam? And don't tell me you studied that in some history class. That kind of history isn't taught anywhere.

Nothing was predictable with Emmerson. He could go from bigger than life to disappearing in plain sight, in an instant. You never got used to him or comfortable, just trusting, and in the Nam, that was good enough.

Well, you're right. Those kind of American history classes are rare, hard to come across. Probably helped that my daddy was one of the original one hundred Flying Tigers into Burma.

Air America officially disbanded on June 30, 1976, having made its last flights over and around Thailand. Later, the assets and the actual business of Air America were purchased and renamed. Evergreen International Airlines, EIA, to this day continues to provide support for US covert operations.

Chapter 6

"Salty"

"Poker night in Da Nang, under a salty cover."

In the Marine Corps, stuff that's been around a while, been used and abused, stood and survived tests of adventurous, sacred times, that stuff and those people are known as salty.

The most obvious sort of salty is a Marine's cover. That'd be the normally dark-green baseball-type hat, with the black anchor and globe symbol on the front and center. In Nam, hats, clothes, and gear stay damp with irritating Asian elements and with the sweat of marines' busy working and operating days. Stay damp long enough and the covers' stain with new abstract white (salty) lines, sweat marks, and thus, the hats (or covers as marines prefer to call them) become "salty" looking. You can tell a marine that has been in Nam for a while often by how "salty" his cover is. Young marines climbing out of the bush "salty" up their covers, uniforms, and bodies, faster than anyone. These guys look tested, experienced, rugged—"salty," hard rice, most ricky tick.

A marine with dark-green rough canvas jungle boots that sport shiny black leather toes and heels ain't very salty. Clean new-looking boots are a sure sign of new issue and of a mega-countdown to a wake-up going on with a marine new to in-country ways. Later, when the marine has been in Nam for a while, at least half a countdown, the dark-green of the jungle boots fades to a sandy looking light green. The boot's toes and heels, once a polished black, gain their own bars and stripes, rips, and gouges from wear of many kinds. From the top cover to the bottom jungle boots, you can tell by looking the newness of a moving or standing marine and thus get a read on how savvy he might or might not be in the warring ways of Nam. In a perimeter line foxhole through evening, or night, by the flicker of falling flares, you don't want to see a leaping new foxhole partner land with a dark-green cover and new polished boots. They won't generally be salty enough to hold their ground in a fire fight, unless made of the rare, sturdy Wilson Street blood and guts.

Other things in Nam, within marines lives get salty, but none more so than the marines themselves. The same young fresh body and uniform that may pass on a trail or in a jeep with a 364 countdown, when at 150 have a whole different look to them. Bodies thin down and take on a different lean and mean most deliberate look. Eyes look back at you differently, keener in their analysis, skittish, always looking to, through, or around you, all at the same time. Grunts just out of the bush are all salty, vacant looking, as if they are dressed green, armed, and irritated zombies, not sure of their existence or their measure of events around them. Salty is a wonderful thing in the Nam. It means you've lived long enough to lose 20 percent of your body weight, have your clothes half rotting off, and earned the right to look like hell, while free of a subconscious that would waste attention analyzing that which makes no sense to analyze in the first place. Salty also means you have a countdown that can be nurtured, rather cherished, and half embraced to a point of some progressing self-satisfaction toward a likely return to the World. The final wake-up becomes painstakingly close enough to actually consider and then the big bird liftoff and back to the World that awakens a latent national spirit that got deeply buried for a while.

By early June 1968, both Emmerson and Rollie were salty. Emmerson was probably born salty, but there was no way from Nam to verify that hunch. A sergeant's black collar pins were chipped, revealing the gold below, and always crooked. Covers faded and sweat rotted jungle boots looked chewed on by Nam stuff. Both sergeants had the salty swagger by June, a swagger easy to notice by anyone looking into the Nam or timid about their own lack of salty or lack of don't-mess-with-me swagger.

June 7, Da Nang was practically a modern city in a perspective of anyone stuck up in Quang Tri since before Tet. Da Nang had everything needed for a good war. Supply guys and Corps purchasing guys had done a terrific job of spending US assets on anything and everything that might remotely need buying and shipping to an Asian war that looked like it would have no end, or actual meaning, once LBJ's "distraction phase" (more on that "distraction phase" in a couple chapters) was long forgotten. In Da Nang, jeeps and clean-looking officers hustled about as if always late for the next mapping or supply strategy session. American photographers with small packets of rolled film strewn on film holding strips all about them, passed by on Da Nang streets as if the next big photo op would jump out from the next dark leaning hooch, and then, they personally would be in a position to "scoop" the folks back home on some new Nam action or some optimistic upbeat theory. There were reportedly lipsticks here and there around Da Nang, certainly in the medical centers, but none had actually ever been seen by salty sergeants half from the bush, half from the dusty never seen, hard to explain, dangerous LZs.

Da Nang had the major airport for commercial jets from United, which most marines had flown in on. Unlike the small helicopter pad at Quang Tri, Da Nang was a major US-style air facility that could accommodate all kinds of aircraft including the small private looking passenger jets that ferried diplomats in and out for their two-hour photo op missions around lunch with other spiffed-up brass. Word was that somewhere in and about Da Nang was a place called Marble Mountain, which was PX land, offering all kinds of American made goodies for sale, just like a big-ass Walgreens, except right here in the Nam. Rumor was the PX was *air-conditioned.*

Marble Mountain had two other strange remnants of commercial America right there in Nam, right in south I Corps, as if the place had no suspicion of actually being part of a massive global teeter-tottering Cold War or part of the saving of Indochina from herds of armed Communists or certainly not part of anything related to the war as it was known in Khe Sanh or Quang Tri or Hue or Con Thien. First, Marble Mountain had a theatre with movies and real theatre-style seats to sit back in. Movies! Right there in I Corps. But that wasn't the extent of it: the theatre was definitely *air-conditioned!* Unbelievable! What a world-class warring supply chain! Would a normal person have any idea of what "air-conditioning" means to a grunt just out of the bush from a month of hot, humid, leechy-crawling, bloodsucking existence? Once on Marble Mountain, everyone went to see a movie, just to sit in air-conditioning for about two hours. What the movie was about was totally irrelevant. If you talked to a marine about being at Marble Mountain, at the theatre, and asked what the movie was, they all said the same thing: "The movie was about *air-conditioning*."

Second, right there at Marble Mountain, in Nam, southern I Corps, were car salesmen from Ford, Chrysler, and General Motors. So they said, if the rumor that Emmerson and Rollie heard was actually true. Rumor was, you could walk right up to those car-sellin' fellows who sat daily on their unfolded car-sellin' chairs and at folded out car sellin' card tables and look at pictures of new American cars. Not green open jeeps with machine guns mounted in the back end! Cars! According to Da Nang salties, you could talk to these car guys and actually buy a new car to be delivered to any dealership in the United States to be waiting at the time of a marine's wake-up and trip home across the big pond. Yep, no one in the entire world had ever created such an efficient wartime military/industrial chain of commerce. American selling ingenuity gone to war, all for the convenience of the soldiers and their countdowns, revolutionary in transporting commerce concept, apparently perfected in product group operations of car building and delivery. The global leader United States's free enterprising and deal making at its guaranteed captive market best. In Indochina, Nam, I Corps!

Reportedly, at Marble Mountain, a marine could buy a tube of toothpaste, go to an air-conditioned movie, and then buy a new car on the way back to the bush or back to Quang Tri or to Go Noi. No one ever explained or asked about cars ordered by marines who never saw their wake-up. Surely, there was a contingency clause in the ordering and fulfillment process that excused the buyer from completing his purchasing obligation if he were killed and thus not burden the grieving family with the unexpected bill of a new car. Car salesmen, right there in Nam, on the sidewalk, with a folding chair just like in the back yard next to the patio TV, unbelievable. Da Nang was a real city! Who would these car sales guys actually be? What mature American adult would go to Nam to sit within a 100-degree, miserably humid day, and hope some beat-up marine would come along with enough money, hope, and survival vision, to buy a car? So the rumor had some holes in it, but the salty of Da Nang swore to the truth of the car-sellin' rumor.

Emmerson and Rollie felt they had a couple days to steal for themselves in Da Nang before they were locked in and relocated back to the north by various sorts of orders that would certainly, eventually be coming their way, and thus, they set about with their brief freedom and constant impulsive planning.

> *Emmerson: Seems they've done it again, Stateside.*
>
> *Rollie: What now? We declare war on Peru or something?*
>
> *Emmerson: Naw, not yet. Didn't you hear? They've killed Bobby, Bobby Kennedy. Word I got is some asshole shot Bobby in LA, after a speech for winning the Dem's California primary. He'd a been elected president, you know. He'd a got us out of Nam yesterday. May have been the only hope for a while to get out."*
>
> *Rollie: No, I hadn't heard. Yesterday?*
>
> *Emmerson: Yeah, I think. Hell, I've been in this nasty dust bowl for almost a year and still can't tell if yesterday is tomorrow or some other sort of yesterday to folks back in the world. Doesn't matter, I guess. Don't change the countdown.*
>
> *Rollie: Bobby Kennedy. Wasn't enough to kill JFK and King and burn fifty cities down and blow up the university of this or that. They had to kill Bobby too. Shot, I presume?*
>
> *Emmerson: I guess, not sure. Ain't it somethin'? You suppose someone somewhere is looking way over the trees, across the planet running this war, while America itself falls apart. Ever notice how all these*

officers we see seem to be just going through motions, trying to act like they have a clue. Frankly I don't think any of 'em knows what's going on, what to do, what to do next, or what not to do. Which means nobody is gonna know how to win, when to win, and pull the plug on this useless shithole."

Emmerson: But, or one big butt, no matter, we're here and might just have a couple days to explore a bit. This is one big-ass base or city or whatever it's supposed to be. And it's payday or so they also say—I asked a couple base homies about payday and they said, "Today." What you say, me and you sniff around and find us a poker game for tonight. Gotta be one somewhere, and I bet at this big place, it could be a doozie, full of our best type of new friend: guppies!

Rollie: I call.

About 6:00 p.m., Da Nang time, America's tomorrow, or yesterday, on a base-homie tip, Emmerson and Rollie gently strolled in the motor pool maintenance building, quietly looked around. Quickly asking a couple questions, they were politely escorted by a fellow marine enlisted through a couple sliding doors into a back room, which doubled as a supply center twenty-eight days of the month. Bingo! Marines of all sizes, shapes, ranks, swagger, salty, hope, and bravado were feeling out the best chairs and tables to play from. This payday poker gaming was soon to begin. Shifting marines eyed new guys coming in to see if visuals could be made of the most probable guppies. While marines and a few other civilian looking characters began to fill eight different tables of players, Emmerson and Rollie took seats at different tables, in a line of sight to one another. Brief introductions that meant zero, quick check of funds, a pot raker ID'd, and cards started to fly by 6:30. Eight tables, seven or eight players per table, times paycheck and savings amounts =

thousands of US dollars to be on the tables, up for grabs, enough floating money to buy a house back in the World or a car at Marble Mountain. This was the "kill zone" opportunity that Emmerson and Rollie had dreamed of in the comparatively small games at Quang Tri or Phu Bai. Da Nang was looking up already, and most of the players seemed quite civilized, largely domesticated from war lives in the controlled safer city of Da Nang.

What war? These guys in Da Nang had no clue about Quang Tri or Agent Orange along a McNamara Line. They had no clue of Hill 881 or the dry creek beds of Go Noi. Da Nang was the rear with the gear, and these guppies looked like it. All happied up, clean, dark-green jungle boots with polished black heels and toes, some had combed hair. What the hell would these guys need a countdown and a wake-up for? This was Da Nang! Emmerson and Rollie had to follow directions past the ball diamonds and tennis courts just to find the motor pool poker game. Mamasans were all over the place cleaning air-conditioned offices for eight-hour work a day officers. Hell, the place looked like Pendleton to a couple Marines from Hue and Quang Tri. There was a Coke machine at the front entrance. A Coke machine! With Coca-Cola in it! Cold Coke!

Emmerson and Rollie knew this poker game was *the* poker game of their whole holy tour of duty, like a new different kind of Angel had delivered them to some sort of Nam respite honey-land of floating pay checks. This was the game that could make their tour of duty riches, all in one night, from guys they would never ever see again. At different tables but connected by frequent glances, the two sergeants set about their business that night of playing the best poker of their lives, showing no mercy to Da Nang strangers anxious to wager their paychecks. It makes a quiet but feel good, calming difference when two sergeants from north I Corps knew they would never again see any of the Da Nangers at the tables that night, strangely adds confidence and extra determination to the play.

To set out on a Nam mission of eight to ten hours of anything seems like an eternity. Nothing in Nam stays the same over eight to ten hours, especially post Tet, especially in the world of moving helicopters, and characters like Fletcher and Stuebe showing up like special needs killing programs, nothing, that is, except for poker games on payday. Poker games at payday are a once in a lifetime capsulized moment to dance on the minds and cards of the unsuspecting. The games are a mini, mental boot camp endurance process. Everyone starts the same; everyone has the same chance at the same cards, except it never works out that everyone is the same. Sooner or later, within thousands of thrown, flopped, or covered cards, the guppies give in to the wizards, sometimes slowly in a mostly folding close held game plan and sometimes most rapidly in a "call, or "all in" hope and prayer type of anti-operational game plan.

You'd think that occasionally, at least once, the guppies would just get lucky, draw some unbeatable cards that they themselves can't screw up. But no, that's not the war zone way it works. Unseen, undiscussable laws of poker nature keep guppies being guppies, losing like they are supposed to lose, as if losing is their own personal calling for the part of Nam life that stays under the radar. Payday guppies live for a very "natural selection" reason, like a food chain without food, just money, cards, and the personal satisfaction of the wizards.

By 10:00 p.m., what was once eight tables of players was now four tables of players, as guppies do their losing guppy thing (leave), and tables consolidate into groups of the night's modestly encouraged winners, and play continues, perhaps a bit more vigorously without the stutter-step guppies holding up routine strategy flop or hit me decisions.

By midnight, what were four tables of players becomes two tables of players, all sitting high and pretty, full of themselves for their winning ways. No more war or stateside table talk. No more stories of the home farm or the home babe or the huntin' dogs. By the time the game is down to two tables, a player can look around and see what he'll soon be up against when there is just one table, knowing the night's money flow will eventually go among just a few class act poker-winning wizards. Emmerson at one table, looked over his hawkish nose and played on with confidence, already knowing he still had two of his own table guppies to fleece, the others at his table knowing a little bit about the game. Rollie at the other table played along flawlessly, raking his pots in regularly, more than his share. And the night pressed on, the rest of the world and the war not even a suspicious afterthought.

More grumpy players abandoned their seats by 2:00 a.m., and the game was down to one table. Emmerson was the greyhound in seat 2, Rollie the immovable statue in seat 6, at a table of eight winners, already at it for near eight hours. By 2:00 a.m., the games are all five- or seven-card stud. No more foo-foo games of hi-low or split this or that—strictly stud poker. Faces behind the cards take on a cast iron determined, kickass look, minds tripping with poker agility strategy with each thrown card and facial expression or shift of playing posture.

At 3:00 a.m. and a new deal, five stud (one down, four up), Rollie made a bigger than usual reaction to his down card and second card thrown up—a Jack—and followed his overreaction with a healthy bet. Four players folded, including Emmerson, not wanting to have a Rollie showdown, just yet, but three players called. Second up card to Rollie was another Jack, two Jacks up, and a hole card all to Rollie's strategic self, followed by a little more vigorous bet, followed by two more folds. The final player in the game with Rollie raised. Rollie called and raised back. The other player called as Rollie rolled his eyes back under his salty poker cover. Emmerson was enjoying the show, other folders glued to the game. The game was nothing but silent, focused, waiting bodies on a fixed plywood table under one hanging light that captured, engulfed, and held the entire developing scene in a grip of poker adrenaline.

Third up card brought Rollie an 8'er, supposedly from Decatur as his opponent received another club, showing three puppy tracks up, all speaking to each other. Four cards into a five-card game, but the real spotlight was on the first up card, when Rollie uncharacteristically made such a big deal of one Jack up, which could likely mean another

Jack in the hole, which to the astute poker player, at near 3:00 a.m., of a long night of poker strategery would mean that the frickin Sarge from Quang Tri was probably sitting on three Jacks, after card 4. Good, but not unbeatable by the puppy tracks building up as an open ended straight in the hand of the remaining opponent for the tidy payday pot of the whole playing night.

The fifth and final card flopped, a 4 slid all dressed up in puppy tracks to Rollie's menace and another up Jack to Rollie. Rollie, high in his up hand, made a solid card salty bet. Could have made a bigger bet but didn't. Suspicious! Could almost be a come-on! A modest bet like that, with three Jacks up is meant to keep the menace *in the game*, not run him out. The menace, four puppy tracks rich on top, within reach of a straight flush, squeezed the dots off his hole card. Looked at Rollie's three Jacks, fingered his dollars and a few piasters off to the side, looked, bitched to no one and everyone, cussed a little, and concluded that lucky SOB from Quang Tri had a Jack in the hole to beat a straight or a flush, all based on Rollie's reaction to the first two cards dealt, one eternally glued down. Silence surrounds the table!

Emmerson could hardly keep his seat, stayed shut-up, lips sealed, eyes straight out and down to the center of the table, frozen. Rollie changed his posture from leaning back to leaning forward, adjusting the trusty salty cover that was as much a part of his head as were his ears. The unnamed menace, soon to be forgotten, unknown for eternity, slowly dropped his hands, his eyes, and probably his heart, and gave into the certainty of four Jacks, propped up by the hoorahs that he could not get out of his mind from Rollie's uncommon reaction to the first two cards dealt. Suddenly, against hope and judgment from the menace, the game had gotten too rich. The temporary menace folded his flush, cards plopped face down right next to the big pot. That was now Rollie's "big pot:" Poker night in Da Nang was a beautiful thing!

By 4:00 a.m., the game had a remaining four winning players, including Emmerson, and including Rollie, the biggest winner. The suggestion of rolling up the tents and packing the mules for the trip home, met with unanimous approval by all the final four enduring winners, happy to conclude with their winnings and living intentions to poker another Da Nang payday night. Emmerson and Rollie stuffed their money away in multiple pockets, into socks, under their covers and any place else they could stash some of the winnings, following the strictest of age old rules of poker: never count your winnings *at the table*. The civilized remaining players all respectfully and cautiously backed out of the motor maintenance supply depot, into the dark Asian, Da Nang night.

> *Emmerson: Let's move, get a little distance from this place. We may not be alone.*
> *Rollie: I'm with ya.*

Uniform-stuffed payday poker winnings, .45-caliber side arms, and M-16s linked to ammo belts strapped to upper bodies, the two winningest Sergeants in Da Nang, on that night, that payday, slipped on through friendlies, passing MPs, in a direction they thought would be toward the huge airstrip.

> *Emmerson: I wonder which way this Marble Mountain place is?*
> *Rollie: Have no idea, but I'm sure these MPs driving around know, might even get us a ride closer. Let's flag down the next one.*

Walking toward what they thought was the airstrip direction, now deep in the city neighborhoods of Da Nang, the streets were pitch dark, not much moving except for rats and island dogs doing their nightly scavenging. Occasionally, a front door was open or was "opening" with short flickers of candle light marking the opening, and silhouettes leaning cautiously outward at the two passing heavily armed marines. Emmerson and Rollie, with one hand on their 45s, cautiously kept the steady walking pace, moving along in a direction they hoped would go somewhere toward the main airstrip or Marble Mountain.

Two advancing lights ahead showed the next pair of MPs the two sergeants were hopefully walking to come across.

> *MP (riding shotgun): What 'n the b-jesus, you guys doing out here?*
>
> *Emmerson (always first to speak and to be in charge): We just dropped in on birds from up north, hoping to find a place they call Marble Mountain, but I think we're lost.*
>
> *MP (riding shotgun): You're lost, all right. Nothin' but Gooks around here. Get in!*

Nam MPs are good guys, especially when they don't have German shepherds with them. Riding around all night in Gook land puts an edge on 'em, probably the most dangerous jobs in Da Nang on a daily basis.

> *Emmerson: Y'all get hit hard at Tet?*
>
> *MP (driver): Hard enough. No one around here knew what to do. These folks live with one foot in Nam, the other in the States. Biggest decision some of these guys make is whether to go to the Officer's Club or go to one of the chippy bars run by the Gooks.*
>
> *MP (at shotgun): Where you guys from? You both look pretty salty. Been in the Nam long?*
>
> *Emmerson: Mostly Quang Tri, but recently some time in Phu Bai, both pre-Tet, and Tet.*
>
> *MP (driver): Ouch. Helluva mess up there, ain't it?*

Emmerson: Daily! We both been flyin' in and out of Quang Tri and I Corps hot spots since last October. Busy-ass places up there through Tet.

MP (at shotgun): Tet was big here but didn't last too long, or so they like to think. The biggest deal with Tet in Da Nang that no one talks about was G-2 estimates about five thousand VC and north regulars worked their way around the neighborhoods and airports, did their damage, killed a few folks, switched to civilian looking clothes, and only about one thousand of them left, maybe less, maybe a lot less. If you watch, pay attention, know how to look into the Nam, the place ain't the same. The faces changed, many more young Gooks around, looking out of doorways, begging in alleys, peddling rickshaws, or just working in the clubs. They disappear in plain sight, all around Da Nang, and we know it. Or at least, we MPs know it!

Emmerson: What's command doing about it?

MP (driver): Don't seem much they can or will do about it. Most of command are waiting for their wake-up, hoping the place doesn't explode again while they're still here, actin' like they are in a special zone of command countdown amidst the pending swirl of the next chaos. They act more like some endorsed, privileged kind of diplomatic countdown, as if that makes their numbers roll along a little faster. They aren't, you know, in command. No one is. This is just a place where they spend each day guessing how much the fuse has yet to burn. No one knows. A month, a year, three years—the Gooks ain't in no hurry. Here in great big Americanized Da Nang. It's just sunrise, dust, hot breezes in the day, less hot breezes at night, and then, the next sunrise. In the meantime, we fly more and more gear in and stack it everywhere there's a place to stack it, except for the part that goes directly into the black market. Out and around the airport, we got enough gear stacked and warehoused to supply all of Asia. Some folks back home are getting rich off Da Nang's black market alone, can't imagine what goes on in Saigon. We build buildings just to stack more gear that then goes out the door. More of it moves in the black market than it does to troops. Everyone knows, someday we'll just walk away from it all, leave it to the last Gook to turn the lights out.

Rollie: We got some gear work to do also, at least that's what G-4 told me. I think our next mission is back to Phu Bai and then off to find some forklifts that got lost on the way. Like we can't kill Gooks without plenty of forklifts.

Emmerson: You guys know anything about Bobby Kennedy getting shot, killed in LA a couple days ago?

MP (at shotgun): Yep, we heard about it. They oughta be killing that lying bastard Johnson! He's the war criminal. He and his tight group of buddies that land and stroll around here once in a while. Look at this place, crawling with corruption and under the table deals all supported by KIA and MIA numbers, tons of bombs dropped by anything they can get to fly something that has a hole in the bottom. For what? Seemed to me like killing Bobby was just kind of a supernatural signal that we're all in the boiling soup, and gonna stay in the boiling soup.

MP (driver): There, there's Marble Mountain. Walk up that road about three easy clicks and you'll see the big PX, the theater that everyone asks about

and wants to visit. It's air-conditioned, you know?
Good luck!

Emmerson and Rollie, talking over each other:
Thanks, guys, thanks a bunch, Good luck yourselves.
See you in the World. Where you guys from?

MPs: Iowa/Texas! You?

Emmerson and Rollie: "Norfolk. I'm a hundred
clicks south of Norfolk, Eastern NC—low country,
hot as Nam six months a year, or at least that's what
I used to think til I got here in this heat.

MPs: Well, we ain't too far from short. See y'all
in the World. Be careful, do what you gotta do. And
count!

Emmerson: Thanks a bunch for the ride and
help. Semper Fi.

MPs: Semper Fi.

Emmerson and Rollie steadily humped the few clicks up the road to Marble Mountain, saw the gargantuan theater and PX-land, and plopped down on the front concrete sidewalk about thirty minutes before the first light of a pink sun behind them to the east. Backs against the wall, the long night that started with a 6:30 poker deal among seventy strangers was finally over—one more Nam story for the memoirs and grandchildren. Seemed a safe enough place to nod off, and the two sergeants were soon sitting up asleep, anticipating nothing, expecting nothing, giving a damn about nothing. They had agreed, as soon as they woke up, "Let's count our money," the generous winnings donated from our seventy stranger best friends.

Marines normally sleep fast in Nam. But this one time, slow to give up the night's poker ass-kicking fun:

Emmerson: How much you think you got? You
were raking a pot every time I looked over, and that
last one with the Jacks must have been a good 'n.

Now you can tell me. Tell your good buddy Emm. Did you have four Jacks?

Rollie (knowing someday there could be a poker playing all-nighter with Emmerson, between the two of 'em, just the wizards): Don't remember! I have no idea how much money I tucked. I just kept stacking and stuffing. We'll see in the morning. How 'bout you? How much you think you put away?

Emmerson: Have no idea either. At least three thousand, maybe four, maybe more. I know it was a great game, maybe my best ever. Hopefully, this place here don't wake up so early."

When they slowly started to stir and open bleary eyes, stacked up against a brick wall in a warming morning in Nam, it doesn't matter what day it is, except for the always important countdown. It hardly matters what month it is. Nam is always the same: hot, fed by warm breezes, distant crashing and booming sounds of bombs or jets taking off, or passing MP jeeps, and skittish foot traffic. Sound asleep in Da Nang for a couple rather peaceful hours was kind of a vacation in itself. Hard concrete was just another inconvenience that would be followed soon by some other inconvenience that might not be as safe.

With a fully lit sunny sky, tinnish-hollow clicks and notching of clicking stuff into place, was finally enough ruckus to awaken the two drowsy sergeants. Sparse foot and jeep traffic out and about soon became busy foot and jeep traffic as the guys in the rear went about their busy PX or supply duties with the gear. Working civilian Mamasans and Papasans scurried to or from their American-style paying jobs. Some other civilians, robust American looking civilians down the sidewalk a few clicks on the PX front side began to set up their mobile shop for the day, selling whatever it was that they traveled half way around the world to sell in Nam, apparently to anyone buying.

Rollie: Emm, you awake?

Emmerson: I am now. You thinkin' what I'm thinkin'? Yep, let's count 'em.

Rollie: You first, or me. Can't both be counting. We'd draw too much attention. You count. I'll look out.

Emmerson: There's a thousand . . . There's two . . . There's three and counting . . . four thousand . . . seven hundred . . . fifty-three. My poker happenin' captain buddy . . . $4,753! Perhaps with another pocket I ain't found yet.

Rollie: Here we go, I think that big pot with the Jacks put me over that mark . . . There's a thousand . . . two . . . threeeeeeee . . . and fooooour . . . Cha-ching . . . High five . . . and six hundred . . . and kicking eight-six more singularos. That's $5,686 friendly new mementos from the Nam! Good God, precious lords of Nam. That might be more than a year's combat pay. I'll love Jacks the rest of my glamorous life! Thank you, Da Nang!

Emmerson: Not to dampen the moment, but what the hell do you do with thousands of dollars in Nam, in Phu Bai, or Quang Tri, ain't nothin' to buy. Can't send it home in a big fat envelope. Ain't no banks?

Rollie: Well, for the time bein', let's just feel it. Here, smell that stack of US dollar bills. Always the same smell, Asia or the US!

Laid back against the concrete and brick walls of the PX, Emmerson and Rollie just sat there in their self-imposed quiet shared victorious gloriousities. Nam, for that day, hadn't got to 'em yet. Armed well enough and suddenly kind of rich, certainly rich by Nam Marine enlisted standards, the two sergeants inhaled the rare kick-ass moment. If somebody would walk by with a cold beer for them, that could be about as good as it gets, for that Indochina warring day.

> *Emmerson: You know who I think those guys down there are?*
>
> *Rollie: The heavyweights in the civvies? Clicking open the chairs and tables?*
>
> *Emmerson: Yeah, those guys. You know damn well they are from the States. Probably runaways from bad marriages or, worse, bad deals. I think those guys may be the car sales guys they told us about. Look, they got stuff laid out, to show folks that stop and talk to them.*
>
> *Rollie: Might be. Stand up, dust off a bit. Let's go say howdy. We got all day. The movie don't start for seven more hours.*

The sergeants, loaded down with weapons, salty covers, and pockets of stuffed cash, cautiously moseyed along the sidewalk, into better sightseeing range, and paused as if hidden in a tree line. Soon, they proceeded on into the combative selling zone, and stared down on the first heavyset, red-faced, bleary-eyed car sales guy happily resting in his reinforced lawn chair, flashy car info all over the snappy clicked together car sellin' table.

The scene was a bit out of place, almost inspirational. Atop the Marble Mountain was a particularly American scene. A pretend Walgreens (PX), a big box of a building, air-conditioned for movies, and plump happy car sales guys, with color brochures of new shiny American cars. The scene itself was of the world they suddenly realized had collectively been left behind, kind of.

Facing the car salesman, the backdrop was Americana. Glass doors to the fake Walgreens, movie marquee posters promoting the next air conditioned movie, and pretty snapshots of classic American symbolism. Cars! Our cars, Detroit cars! The crazies back home can kill Kennedy's and kill King and burn up cities, but they can't stop the industrialists from making things nor can they stop military folks from buying those things. The scene was safe, refreshing, optimistic, reassuring until you turned around and faced the other way, down the mountain. Facing that other way, away from PX-land was the hustling chaos of dashing jeeps kicking up Nam dust, expressionless Gooks moving with heads down. Beyond was the perpetual poverty of the villages and outskirts of Da Nang that would change a flimsy existence in an instant, depending on the prevailing powers.

Facing out from the US buildings of Marble Mountain was Nam capsulized. Modern airstrips, huts, forklifts moving gear, young dirt poor Asian moms with babies on their hips—all with no hope of a peaceful future of any kind, unless they escaped on a boat to nowhere, then to another boat, then another. The three car sales guys sat in the shade daily, meeting US soldiers, passing their own time, and seeing Nam at its most "confusing" opposites. Truly, the more the place changed with American strength and warring ingenuity, the more it stayed the same in Asian cultural paralysis.

Within a few lazy Nam minutes, Emmerson and Rollie were getting along famously with the car sales trio as if destined for partnerships that warming morning in a hemispheric flip of conflict fate. Of course, really good car sales guys born unto their talented selves are by nature to befriend anyone with thousands of dollars stuck in or hanging partially out of passing pockets. The two marines just sucked up the fun of talking to guys who could actually carry on a conversation and who had been back in the World just recently. Emm and Rollie learned that California was still California. The Midwest seemed to still be growing corn, and of course, folks in Detroit were still designing and building cars, yet unscathed by the creeping disposition of political industrializing chicanery that would begin to undermine all of it.

Not long into post-introduction niceties among the small group of new best friends, Emmerson decided to spend his nightly winnings on a brand-new Mercury Cougar, maroon, convertible, to be picked up in Norfolk about October 10. The Ford car sales guy drew up the papers and got to the "How and when would you like to pay for this shiny Cougar there, Sergeant Emmerson," all part of the fair exchange. The clever Emmerson always ahead of the uptake calmly asked the amount of payment that would be due to take possession back in good ole Norfolk. Mr. Ford/Mercury, car sales guy, scribbled away at his figures in a contemplative struggle as if it were his first rodeo, figured all the options and add-ons, pretended to throw in some meaningless goody like high-speed, super stealth windshield wipers and handed Emm the scribbled note.

> *Emmerson: Hey thanks, good buddy. If that's all it is, I'll just pay for the whole thing right here and now, if that's OK? Is this figure correct? Includes delivery to the Norfolk dealership? $3,852? That it?*

With a hesitant nod from the Mr. Ford car-sales guy, now a stateside Buddy, Emmerson started pulling out stacks of money to begin his Cougar count.

> *Emmerson: There you are, good buddy. $3,852, as agreed. Oh, just one more thing. If that car ain't there, in Norfolk, October 10, like you just promised. I'll find you and frag your fat ass. You know what fraggin' is, right? Deal? Just kidding.*

In all of Nam, who'd a thunk of winning enough poker dough pocket change in one night to buy a car, an MP escort to Marble Mountain, and *ending up with a dream car to be waiting for the post wake-up, rat there-in-good-ole, can't-wait-to-see-ya-Norfolk!*

Having been shown the way, Rollie scootchied on down the sidewalk a super short click, past the Mr. GM new friend, and on to the smiling Mr. Chrysler car selling guy new friend. Rollie knew what he wanted, knew he had the cash, but didn't want to make the sale too easy especially when there were still six hours before AC movie time. Rollie raised a grin from Mr. Chrysler and then bounced back to Mr. GM's premature grin, then back to Mr. Chrysler, then to Mr. GM, then off to the side for a private discussion with Emmerson, all while facing the walls and openings to Americanized style business-looking places; with the real, poor, nasty, killing Nam to his back, almost out of sight for the moment, and out of mind, almost.

Hoping the appearance of buying uncertainty would have a pricing effect on the waiting Mr. Chrysler car-sales guy, if that were at all possible, Rollie slid over and leaned into Mr. Chrysler and his unfolded, clicked together dealership.

> *Rollie: Tell me about that lean, fast, chick mobile right there, the Dodge Charger. I'm looking for a car bad enough to cruise through campus with the windows down, and the chicks'll jump through the open windows for a couple smooth rides.*
>
> *Mr. Chrysler: Young man, you have most intelligently nailed that car's most astounding feature. Chicks jumping through the windows are exactly what the reports are from new 1968 Dodge Charger owners all over America, especially those who are Nam veterans. What color would you like yours to be?*

In no time, Mr. Chrysler was into the trial close, the paper work and detail of the sale. White body, with a black vinyl top, dancing chrome wheels, 383 engine, with a four-barrel carburetor, four-speed on the floor, bucket seats with a console—and super, fast moving power windows, seemed appealing priority features. For pickup in Raleigh, North Carolina, October 17.

> *Mr. Chrysler: Congratulations, Sarge. You've picked the finest car on the American roads today,*

that car will only come to $3,684. Please sign right here. And, Sarge, how would you like to pay for this dream car?

For a while, time stopped. Within the whole Americanized scene, it was as if the filth and danger of Nam didn't even exist. As if Khe Sanh and Quang Tri were distant long forgotten instances of passing bad dreams, as if what was just behind them wasn't just behind them. As if the two sergeants weren't draped in weaponry and ammo for killing or defending. For that one moment, on that sidewalk, with those strangers and a good buddy, on June 9 or was it June 10, the all-important countdown was suspended at one hundred and thirty something.

Rollie simplified the paying issue by laying out stacks of poker winnings and letting Mr. Chrysler do the counting. Just a real content feeling of accomplishment, almost a happy Nam moment washed over the whole group, even over Mr. GM who was zero for two on his new car selling day joined into the happy moment. Sale and paperwork complete, Rollie's two grand of change tucked back away and a signed sales agreement as proof that the whole deal actually happened. He and his buddy, Emm, turned to walk away into their Marble Mountain day and maybe some air-conditioning, hopefully toward the coldest Coke ever poured down a dry throat.

> *Rollie, who was a few steps away, turned to look back at a glowing Mr. Chrysler: Sir, thanks. You do understand it's ditto on the frag-thing, if that car don't show up.*
> *Mr. Chrysler: I understand, Sarge. It'll be there! You just be careful driving around with them windows down.*
> *Rollie: Gotcha. You take care, big guy. Thanks.*

For the two sergeants from north I Corps, Marble Mountain was everything that they had heard it to be. Hard goods American style right there in Nam! Some unremembered movie about noon that day was nice and cool, with a Coke. Walgreens was loaded with stuff like soap and tooth paste and powder to dry up some stinking body stuff at least for a couple days until the powder ran out. Marble Mountain was a dream place, a mini-R&R, and new cars—all financed by Da Nang's eager guppies. Semper Fi!

If only the two sergeants didn't have to turn around to their reality for four more staggering months, including heading back up to I Corps north. But they did have to turn around, soon, the next day. Sergeants Emmerson and Rollie would head straight into their final Nam experiences, now with a little more faith in their angels and visions of their waiting new cars, windows down.

That very evening, Rollie found a C-130 headed for Phu Bai and jumped aboard. C-130s to Phu Bai or about any other Nam base were easy to catch from Da Nang. A constantly busy supply chain of war things from the World into moving or fixed Nam locations always needed moving from one lost place to the next soon to be abandoned place. The supply guys, in the rear, dutifully massed around the Asian side of logistical operations, logistically completing deals made months ago on the other side of the world by practiced war stuff logistical deal makers, kept all streams of stuff moving in every direction.

Emmerson would catch a couple MPs for a ride over to some parked Air America props at the vast long airstrip, trusting that his pilot buddies would be close by and ready for any planned or unplanned missions, especially a milk run and drop up to usually friendly Phu Bai.

Both had agreed to meet at Phu Bai in one day, back at S-4, and see if those rumored orders to find the forklifts were still real, or if new priorities had come up and along some always invisible command line. Both sergeants feeling short but not that short, strong but not invincible, "salty" but not yet pickled.

By June 11, back within the barbed wire perimeters of Phu Bai, Rollie was first to discover the rumored order to find eight lost forklifts was not a rumor. S-4 command Phu Bai indeed had some forklifts coming, and wanted them. Trouble was, the search would be to the north, back to Hue, perhaps then east on the Perfume River, maybe to blue water. Some place between Hue and the big cargo ships bobbing pleasantly with the rhythms of the South China Sea the forklifts had reportedly been unloaded and then lost track of. True Nam logistical SNAFU processes! It was not uncommon for one unit to commandeer certain supplies from another unit for their own use. Worse yet, the entire country seemed to have an entire black market subculture mentality, as if anything within the deals and supply lines was fair game. Papers get lost; stuff gets lost and blown up or sunk. When it comes to supply lines, salty "Tops" can be quite creative in supply management procedures and paper trails. After all, who knows? Who really cares?

Rollie, of course, was familiar with Hue, carried enough stripes to move around with some freedom and authority, and salty enough not to get killed before he found the phantom forklifts. He was to head that way just as soon as he could get organized and study some sort of travel and search plan of operations. He also wanted and needed Emmerson to go along, so he waited and checked in with the Air America renegades two, three times a day.

Waiting on Emmerson was always an uncertain tempo of a different kind. Emmerson did nothing normally, within a predictable timeline. No one even knew from where he received his operating or mission orders, and he would never tell. Never did tell! It hardly seemed real that he was even actually in the Marine Corps, maybe just wearing the uniform with a made-up military ID number and shirt pocket name tag, always armed with small arms firepower. If the Marine Corps had a "freelance" ops man, it was Emmerson. But as usual, Emmerson did show up, at S-4, front and center to Rollie and their pending orders—naturally ready to go, seemingly intrigued by the challenge of the unusual mission. He'd not been to Hue before, and suddenly, Hue seemed important to him, a priority.

One quick late afternoon and evening at the Phu Bai Sarge's Club with a small herd of salty dogs, the two would create their operations and travel agenda plan and be ready to go north by the next morning, traveling the necessary air clicks that it would take to reach Hue. They'd catch a helicopter ride from one of Phu Bai LZs to the Army Signal Corps communication center just southwest of Hue and meet with a Captain Guthrie, who supposedly would know the current status of areas and general travel in all of I Corps, but especially around Hue. From there they'd find a grunt platoon patrolling into or around Hue, hopefully with a CO who had intricately become familiar with the area, where to pass through, and where to stay out of. "Mission Forklift," of all things war-like, would be underway. Seemed a strange priority, finding lost forklifts, but orders were orders. Maybe the trip will be more secure with Tet now a few months passed. Maybe it won't be much more than sightseeing parts of Nam, with smiling, grateful Vietnamese peasant homies welcoming the two sergeants every step, singing patriotic American songs, throwing flowers in their brave liberating paths. Maybe not!

The communications center at Hue, staffed and managed by the army, knew everything I Corps and could catch Rollie up on places he had flown into back in the middle of the Tet chaos. Khe Sanh had been brutally defended, magnificently oversupplied, and then abandoned. Con Thien remained the most blasted and ripped spot on the earth for 1968 as plans were being made to abandon that hilltop LZ overlooking the McNamara Line in favor of mobile marine and army ground recon who would work in and out, owning no ground for very long, just identifying North Vietnamese Regular movements and calling in massive aerial bombing tonnage when necessary or the urge struck or future reports required.

Rollie quickly learned that not much in north I Corps had changed or could be considered improved for the better. Reports from Quang Tri, just a few clicks up the road from Hue, were same ole. Lots of Huey/Chinook traffic all over the place, dropping grunt troops in here and there, picking up wounded marines and the dark-green zippered body bags of those whose countdowns had prematurely violently ceased. More and more munitions traveled by any means capable, creating the constant need for greased supply lines, which demanded more and more in-country Wilson Street boys. Whatever the mission, or whatever the orders, Rollie would stay away from Quang Tri, feeling his luck in that place had run plum beyond what an angel could shield against.

Emmerson laid down his communications center head phones after talking to someone, somewhere, and sporting a brand new snub-nose .45-caliber machine gun acquired from other unnamed sources, stated his eagerness and readiness to sightsee Hue and find some extra special super-duper forklifts. B Company, Fourth Marines would be moving into Hue toward the east Perfume at noon. The two forklift hunters could join B Company and then break off toward the east, up river toward the coast, or wherever they thought forklifts would be hanging out. Army Signal Corps would communicate their mission to all friendlies in the area and see if they could get a directional hint that might save some time, effort, and perhaps save their lives from some smart ass Gook sniper hanging out around Hue still hungry or feeling froggy. The walk back into Hue was spooky for Rollie as with each step he tried to explain to Emmerson the Battle of Hue, just five months past, and the constant bone-chilling smells, heavyweighted air and red clay holding all boots from each step out of one clay hold into the next sticky, infected, toxic clay step.

B Company moved with precision, tuned to and part of the dangerous landscape. They moved quietly and deliberately through bombed, blasted, and shot-up neighborhoods. Exhausted, frightened Asian eyes leaned out from doorways or from the partial safety of short walls and glared at the marines as they passed by. The human Asian eyes looked no different than the looks of the ever present scavenging island dogs who seemed to live through it all as if being their own special kind of drifty ghosts of the spent landscape.

Everything Asian in Hue '68 was just trying to stay alive by animal instinct, with no plan or real hope of a better way, or a better day, unsuspecting that anything would save them from some eventual catastrophic demise. Asian eyes, in Hue '68, carried no hope at all, were numb, beaten, unconcerned about who would win a war they saw daily but truthfully had no idea about.

The scene didn't bother Emmerson as much as it infuriated him with the uselessness of the whole situation, realizing at some point five months ago in order to save Hue, it had to be turned to structural and human rubble. One look was all he needed to understand that Hue was merely a representative snapshot of the misery and hopelessness of the entire wannabe country. Emmerson and Rollie walked with B Company but felt totally separate from B, knowing the escort would soon go in their own ordered direction, and the two of them would be left alone somewhere deep within Hue, among waiting uncertain stark elements. The place still was stinking of death. It was a place where something "good" happening was inconceivable, not even a remote possibility. Suddenly, the mundane task of finding forklifts fell deeply back into the uncertainty of the war where every wall and curve presents a great new possibility to prematurely conclude the countdown.

Soon, the majority of the spread out B Company was at the Perfume, just aside the shot-up, pocked, beaten walls of the historic Citadel, just fought to the death over by young determined mad marines who would not be denied the victory of their mission. The Perfume was heavy, layered with curves of various types of surface scum, reeking of smells left behind from the late February battles. Barbed wire stretched around openings and over what was left of bridges. Depressingly, Rollie knew he had returned to a scene he had hoped he would never feel again. The visual impact of a time passed reached deep inside of him grasping his conscious and subconscious feelings. Broken, torn things still lay about, including sunken uniforms of once VC and NVA, beaten in the late February showdown with the marines of the Fourth Division. Rollie tried to explain it all to Emmerson but knew the experience could only partially be related, never actually felt by anyone not there, just like the other million stories of Nam from Tet and the rest of 1968.

B Company had orders to search (and destroy) within the Citadel, clean up anything left to clean up, leaving the two sergeants along the Perfume to choose a direction and regroup within their own plan: The silly plan to find eight missing forklifts that would more easily move vast tonnage of war supplies from point A to a point B around Phu Bai. Forklifts! In Nam! Americanized industrial supply efficiency, forklifts that require tires, fuel, parts, and mechanics that know how to use the parts, while Gooks move massive amounts of fire power all over the damn place by foot, hard and lean sweating, obedient to a cause Asian backs.

> *Rollie: How many forklifts you suppose it took to win WWII?*
>
> *Emmerson: Huh, not sure they even had forklifts in WW II. Germans probably did.*
>
> *Rollie: I bet I've seen fifty forklifts running around Phu Bai right now and supply needs eight more, bad enough to have our short asses up here along the Perfume. This place has got to be crawling with Gooks . . . and we're walking around looking for forklifts.*
>
> *Emmerson: You're looking at this thing all wrong. You see, it isn't the forklifts that are important. Nobody gives a rat's ass about forklifts! Nobody does. Like you say, there must be fifty, maybe one hundred forklifts running around Phu Bai right now. It's about* deals. *Some forklift sales guy, just like our buddies Mr. Ford and Mr. Chrysler, are running around the Pentagon with midsummer forklift sales specials. It's deals. You know, buy one now, get one free this fall kind of a*

deal thing. Or 25 percent off, if you order in time for the next Tet Offensive. Plus, a 25 percent kick-back/wrap-around to the purchasing agents favorite political fund, matched six months later with an equal order for more forklifts. See? Get it? We're just at the end of the supply chain, which needs to stop by the way. All of a sudden, this milk-run mission to find forklifts, of all things, is starting to feel like Fletcher and Stuebe stuff. It's one of a million stupid ways to get killed.

Rollie: Thanks, I really needed to hear how insignificant we are and how far down the human war chain we have slumped to. Well, we're here. Let's follow the Perfume east, find a camp or an LZ, and see if we can figure out what's where. Find a way to get from this brown water to the blue water guys that probably know what's going on. If at each camp we call back to Guthrie, he said he'd keep track and see what he can locate. He may be the best shot we have to keep moving in the right direction.

Emmerson: Speaking of Guthrie, did you get a chance to talk to him much?

Rollie: No, not much, just about hitching in with B Company and likely directions and procedures. Why?

Emmerson: Well, I did . . . had a chance to talk a little bit about back in the World. Did you know that America, NASA, is preparing to send a manned spacecraft to the moon? Next year, Guthrie said! To the moon! Now I'm telling ya, we sit here in the arm pit of the globe, walking Gook infested trails, looking for stupid forklifts, in a war no one has a clue about—and smart folks, with other kinds of US military/industrial stuff are gonna fly to the frickin' moon? What's wrong with that picture?

Rollie: No, I didn't know anything about that. You think it's true?

Emmerson: Well, I don't know. Guthrie seemed pretty smart, informed, can't imagine why he'd care about foolin' a couple stupid sergeants out all over I Corps looking for some steel on tires with long forks out front. Or I suppose he could figure if we are this stupid, he could have a little fun with us going to the moon story, like we may just as well be on the moon, right now. Might rather be! Not sure, the guy had a strange logic to him, but maybe he's a little desperate to have some fun with a few passing leatherneck guppie sarges.

The two make-do sergeants traveled on foot east along the northside of the Perfume, eventually to the edge of Hue. Facing the sparse sandy country side on a trail that could include anything, it seemed certain they would spend a night back to back, locked and loaded, at some reasonable vantage point. Au contraire, for these two nothing was normal!

Before the Asian late day haze of predusk would settle in, the Perfume ahead became full of the deep sound of working diesel engines, moving deliberately west, toward Emmerson and Rollie. US diesel engines were easy to identify compared to the putt-putt sounds of Gook sampans that move around coastal rivers doing their hidden business. Soon, the heavily armed PT boat came into sight: dark, armed, solid, a whole different type of war personality from what was going on in the interior. The two armed sergeants cautiously showed themselves on the north riverbank, and the PT gently swerved toward them, then coasted up and reversed engines to a stop, all machine guns manned, at a ready, pointing in every river bank direction.

> *PT captain: We're looking for two marine sergeants. You look like them. Cahill and Emmerson?*
> *Sgt. Rollie Cahill: Yep, that's us. Super glad to see ya!*
> *PT captain: "We got orders to find y'all and pick you up. Get in. We don't like being up here, this close to Hue, so jump in, and we'll head back and drop you off at the Army Camp Diane set up about five clicks down river, a couple clicks in from the South China.*
> *Cahill: We're in, thanks.*

And instantly, the war, the mission, short, was better, kind of OK again, a fortunate reversal of expectations for the night ahead that the sergeants were mentally preparing for another "Nam surprise." The quickly arriving night would not capture them in the bush this time. Suddenly, Emmerson and Rollie had new best friends, armed and mobile, they knew where they were going, and the night looked OK, at least for a while. The river scum had cleared this far up river from Hue, as the diesels purred gracefully east, away from Hue, diesels gliding effortlessly on the brown Perfume. Machine gunners on each side, never flinched, never looked up to see the new passengers they had been put at risk to find and retrieve, ordered again not to care what lost roving bodies were stupid enough to even be out there. The scrubby-pathed shorelines slowly but steadily passed on both sides of the river. There were a hundred places for a sniper to hide in and do his killing work, then disappear into the bush, if they could, before these poised PT gunners would unload fifties on them. The war in Nam changed constantly; no one ever knew what was next or why. Nam on the ground, or on the Perfume, was all about being ready, agile with quick reactions and weapons. All about surprises, constant surprises!

PT captain: There you go, guys, Camp Diane, set up by army lead teams about two months ago. You're looking for Captain Tracy. Good luck!

Cahill: Thanks a bunch, Cap. You been on this river long, too long?

PT captain: I've been PT'n troops, command, recon, ammo, bales, and green zippered bags up and down the Perfume, I Corps coast, and out to cargo ships my entire Nam life. We don't get in the bush much. Picking you guys up is as up river as we try not to get. This is a whole different type of war out here on the water. When Huey and Chinook guys get hit, shot up a bit in I Corps, knocked down, they always head for the beaches. We pick 'em up if we can get to 'em. That's what we live for. All this other stuff is just milk-run stuff. But I must say, we don't see dumbasses like you guys out wondering around very often. But orders were to find 'em, so we did.

Emmerson: Bet not. Hopefully, we'll never meet again. What's your name?

PT captain: Magsamen, from Nashville. Good ole, beautiful Nashville. Be careful. You guys short, how short?

Rollie: Too short to be back up in Hue looking for stupid forklifts. About 121, maybe less, lost track. Can't wait for that 100.

PT captain: Ten-four, after my wake-up and bird back, I'm gonna stand on dry Tennessee ground for a while, dry American ground, look into Mrs. Mags, make sure she's good, then she and I'll have some fun living.

Army Captain Tracy was easy to find. He'd been contacted by Captain Guthrie, let in on the now infamous hunt for the "8 forklifts" mission, and had been told by the Navy ship just off shore that the forklifts were unloaded a month ago, and moved down the coast to Chu Lai, apparently by some sort of SNAFU mix match of paper flow. Furthermore, Captain Tracy had arranged for Emmerson and Cahill to be picked up first thing in the morning by an Army Air Cav Chinook and taken to Chu Lai. A Major Buzan, S-4 Chu Lai, would be looking for them later that day. In the meantime, Emmerson and Rollie could enjoy all the accommodations of Camp Diane, named in honor of the captain's mother, a Red Cross nurse of many years and other past wars. Not wanting to take a chance on missing the morning ride south, the two sergeants found the small chow tent and then found the camp's LZ to settle down inside the convenient coastal security of the guard bunker.

> *Emmerson: You know, bud, what I'd wish for right now, if I had one wish in all the world?*
> *Rollie: Oh goodness, I can't imagine. What?*
> *Emmerson: I'd wish the forklift sales guy and the Pentagon Full-Bird that signed orders for these forklifts, probably a year ago, I'd wish part of their duties was to deliver the damn things and if the forklifts were lost, those milk sops would have to find them. This crap would not only, not get lost, it wouldn't even get ordered, for fear of having to fulfill the small print issues on the orders to deliver them.*
> *Rollie: Super wish, super idea. Probably have a few Congressional snags in implementation, but you hit on something, something bigger. If the whole war were run like that, clear to the top, this mess would end by Monday. What day is it anywho?*

Forklifts? How much stuff wouldn't get moved around if eight forklifts are never found, which they probably won't be? Truth is, it won't matter. Cahill had to keep reminding himself:

> *It isn't about the forklifts. It's about the deals!*
> *The entire frickin' war is about deals, must be. Deals*
> *of all kinds, and flavors and wrappings! There's so*
> *much crap moving in and around Nam, it probably*
> *takes more deal makers at the Pentagon than it does*
> *sergeants and S-4 officers to hunt the stuff down and*
> *keep track of it. It's not even a fightin' war any more,*
> *maybe never was, it's a deal-makin' war!*

Nam was turning into a churning industrial use permit system of flowing parts and paperwork. If you paid attention, Nam seemed to be more and more about ancillary camp maintenance and transportation than it did about guns, ammo, bombs, and gutsy marines to fight the actual battles. This was a little different type of military/industrial relationship right down to the lumber yards and sporting goods. Wait until this newfound war supply niche matures! Then what?

Dawn always comes to Nam among tired, bleary—"Here we go again" eyes, hearts and dry mouths. Rollie's trained, salty senses picked up the early sounds of Chinook blades coming from the Southeast, long before a visual could be made.

> *Rollie: Hey bud, listen. Here we go. One day*
> *closer to that maroon topless Cougar.*
> *Emmerson: Don't use the word topless! OK?*

The army's yellow and black First Air Cav logo on the front of the Chinook was a blessed welcome sight growing larger in the sky as if pulling along the rising pinkish brightness from the sun further

DICK FOX

to the east. Quickly, helmeted crew with the same yellow and black patches helped the sergeants aboard. Just as quickly as the bird had arrived, it lifted and tilted nose-down forward, back toward the sea and the direction from which it had just arrived. Two hundred feet, nose-down, blades thumping faster, the big bird leaned through the morning air, back toward the coastal rising sun, crew locked and loaded, nameless hidden pilots doing their daily First Air Cav work flawlessly as they had done and would continue to do for thousands more warring days in The Nam. Six hundred feet, Emmerson and Rollie tucked tightly in cargo straps could see the landscape below passing quickly by. Eight hundred feet and the sea to the east showed itself a colorful rolling blue, strands of scenic whitecaps as normal as any US coastal whitecaps. The bird leaned right . . . to the south . . . down the coast, and for the moment, things in Nam seemed OK, almost thrilling, surprise-free.

Calm moments in Nam don't last and are never predictable. Tat-tat-tat-tat! Tat-tat! And the crew on the right, across from the two sergeants, urgently started firing down, unloading the '50s fire power as the bird's radios started an urgent chatter. Rollie had heard the tat-tat sounds before in his copter days, it was small arms ground fire hitting the sides of the Chinook.

Rollie (yelling): Hang on, Emm, we're hit.
Strap in tight.

Through the cockpit opening, they could see two pilots, frantic with the business of keeping the bird in the air. The Chinook, slightly lowered, leaned left toward the coastline, lowered more, and the crew hand signaled the two sergeants that the bird was going down. Right there. Ten minutes off Camp Diane. And it did!

Pilots, crew, and sergeants rode the thing down into Asia, with a mega-womp, huge rotor blades cutting into and tearing up anything within their centrifugal reach. Crew gunners thrown violently in every direction, two didn't get up. Two did and immediately scrambled to their machine gun assignments. The other two downed crew slowly started to move, cautiously testing arms, legs, necks, and heartbeats. Rollie had seen this act played out before, unhooked, and leaped to the rear to the unmanned fifty. There they all sat for a few seconds, gathering their thoughts and nerves, appraising the situation, two pilots at their radios and instrumentation work in the front. Emmerson unhooked, grabbed his 16, and snub nose .45 Uzi-looking weapon and was out the right side to the sandy scrub ground in a flash, first to form a crude perimeter defensive position.

All weapons locked and loaded, one pilot came from the cockpit, ordered two crew and Rollie out the side, one to the front, one to the rear, Emmerson where he already was would be in the middle, all personnel measuring all things west of the downed bird, the remaining cockpit pilot busy on the radio, two crew still on the side door 50s. Thoughts of forklifts and easy morning milk runs were long gone. The second pilot, Major Rund, grabbed remaining aircraft 16s and ammo belts, and leaped with the rest of the crew off the right side, into the sand, seemingly in the middle of nowhere-Nam. All eyes back to Rund for a direction or an order, or some sort of regroup and plan. Everyone knew what was next.

Gooks that see downed birds swarm from everywhere to the sight of the crash. Downed aircraft were the special work of VC and north regulars. There was nothing they liked better than to capture an aircraft and any crew, such work being their symbolic reprieve for the damage aircraft do to their countryside, people, and determined, patient Asian processes. Armed, hungry Gooks would no doubt soon begin to appear among the moving scrub brush of the near coastal plains, and the downed Americans would be their once in a warring lifetime target.

Just as determined as Gooks swarming to downed aircraft, are American fighters from other Air Group units, to rescue anyone shot down, and do it ASAP, as the war's #1 priority, when called upon, the only priority at critical times. Rund gave quick orders to regroup and move east away from the downed bird. There were eight of them in the escape, six Army Air Cav, and the two marine sergeants, all trying in their own ways and worlds to get shorter, while doing their tough, deadly vital work. East was the South China Sea a short click or two, unlikely to hold any enemy groups of much size, the sandy landscape being too much in the open. A good thing and a bad thing in this situation but move east this half-size squad would do. First a half click, then another half click, marines in the middle, a major and his trusty crew chief always in the rear looking back. Rund was certain their situation and location had been radioed clearly and was equally as certain mad new Air Cav birds would be on the way, but he didn't know from where they would launch, and thus, the timing of arrival and rescue would be impossible to calculate. He was certain the radioed return orders to immediately clear away from the downed bird were so Huey gunships could arrive first to strafe the area of any advancing Gooks but also to lay a couple rockets into the downed bird and destroy any assets from being left in degenerate Gook hands.

The good news was, the pilots, crew, two marines had all day. That's the beauty of being shot down by 7:00 a.m., you got all day to figure out how to position defenses and survive the next night. *Getting shot down early in a day is a real survival advantage.*

The mostly hidden little group of air-crashed survivors laid spread out prone to the terrain, looking back to the site of the crash and the likely direction of any enemy ground pressure, the South China Sea, just a couple short clicks or less behind the poised group. Small arms pop-pops, from the area of the downed bird, began to break the quiet. Likely ground Gooks approaching the crash site, meaning they would soon be onto the sandy trail of Americans surely hidden in the sparse brush to the east of the controlled crash site.

Emmerson: You OK? Loaded?
Rollie: I hope I never see another forklift. Yeah,
I'm good, good as I get in this shit hole. You?

Emmerson: Hell yes. I gotta be good. I gotta new Cougar to pick up. These Air Cav guys look like they know what they're doin', we got enough guns and ammo . . . It's just a firefight for our lives and an emergency evacuation pick up by some birds that might, or I suppose might not be on the way. That's all, just that. We got all day to figure this out.

Rollie: Listen, I hear blades a-ready. I hear lots of blades.

Rollie: Whoa Nelly, Emm, look behind you.

Low, over the scrubby bush coastal range, just coming off the coast were a squadron of yellow and black First Air Cav logos, noses down, spread two in front, six wide behind them, moving fast, a friendly, strong, brave, U.S. ass-savin' sight to behold. Just above the scrambled crash survivors, the two lead Hueys let go with four rockets each, secondary explosions marking a hit on the downed Chinook, destroying the bird and anything remotely useful inside, or close around. As the next wave of six Hueys approached, two broke off to the north, two to the south, with two straight ahead. Within seconds, all six Hueys were firing down upon Gooks rushing the crash site for their own war trophies. It was a beautiful sight, cut short by the third wave, which were two more guard Hueys and a beautiful First Air Cav Chinook landing at the sight of Major Runds location, marked by the yellow flare thrown close, just wide of the eight crashed survivors.

Guest marines in first, crew, then one officer pilot, and then Rund, and with the last step off the sand, the rescue Chinook lifted gracefully, did the midair pivot toward the sea, and laid a nose-down, all engines and jets forcing the quick escape and return trip from the bush. The eight lead Hueys remained circling with exquisite displays of American fire power, slow to give up their chases. The rescue Chinook and two escort Hueys were soon over the rolling blue South China Sea, all crew standing down from the side guns, enjoying the view and the rescue accomplishment, all before 8:00 a.m. on another day in the Nam.

> *Rollie: Where you guys out of.*
>
> *Chinook crew chief: We took off this morning from Quang Tri, but we base out of Chu Lai.*
>
> *Rollie: This things not going back to Quang Tri is it? Tell me NO!*
>
> *Chinook crew chief: Naw, we're headed back to Chu Lai. We've been up in and out of Quang Tri for five days, that's enough of that place. Hard to think some of them marines been up there since Tet.*
>
> *Rollie: I know. It is hard to believe, sure is, very hard to believe. Chu Lai, super!*
>
> *Emmerson (shaking his head in disbelief and talking to himself): "What a war! One minute stuck on a riverbank in Hue, the next saved to Camp Diane by a navy PT boat with orders to find two pitiful lost sergeants, the next moment shot down in an Army Chinook by lost Gooks out target practicing, then suddenly up and out in an emergency mini-airlift. All within twenty-four hours and this birds on the way to Chu Lai? Where we were supposed to be, in the first place? You are one luck-filled, angel-squeezed mother-dupper! It ain't payday, is it? We could clean that place out too.*
>
> *Emmerson (again, to no one in particular): Out here fighting the threat of world communism, which must certainly fail when meeting two wandering marine sergeants and their eight lost forklifts. And now, this surprise short cut to Chu Lai! What a war!*

The coastal ride south at about six thousand feet, morning sun panoramically lighting the Nam shoreline to the right was glorious, inspirational, past Phu Bai, and then south past the opening to the Da Nang bay and sprawling Da Nang air and ground assets, Marble Mountain glowing in the midst of the American warring busyness. Thoughts of robust, grinning car sales guys from less than three weeks ago filled the grins of Emmerson and Rollie Cahill. Further down the coast, ordinary sun-filled beaches and unique geographic fixtures took marine and Air Cav minds off their work of war. Perfect rhythmic waves splashed the shore lines as if controlled by some wave machine at a busy American water park, the shallow waters dotted with locals doing their morning duties. This was a Nam seen close up, like Emmerson or Rollie had never seen it before. Perhaps there was hope for these people, perhaps they had a future, if people would just let them be. They'd figure it out, their way.

The big First Air Cav Chinook glided with long blades thumping against the morning Asian air most gracefully down the coast. The two escort Hueys were soon joined by the eight other attack Hueys who had gotten bored blowing the hell out of the downed Chinook and the creeping up Gooks at the crash site. Major Rund, hand over handed up to the cockpit, nodded a half dozen times, and returned to his crew with certain explanations of what was next in their army air lives.

Anticipating a landing at Chu Lai, new to them, Emmerson and Rollie had no plans. No one related to their specific mission knew where they were, why they were where they were, or expected them back. Plus, against all odds, they were somehow going to land in the very place they were told they would find their precious eight lost forklifts, the freelance search having long ago lost its appeal. All they had to do was find a Captain Buzan, sooner or later, which under the circumstances, could take a while.

Army Air Cav folks had more war stuff to work with and move around than Marine I Corps folks had, or so it appeared to the two sergeants. Chu Lai was like a perpetual, unbroken PX land, only broken in the landscape by soccer fields, basketball courts, and a ball diamond. The two salty marines just walked around a while feeling alive, grateful for their shifting good fortunes on the trails to Hue and then out. Now late in the day, the two poker wizards learned it wasn't payday in Chu Lai, but there *was* a well-stocked Sergeant's Club. Captain Buzan could wait a day, maybe two, as Emmerson and Rollie stepped out of the bright Nam, Chu Lai sun into the tent acting as the Sergeant's Club, in search of Nam's traditional relief of all pains, frustrations, and heartaches—*salty dogs* (vodka 'n' grapefruit) Nam style, with about 115, and a wake-up, or there about, close enough, who cares for a day or two.

Rollie still had over $2,000 in poker winnings, to share with his new Sergeant's Club Army buddies, which made a fine start to Chu Lai introductions. Emmerson was just as healed, right there in Chu Lai, of all places. Let's see. It was Phu Bai four days ago, then Hue and the Signal Corps. Camp Diane in some lost place that will be abandoned and swept away within a month and end the day one hundred clicks down the coast, past Da Nang and the car sales guys, and now in a wonderful Nam place called Chu Lai. Big place, supply/gear guys were working hard here also. What they say is certainly true, if you just let it happen: "Join the Marine Corps. Travel to exotic places. Meet new people!"

> *Emmerson: Buddy, you ever think that if those frickin' forklifts are here in Chu Lai somewhere— you ever think these army guys won't want to give them up so easy to a couple marine stragglers, carrying no orders—marines who owe the army their lives right now. How 'n the b' Jesus we gonna get eight forklifts up the coast to Phu Bai anyway.*
>
> *Rollie: Truck 'em, I guess.*
>
> *Emmerson: Truck 'em? In a convoy? Up these dangerous roads? All the way to Phu Bai? Through Go Noi? Then Da Nang? Ahhh, man! You do realize that at night the Gooks control the entire countryside? You know that, right? We gotta think*

about this, talk this over. I'm sick of forklifts already, and we ain't even laid eyes on 'em yet.

Rollie: Let's just see if they're here first. Then we can plan up. In the meantime, I'll buy—Hey, Sarge, give us two king-size salty dogs, with that stuff they call ice.

Emmerson: Look at this place, these guys. They got ice in their drinks, white T-shirts, hair all combed. Let's take our time, hang out, eat up some countdown. Here's to you, bud, thanks for the memories. That's the only shot down bird crash and escape down a coast that I need for a while, OK?

Rollie: My thoughts exactly! Notice how clean these guys are! This place is a little like the World. Maybe they know what's goin' on around Nam, back in the World. Maybe there's a lipstick or two around."

Emmerson and Rollie hung for another day, making cozy the back room of the Sergeant's Club at night, surveying the large Chu Lai base during the day, until 5:00 p.m., salty dog time. They didn't have to go find Captain Buzan. On the third day of glorious, calm, laid-back life at Chu Lai and the Sergeant's Club, Captain Buzan found them. Seems yes, there had been some confusion among S-4 operations, when eight new forklifts had arrived on landing ships from the large cargo transport ships off shore. The forklifts showed up a month ago, quite a surprise. Of course, the paperwork was long lost, but the forklifts weren't. Buzan explained that they put the surprise, moving, lifting beasts right to work, guys moving gear around felt blessed, kind of got used to them, real fast. Then four of them disappeared, and no one knew where to. They just vanished, driven away in the night, or just poofed away by Nam forklift poofers. Probably off to some other unit. But the good news was, the other four were right there at Chu Lai. Buzan advised the two marines to relax, enjoy their salty dogs, with ice, and he'd prep up the four forklifts that they could take possession of in the morning, or the next morning, whatever suited the two marine sergeants among their lack of priorities. Meet y'all at S-4 whenever you can get up and around to it. Enjoy the new mess tent for breakfast, and "he'd see 'em, when he'd see 'em."

> *Rollie: What a nice guy, this Buzan. How cool is that, the army saves our asses, and they get four of the forklifts, and the marines get four. Perfect! I don't even care anymore.*
>
> *Emmerson: Sarge, what 'n the hell we gonna do with four forklifts?*
>
> *Rollie: I think there is an upside here. I see the great forklift light in the sky.*
>
> *Emmerson: This'll be good. Just a second. Sarge! Two more of our doggiest salt friends. OK, what? What can possibly be an upside?*
>
> *Rollie: Them folks up in Phu Bai long forgot about us. I'd bet good cash there ain't one Phu Bai brass that gets up in the morning wondering where good ole Rollie and Emm are at. They'll be startled to hear we're still out here on the great forklift search trail, alive. We just slow down the process, take a few days to figure out how to move the things, wait for guidance from Phu Bai S-4. Put the transportation problem back on them. In the meantime, good ole Army Sarge Club guy here will take care of us, and we spend a day or two on the Chu Lai beach, perfecting body surfing techniques. We'll just figure it out later, in a couple days, Buzan don't care. Gives him a couple more days to work his end! Besides, if we dilly-dally around long enough, maybe two more will get lost, Nam black market style.*

> *Emmerson: If we're gonna hang around, we better not fleece these guppies on payday. Could make the wait very long and tense. We don't need the money anyway.*
>
> *Rollie: Good, a great part of the delay plan, something not to do. Excellent judgment! Anything else?*
>
> *Emmerson: Yeah, tomorrow I'll lean over to the main strip and see if any Air America guys are expected in. I may have actual orders and work to do, if anyone knew where I was.*

Late June, the two sergeants had practiced body surfing, downed about two hundred salty dogs amongst themselves and a constant stream of new army friends, spread a little Da Nang money around Chu Lai and even delivered a couple trays of the Dogs to Army guys peeking out of bunkers during a brief happy-hour mortar attack. That sort of service paid quite well in tips from the tipsy army run and fun guys. Tips quickly turned back into Salty Dogs for all. Now part of the Army Sergeant's Club core crowd of steady patrons, Emmerson and Rollie knew they had to move on from the impromptu R&R. Again, a plan fell into place, although a little tricky.

June 27, Chu Lai, Sergeant's Club:

> *Emmerson: Rollie, [Yo, Sarge, give us a couple salty dogs]. What's up? You gettin' anywhere on moving those four lifts?*
>
> *Rollie: Yep, I am. How 'bout you? Any new orders coming your way?*
>
> *Emmerson: Yep. You first.*
>
> *Rollie: These guys have a convoy gearing up to leave in two days, to Da Nang. They'll load the lifts on a flat bed, deliver 'em to Marine G-4 in Da Nang, then it's up to the Corps to get them up to*

Phu Bai. I'll catch a bird from there. Simple, clean, easy. All we gotta do is keep from getting killed on the convoy to Da Nang.

Emmerson: We? I won't be goin'! I told you, I'm not goin' on any cross country, convoy line up 'n' get shot sightseeing country tours. Besides, I got new orders, kind of big stuff.

Rollie: I had the feeling I'd be finishin' this forklift job all on my own. That's cool! I can do this. Besides, no sense two of us out there, going through Go Noi" What kind of orders? World orders? You're outa here orders?

Emmerson: Yep, outa here! No kiddin'! I'll hop an Air America tomorrow morning, be in Da Nang debriefing for a day, then over the big pond.

Rollie: Cool, man, that's terrific, Sarge. Two more salty dogs! Hey, guys, Emmerson here is next to a wake-up. He's gonna miss all us salties that'll hang and try to finish up some war stuff.

The Sergeant's Club was one big round of applause, at-a-boys, and a king size pitcher of salty dogs, passed for the pouring, then another, also passed for the pouring.

Rollie: Can you tell me about your new orders? Or is that top secret like everything else you slide in and out of.

Emmerson: Oh, it's top secret all right. Let's take that table back there, way in the corner and I'll tell you anyway, you deserve to know. Besides, this is too juicy, you won't believe it. I don't believe it!

The kindred sergeants grabbed half their change, a full pitcher with ice in it, cups, and moved out off the line of conversational fire, alone, to the corner of the now familiar Sergeant's Club tent, Emmerson accepting congrats from all his new army buds on the way.

Rollie: I can't imagine; What now?

Emmerson: This one has really surprised me, glad to do it, cause it's out of the Nam, but a real change of pace. I'll be at Pendleton for a month or less, debriefed on anything Nam. Then briefed on domestic issues, the politics of the war, what is or isn't going on in radical protesting groups caught up on the whole domestic protesting mess that we keep hearing about, but never really know about. Then, presuming all that goes well, I have a specific mission, along with about ninety-nine other active duty guys just returning from Nam. They want me while I'm new out of Nam, trained, not yet domesticated, a little edgy I suppose. You ain't gonna believe this.

Rollie: I've seen you work the edges for about a year now, worked on the edges with you—I'd believe anything with your orders.

Emmerson: I'm to go to Chicago, be there by August 15 or so, and stay at the Hilton on Michigan Avenue. You know what's in Chicago in August? Of course not! By then you'll be too short to give a damn, tucked up in Phu Bai waiting for the ride to Da Nang and your own cross the pond lift off.

Rollie: No, no I don't know what's in Chicago in August that they'd want you for. What?

Emmerson: The Democratic National Convention! I don't really know a lot of detail, right yet. But apparently, they expect the convention to be one big war protest, riot and head bashing, perfect for returning Nam guys. Kind of the culmination of all this other broken up protesting that has gone on and we hear about now and then. This seems to be the big one, violent, all kinds of broken groups smashin' things, burning things, tearing Chicago and Convention things up. Seems FBI work has learned all these radical groups have centered on the leadership of some sort of group of seven, all coming together in Chicago. Apparently, the Chicago police are bullin' up. The National Guard will be called out and the Corps is putting about a hundred Nam Vets on the ground, undercover, to plant rumors and persuade potential riotous groups to move in different directions for all the wrong reasons. We're supposed to kind of infiltrate the radicals and prod the long hairs and idiots like cattle into waiting control areas, which can then be surrounded. How's that for orders! Should be a blast!

Rollie: In Chicago! You got orders to stay at the Hilton Hotel, on Michigan, in Chicago and trick a bunch of hippy fools. How natural! Perfect, should be your specialty anyway. How do you get this kind of stuff? How does this kind of order come down to your flyin' around ass?

Emmerson: Just lucky, I guess. Well not really "lucky." It's part of the Air America connection. In fact, I'll be joined in Da Nang by some sort of group of select marines, and we'll all prop-hop our way to the World on some new Air American bird. They figure I'm too short to waste here in Nam, plus I get out of the Corps at the end of October anyway. Pretty simple! While I'm all warred up, edgy, they'll let me run around Chicago up to September, then I go to Quantico/Norfolk for a new Cougar, and its happy trails. Kind of a perfect way to unwind and step back into a life! May get to knock a few war

*protesters' heads around on the way out the door—
kind of a dream finale.*

*Rollie: While I'm bouncing my ass up Highway
1 on Gook ambush watch, with four forklifts that
will get blown up before we ever see Phu Bai, you'll
be landing in San Diego. Am I delusional on this,
or is that what I'm hearing? Never was a "fair" war!
Quang Tri, Khe Sanh, Hue, chasing forklifts and
you got orders to check in at the Hilton Hotel on
Michigan Avenue in Chicago. You know how many
babes will be at that convention, or just in the protest
crowd—thousands, that's how many. I swear!*

*Emmerson: Drink up! It's all on me today. One
more night in the back room, and hello Da Nang
and new Air America flight buddies. At liftoff, I'll
tip my cover to you and your wake-up.*

*Rollie: Yeah me. Thanks. I suppose that's the
best we can do. Look, we both should be back in
the World on the east coast by the Holidays, maybe
settled some. How 'bout we meet up over the
Holidays, if I don't get waxed on this convoy. You
got a lady waiting for you?*

*Emmerson: Not any more. I got that letter
eight months ago. You?*

*Rollie: Hell, I got my letter in staging, before I
even left the World. It's just as well. I'll be different,
maybe real different. No babe would want me for a
while, maybe a long while. Like a thirty-year while,
if not a longer while."*

The whole convoy/back to the world/debrief/brief/back to Phu
Bai plan worked as well as loose-end things like that can work in
the Nam world of SNAFUs. The next bleary-eyed Asian morning
arrived as usual, right on time. Rollie and Emmerson headed to the

Air America idling prop engines at the airstrip. The two sergeants said their good-byes without eye contact. Spoke briefly of the futility of everything or most things Nam and the apparent chaos and confusion of the domestic side of things, at least as much of it as they could grasp. Emmerson asked one more time about Rollie having the four Jacks back at Da Nang payday game night but expected no answer, which is exactly what he got.

Emmerson pointed out some new fresh-looking guys passing by to their full in-country and countdown of a million days, then tipped their salty covers to one another in half salute, as Emmerson gracefully pivoted and danced over the asphalt tarmac to the waiting silver prop, disappearing up the ramp and into the dark hole for the first leg of his long awaited trip to the World. The Air America prop was a beautiful flashing silver sight as it taxied, accelerated down the runway, lifted, and leaned left, up the coast, toward Da Nang, with its unusual, brilliant piece of American ingenuity and human history as a special cargo—Emmerson!

Thirty-three years would pass before the two sergeants would meet again. In Oregon on the coast, with a singing Heather. And that's a whole different worthy story!

Rollie had one day before his next Nam adventure, which would be the convoy north from Chu Lai, escorting four forklifts through lowlands and Go Noi. The forklifts, as a bottom line war footnote, meant nothing to anyone. The whole forklift search and retrieve mission was just another ops outing to be checked and forgotten. The start, ops, and finish was just part of Nam life where no one made friends, not real friends that you knew would be lasting, or the kind of friends that would share lives and growing families like back in the World. Too many people died or were transferred to different units on all kinds of emergency special operations to allow development of friendships. Those that didn't end up in a heavy green body bag rotated to the World at their wake-up. Either way, having a friend was a passing, temporary situation. Nevertheless, when two guys that have a good deal in common get matched in tense, life-defining situations, a deep strange type of friendship through respect develops. Teammate/buddy system closeness is part of the process of depending on someone besides yourself. What develops personally is just a natural, rather gravitational process when in the midst of war's chaosing.

Before Rollie could even walk through Chu Lai and check in with Captain Buzan at S-4, he knew his life would be different once that Air America flight took off with Emmerson. He didn't know exactly how it would be different, but he knew it would be. Deeply dreading forklift watchman duties in an army convoy was only on the surface of Rollie's changing feelings. The convoy would move, move as best it could, and probably get to Da Nang OK. Buzan says the convoy will have constant First Air Cav support, with Huey birds and their gunners in constant flying surveillance, with constant eager fire power, from the constant itchy fingers of crews.

One last night at the Sergeant's Club was full of conversations with new army buddies, all inquiring about the absence of Rollie's wing man, Emmerson, which, of course, could not be truly explained. Rollie knew his gut had changed. He felt his right arm or something more had departed on that Air America bird also. He also knew that after this last night in Chu Lai, he might not see ice in a drink again for a good while.

Forming an army convoy in Nam seemed somewhat akin to what it must have been like to form a wagon train to cross the unscouted American plains in about 1860. Same ole hot morning sun and swirling dust kicked up by the mass movements of convoy vehicles and boots rushing to assignments. Buzan would be in the lead jeep which would be heavily armed. After Buzan at point, there would be three supply trucks, then another heavily armed jeep with a .50-caliber rear mounted. The convoy went that way for a half mile, three trucks, then a heavily armed jeep. The scene could be confused for a cross between a wagon train and a moving parade of some sort, if it weren't for the seriousness of all things Nam.

Rollie tucked in the front right seat of his truck cab to ride shotgun with his new army friend from the transportation pool driving the big diesel with a flatbed and four forklifts strapped on tight. What a strange load for a war scene, forklifts, almost embarrassing for the only marine in the convoy, but better than hauling explosives. Buzan, followed by a half mile of moving military/industrial apparatus, got underway north about 9:00 a.m. How hard could it be? Up the road about twenty clicks to Tam Ky, another twenty to Hoi An, across Go Noi and into Da Nang, with an ETA near dusk—if everything went OK.

Rollie's body was inside the slow moving, low geared crawling truck, but his mind was elsewhere. He couldn't help thinking of Emmerson, already in Da Nang somewhere. Maybe they'd run into each other, probably not. Emm's probably already on his second Air America leg with a couple dozen other crazies on their way to Chicago to further confuse the already confused. Rollie could not shake the feeling that his life had a new direction. The semi-driver didn't even seem like a real person. He was there, right there with him, Rollie could reach over and touch him, check his realness, but he wasn't really there. The scene was not a scene he felt within, being certain that at least for now, in this portion of his marine life in Nam, he was actually the angel. The angel was him, looking down at the whole crawling, kind of organized scene. Rollie felt above the moving convoy, looking at the dust and moving pieces of dark-green war stuff. Buzan, way up front, was plenty capable. Rollie liked Buzan, trusted him. The whole surreal scene and action just seemed out of place, unnecessary, not contributing to any special need or cause, just another pile of risky actions, almost for actions sake. Similar to the whole Nam war! Rollie and his ghost of a driver bumped along, amidst a group of strung out strangers also bumping along together in the same direction.

Two hours into the convoy experience, Rollie learned a couple new things about army transport SOP. First, any pause or stop, dozens of armed infantry scrambled out onto the narrow roads and paths, weapons locked and loaded—a good sign. Sometimes, the convoy travelled slowly through populated hamlets and small villages, but mostly the convoy was on elevated dirt paths, looking out to tree lines, or down to rice paddies. The army vehicles took the entire width of the narrow path, requiring oncoming Vietnamese, often with water buffalo or push carts, to move off the path into the ditches and canal fingers. Eyes stared back at the convoy, eyes that talked, and said things about unwelcome Americans in Nam taking up all the road space. No one could possibly know what was in the next tree line or where the next land mines were set to rip and blow things up on the road north to Da Nang. Then Rollie saw the truck just ahead, swerve quickly left, then back to the path, just missing the thin ancient looking Vietnamese walking in the same direction as the convoy. Then, the truck ahead jerked again, the exact same quick truck jerk as before.

> *Rollie (to the semidriver): Hey, bud, what's that about? Why would that guy ahead jerk his truck like that? It looks intentional.*
>
> *Semidriver: Well, it is intentional. He's maybe one of the sickos, thinking he's having a little fun.*
>
> *Rollie: What's the fun part? Looks stupid, dangerous from back here.*
>
> *Semidriver: Some of these truck drivers play a sick little game. When there's a Gook on the narrow road, especially an old Gook that may not hear so well, and they're coming up from behind them— they do a quick swerve like that to see if they can catch the back of the Gook's head with their mirrors. Every now and then, they get one and bash his head in. It's a convoy-thing!*
>
> *Rollie: Terrific, kind of a special unintended consequence of Vietnamization? My god, what have we done? What are we doing?*

Buzan's convoy crawled further and further north, certain 12-Xs occasionally darting quickly left here and there, spontaneously, or so it seemed from behind them. Huey flights guarded the long chain of moving army gear and Americans constantly, lending a sense of security to the whole out in the open crawling wagon train. On schedule, it looked like the convoy would reach Tam Ky by noon, pretty good time, and pretty non-eventful so far, except for the deplorable-looking locals, hopelessly lining the roads and crossroads. Rollie stayed calm, stayed locked and loaded, his angel in the semitrailer truck front seat with the driver, he himself above it all, with a full view of the ridiculous scene of moving millions of dollars' worth of assets through an impoverished third-world country from one place to the next place. Soon, Rollie would learn of another way for a convoy to entertain itself through the Nam countryside.

Approaching Tam Ky was like approaching any other lost, hopeless Nam village. Vacant hungry eyes stare up at the vehicles' militarized passengers. Behind them, elderly black-toothed Mamasans and Papasans lean on rakes or hoes or anything leanable. No young male faces populated the villages, none, anywhere. Island dogs, perhaps the distant cousins of Hue island dogs or island dogs all over the world, patrolled the sidelines and shallow ditches for a quick opportunity to inspect and scavenge anything dropped from the convoy. Island dogs realize that US troops drop more goodies than ARVN troops. Army troops scurried about in the back of the truck just ahead of Rollie's semi, and soon raised the dark-green cans from C ration boxes. As village children scampered to the road side begging for any food or anything thrown from the convoy, the army guys went to work. Like throws from deep short, army regulars then threw the C ration cans into the crowds of begging children. For the price of a bash on the head or body with a green can, a Vietnamese child could run off with the can of something to eat for that day. The hard throws of canned goods into the crowds of children did not deter the hungry kids. The kids lined the path of moving American assets through Tam Ky south to north, army regulars bashing them with thrown cans at their bashing pleasure. What fun!

> *Rollie: Is that normal . . . throwing C rations like fast balls at the begging kids. Is that normal convoy fun also?*
> *Semidriver: Well, it didn't used to be but seems to be these days. I don't get it. I don't allow it on my truck, but there it is, you see it for yourself, part of it, part of the whole mess of a war, like it or not. Sorry you had to see that.*

Rollie's mind went all a-wonder in the confusion of the scene and his sunken gut feeling that now dominated his emotions and thinking and his attitude for the few remaining days he had left in-country. Leave the angel in charge today! Angels know better how to process and rationalize such awkward, cruel realities. My goodness, what are we doing? How did it get this way? These guys know better! Get me back to the Corps and the States!

Some tight road spots slowed things down for a while and then south of Go Noi a couple mortars broke the afternoon silence. With the incoming mortars, First Air Cav Hueys eagerly pulled off the convoy to do their protective duties. The sizzle of rockets returning fire echoed in the distance, followed by predictable explosions. Soon, the Air Cav Hueys were back patrolling ahead and behind the convoy, pilots happy enough for the diversion and target practice. So good so far in convoy life! By late afternoon, Freedom Bridge, connecting Go Noi to the south edge of Da Nang, was a welcome sight. Soon after the bridge, the sounds of phantom jets taking off and returning to Da Nang were an even more welcome loud familiar warring experience straight from busy friendlies. It wasn't *the* World, but Da Nang was always a step up toward civilization. Da Nang life would do for now.

For Rollie, the sight of Da Nang was a sweet and sour experience. He had arrived to turn over the precious forklifts to anyone else in logistics admin that he could get to take them and create some sort of a sign of a paper trail but at a price paid. Rollie had learned way too much about a different part of the war and what the whole outrageous total scene had evolved into. The convoy trucks and equipment delivered would soon be lost in the vast supply warehousing network of Da Nang. The four forklifts might or might not actually make it to Phu Bai. Heck, by now, ships in the South China were probably unloading eight more, half of which would be lost in the Asian black market now an accountable, expected part of the whole supply system. But that isn't what mattered.

What mattered were the deals made back at the Pentagon or some other lower military/industrial point of collusion and then more deals. Rollie now knew too much, carried too much salty weight of Nam's realities. Plus, he'd had a drink with ice in it and hoped that part of civilization might have reached Phu Bai by the time he got up the road that far. He'd been gone nearly a month. Seen Hue again, which was one time too many. Just like they say about life in the Corps, he'd traveled to exotic places and met new people. He'd shipped Emmerson off to Chicago of all places to the Hilton Hotel. It was time for Rollie to introduce his own strategy of *declining intensity*, using his salty sergeant status to lay low with his precious countdown and trust his personal angel to help ride this out.

Da Nang was pleasant enough but way too many picked guppies walking around that might recognize one of the guys that cleaned house in the payday poker game just a few short weeks ago. One of the most active Da Nang area helicopter LZs was tucked in the far Northeast corner of the airstrip and would eventually have some sort of bird going to Phu Bai, a good place for Rollie to hang. Having dumped the forklifts, Rollie caught a jeep going northeast and was soon dropped at the transient LZ. Two hours later, one of the large CH-54 marine cargo birds from Marine Air Group 36 was headed to Phu Bai. Rollie jumped aboard and strapped in for the scenic ride out Da Nang bay and up the coast, absolutely feeling that this was the first day of the rest of the days of his countdown. *A day that was a long time coming, the one day that would divide Rollie's Nam past, from his Nam future.* Beat down by his long war, Rollie felt a strange sort of jittery invigoration. Like he would make it, meet his countdown, and his next visit to Da Nang would be the first leg of the trip home. He could almost feel the sight of the California shore approaching, except it was still the shoreline of Nam.

Always expecting the changes of Nam, Rollie soon discovered, in fact, that Phu Bai had changed. The base was bigger, ever expanding, more Big Red One Army patches and logos moving around everywhere in jeeps and on the ground, and more First Air Cav yellow and black patches in the air and on the ground. No longer did marines dominate the moving, shifting landscape. There was one other big change. A quick check at the Sergeants Club showed they had added a little electricity to the tent and with that came coolers for Falstaff and Ballantine beers—*and ice*! Ice from an "ice machine"! An American ice machine that just sits there and groans and kicks out buckets of ice, all day long, nonstop, for salty dogs, now the main nutritional staple of the war for spent sergeants now hoping to only join the boys in the rear with the gear with the more laid back part of warring. Rollie actually reported into S-4, as if he were going to work with them on useless daily chores of coordinating war stuff, more telling the staff what he would do than asking. Rollie nailed down an S-4 desk duty, then jeeped his way back to the Sergeant's Club where he nailed a bartending duty he hoped would last a couple short months to prewake-up.

Back in Phu Bai, Rollie would mostly keep to himself, listen his way through the days, avoid any travel, except an occasional *for sure solid* milk run. The Sergeant's Club was the perfect place to learn what was going on all over I Crops and to get news about the World with new guys coming in, especially sergeants. Sergeants were traditionally the center pivots between enlisted and officers. Enlisted needed sergeants on the uptake; officers need the sergeants on the downside of war's demands, needs, and credentials. In all of Phu Bai, if you wanted to know what was really going on, go to the Sergeant's Club. Or better yet, go to the bartenders at the Sergeant's Club.

Into August, post-Tet, and then into September, life in Phu Bai was as predictable and steady as Rollie had ever experienced in Nam. Paper, things, news, stuff, troops, and buckets of new ice, all came and went, all a part of Rollie's life of new comforts, declining intensity. VC and North regulars seemed to have retreated to the mountains and valleys to regroup or were hiding in plain sight in cities like Da Nang, awaiting new orders and new events, inventing their own next unification episodes. Phu Bai itself was calmer, just as much air traffic, night and day, but the place now had a different, slower pace about it, as if settled into a routine of feeding troops, burning diesel fuel in half barrels from the latrines and outhouses, and moving equipment in multiple busy cross fitting directions. There were fewer stories about scrambles to one LZ hot spot or another. Reportedly, there were less dark-green zippered body bags in and out on their lonesome, depressing way home. There were still the usual fights at the enlisted club, but that was expected. In fact, it would have been unusual if a week went by and no fights were reported at the enlisted club. People would worry that the war had lost intensity.

If you'd been in Quang Tri for six or seven months, life in Phu Bai, early fall '68, was a breeze. Days flipped by on the calendar. Rollie, with his angel, could feel the wake-up, practically taste it if he kept his eyes closed long enough and did taste-concentration thoughts. S-4 work was routine, unchallenging, and safe. Occasionally, S-4 staff would clear the desks toward evening and show a movie, right there in their tent work space. In fact, a movie showed quite regularly. It was Dr. Zhivago, shown over and over and over and over, mainly because of the blond Russian beauty Lara, every marine's dream babe. Just the movie sight of her quieted the whole tent. Bartending at the Sergeant's Club was a hoot, almost too hooty. The salty dogs rolled out each day, and a guy could get used to them if not possessed with good ole portions of country-boy self-discipline and judgment of a descent nature at the very least.

Then, mid-September rolled into view, straight ahead of the wake-up, and Rollie received a slight swerve in his Nam countdown road. Rollie got two letters. One was from home, the other totally unexpected, from Emmerson.

There had not been many letters from home that year or ever, none since Tet. Rollie had actually wondered why, fearing something was going on that was more important than his Nam workload and Marine Corps tour of duty. At this point, Rollie was twenty years old, and he was right about something else going on.

> *September 18, 1968*
> *Dear Son,*
>
> *We hope this letter finds you as well as possible. Your tour of duty will soon end, so we all presume you will return home, around mid or late October, or at some point near then. Although you have been constantly in our thoughts and prayers, I am sorry to say home today, is not the home you left when joining the Marine Corps. A month ago your mother and I completed a separation and divorce process. Several things go along with that whole mess that you may feel the need to know more about some day. I presume you have enough to think about now, still in the Vietnam war mess.*
>
> *I've moved, and the house was put up for sale, and has sold. The new owners are in the process of moving in at this time. Your mother made arrangements for a small apartment near downtown, but at the moment is not there. Her anger and anguish has led her to some extreme actions, and thus, for her own good, she has been temporarily*

placed in a mental institution in Jacksonville. They say for a few more months.

Your mother had cleaned through your remaining possessions that were in the house. There isn't much; mainly just some clothes that may or may not still fit and some sports equipment.

I have also rented an apartment with a lady I have been seeing for quite some time. You don't know her (Priscilla), but you are certainly welcome and encouraged to stop by when you get in the States and back this way. I presume with your return, you will be discharged. I'll be most interested to hear about your plans for the future and whatever you feel you can tell us about life in Vietnam.

Stay safe—you've made it this far. We hear it's a real mess over there, but things have quieted down a bit lately. Well, it's kind of a mess here, back in the States also. Ride the high tides and see your way. I'm sure you have a bright future.

Love—Your Dad

Rollie could only lean back on his bunk and soak in the letter's unexpected, vague meanings.

Ah'll be damned! First of all, home was gone. No walking back down Main Street, up to the porch and rocking away a first few afternoons, feeling the air, breathing, resting, feeling safety and the greatness of my old neighborhood and country. There was no home, none, gone, and all my stuff with it. Now what? The World and discharge papers at Pendleton will only pay a few hundred bucks and a trip home. At least I have a new Dodge Charger waiting, I think. Nice of Dad to write . . . the bastard!

Emmerson's letter was next.

> *This'll be good. He's probably bragging about picking up his Cougar convertible. Kind of strange, to know Emmerson ten months and feel more familiar, trusting, comfortable with him and his ways than with Dad! This war twists a lot of things, as many unseen, as seen, apparently some time for the better.*

> *September 10, 1968*
> *Hey Bud—to the Great Sergeant Rollie, USMC—*
> *I don't think I'm much good at being a pen-pal, and don't intend to be. But, I had to write you this one time, with a little heads-up. Here's the truth—the World ain't what it used to be, won't be what you expect. Trust me!*
> *I've been here in Chicago about a month, take off for Quantico tomorrow and discharge. Chicago has been a mess, a state-side street violent mess, at times not much different than some Nam days we worked and fought through. Everybody here hates everybody else, just like in Nam. The cops hate the hippies, the Democrats hate everybody, the blacks despise the whites, the hippies move around in and out of dark places like rats, encouraging the staggering, counter-productive hatred. TV and newspapers record it all and distort it all and send more hatred and sensational emotion back to the public as if some sort of spirited revolution is under way, when all it really is, is a bunch of spoiled loafers trying to reconcile lost values.*
> *Our work, here, right in the middle of it all, for us undercover agitators, is easy, compared to*

Nam. We sneak out a Hotel side door near evening, blend amongst the hippie trash and most active of the protesters and spread as many stupid, radical, misdirection rumors and lies as we can think up. That parts been kind of fun! Lots of hippie babes could also be fun if they weren't such a bunch of nut-bags.

I think what I see here has become America, and I fear it is rather permanent. The assassinations of King and Bobby that we only heard vaguely about in Nam are true real live influences in the protesting crowd. Nam of course is the protesting elephant in the crowd. These low-lifes will never serve, but they can't help hiding behind some righteous cause to deflect any non-service, anti-patriotism criticism, and they get away with it. The people and the politics wrapped around this whole cluster all seem fake to the core. Nothing is the same as just a few years ago when patriotism and pride of service drove many of us to causes we knew little about, other than it was our time and our duty.

If/when America comes to some sort of unified common ground on such national issues from these new domestic distractions and misgoverning, I feel it will be too late. Too late-isms will have taken a societal toll, and once released cannot be put back. The haywire behavior itself will have spawned new types of radical leaders who will eventually rise to the top in certain places not consciously guarding against internal trends of radicalism.

Rollie, this will not change, this craziness here at home is here to stay. I fear it is the new normal of American attitude that will divide our country racially, economically, politically, and domestically in yet unseen fundamental ways for a long, long time to come. This attitude and behavior is a new kind of irresponsible bad temperament for our nation to endure. There are those among us who will make misguided causes their personal industries. And you know what? We have done this to ourselves. I think it started with the JFK assassination, but deep down, Nam is also one of America's cancers. This turmoil is not the work of Lenin, Mao, Cuba, or Khrushchev. We've sadly, in reality, done this to ourselves.

I did not want you to return and expect a walk in the park. In fact, for the crazy Dems, Grant Park on the Chicago shoreline near the Hilton convention center is the center-pivot of discontent and violence between protesters and Chicago cops, with National Guard the clubbing backup. The public head bashing is the daily normal scene down at the Park and surrounding areas. How strange for us Vets here, who couldn't wait to get home, to stand down, relax, and regroup, and gather new visions of a future in our America, or what we thought was our America.

So, buddy—don't think it's over. In fact I fear Nam and new waves of blasphemous, unaccountable politicians are unfortunately the future for some time to come. LBJ is nowhere. He'll slither out of the White House leaving international and domestic stains galore, go home to Texas and die in shame, draped in guilt—and good riddance. Too bad he can't take a few busloads of politicians with him to their dark holes of shame.

Here's the only meager advice I can lend: Do not expect to be well received! Just come home and observe, listen, and gather a new steady pace about yourself. Do not wear your uniform across country,

*especially in the airports and cities. Don't even
attempt to tell people what is going on in Nam, it
will just cause you pain and frustration, and they
don't give a damn anyway. Suck it up, find your
way, and trust there will be a day. Get your new
Charger, and get the windows down.*

*I'm off to beauteous Norfolk. Be careful! This
thing won't be over for guys like us for a long, long
time.*

Semper Fi—Emm

Two new, late-September letters and home was gone with
America leaving. A lot of guys would re-up, unable to return to the
World, fit in, and adjust to an acceptable mentality. A whole year of
fighting, trusting no one and trying to stay alive a hundred different
ways would have eaten away the parts of young men's bodies that they
once trusted. Indecision would be the normal behavior for individual
veterans of Nam. Perhaps too many dreams hang heavy in night air
to allow the Nam Veteran to steadily acclimate and proceed forward
with life's mundane issues.

War protesters! On the streets, on campus, perhaps in homes as
invited guests and at neighborhood bars, Rollie could not imagine
how that would possibly work or settle with veterans. At that
moment, he considered extending his enlistment. He'd already been
told he was up for a promotion to staff sergeant, and two years of
duty at San Diego, MCRD. Staff Sergeant, at twenty-one years old,
war veteran—salty.

That crazy re-up feeling drifted away when Rollie folded and
placed his letters away, realizing after the two years at MCRD, there
would still be a Nam war to be ordered back into. He strolled back
over to the Sergeant's Club, his own personal friendly confines of
that time. One pitcher of salty dogs later, with some new sarges in
from up north, and Rollie forgot about the reenlistment temporary
insanity. Rollie knew this war would go on and on. There were no

signs of how many body bags are enough body bags for politicians to come to some war ending conclusions or policy wiggle room. If anything, shipments of new war goods and materials into Nam from the States were increasing. Deal makers at the Pentagon and Capitol Hill were now at their most glorious deal-making peak, fit, agile, in tiptop deal-making shape. Vietnam would surely tilt into the South China Sea with all the hardware and goodies shipped into camps, hoisted around on new forklifts or disappearing into black market chains of underground activities also now perfected.

As good as San Diego/MCRD sounded, Rollie knew two years as a staff sergeant would end in another promotion to a Gunny, and that would lead to new orders back to the Nam. One angel had worked, done the angel job, perfectly. Rollie knew he'd never get another angel for a new Nam tour of duty. Just another couple weeks at Phu Bai and Rollie would be too short for his legs to touch the sand. Watch, listen to the stories, look into the Nam, and wait a little longer, just a little longer, just a few more hot days, dusty rides, mindless pitchers of salty dogs and sandfilled rising Asian suns.

A few days after Rollie's welcome-home-to-no-home letter from his dad and the America-ain't-what-it-used-to-be letter from Emmerson, Rollie was at his S-4 duty desk when two MPs entered, braced themselves, no-nonsense MP style squarely in front of his desk:

> *MP #1: Sergeant Cahill? Let's go. Now!*
>
> *Rollie: Hi, guys, thanks for the kind greeting. Go where, for what?*
>
> *MP #1: You need to go with us. What for is none of our business. It's just our orders, Sarge, to come get you! We follow orders. Do not concern ourselves with—What for! So let's go. Our jeep is out front. Now!*
>
> *Rollie: Like I said, nice meeting you. I'm fine. Thanks for asking. OK, let's go.*

In Rollie's cautious Nam mind, maybe short wasn't short enough. Surely, there would not be one more crazy-ass mission. Surely! The go-by-the-book MPs escorted Rollie, post-haste, to his barracks-style tent and cot, helped him grab all his stuff for his duffle, and piled back in the jeep, everything in too much of an MP giddy-up to feel good about.

In the Corps, there are times to lead, times to follow, and most of the time just shut up. Shut up and follow seemed good choices with these two MP-trained body snatchers, who soon pulled the MP jeep in front of the Command Center of the whole big bustling base of Phu Bai.

Damn—they're gonna put me on a frickin'
plane to God knows where, for some half-ass goose
chase of a miserable mission.

Rollie was half-expecting a smiling Emmerson to be waiting for him and an idling Air America prop poised for some sort of escape from Nam and the whole near fiction scene of some sort from the past repeated all over again. Being in and out of Phu Bai for many months now, Rollie had never even seen the actual Command Bunker, let alone the inside of it where the full Birds, half Birds and top I Corps brass popped in and out during their quick, dodging, two-step visits to I Corps. Rollie had no idea top command even knew he existed. Maps covering every inch of the bunker walls, communications gear covering every inch of everything else, leaving the serious looking robotic officer bodies that appeared in charge to the rest of the bunker. Two MPs planted Rollie in the corner, just inside the entrance, threw what was left of his gear at his feet, mentioned something about "be careful out there," and disappeared as quickly as they had appeared twenty-six minutes ago at S-4.

"Be careful out there?" "Awwww man: Out
there? Where? Surely not! Can't be! One more trip

to the bush? My angel is worn out, beat up. We both are. My time is up. I'll never make it through another run up through I Corps rocket belts and hot LZ landings.

Colonel Kelly: Sergeant Cahill, over here— this map here. Glad to meet you. We've not met, but I've heard of your work and missions, your efforts at and around Quang Tri and up through I Corp outposts at Khe Sanh, Con Thien, Camp Diane. We understand you know that area well, know Hue, and just about everything in between.

Sergeant Cahill: Yes, sir, I suppose I do.

Colonel Kelly: We were told you did. We need someone salty, knows how to get around, knows Gook land, knows hard rice methods, and how to work with the army. We need someone who can look into the Nam, feel the things that other new guys can't see or feel. Thank you, Sarge, for your hard work!

Sergeant Cahill: Yes, sir, I suppose I do know all those places, apparently all too well.

Colonel Kelly: Look here, Cahill, this map here. You see, here's where we are in Phu Bai. North, as you know is Hue, and your old home town at Quang Tri. And down here is Da Nang. You see all that."

Sergeant Cahill: Yes, sir, I certainly do know it all, quite well. See it clear as you and I standing right here in front of these maps.

Colonel Kelly: Good, Sarge, excellent. We were told you are a sergeant of clear vision, good judgment, with enough guts for any mission. Now here is what we need you to do: take these very valuable, important papers. Guard them with your life. There *is a CH-54 waiting for you on the tarmac, should be idling right now, waiting for you and these papers. The MPs will run you over to it. Son, that big bird is going to Dan Nang, right to the airstrip. Take these papers and tomorrow morning. Deliver them to Captain Loftus. He'll be at the foot of the gangway to board United flight 911, on the way to LA—Sarge—you are out of here. Congratulations, you're a good marine!*

Sergeant Cahill: (Dazed, roused, always faithful), "Colonel Kelly, I don't know what to say. I thought I was off to the bush one more time—I'm home? To the World? Today, and a wake-up?"

Colonel Kelly: Go, son, you've earned it and much more. Just go, before that 54 gets tired of waiting on you.

Sergeant Cahill: Yes, sir, would you, or somebody here, do one small thing for me? This is kind of sudden. Obviously planned that way! I have some funds stashed at the Sergeant's Club where I hang out, bartend a little. And I have these piasters here in my pocket and here's a little hunk of cash. Would you have someone go by the club later today, maybe about 6:00 p.m., and just lay all this cash and my money stashed at the club on the bar—and tell all those sergeants I said good-bye. See 'em all Stateside. Is that possible? Can someone do that for me?

Colonel Kelly: Sarge, I'll do it myself, my extreme pleasure, might even kick-off the first round. Now go!

Sergeant Cahill: Yes, sir. Semper Fi! Thanks, thanks a lot."

One more helicopter ride—lift gently with the big long reaching powerful blades of the Marine-54 and the familiar forward lean of the bird—pilot, crew, and one special passenger. Grinning crew, in on the trick of the special trip, first leaning in to greet and grip Rollie, then leaning out, back on the 50s and ammo belts. The bird leaned forward and then gracefully right, then gently higher, floating and moving with solid, victorious military power, shoreline showing the way south one final time. Four thousand, then six thousand feet, and Rollie would stretch to see his last, final departing views of Phu Bai and the rolling landscape to the west that soon met with foothills and mountain ranges full of encamped, waiting North regulars. An adjacent scene of water buffaloes prodded along by young kids with sticks on the dusty paths, through the knee-high flooded rice paddies. It had been a year, but nothing had changed in Nam, except for more American Wilson Street Boys, and bigger and bigger US bases overflowing with equipment. The nights still belonged to Charlie!

This 54 was one more ride, one more, but the one out of the crazy Nam countryside into Da Nang, maybe then to Okinawa or maybe straight to the States, more riding and floating in the skies, above it all, across the pond to California, final in-country Nam floating, effortless, last copter ride of a blessed individual historic journey. Ending one phase, beginning another!

> *"I've made it. My angel and I have seen it, touched it, and breathed all the heat, sand, and violence. We have seen enough hate and killing for a lifetime. We'll lean back, breath, pray."*
> *"Now what?"*
> *"Where did the angel come from?"*
> *"Why me?"*

No one ever knows how long it takes for war's personal counterbalances of regret and self-deprecation to set in, that constantly aggravating self-imposed inner feeling that you didn't do enough, could have done, should have done more. The 54 lift and flight from Phu Bai showed the country of Nam clear and open, ongoing in its endless struggles from one generation to the next, passing through a society of corruption, through war-lord hands with the weaponry of fake, false, greedy pretend governments. Quickly, Rollie could only think of the marines and Wilson Street Boys he was leaving behind, in a million different situations of the emotionally deep useless killing messes of Nam.

> *Those guys are out there, some in a fight for their lives right now, this very instance, while I float effortlessly away. Some went to the bush, just this morning, will return from the day silent forever, in a dark-green zippered body bag, to be shipped home to a family burial like another piece of military/ industrial freight. Then, back in the Nam, the same fight, with different names and terrain, will be repeated tomorrow, then repeated the next day, as new warring tools arrive daily from the military/ industrial armchair providers.*

None of it had mattered nor changed a thing. This was not the way of rational countries and competent leaders of good people. What nation would ever trust America again, after we spent everything on an undefined mission with unethical human fundamentals? How do an individual and a nation spit this out in order to gain some coordination and confidence to put one foot in front of the other with any righteous confidence or national self-assurance and pride of service for a future?

Rollie had heard of various jungle prison camp hells that contained breathing souls, hearts, and minds of those Americans captured and not yet killed. How long would those guys go through their special hell, while politicians fritter away with maybes and fictitious scapegoats, gonna-be peace talks that paralyze their strategic decision-making duties that could free all these guys, and free the families and friends who cling to suspicious hope? Rollie had also heard of the Hanoi Hilton, the prison camp in North Vietnam, in the enemy's capital (Hanoi) where downed pilots and American prisoners of higher rank were kept like caged rats and debriefed vigorously by torturous Asian prison Gestapo and guards who stopped at nothing to pit one American against another, or pit any one individual against their own natural patriotic spirit. What must the future of those lost prisoners look like and feel like, and the futures of their families who must know nothing of their imprisoned realities. Why don't we go get them? Why don't we end the war? When will the body bags mount so high, that America's bent, distorted leaders can't see over them to see the actual war for what it is, and thus become strangled by the grief of their own blind warring indulgences?

Flying "out" was not as calm, fulfilling, and self-satisfying as Rollie had dreamed it would be. He suddenly knew he was leaving a part of his gut behind, leaving other pieces of conscious thought and prayer with guys all over I Corps stuck in some vague concept of fighting the advance of someone's idea of communist aggression, which in the end was all a meaningless, covert, political distraction. Rollie suddenly understood what Emmerson's letter was trying to tell him. A lift, lean, and flight up and off the ground you were standing on in Nam is big, real personal step in a correct direction, but it ends nothing, not really.

To survive Nam, you have to "look into the Nam" and somehow fit into a personal pace of survival. A marine, in particular, must hold to a sworn intent, and thus inhale and hold the war's way of life within, in order to understand how to stay alive, while leaving no marine or American behind. But the eventual exhale only spends part of what was held within. Parts of Nam stay inside, a down deep kind of staying. Rollie was just on his way to Da Nang, not even out of country yet, and he suddenly felt his new reality from what he had done, toward what he thought he would and could do with his soon to be twenty-one-year-old homeless life.

Maybe Dad's letter is a message that the Marine Corps should be my new home. Well, we'll see. Read Emmerson's letter a few dozen more times, and we'll see, see how long, where the next chapter is, get in a new Charger and put the windows down. Maybe there is a babe out there waiting, to partially help remove some of this evil, self-imposing heavy gut feeling of doubt fed by hate.

There was nothing to the Da Nang trip on this visit, just in, then out. Lean against this airport hangar wall and wait until sunup. Find Captain Loftus, show the personnel file from Colonel Kelly, and all aboard. This is the actual "wake-up." It got here; it is right now!

I wonder how long an angel stays with you, after you leave a war, get discharged? How do you suppose that works? Does the angel just float away in some softened night air to another needy shoulder? I could use an angel for a while yet or so it appears. I know! I'll ask Aunt Marge. I'll call her from Pendleton or Oceanside. She'll know. I owe them a call anyway.

Brightest and earliest on the Da Nang tarmac, October 2, 1968, and suddenly, the morning Asian heat mattered not. Rollie did not have to find Captain Loftus. Loftus found him with an MP jeep and bullhorn, as if searching through airstrip buildings and assets for some VIP. At attention, and the snappiest salute ever, Rollie presented himself and his papers and was immediately escorted to the foot of the gangway leading up and into the darkened doorway of the long-awaited United flight. Rollie took a last look back, down, saluted Loftus again, took a second last look, then a glance over toward Marble Mountain, turned around into United, and witnessed the brightest most loving sight he thought he would never see again.

There, facing Rollie were six of the most beautiful lipsticks he had ever hoped to see in his life. Helped by two pilots who made a special effort to join the personal welcome, Rollie was escorted and hugged to his United, travel home seat up front behind the cockpit. Only then did the pilots tell the lipsticks to allow the others to board for the trip home to the World.

There are happy, touching, stirring types of flights of vacationers or groups on their merry way to Vegas or to weddings or conventions. Happy flights of all kinds, all over the place stimulate passengers into cheers or applause of sustaining spirits for that mission or flight or entertaining event ahead.

Those types of happy-go-lucky flights don't begin to compare to the flights out of Nam for war-weary Nam vets! The worn, beat-up, flitting bodies and personalities of all kinds of army and marines in the process of rotating out of Nam at lift-off out of country, to the World, are a sight to behold and experience. No one actually trusts the moment, although six lipsticks stand grinning, to ensure the truth of the moment. It is practically too special to actually be real, uplifting in their survivability and pride of service on one hand, depressing in their skittish looks and half reluctant reactions on the other hand. The 120 bodies, with 120 different Nam war experiences and stories, all rather stunned and willing to pretend to be orderly in their search for their United seat home. The 120 bodies, with 120 war gut feelings and visions, outlooks, and expectations, hatreds and confused angers. The 120 Wilson Street Boys who think they can now go someplace better, someplace they deserve, have earned the right to be, wherever that place is, different experiences for different attitudes in different shrunken bodies.

There was an instance, on this journey, when none of the unknown future or the past mattered. An instance when 100 percent of the human cargo would come together, touched by the movement, 100 percent of the time on United flights out of Da Nang. That instance is the very instance that peculiar group of passengers collectively feel the dash and acceleration down the runway and the pilot blasts his cabin message over the United loud speaker: "We're airborne—out of the Nam!" At that moment, 120 different war-beat American veterans come together in the loud happy cheers, and grins, and pride of service, like no other moment any of them will ever again experience. The plane fills with the reaching, handshaking, shoulder slaps and grinning of new types of American men. These are the survivors, and for that time, on that day, in that plane, with those six gorgeous American lipsticks, life was on the way to being good again, on a way to trying to be normal again, safer again. Some of those lives would actually reach a satisfactory human normal, some wouldn't ever, and others would for a while, then for a while not. Regardless, at that moment of liftoff, nothing of deeper thinking mattered.

United circled Da Nang harbor and gained altitude while salty veterans slowly settled back into seats, trying to get a feel for how to relax, and how to react to a lipstick passing with a smile, her rotating hips rotating all the way down the middle aisle. Now off shore, gaining more altitude over the picturesque blue South China Sea, the pilot broke the heavy new silence of the flight.

> *Pilot #1: Gentlemen, off to your right. You'll see one of America's most distinguished displays of global power. That is the aircraft carrier,* USS Enterprise, *with enough fixed wing weaponry and trained brave pilots to wreak havoc on the enemy like never before. All of our troops will be coming home soon.*

A new round of cheers filled the plane with the temporary foolish hope that something in Nam was going to be accomplished soon. A United pilot's practical guarantee that for all the lives lost and hardships spent, and for all the assets and political lies that it has taken to sustain the war in Nam, and for all of the tearing apart of the core of American values—for all that—this pilot, that guy right up there, says all the troops will come home soon. What a guy!

That flight 911, beat wings and Boeing jet engines across the Pacific west to east, so fast and far the flight would get over going east and concluded in the far west of the United States. Discharge, processing would take a mere two days. Just a little debriefing about several things, papers passed, and more papers to be filled out, and one signed.

Rollie felt the warm California sun and breathed the cool air that sunlight passes through in California but somehow doesn't warm. He now tried to stand firmly, where ever he stood. In the street, he watched cars go by and measured the happy Americans in them. No longer was it an epiphany to see a lipstick. They were everywhere, like a regular part of the population. Some stared straight ahead, but some looked back and even smiled. Rollie had no idea how he appeared to others. He presumed he appeared awkward and out of place. He'd lost weight, everybody does, but he felt OK, inwardly strong, didn't feel weird, only out of place. One night in an Oceanside hotel, and then, he'd head to LA for another flight east. He saw a lipstick in the drugstore next to the hotel and said, "Hi." The lipstick looked back, looking Rollie right in the eye, and said "hi" back to him. Rollie thought that was a pretty good start while fully realizing this boy/girl thing was going to be quite difficult.

At the hotel payphone, Rollie reached a telephone operator and information for Coronado, looking for the number of Marge and Art Cahill, on B Avenue.

Marge: Hello, this is Margorie.
Rollie: Aunt Marge, this is Rollie. I made it back. I made it kind of a week earlier than I expected.
Marge (yelling backward into the house): Art, come quick. It's Rollie. He's in the States. Rollie, honey, where are you?

Rollie: I'm in Oceanside for the night. I just didn't want to stay on the base at Pendleton. I'm discharged. I made it. Going to LA tomorrow.

Marge: Rollie dearest, our prayers have worked their trusty mystic ways. We are blessed! We traveled with you each day, each evening, as best we could anyway. We watched all the dreadful news, especially through and after Tet. We knew you were there in the mix. We could feel it.

Marge: Art wants to say hello. Here's Art.

Art: Hi, Rollie. Rollie, thank you for your service, from the bottom of all the hearts here in Coronado and across the country. Son, we loved you every day, prayed for you, and those prayers helped deliver you back to us. I'll let you talk to Marge. Everybody always wants her angelic voice over mine. Bye for now. Marge!

Rollie: Well, thank you. Thank you both. By the way, have you heard from North Carolina?

Marge: Yes . . . yes, we have, have heard too much all along. Don't know what to make of it all, and obviously, you don't either. Rollie, we know your home is gone. We are aware of that. Where will you go? What will you do? I know all of this is new and will take some time to settle into, but you know you can always come to our home. Art and I would both treasure to our deepest souls helping you get started again. Would you consider that?

Rollie: Yes, I would consider that, but that's not why I called, of course. Besides, I have a new car to pick up in Raleigh, a brand-new Dodge Charger."

Marge: Oh, holey Moses, how does that happen? You just got here.

Rollie: It's kind of a long, very hard to believe story. Would you believe I won enough money in a poker game in Da Nang one night to buy a brand-new car?

Marge: I think I would believe that, but I can't imagine a car dealership in Da Nang.

Rollie: There wasn't a dealership, but there was a Chrysler car salesman at the big PX in Da Nang, just sittin' out front at a card table—that was his own personal dealership. So I gave him about $4,000 of my poker winnings, signed some papers, and hope to hell he was legit. Marge, the war isn't about fighting back Communism anymore. It's about something else. I'm not sure what.

Marge: We kind of know what you mean but not firsthand like you. There isn't hardly a day goes by here in Coronado that we don't have just that conversation, with local military friends, and customers at the TV shop over on Orange Boulevard. I hate to say this, but the whole thing is beginning to look like a huge national disgrace. But let that be for now. When will we see you?

Rollie: I don't really know. I'll fly out of LA tomorrow, to Raleigh, find my car, go by the old home, pick up what's left of my things—and then, I don't know. All that aside, I have to ask you something—something really important. I have to get this out and see if I can come to an understanding, or partial understanding.

Marge: What, Rollie? What could I possibly help you with? Anything!

Rollie: In Nam, I had an angel with me, sounds crazy. I know I did! Shortly after I could see what I was in for and up against for the year in-country, from then on, I felt an angel was with me, every day and night, always, everywhere. I even remember the evening that I first had the feeling. Was it you? Are you the angel I could feel? I think it was you. It was a strange feeling, like sometimes, we were one, and other times, we were separate seeing, feeling different things. The feeling was real, very true to me. It carried my weight when extra weight needed carrying. I think the angel guarded my actions, many times, was often some sort of a shield. The angel did all kinds of things, probably things I'm not even aware of. I came to conclude the angel was your spirit, somehow with me. Was it? Was . . . Is the angel you? I have no other choice of reasoning. The angel had to be you. Do you know?

Marge: Yes, the angel was me. It was a strange feeling for me also, that I had to be content with, understand the pace of. I had a strange feeling also, that many days were half me, half-distant angel.

Rollie: How long will you be with me . . . as my angel?

Marge: I think a long time. Maybe a very long time. OK?

Rollie: "Of course, OK! I've only been in the States a day. I have to admit I feel a little lost, like I don't fit, or won't fit, anywhere. I even had thoughts of re-upping, but I know I'd end up right back in Nam, and I'm afraid I'm worn out from that, my angel probably is worn out too.

Marge: You are worn out. Stay put. Look into your new World. You will never fail. You're too full of America, just like Art and I were twenty years ago, coming to a new job in a new corner of America. Never forget we are here. We will always be here, drive that new Charger to our doorstep whenever you are ready.

Rollie: How will I ever thank you enough? I know you have a lot to do with why I am here, alive.

Marge: You won't because we don't ever know what enough is when it comes to wars and the deepest of inner emotional feelings. You go! Go on and be yourself. You and I both know we will meet again in the glorious, blessed sun light of future lives.

Rollie: Do you have any idea what my angel did, did for me? I never even spoke of it to anyone around me. I knew no one would understand. I'd look stupid or worse yet a little touched. I would have never returned alive without the angel. I know I wouldn't. So many aren't returning.

Marge: Rollie, honey, yes, I do know. I don't expect you to understand this, but it drained me. Angel work can be hard. At times like Tet, I spent every night with you, I did. It even wore Art out. He didn't ask, but he knew. Rollie, I don't know how it works either, spiritually, how God's hand reaches so far across such distances to different worlds, from one person then to another. And you know what—right now—I don't care how it works. I'm just raised and lifted, floating on clouds through the heavens with a giggly spirit. I sense we will always be some kind of one person, you and I, always connected. Look, you are about twenty-one now. You go. Go find what you deserve. We will always be here, easy to find, always with you. Go! Go collect yourself and your thoughts, and your goodness, and your skills. That angel ain't goin anywhere. We will see you when we see you! We are so very proud.

Rollie: OK, I had to ask, try to understand or find out. Bye, Marge. Love you!

Marge: Someday, right here in Coronado, we'll sit at the Bay for lunch. And I may just grab that angel right back off your shoulder. Bye, my love!

Chapter 7

The Domestic Wake of War's Phantasmagoria

"Deepest challenges and fears stuck inside
forever is a long time to be lived with."

The small print of an airstrip just outside the village of Quang Tri was a place not to be in February 1968 or for that matter a place not to be pretty much any other time for Americans. For US warring assets, Quang Tri itself was a nonstrategic, strategic helicopter landing pad and short airstrip outpost, appearing to be a military afterthought. The strip and small camp surroundings were "Quang Tri" in name only. The real village of Quang Tri, one of many local provincial capitals displaced about the country, was a couple clicks north of the camp and air pad, on Highway 1. Marines stationed at the Quang Tri strip rarely went into the village or mingled with its population. It was assumed that this close to the DMZ a good deal of the peasant population were Viet Cong, undercover bad guys, smiley pleasant in the day, calling in mortar target locations at night. The camp itself, with Highway 1 a quarter click off the east side toward the South China Sea, was all Marine Corps, except for passing flights, special forces, or recon ground troops who would wonder into the area and hang out for a couple days to gather their nerves, thoughts, weapons, and survival assets.

Quang Tri's lifeline to the World and Command was Phu Bai, where Marine Air Group headquarters for I Corps resided and literally called the shots. Most marines first entered Quang Tri by air, so close to the south edge of the DMZ, entering on foot or as part of a motorized convoy was usually a bad plan. The strip was the epitome of the Corps' "troop level" basic philosophy all over Nam: "You only owned the ground you were standing on." In Quang Tri and a thousand other remote sand piles, marines survived inside their own perimeter. Anything outside the rolled barbed wire and claymore trip lines was Gookland, where Charlie made up plans for the night's attacks or just the harmless night's harassment.

A pilot that was good enough could drop a C-130 into the short Quang Tri strip, but otherwise, the place was for the marine Air Group I Corps helicopter traffic and plenty of it. The small strip was nonstrategic in its lack of size, lack of actual human marine firepower, lack of significant weaponry, and lack of any sort of apparent importance to location. The place was built or, more accurately, thrown together, in late '66 on a sand pile along the Quang Tri river, just kind of there, so it had to be protected and be a part of I Corps implementation of shifting war college brilliance and the never certain string of Nam war strategies. The stretched sandpiles that made up the Quang Tri strip and camp were someone's idea of a place to be as an outpost against the spread of Asian Communism, plenty of Wilson Street Boys coming and going to keep the remote place war active and defended. The airstrip and base had no "rocket-belt" defense planning.

The Command bunker was like an oversized, sandbagged outhouse-looking nonstructure, half above the sand ground level, half below. Modest ranks of officers and their NCOs held the Command bunker together and operated as best they could, constantly studying maps, hourly chatter with higher command in Phu Bai and Da Nang, or aboard a ship to coordinate the daily chaos of moving troops and assets and predictions of enemy pressure. Bottom line: Quang Tri was one more Nam dung-heap that no one would ever know much about, care about, or remember except for the few marines stuck in the place and maybe their far away families who may have noticed the strange spelling in a letter home, insinuating some weird, nondescript temporary location of their at-large family member working in one more of the Nam's fractured, dangerous targets.

Quang Tri was strategic because the non-descript place was just ten to fifteen clicks South of all of the key hot spots on the southern border of the DMZ and just eight clicks north of the more strategic ancient city of Hue. It was connected on the East side to Highway 1, the only passable road of anything South to North in I Corps. The Quang Tri strip and collection of tents and bunkers was half night-fire Gook-bait, and half operational. Sure, the airstrip and assets were used, plenty, but once a marine was there, within the isolation of the small base, ya kind of had to ask yourself:

What would happen, or not happen, if this place didn't exist?

The painful realistic answer was always the same: nothing. The place just didn't matter, not really, unless you were physically part of it, owning the ground you stood on. However, ironically, in the painful US warring ways of Nam, not mattering didn't really matter to far away faceless strategic commands. Lots of places, especially in I Corps, didn't matter. The LZs, firebases, and small camps were built up, fought over, and then abandoned, one after another, each requiring a certain supply of body bags symbolizing the prices paid to complete the extrication process. One would then assume the body bags didn't matter to Command either. Those lost places were largely just part of the "strategery" of "busyness," doing "something," first with one brilliant warring fancy terminology, like "Vietnamization," then with some other fancy name, multi-syllable coining of Indochina strategy brilliance. It was all just pretend hustle and bustle of military advantage seeking of some sort, to make people up the chain of commands feel better about their back-ass-ward indecisive confusion, and uselessness.

The Quang Tri airstrip itself was buckled together steel sheets, laid by the workaholic Seabee bunch that race in, build stuff, and disappear to build other stuff in other temporary places that don't matter but are super key to American advantage for the moment up until the instance of not being key and then also abandoned.

Quang Tri itself, the actual place where the marines lived and operated from, was sand. White sand was in some places, darker sand over there, and then darker sand further out from the river. Deep sand! The further from the white sand center of the base you got, the stretching, sinkable line of sand sight was broken by sturdy Asian clumps of healthy weed cover. Most of the sand just lays there like it was supposed to over thousands of years of Asian sandy ways. Not so any longer, starting in 1966 and through 1968, the sand at Quang Tri would be on the move, mobile, aggravated, whipped-up sand—sand with a war-based sand-blasting attitude. In those special years, Quang Tri sand mobilized and constantly moved, as dozens and then hundreds of Marine Corps helicopters landed, then took off and more landed, all day, into the night. Early pink eastern sky line, furious daily helicopter mission launch action, whipped the new day's sand-blasting all that new day, then the next day. If the sand was resting too long from a Marine Air Group (MAG) breather, First Air Cav helicopters from the army air mobile guys passed in and out of Quang Tri, kicking sand into faces, clothes, vital M-16 hardware, and through any tent or bunk or mess hall. Quang Tri sand blistered and blasted marines and their equipment the most when the occasional C-130s used the short strip for their brave, vital missions of supply or life-saving. C-130 tsunamis of sand were altogether different. When those big boys took off, everyone would just hide, get down, low, out of sight, cover up. In the open space of an airstrip, everything around that's not nailed down goes recklessly in the opposite direction that the C-130s do.

As a normal part of marine life at the Quang Tri airstrip, sand was in your socks, under your cover as part of your hair, in your nose and ears. Sand was in your C rations or mess kit. Sand crunched between teeth at a predawn tarmac C ration breakfast and found a way up, in and around everything. Every other day, marines dumped the sand from their cot blankets, dumped the sand onto the sand floors of their tent or bunker, so the sand could whip up again, into boots and skivvies and find a sand way back into the cots and blankets. New marines to Quang Tri quickly learned to hate sand, just as the grunts were learning to hate the constant monsoon rains and leeches that squirmed on the jungle floors and seemed to follow them from one beat-up, useless jungle location to the next. Sand was another sort of persistent enemy that owned the ground, was the ground, at the very least a constant harassment that wears, erodes, creates misjudgments, and keeps attitudes at a high level of directionless irritation.

There *was* one good thing about the sand at Quang Tri. The same sand that irritated the hell out of everyone also filled the dark-green Marine Corps-issued sandbags, and the sandbags made walls and covered dark damp holes in the ground called bunkers. Neither mortar incoming, nor rocket incoming, nor artillery shrapnel would normally penetrate through the sandbagged walls. Russian AK-47 bullets wouldn't pass through walls of sandbags and thus what was slowly torturing the marines of Quang Tri would occasionally save them. Just one of war's crooked ironies. Like certain salty marines would say about their American women, in cranky nostalgic Nam moments: "Can't live with 'em, can't live without 'em." Sand! Enough sand, too much sand, sand always in the wrong place, always too deep to walk or run across, always aggravating a moment that needed no further aggravation.

After the country-wide tumultuous kick-off of the enemy's warring showmanship in Tet, late January, '68, life for marines at Quang Tri had two distinct twenty-four-hour activity cycles. Toward dusk and through most of the night, until early, early morning, marines either guarded the perimeter of their small air base, or were getting ready to guard the perimeter, always going to, or coming from some remote, sand-filled, shit hole, tense, dark line duty. Marines would lay, sit, squat, prop up, and stay awake all night within the sand. They would stare long strange sight paths hours at a time across sand formations. A person staring enough into timid nights with floating, flickering flares and passing moon beams will create a self-imposed illusionist sensation that things that couldn't possibly move, do move. Those Asian clumps of weeds a half click off the line jiggle sporadically in warm dark breezes, one at a time in coordinated strings of jiggling as breezes stretch across the darkened sandy landscape keeping all things nervously alert. Out of place nights with unfamiliar sounds and uncertain landscape test bleary, spent eyes, which then test nerves, which reach deeper and test souls, reasoning, and then test faith.

Toward 4:00 a.m., those same marines return in short low dashes to their tents, to reinvent their core Quang Tri purpose, and switch from ground gear to air gear. Flight gear equipped, the exhausted air crews head for the tarmac and dawn flight plans to climb aboard fueled waiting Hueys and assist fighting and dying marines all along a southern DMZ line from Khe Sanh to Con Thien and any LZs or single ground units in between that they might be able to reach with Hueys supplying ammo in and wounded out.

Life for Air Group Marines at Quang Tri was that simple— listen, observe, be ready to fight, and survive on the ground at night, do the same from the air in the day time. Sleep in twenty-minute increments four to five times a day, whenever you can. Crunch sand in your teeth whenever some food source was available and could be released from the hard green C ration cans. Then rot within the persistent humidity and sweat inside marine issue skivvies, under salty covers (hats or helmets) for most of the rest of the day. Sounds simple enough! It was a war, broken down to basic Nam I Corps, Tet elements! Each day was a Nam learning curve to exist until the next day, to then do it all over again, all the while counting down to a "wake-up."

Marines at Quang Tri knew each other, bunked somewhat together, but saying they were "friends" would be a civilian style overstatement. Crews regularly shifted from one Huey or Chinook bird to the next in the day and night. Perimeter duty made strange foxhole mates constantly. Trust in the fighting skills and stay awake fortitude of the next new foxhole body was a hope and crap shoot. People/marines just handle themselves differently under different pressures. Throughout Quang Tri, spontaneous yells of "Incoming" from enemy mortars and rockets created scrambles and unpredictable dives into ditches, bunkers or between sandbag walls. When diving in a low lifeline into your foxhole or bunker a marine's best friend was the guy with the most weaponry and ammo strapped to his diving body.

Helicopters were a new symbol of American warfare perfected in their use for Nam as were several other types of weaponry and war assets engineered in America after twenty straight years of war and warring preparation all across the globe from Europe to Asia. Helicopters were most important to marine life and rescue in I Corps and the traffic in and out of Quang Tri became a high priority. Tarmac-parked birds were a constant, irresistible target through post-

Tet nights for enemy mortar and rocketry around the Quang Tri rocket belt. Marines all over I Corps geography needed and depended on the helicopters and were seriously committed to guarding them, first with sandbag protection, then with sentries looking into each night for a running suicide Gook with a satchel bomb strapped above his Communist ass. No fifty-five-gallon fuel or oil drum was emptied of petro, without being immediately filled with sand and laid in lines to guard parked helicopters.

Filling fifty-five-gallon drums with sand and their tarmac placement in lines to guard the helicopters was one of Quang Tri's mini-industries. Tarmac guard duty was a bit like sleeping with dynamite. Your duty was to be at the exact site of an irresistible Gook mortar target. You knew things would get busy, get hot. It was just when, at what moment, that was always unpredictable. Salty tarmac guard Marines perfected the listening art of detecting incoming mortar and rocket fire after launch from the rocket belt, but before it hit Quang Tri ground. A tarmac guard would rapidly develop a new sense of identifying flying kabooms, before they kaboomed, normally giving them 2-3 seconds to take diving cover.

On the edges of the Quang Tri strip Marines bunked in 20' X 20' dark-green canvas tents, on white sand, a couple of support poles down the middle and along the sides, flaps at each end to enter, or get the hell out of there. Big dark-green tents for resting, sleeping and keeping Marine stuff, stuck out on the white sand like mortar bulls-eyes. 6 short inches, or closer, from the outside of the tent canvas sides, Marines built sandbagged walls about 3' high, just high enough so that razor sharp shrapnel exploding on the outside, would shred the tent just above the level of the top of the cots inside, plus a Marine's laid out body height. Split sandbags with leaking sand, were rapidly replaced no matter how far down the wall they were, with great replacement enthusiasm. At the tents two end exit or entry flaps, L-shaped sandbag walls kept exploding enemy shrapnel from shredding the bodies inside in a direct line through the tent opening.

These filthy, regularly sand-blasted, usually shredded tents were home, where Marines unlucky enough to be sentenced to Quang Tri tried to sleep occasionally and where they kept their stuff; ammo stuff, strange weaponry stuff that was found or thrown on a Huey at some frantic moment in an emergency landing or lift off. They kept a lot of stuff in a dark-green duffle bag, made for slinging over a shoulder and a quick jump on a Huey, just in case relocation to another nonstrategic camp or LZ was the order of their strategic moment.

With ten marines to a 20×20 feet tent, each marine had a short four-foot width on his side of the middle aisle and normally a short attitudinal fuse. Five cots to each side left a marine with cot space two-foot wide, and two more skinny feet to stand, or sit, and keep or contemplate his armfuls of marine combat and survival stuff. Two feet was also enough space to "hit it," if some other marine somewhere yelled "incoming" or a rocket womp or mortar thud interrupted a quiet war moment, which happened most often all through February 1968, then through March. The tents and marines were also filled with tension and irritation that spilled outward on occasion from any source of frustration that added to a Marine's Nam weight of existence. Scraps between marines never seemed to last long, no one had the energy to scrap for long. It was more snarling than scrapping that settled unsettled moments among tent mates. The sandy place existed within shifting levels of tension Quang Tri style.

At Quang Tri, in February, 1968 a "day" was something you tried to get through, just tried to survive. There were probably worse places, like the Hanoi Hilton, or five hundred feet off a carrier deck prelanding an A-6 at night in a rising and falling South China Sea, moving twenty-three knots, south by south east. However, each true grunt believes their particular "hell" is a hell like no other, which is their grunting privilege.

Twenty-six nights (maybe twenty-eight, maybe thirty) in a row after Tet, Quang Tri was probed, attacked with Gook ground harassment and more serious actions or pounded with enemy mortar or rocket fire. Twenty-six nights in a row, into late February, marines "hit it," dove into bunkers, or raced to the perimeter in the dark monsoon night or among moving shadows provided by the temporary sparkling light of friendly flares. Twenty-six nights in a row, marines locked and loaded, looked into Nam nights to see the Nam, moved low, and then occasionally looked up to the stars with their angels, looking for a sign of sanity or reason or confidence. Then for twenty-six early, prelighted dawns, most of those marines slipped quietly and low back to tents, trading helmets and flare pistols for flight gear, then a little more upright, working their dark way through camp QT to the tarmac for the first revs of Huey engines, all while looking for signs of pink to the east that would be the official, unofficial notice of having survived the night and into a new Nam day.

Early dawn tarmac wake-ups marked individual relief on one notion for having survived the night but turned to more adrenaline in the next notion, preparing for new flight plans. Pilots would emerge from their own dark hideaways with crew orders and maps like dutiful leaders, armed with side weapons, saddle up, and start dash board clicks to wake-up the stretched bend of the copter's blades. The long, sleek, powerful blades would slowly whine with resistance and always groan to a start, eventually whipping up their own Nam wind and the previously still sand, as the pilot and crew preflight chatter would ramp-up into instruction and at-a-boys and brave talk concerning the day's early mission. At those fleeting moments, life on a Huey crew was good. Door guns click with their checks, ammo strings strung through the guns and clamped. Helmet mouth pieces connecting crew to pilots, tested, then tested again in a unique flight crew jargon rhythm passed down by pure instinct.

If enough morning pink graced the small camp at liftoff, airborne marines off to the first day's mission could see ground marines moving as smaller and smaller hustling dots from perimeter positions back into camp and daytime duties. More flight crews heading to waiting birds emerged from other worn, partially shredded tents. These crews would be headed in a different liftoff direction to some other remote

LZ or maybe down the coast. In the early mornings, huey crews knew little of their day's missions. Until the briefed pilots plopped up front and spread the good news, the crews knew nothing of the missions to come and largely yet to be designed in strategic approach or exit, that detail is always a spontaneous work in progress. Spreading the news for the first mission was a time in the day that was critical. Crews and pilots paid the strictest attention, making sure everyone understood everything they could through there split-second radio chatter.

First, early flights were the best, freshest, even for worn out crews. After the chatter and the weapons checks, fresh morning breezes from turning props would lift all crew spirits. At liftoff, a broad view of the landscape below created a little hope that a bigger world was out there and would someday be reached, then embraced. Such illusionary feelings of transcending the weight of the moment helped with the presumption that eventually all marines would climb high enough to see something besides Nam.

Marines are like most other groups of people, maybe, kind of. They react to certain situations differently, just like street or home folk do. In Nam, once you realized there were no days off or "downtime," a marine could acquiesce to his own pace of survival and find an emotional personal zone to reside within, keeping highs low, and lows high. Flight life somehow had a spiritual mood 99 percent of the time, maybe because of the vision, beat and pressure of the blades lifting your life up, carrying lives along an unseeable path, dropping them, twisting your life amidst the air, and then saving lives. For some, Air Group Marines life was all about the power and rhythmic sounds of the bird's stretched powerful blades. A flight crew marine could be up all night along the perimeter, soundly asleep on the tarmac, and then wide awake a second later with whips of a couple Huey blades announcing a time to mount up. If there were only a way for copter engineers to design blades powerful enough to lift a bird, but respectful enough not to sand blast everything within fifty feet.

Copter engineers did design one very unique feature for both Huey and Chinook blades to perform all on their dutiful own. Some pilots and crews preferred transit time (time from one location to another, preduty or prebattle) to be low, just skirting ground positions. The engineering-challenged would believe that low altitudes would then leave less distance to fall from the air and be crushed to death when struck by enemy fire, as if falling seven hundred feet, at Mach-falling speed would shatter every bone and kill a crewmen less than falling seven thousand feet in a death spiral to an unforgiving Asian landing grave. However, most such transit/milk-run trips were flown at eight thousand feet. The engineering theory being: those long powerful copter blades are designed so that, if a bird is shot and disabled, in the rapidity (through thick Asian air) of the drop to earth, the passing of air through the spinning blades would alone cause a sort of copter lift, or less rapid fall. The rapid fall (presuming the disabled shot bird was falling in a lateral position) would cause the blades to turn faster, just rapidly enough to gently set the copter to the ground in a modified more controlled crash, rather than with a full copter body slam crash to earth guaranteed to kill everyone inside. Theoretically, with this little engineering "rumor" tidbit, flight crews could fly with more confidence at eight thousand feet, in full view of long range enemy killing intentions.

Another slight survival caveat to the greater flying altitude was that any Gook smart-ass with a new Russkie RPG would clearly see the eight-thousand-foot target to be out of his range. Just the discussion among flight crews of the engineering rumor of falling from the sky was momentarily fulfilling for a while until the crews actually thought about it. In reality, once you've seen a falling helicopter hit, ground or tarmac, and spinning blades drive into the surface at all angles, violently twisting the fallen helicopter into pretzel style steel, rumors of the potential engineer designed gentleness of controlled crashing kind of evaporate, at least for the realistic. It was generally concluded that there was no such thing as a controlled crash in Nam. A "controlled" crash was for some other crew story in some other war, although it is generally accepted that carrier landings by A-6s hook and cable style, were all controlled crashing.

Marines at war have other things in common with humans, other things beyond the apparent. Marines' brains, in war, are constantly processing issues of major concern. In war, the issues change rapidly, instantly, no plan seems to last very long, the enemy other guys just don't cooperate. Bombs explode where they aren't supposed to, in amounts unpredicted. Stuff burns, breaks, is blown up; the stuff that was supposed to be of great support. The overworked, combat-fatigued brains constantly search for solutions to huge lifesaving problems and to smaller life convenience issues like digging out and then spitting irritating sand caught between teeth. Marines' minds work consciously responding to issues and subconsciously appraising or resolving issues from the past or around the fantasies or speculation of the potential future issues. The mental predictions of the unpredictable never stop. A Nam marine's life is a reactionary life, only partially in control, only occasionally making human brain processing sense.

Within the marine's Nam life, experiences and events pile up at the brain's gate. Deadly, tense events pile up rapidly at a time like Tet. Flying missions, then perimeter duty, then "incoming," the outlet for the counter/corresponding emotions in reaction to those events become an emotion packed, subconscious mental logjam. Unfortunately, the emotions don't then disappear from the logjam; they don't then just sweat away in the next rising sun, daily Nam heat wave or with any particular understandable timeline. The emotions embed, seep into the marine's veins as a silent, patient virus, long term, waiting in an unknown cerebral gut hideaway place, unfelt, often for very long periods of time, even for lifetimes.

Even "disarmed" emotions from warring events cannot just disseminate, disperse, stand at ease, and separate from the veteran's existence. The human experiences become a peculiar sort of inner wisdom in some cases, inner turmoil in other cases, or inner warnings in even more cases. There will likely be times in future life when these subconscious experiences arise in the form of a personal inner symbolic language that is designed to review or recommunicate these past events that the uncontrolled subconscious considers (incomplete). This seems to be needed, to in some way resolve the past dangerous moment's incompleteness. These unpredictable episodes of subconscious review intertwine the veteran's imagination with the actual events of the past.

Just as there is an outward angel vaguely lending to a safer way, there can be an inner demon that will not let go of unexplainable, unresolved events. The demon in one instance is an inner warning of danger. In the next instance, the sensation can be the "actual" situation of a past event, symbols of the situation, or moving, acting fragments of the situations. The veteran soul is simply the awkward, unknowing carrier of situations unresolved. The Veteran is the carrier of the occasional situation sensation force, moving a person unexpectedly in directions not anticipated, always unannounced.

These inner warnings of danger are often in the form of *dreams* or in the form of an awkward "phantasmagoria," moving, color dreams, or fantasies of the dreams sensing the unresolved never seen danger below the surface. *Dreams* that unfortunately can play out in slow, torturing motion, extend the actual unresolved moments into the sweat of palms, and into erratic violent motions to extricate and separate the body from the surprise subconscious attack. Once the *dreams* begin, the emotions can grow like a reactionary cancer, war dreaming begetting more war dreaming, recalling hidden demons that become unleashed further up the personal subconscious ladder.

Ten marines to a tent never evolves into 10 Wilson Street Boys, all on the same Nam page. Too many different faces come and go. There are too many personal issues and war duties to create any real brotherhood other than the type of brotherhood from a scramble to the bunker or a dash to the line to support one line of foxholes or repel another threatening action further down line. With ten marines to a tent, you pretty much will have ten different personalities, ten backgrounds, ten expectations on how things happen, should, or would work or not work, in the vague realities of a hundred different nightly scenarios. You get ten different timetables of reaction to crisis or prevention to crisis, just like ten different baseball athletes have ten different bat swings through the strike zone.

Then, the close *szzzz-womp* of a night launched rocket, and the tent scramble of the ten marines begins. A scramble to hit it, grab a weapon, decide if the rocket is followed by ground fire, more rockets, smaller mortar fire, artillery, or all of the above. Three-foot high sandbag walls protect cots, bodies, and the stored weapons under the cots, if the rocket lands "outside" the sandbag walls around the tent. The bags protect the emptied open boots, pictures from home and other stuff from the world—the rest of the tent, above the three-foot line, is shredded, and so is anyone caught standing at the moment of the enemy rocket's deadly *womp*.

"Incoming" yells, echo down one row of tents, then from another row across the sand and dirt dividing path. Everyone in camp wonders if the front gate is manned, armed and awake, if enough Marines are there to make the difference and hold the position against a front gate ground attack that is surely just a matter of Gook time.

"Incoming" yells, elbows and ass-holes immediately move, scramble, some move to the lines, some fly to a bunker, some hit-it inside the tent in their 2 foot hit-it space. If not scrambled, all bodies wait motionless for a hint or an instinct that helps to predict a sort of detail to the sudden threats for the moments to follow.

Lighter mortar "thuds" peck away at parts of the dark camp, signaling mortar Gooks are working with the rocket Gooks, which is a sure sign of a coordinated attack; maybe with ground Gooks holding their positions, which is a sure sign of a ground probe sooner or later along some target camp perimeter line. Grab flares, pop one, for show; just to show an alerted armed ready.

Sandbagged covered bunkers outside each tent of 10 Marines are pitch black, dark, damp crap places inside for one purpose only, to survive a mortar or rocket attack. The bunkers are holes in the sand, crawling with living Asian sand things, with a front angled entrance big enough for a scrambled diving Marine to launch his body into, roll down and then right, into the deeper dark hole of the lifesaving bunker.

Szzzzz-womp. Another rocket! One marine bunker dive into the dark hole, then another, then another, and soon half-dressed, bootless, startled marines pile up against each other rolling down and to their right. The next marine aims his dive too high, the middle of his skull crashing with the bunker's steel top plate of support, which was stolen from tarmac construction assets, to support sandbags stacked three-foot high as the bunker impenetrable roofing. Soon, the tight bunker is full of the smell of the skull crashed marine's warm blood, as well as his groans and squirming efforts to compensate for the pain. Soon, the marine becomes sticky wet with the blood from his own self-inflicted, too high skull cracking head wound dive. (Never dive into your bunker too high, always error your dive on the low side.) He's new. We forgot to tell him, "Always dive low." The incoming bunker-dive blood wound somehow spreads in the confusion of the tangled bodies now untangling, and the next marine flies through the slanted hole and rolls, then another, piling against and around the cracked bloody skull.

Another rocket—*szzzzz-womp!*—and Gook mortar tubes walk a few more exploding mortar thuds across the bare Quang Tri landscape, blasting sand and shredding tents, jeep tires and latrine sides. The deadly enemy fire shredding anything else the shrapnel can reach into and wrangle and rip apart. Womps and thuds, eventually also shred minds, all minds eventually.

Sergeant Dickerson soon made his dive inside his tent's bunker with seven other marines, one bleeding profusely, moaning just as profusely. Eight marines in a dark, damp, sandtrap of a hole in the ground, in Indochina—ten thousand miles on the other side of the globe from Main Street or Wilson Street or any other World Street. Ten thousand, likely the number of political lies it took to put and maintain these marines in their filthy dangerous positions. Two marines missing, presumed either headed for the gate, or the perimeter, or some other defensive position, always presumed at work, out there amongst whatever is out there on the way. Maybe they dashed to support the front gate, maybe to the tarmac, maybe on their own special journey.

Szzzzz-womp!

In the distance, the increasing rapid echo sounds of blades against the night air, signal that at least one squadron, or parts of a squadron, made it to the tarmac and are revving up to get in the air, possibly to spot mortar or rocket launch firing sites and provide some return rocketry and .50-caliber payback.

No one knows whose squadron. *Thud. Thud. Thud-thud.* Gook mortars walk past a different area of the small Quang Tri base, possibly down a different row of tents and their adjacent bunkers.

Inside the bunker:

> *"Jenkins, you OK? Your head smashed? You gonna live?"*
>
> *"Don't know. Bleeding bad, blood all over. Can't see through. Bad stuff man. My head is bulging."*
>
> *"Anyone bring a weapon? We got ground fire. We can't all be in here unarmed."*
>
> *"Naw man . . . No . . . Not me . . . Me neither . . . Naw . . . Shit no!"*
>
> *"We got no weapons, not one?"*

A squirming mass of tangled marines, push against the bunker walls and against one another to untangle, to find individual cramped sand spaces while the "incoming" pauses.

Dope-ass in the back, Mr. Chicken-dung in the corner, uncontrollably trembles with fear, shaking madly, with a disgusting low quiver of a child's whine. His fear having taken control of his entire body, the possibility of any useful body motion paralyzes him within his own shaking fear. Useless to himself and to the world, a pitiful behavior, in Indochina, in Nam, in Quang Tri, in a frickin' dark damp hole in the ground, filled with sweat, heavy night air, the smell of Jenkins' blood, the sound of persistent enemy night rocketry.

The awakened Asian starved bunker bugs begin to move around to do their natural irritating duty of feasting on the newly arrived exposed fleshy parts of the unexpected bunker intruders.

> *Dickerson: I don't hear anything, I'll go. Go find my 16, 45, bring back whatever else I touch that will shoot something. You guys stay right here. Don't go dancing down Broadway for a beer. Ya hear? Be right back! If this goes OK, I'll get some more weapons on a second trip, we'll set up our own perimeter right outside.*

Sergeant Dickerson slipped up the bunker's slight exit incline into the dark as occasional pops of small arms fire were the only outside sounds now. The exit that was, moments ago, a survival entrance decline opened out to a few line flares flickering in gaps between the passing low clouds. A few short clicks north, more small arm's pop-pop. Then Dickerson proceeded, low, within the sand that had suddenly reversed a nature's normally rude manner to become an ally.

In February '68, Dickerson was "short" to Nam, fifty-eight days short, short enough to be filled with a dreamy imagination of the World he would soon sit back and see, dreamy smells of ladies to be met, touched, and sacheted, and short enough to create illusive make-believe sounds of crowds at a Saturday football game. Short! Finally Short! How sweet is "Short"? Dickerson's mind and emotions had inadvertently turned a page from Nam to his future, to his awaiting, promised day of a wake-up, all back toward the World, toward a rising "American" sun, very strangely, the same sun as here in Southeast Asia.

Dickerson didn't need one more sand low crawl through a shredded tent, under ground fire, in pitch-dark, to find a weapon, and didn't need a new bunch of Viet Cong or North Regulars dashing around the Quang Tri airfield popping at marines and sapping valuable air assets. He didn't need any of it anymore. He was full of it a' ready, had been full from the day he stepped into the sandy outpost of Quang Tri, with 242 and a wake-up.

Dickerson had a future past the next 4:00 a.m. flight plan, which would be off to some other stranded, tortured bare dirt LZ full of marines who had also "had it"—"had it" with a war that made no sense to anyone, a war of people just going through war motions for survival in Nam, for promotions in DC, or at least those still alive in Nam after Tet and not yet wounded were war-motioning. The others had already paid the price, had moved on, earthly or heavenly.

Logical choices were rare when "it starts," when the thuds, pops and womps set up the night, "logic" simply becomes reaction. Reaction is what matters, and Dickerson was reacting, did react, and kept reacting.

Dickerson's volunteer personal mission for his weapon started that attack night with the low, six-foot crawl through the sand toward the tent's back flap opening. A short crawl by ordinary measurements, a marathon crawl under attack pressure. That night was different, with rockets to mortars to small arms, there is no such thing as a short crawl. Pitch-dark, just the pop-pop with the sizzle of tracer's deadly passing about five feet up in the night air and Dickerson crawling. No other sound broke the tense estranged silence of mortar and rocket attacks pause, just the sporadic pop-pop, then more pop-pop from ground shooters picking and darting a shooting way around camp positions.

Slightly drifting monsoon cloud cover darkened the night more than usual, with splashes of gray light escaping from the heavens to Quang Tri through breaks in the passing low clouds. Enough splashes of the vague moon provided lighting so that Dickerson could see a tent opening to crawl to, and through, into a darker place.

Three cots to the right, three spaces between,
then space four, cot four, mine, my space and cot.

My 16 is under the cot, at the head. Belt and 45? I left that hanging, hanging on the tent ring, up on the pole, just above the head of the cot. 16 ammo belt should be right there. I think I had four to five grenades still attached. Five, no, four.

Stay low, lower than low, inch along slowly, inside the flap.

First open space, check. Feel each cot leg, there's one, two legs. That means one marine space. This space is open. One leg, two—that's two marine spaces.

Sand, how you s'posed to crawl for your life in this heavy sand crap, makes life-crawling dangerous!

Szzzzz-womp!Pop-pop . . . Pop. Pop-pop. Szzzzz-Womp!

Damn, sounds like more small arms, that means Gooks in the wire, on the ground, inside the line, damn. How many cots was that? Two, I think. Damn, or was it three, damn sand!

This is taking too long, too much can be going on.

Crawling is heavy, low work, sweat pouring, sand caking against clothes, collar and sweaty, sticky skin parts.

Here's a space, another cot, one-two legs. The next one is mine, if that one is three?

A space, this must be mine. Pops all over camp—voices. "It's on this time. They must be in. I need . . .

Is this my space? Cot? Must be! Reach, feel, slowly, low, just feel for the M-16, it will feel like money or love or love of money with gold, precious. Where is the frickin' thing?

This Quang Tri night attack felt different, crashing, rushed, and hungry. Heartbeats vibrated to the brain, then bounced about. Sweat poured.

Dickerson lay prone as part of the tent's sand floor, silently, totally still, sweating, head down, a massive heartbeat, lifted then fell, then lifted. A slight lighter gray altered the shade of suffocating tent darkness. Air was difficult to catch. The new, different thuds were Dickerson's heart beating wildly.

Ka-thud!
Ka-thud!

The lighter gray at the flap spread slowly, cautiously, sparingly, through a little more of the tent's interior.

Dickerson was nerve-rack-calm, stunned, paralyzed, could not see anything up. Suddenly, he felt the strange sensation he was not alone. His heart hammered alerts to his chest and lungs, then to his brain and out to hands and feet needed for crawling, his heart threatening to leap out through his dry, gritty, sand-caked mouth.

Don't move a fraction, feel a little further for
a weapon.

Darkness gripped the tent in firm Asian blackness, everything on earth was suspended. A little night light gray again, someone else's light boot shuffle step. Then, completely still and dark again. Sweat rolling.

Feel, just a half inch at a time, touch something
that will shoot bullets.

Sweat poured from Dickerson, blasting heart ka-thuds threatened to announce his life in suspension, as part of the tent's sand floor, between cots three and four, meshed in the deathly Indochina elements.

Gut-wrenching Nam air, too heavy to breathe, threatened to choke Dickerson's gun retrieving intentions.

> *I'll never, ever, go anywhere without my 16, so help me God!*

Another half-step shuffle sensation. A shuffle from the suspected tent body, not seen or heard, just somehow felt!

> *Someone is here, with me. There! A slight shadow. A shadow for sure!*

Small-arms pops filled the air from far away parts of camp. The world outside that tent was hustling in different directions.

> *Who was it inside the camp, inside the tent?*
> *Gooks, inside, inside the front gate, inside the perimeter?*
> *Stillness, then feel, listen for another shuffle of sand, tick or a click.*

Quang Tri's stingy rare night gray light flowed further into the tent from the partially open flap. Someone *was* in here. Dickerson knew for certain now that he was not alone, knew he was still unarmed. Through a corner of his left eye, Dickerson leaned to slightly see up, in a direction back toward the tent opening he had just crawled through, seemingly an hour ago.

> *How can this be? I know better than to leave my weapons for a dash anywhere. I'm trapped. I don't even know if this is my cot and space, my stuff, where my 16 should be!*

The silhouette from the body that Dickerson knew was there, with him, finally showed within the shadows and flashing glimpses of gray outside light. He was here! In the tent! Helmet outline, armed, stationary, a body also in suspension. Then, another half-shuffled step, closer to Dickerson's prone helpless, weaponless last position on earth.

Sweat poured from Dickerson, a twenty-one-year-old American heart tested to full beating, raging, leaping capacity.

> *This is it! Fifty-eight days to a wake up, and I run off without my weapon, run like a kid from a firecracker. It's my own fault. Damn!*
>
> *I can feel this guy breathe. Soon, he'll poke around with his AK. Can't be long. I'm dead, screwed, helpless here in the sand I hate.*
>
> *Angel? A beautiful angel!*

Time, ka-clumped the atmosphere, second by second. The war outside the tent was now also on the other side of the earth in slow motion. This moment, right now, this is Dickerson's moment. This is it!

> *The shuffling half-steps, very close now, right here, right here on top of me!*
>
> *Reach the frickin' gun. It's not here? How can it not be here, my 16s always here?*
>
> *The enemy is here, right here, at the end of my cot. His Gook breath calm. Eyes staring down.*
>
> *Can he see me in this low dark last place on earth? Maybe I am part of the sand now.*
>
> *Why doesn't he shoot me . . . He's just looking, right at me, I feel his eyes on me, like a ghostly veil of transfixed blindness, looking but not seeing.*

Fifty-eight days, and I lose my weapon so this asshole can sneak around and plug me like a rat trapped in a barn corner.

I'll give him five more seconds to kill me, five more, then I may as well make a fight of it . . . Two . . . That's three. He's looking down at me . . . Four . . . K-bar his ass!

Dick, Dick honey . . . Quit it. Stop. Wake up! You're OK! Quit! Wake up! Now!

Stop! Stop it. Wake up!

Dick. It's your dream. It has you, again. Breathe! Just lay there and breathe.

Wake up, honey! Look at me. It's me! It's Sophie!

You're twisted, wet. Let go, baby! You're OK. We're all OK! Nam is OK. Your buddies are OK! Look at me!

See? It's me! *Feel this soft touch on your face. It's the only touch you need right now.*

Sit up . . . Breath . . . Lean to me. I'm here. Sit up. You're OK. Breathe more! Deep!

See?

Let's straighten things up, get you a dry T-shirt. Come on.

Stand up, Sarge!

Dickerson, honey, you gotta find a way. You're gonna hurt somebody, hurt yourself with your dreams.

In that awful bunker and tent again? Weren't you?

I heard you in your night, same ole struggle, same ole. Heard it all, again.

Bad guy interrupt your search for a handy M-16 and a few grenades?

You're exhausted, soaked, trembling—just breath. I'll get you a big ice water.

Are we gonna be doing anything about this? It's thirty-three years now. How long can it last?

Dickerson: Sorry. I'm always sorry. I don't know, don't know what brings it on. If I knew I could . . . could, stay up all night, or take walks, or sleep with the dog. Did you get hit?

Sophie: No more than usual, glancing blows mostly. You aren't as tough as you were anyway. I'll be all right, but you won't be. Besides, I'm getting used to it. When I hear you go for your M-16, I get the hell to the other side, or out.

Sophie: You must deal with that night. You have to. It will kill you some day. You know that, don't you? Maybe kill us both. Dick, that night is gone, long gone, gone forever, over, you made it. You are right here! It's overrrrrrr!

Dickerson: I wish I could believe you. I'll try, would try harder, if I knew how to try.

Sophie: I've suggested how to try. You won't do it. You always have an excuse.

Dickerson: I'm not doing that. It's not the same. People just don't understand the Nam. It won't mean anything to a lap dog shrink. They'd give me some drug to take before bed. That ain't gonna happen.

Dickerson: I don't understand it any more than you do. It's the subconscious that hammers me to get out, in some sort of weird standby time system separate from any other aging or passing time periods in our lives.

Sophie: So what do we do? Should I slap you upside the marine jarhead each night about 9:00 p.m.? That'd be kind of fun. Take that, you ancient, flying war dunce!

Sophie: Follow a backhand head slap with a quick judo kick to the groin, just for nighty-night sake. What? What can we do? I agree! No drugs, no sleeping pills and such, that's just another kind of hell.

Dickerson: Something will happen, eventually happen, something that sets all other moments aside, separates the past from the present, takes the place of all the other demons piled against the subconscious demon gates.

Dickerson: Something will happen, and I'll be free. We'll both be free! I can feel it.

Dickerson: We just have to wait. Let it happen. It will happen. I know it will. It just isn't time yet!

Sophie: Sure, great, maybe within the next *thirty-three years.*

Sophie: How long does Nam hold on?

Dickerson: We don't get to choose, or we'd all just drop it on the Nam shore, like a piece of used equipment not needed anymore. The stuff crawls inside, the close calls, the body bags with silent fixed faces zipped inside. People don't see that part, ever. But it's real, always real.

Dickerson: Something kicks this off in me. What have I struggled with lately? We just need to figure that out.

Sophie: So we do. So we think we do, think we know what stirs up the demons. Say we figure it all out, then what?

Dickerson: Well, things settle again, just settle, then it's time!

Sophie: Time for what?

Dickerson: You know, time!
Sophie: For what?
Sergeant Dickerson: Time, the temporary cure.
Time to "Treat the queen like a whore, and treat the
whore like a queen!"
Sophie: I shoulda known you'd come to that.
Sophie: There's a pink glow in the east sky, a
new day. Go punch the coffee.
Sarge: We'll find that M-16 later!
Sophie: By the way, which am I?
Dickerson: Same as last time.

Domestic Nam lingers and drags through unseen parts of American daily life as an uninvited Domestic partner, probably forever for some, increasingly a shameful part of American history to those who give the era a truthful analysis. If there were such things as "national dreams," not just individual dreams, those dreams would act as baselines or at the very least fundamental rules of the macro types of warring engagements. One could suppose that national leaders indulge in certain types of Nam-like dreams on their own in new places like Afghanistan and more subtle warring national adventures as in gun-running to Syrian rebels or other Asian developing hot spots.

But do they, really? Do you think that in the days of Nam, LBJ, Abrams, McNamara, and hundreds of occupants of Congress really give a damn about the drafted grunt who sat in the dark rains of the Central Highlands, waiting for his own personal pop—pop, and then care about that guy's dreams? Do you think McNamara really gave a damn about life's lasting irritations from Agent Orange, and that infection as well as the mental infections?

Do they really? Do you think Hillary and Chuck and a hiding socialist called Obama give a damn about Benghazi, Afghanistan, or Mexican gun-running or Nam Vets?

For those on the ground in Nam, in the mix of a confused American half-ass commitment, a piece of Nam breaks off inside them, at least a little bit. One small piece at a time punctures an individual's future perspective. The pinched-off bits burrow into hearts and souls, festering, awaiting a chance to react. Some reactions become prolific behavior, some lay dormant, unspoken of, unsuspected, forever. Until someone wonders, "What in the hell got in to him?"

Lasting individual life dramas from dates in Nam are impossible to pinpoint through decades of family life or a lasting, multitasking career. The experience is more like a string of tiny weights attached to situations or attached to heartfelt enthusiasms left unacknowledged.

The multiple tragedies of the misspent era surrounding Nam are both personal and nationally shameful, although shredded in distractions as America building and maintaining, or America dividing and tearing down, occupies the progressive fragments of contemporary parts of domestic societies and atrocious modern day political behavior.

> *"Phantasmagoria" can be whatever it is that you want things to be: scenes real, or scenes imagined, and unbound, in always shifting figures and impressions, where reality meets imagination, in a subconscious world of gray half-visions.*

Chapter 8

America's '60s Crossroads

"The truth about Nam."

By the 1960s, America had been at war virtually the entire twentieth century. Not always in the fights, wars aren't like that. So much of warring is preparing for war, making and building war stuff, putting together the millions of deals behind the scenes to be assured the coming war will be a good one, well fought, blowing lots of things up. Then, there's the challenge of getting there, to the actual location of the war that is planned. Getting there is not as easy as it sounds as wars are uncertain logistical endeavors from the politicians' top podiums to the bottom of the numerous supply chains. An excellent military can plan a war in one place and end up in another (i.e., a war in Europe can start in North Africa). Then there is getting back. Some armies and governments work at getting back a long time. Making excuses for wars, fooling the timid public, then burying the warriors and telling their families about the good causes and noble, brave efforts spent on the way to their loved one's heroisms is all a part of the war process that takes time and more effort than one thinks.

All these warring actions and reactions, and unsuspected thousands of other more detail-oriented actions and reactions are a part of going to and being at war, then mending the war's fractures. Following this, of course, is the rebuilding, while preparing for the next war. To be in one national war cause after another takes fluidity and considerable espionage intelligence to drift and gravitate from one war, in and out, and to the next, all while in a democracy of which the fundamental government/populace relationship requires some degree of public acquiescence to the war process drawn up by the leadership of the era. In a democracy, the public must be dragged along into new wars quasi-convincingly, at the very least begrudgingly. One continent for one war, then across the globe for a good, well planned and equipped warring invasion on another continent that was previously not even considered of sufficient corruptible opportunity to be a location worthy of the next war plan and national commitment (i.e., Europe, North Africa, back through Europe, across and around the Pacific, then to Korea, down to Nam, and back again to the Middle East), war is remarkably transferrable for all its vast necessities, predicaments, and requirements if the warring leadership has enough hard assets and soft truth to convincingly sell within the aggregate war plan. At the bottom line, we must have wars, as warring is just too profitable to avoid, as long as the basics required of war are available.

Governments, people, politicians, populations, industries, and militaries cannot do a half century of warring without drifting into chaotic, selfish, corruptible opportunism. Constantly debating the options of freedom, socialism, communism, fascism, and tyranny while differentiating the wolves from the lambs' clothes, societies can barely put one acceptable economic foot in front of the other, let alone manage to organize supplies and means for killing one decade after another. Creating the immovable foundations of stability necessary for a country to back up war's mobility demands, often reveals new cracks and depths of political and supply-side gaps, breakdowns, and good ole institutional corruption.

Hitler did his warring the old-fashioned way. Hitler and the Nazi's mobilized an entire modern-day country of the times in manufacturing and soldiering (air/land/sea) to invade and steal away with anything throughout most of Europe, sub-Europe and North Africa that wasn't nailed down—including souls, minds, and millions of human futures.

Once civilization warred through the '60s, largely capitalized by atrocities from Nam, freedom loving countries realized you didn't at all have to be a Nazi to steal things, corrupt societies, and expend their expendables. Politicians of freedom-loving countries could justify invasions in all kinds of new creative ways, ramp up commercial systems, excite public opinion, and merrily war right along, while casting blame in multiple, sometimes fictional misdirection and raking in new kinds of warring bravado and new mysterious types of war dividends.

Nam was the perfect example of America's core values being hacked apart, including logic, truth, and the relationship between the politicians of a dark government and the general trusting population. Since the hard times of Nam, for a while, the hacking apart slowed, almost stopped, but nothing societal or of our nation's core values was really repaired or put back together for various reasons. Forty years later, the hacking has been energetically resumed and is generally accepted as standard operating hacking, albeit a different, deeper, more thorough type of ruinous inner country hacking, hacking from multiple levels, by multiple hackers, stealing from one end and building labyrinth angles and levels to the war troughs that suck in new hackers toward another end. Truth is, the hacking and national value bending started and became perfected in the '60s when America gave up truth and goodness for façade chasing and transforming scary political leadership into blatant criminal enterprising, using bombastic rhetoric as the cover-up drapes shielding the public from truth. We'll look deeper into that as a part of this Domestic Nam chapter of final thoughts and feelings.

In Vietnam, specifically South Vietnam, theoretically, communism had to be stopped. Yep. In Nam! Nam was to be global Communism's Thin Red Line of the times, the Nam on the other side of the globe from America, that Nam, commonly also known as South Vietnam: the country with the ancient rural culture, half Catholic, half Buddhists, half many other societal dimensions that would never be understood. Thousands of isolated huts and hamlets connected by dirt paths, tunnels, and rice paddy dikes, writhing within its own isolated water buffalo wars for centuries. A-right, a-ready, a good suitable war place for dumping vast stockpiles of paid for ordnance and testing the coming evolutions of future weaponry. South Vietnam, by American standards, an uneducated third world, was entangled for centuries by their own sandal straps.

In the infamous '60s, the country of South Vietnam would become the Global Communist fighting target hot spot, despite that one of the world's most aggressive advancing Communist systems (Cuba) was entrenched and subdividing ninety miles off the South Florida coast. Nam was described as a globally dangerous, sticky, infectious, teetering, backward leaning domino, which if fallen to the basics of Communism, would domino crash away to world obliteration and endless misery for populations of all sorts in numerous countries and there soon to be entrapped populations, which would then or later, strangle America itself. (About as legitimate a theory then as the hoax of global warming is today.)

Communist dominoes would crash across mountains, crash through Indochina and sub-Asia, across vast oceans, infecting Latin America for sure. Tsunami domino crashing would gain steam on a path up through California and Arizona, infect the vulnerable without them even knowing they are being dragged domino-infected to the brink of some new style brainwashed capture by the Communist entrapping subconscious clutches. A risk far too dangerous to overlook or avoid, too ominous for the new self-righteous leaders and weapons manufacturers of the free world to turn backs on. We would stop all this Communist nonsense in a country no one had heard of. We'd stop Communism in South Vietnam, with Wilson Street Boys and ka-jillions of American dollars.

There are always contingencies to transporting war's intentions. We wouldn't stop Communism right there, in South Vietnam, until we needed that '60s political diversion distracting the American public from other domestic infections. Communist stopping is a big business, far beyond just standing armies against one another. There must also be politics, political theory and configuration, and reasoning with subreasoning toward some sort of long range astute domino balancing calculation from reliable Chiefs, who nudge the first dominoes themselves.

America would not then and does not now have to tolerate such Communist/Fascist/Jihadist domino teetering threats. America had, and has, hard manageable resources and Wilson Street Boys to fight such dominoing evils anywhere in the world at any time. So we do! The '60s happened so fast and furious we couldn't even keep track of the inter- or intra-US domino crashing and prioritize the growing, creeping systemic evils lining up to be dealt with. The good guys weren't wearing white hats, and the bad guys weren't wearing black hats. In the '60s, all the hats were gray and too many heads under them wear opaque. The Wilson Street Boys started the '60s with their own multicolored baseball hats and ended the '60s with dark-green, heavy army/marine-issued combat helmets, while '60s American politics were reversing and becoming inside out and upside down, becoming sickly, distracted, infectious at a staggering rate of infecting.

Within the research and translations of the events chronicled herein, one can become awakened to an entirely new universe of multiple *new realities*, current and historic, largely based from consideration of the Domestic Nam. These are important to consider because they affected that time and continue to have a chilling effect now today, and it looks like for quite a while to come. Today, starting 2015, there is not a fundamental standard of American living that is not under attack. Marriage, the military, basic supply-side economics, religion, education, drugs, the right to arms, truth, health care, all dangle by Constitutional threads by the latest liberal versions of government. It all started in the '60s when American leadership gave up truth as a core governing value, and the Domestic Vietnam was that first major domino to shake, rattle, roll, then fall.

Reality #1—The Hidden Attitudes of Vietnam Veterans

America's war attentive politicians had access to an unending supply of Wilson Street Boys to fight their '60s war in Nam via the national draft. Ramp up a cause, tweak the industrial contracts and supply lines, build the distractions and sideshows, and we'll find the meat at thousands of different draft board offices from Maine to San Diego County to put fighting boots on the ground opposing any peep of Commie aggression or threat of aggression. Wave some flags, do a couple fly-overs, dress-up the marching bands and most patriotic young Americans of the early '60s will charge any hill and bless any parachute drop in a patriotic mission or patriotic fervor for love of country and pride of service in the name of nation protecting and freedom building. At least, that's the way the '60s started, still in a post-WWII/Korea world leadership frenzy, not yet diminished or diluted by politics as usual declining to criminal enterprising and not yet diluted by separating population segments and then pitting them one against the other for goodies to be given away, someday, maybe.

If one pays attention to the current Nam veteran landscape, a couple things become quickly apparent. First, there are an extraordinary number of imposters out and about on the Nam issue. Google "facts of the Vietnam War," and you see a multitude of individual facts, among which is an estimate that for every one actual in-country Vietnam Veteran, there are five imposters, defined as people close enough to the "Vietnam Era" in age, to claim some sort of combat experience in Nam. One can assume that sort of trend is not limited to individuals but extends to Internet groups and fundraising websites "for veteran's causes." A Nam Combat Ribbon does not necessarily mean you fought in Nam or were even in the country of South Vietnam. Thanks to more politicizing benevolence, if you stocked an O Club bar in Okinawa or Japan (thus in the Vietnam Warring Theatre) with the latest greatest drink mixes, you get some of the same Nam uniform ribbons as if you were on Hill 881 at Khe Sanh. Or worse yet, if you were a cook at any cozy base in America, you were known to be, and agreeably within, and bravely positioned, in the armed services in the "Vietnam Era," as if being a cook in Texas is somehow more dangerous because five hundred thousand other guys are stuck in the fighting dominoing muck of Southeast Asian rocketry, monsoon rains, and damp suppressing Asian heat. Time Travel Liberalism pulls us all cockeyed into the same forty and eight societal rail cars, so one net can be thrown to equalize and standardize the throwaways of the Vietnam period. Add time, decades of time, lost reflections, misdirected reconstruction of history, and the true veterans of the actual Nam fighting become part of the mixed-up hectic '60s past, with no particular relevance to anything teachable or socially sustainable.

Deeper in the human mix are the actual veterans of the fights and battles of Nam, ground and air. These guys are the real, walking, breathing, *dreaming* Domestic Nam—unanimously quiet among us. These guys carry the individual hidden real burdens and business of the entire American episode of Domino Falling Nam and Southeast Asia military/industrial politicizing, profiteering and death. These guys could not drop Nam at the shore's edge before a tarmac liftoff east, toward, then beyond, a new blistering Asian rising sun, back to America in 1968 or '69 or '70 or beyond. These guys had no processing from warring to civilization, or PTSD psychological cleansing nonsense, or methodic reacquaintances with civilization, friends, wives, and families. Back from Nam was a veteran soldier following a personnel file folder passing process from a baking in-country tarmac, through Okinawa, then California and a flight to Homeville, a bus ride, and a gee-whiz walk down Main street, all in five days from the burning blood smell of Hue, the blasts of Go Noi, or a carrier launch and SAM air tag.

Talk to the real veterans of Nam. At first, you get a fundamentally similar story of somewhat guarded, individual Pride of Service. At least, that's what you get on the surface. Strangely, what you see is not what you will get. If you sense what the depth of the conversation is really about, you soon sense that the conversation is too polite, too surface, a little too la-de-da for the depth of the subject matter. Listen with care and respect to the conversation about Nam events, and you will eventually sense the conversational tone is a broken record pronounced as a screen, very much like the confining net of a batting cage that would be shielding something more valuable within. You can see through it but cannot reach into it. There is a sense that the conversation of Nam is much more personal, more intense, more heartfelt and more underlying violent than is being casually expressed.

The universal impression of millions of friends and families is that Nam Vets do not talk of Nam, they just don't and won't. Radio and TV shows have researched and some have implemented programming based on Nam stories and events, opinions, or conclusions. The shows go nowhere. Show producers say this is because Nam Vets clam up, won't talk, and only present the token silent screen of whatever is beneath their surface. What would be from the gut, remains in the gut, while the Nam vet tries to determine which inquiry or which listener may or may not be worthy, assuming in the beginning that very, very few are worthy.

Truth is no! They don't talk, and there is a reason. But that doesn't mean they won't talk, and when they do, they have plenty to say, and it is riveting.

Nam Vets will talk, if you give them a slight chance, but *only if they trust you*. But the trust does not come easy. It is not "given." That kind of trust is difficult, timid, and harder to gain than the teammate or traditional family/marriage kind of trust. The Nam trust is like a veteran momentarily splitting his heart, and letting you in, but only in so far, for so long, and only if it feels OK. Like a skittish cat anticipating a leap from a roof or high window, they can call off that leap at any flick of an instance. The trust, at best will be very temporary, always fleeting, forever fleeting, a trust-door to be closed by any passing breeze or cause, just or unjust, real or suspected. A conversation with a Nam Vet, about Nam, is a temporary chit, unilaterally callable at any moment. At least, that is the way it is with the real Nam Vet. The imposters talk on freely, endlessly, usually until the listener senses something is not right.

To a Nam vet, questions or inquiries about the Nam War from a casual citizen or a passing friend, a bar stool acquaintance, or distant relative are just flukes and meaningless flitters of irrelevant conversation yapping. Participating in the Nam speculation of conversation is just a lower level of emotional gossip, leading nowhere for anyone, except dredging to uncover misunderstood emotion that needn't be uncovered and cannot possibly be explained properly. Talking about Nam is like talking about the dying details of deadened relatives. To the Nam vet, eventually the unsuspecting listener will simply nod "uuuh" or "aaah," take another drink and conclusively pronounce: "How 'bout them Bears." Why go through the humiliating process?

What does it mean in 2012, in America, when some job candidate dude, all prissied up for the interview includes, "Vietnam Era," in the military experience portion of his resume. Perhaps in reality, it means different things to different people, no doubt it means nothing to some people and is totally overlooked. To a Nam vet, on the hiring side of the interview desk, experienced, perceptive, hardened in the real world of Realville, a resume reference to "Vietnam Era" means:

> *I (the candidate) was never really in South Vietnam, in the war, but for some reason, I want you (the interviewer) to think I was. I know it's phony, it's really crap, but I can't help it—I want you to sense or suspect that I might be one of those silent, undercover heroes, like you hear about, one of the real Nam Vets. You might even think that at one war moment I peeked over a rice paddy line lowering my M-16 for the coming attack, looking into a dangerous thick jungle tree line, bravely, patriotically for country and family. So I'm willing to risk this false hallucination by extending my mundane, chicken-shit background in a bit of a heroic illusion, hoping to fool you a little bit; hoping to trick you into potentially thinking you are hiring a hard core, patriotic Nam Veteran, of a misunderstood era. It's just a little lie, not even a lie; really, there was the era.*

In America, we have come to commonly alter stories of national history, distort causes pre-action and post-action, and we tolerate imposters. In fact, we practically encourage imposters. While thousands and thousands of Vietnam vets live with the effects of Agent Orange and their dreams of another time, the US Veterans

Administration employs a posture of delay and distract and Texas Two Step in relation to Nam vets benefits inquiries. Today, the big thing is PTSD—post-traumatic stress disorder. It's PTSD this and PTSD that, as if the whole world is soon PTSD benefit qualified. Today, sexual harassment qualifies for military-related PTSD benefits: thirty-five thousand claims in the past three years. And people wonder why the Nam vets clam up to themselves, or among one another, refusing to participate in the public boiling points of Nam or veteran conjecture.

The Nam vet will talk but will be guarded, edgy, shifty, and aware of a talking exit at all times. The conversation has to be trusted, guarded, leading to something besides gossip or useless bar room chatter. And when they talk, here's what you get:

The Vietnam vet first and foremost has a deep committed, silent Pride of Service. The patriotism of intent of service and duty that the Nam vet embraced forty-five years ago at eighteen, nineteen, or twenty years of age, entering the draft board or working through basic training, is still there and is a remarkably vivid personal core inner vision of sustainable commitment.

It is the survivor's rite of passage to add relative levels of intensity to that Pride of Service with each passing year. The experience and the Pride of Service of that youthful period has likely become part of the human foundation of the individual Nam veteran's life and times then, now and forever.

However, talk further in a Nam vet conversation about the battles and prepositions of Nam, talk about America's commitments and lack of commitments of the times past or present, and the tone will begin to shift. Give them the chance. Let the shift occur, and if you have a seat belt, buckle it.

Without attempting to paint with the broad societal sector brush, a longer talk with a Nam veteran about Nam, the '60s, about Tet, and about coming home, consistently reveals the same overwhelming general human points. Nam Vets are pissed! Really pissed! Nam vets have learned the magic balance of love of country, while despising the leadership and leadership peripherals of the Nam era. In addition, they largely are attuned to the increasingly decrepit national leadership in times since, especially in comparison to the perpetual stupidity and criminal enterprising of a decade of US troop occupation in remote Afghanistan—another useless effort and expense, doomed to an identical conclusion as Nam. It is not that we don't learn. We do learn as working, living, loving "individuals." It is what we as a national operating government body are not learning, or not heeding, through distracted and criminal contemporary leadership that is the modern-day pit of punji sticks.

Within the Nam vet population, it is magnificent that all these guys are so different, different experiences, different lives, different attitudes, different pasts and futures, while being remarkably similar on Nam. A long unstructured conversation can drift in and out of many issues and recollections, temporary episode summaries and feelings about missions or lost buddies, or just what and the hell was supposed to be accomplished for the brutal risks and extensive costs expended.

Once a conversation with a Nam vet goes from the Pride of Service phase into the "I'm still really pissed and getting more pissed with each passing year" stage, just shut up and listen. In fact, if you *aren't a Nam vet in the conversation, you have to shut up and listen, you likely won't qualify to participate right at the early parts of the conversation and "I'm pissed" attitude building.*

The "I'm still really pissed" stage is loaded with spare clips of full metal jackets. Remarkably, Nam vets will recall vast amounts of their service detail from forty-five years in the past, at a time when they were displaced to an "otherworld," possibly in their late teens, long before families and careers would become life's priority. Facts and emotions from Nam will rush like a downhill avalanche or a flash flood through a narrow mental canyon space. Nam vets are loaded with perceptive wisdom from the Nam years and how it all relates today. Nam vets that have driven trucks for forty years, managed hardware stores, or worked at caterpillar assembly lines can recall and rationalize multiple complicated '60s issues that today's political imposters seem to have no public clue or morality about.

The silent forum of Nam vets is deafening, if you find the crack and are let into the reservoir.

Realistically, most folks don't really care about Nam anymore and thus don't really care what Nam vets think. Today, America is fractured, and there are more and more people lining up to do more fracturing, led by a fracture practiced president and Congress. However, one thing with Nam vets is a certainty:

It's OK to be pissed, while full of Pride of Service!

In fact, Nam-pissed and Pride of Service are realities, neither of which could evolve over time in any other way. It is what it is!

"Pissed" is a good thing because at the foundation of the feeling or sentiment is reality and experience and the truth of Nam and hope for no more Nams amidst better more fundamentally reasonable days. Someday, if enough people concern themselves with Nam realities and how Nam got that way, maybe America's leadership will have an outside chance at acquiring the fortitude and wisdom to prevent new atrocities, new blunders, wasting assets and lives and avoiding global, national embarrassments. At least, the Nam vet, pissed condition is a real basic outright "Pissed," true and unable to be distorted. Nothing squishing in the feeling! You'll know it when you see it. (In fact, there just may be lots of Nam Vets, with special stories and perspectives, who would now like to talk—given a trusting forum.)

Reality #2—America Changed in the '60s, and ain't goin' back, ever.

The explanation for the big question, "Why Nam: How did we get involved and why did we stay involved for so costly and aggravatingly long," is a difficult, subjective challenge of blending multiple historic '60s issues that on the surface, do not seem to be intimately related enough to offer any key answers. While the boys on Wilson Street were growing taller and reaching further, America was in a massive post-WWII, cold war environment as an overriding, national environment. In addition, the country had reached new levels of interconnecting fixed and intellectual assets concerning itself with new issues in aerospace, national and international political propaganda ideology, drug trading and gun-running. In the '60s two megadomestic issues were beginning their mega-clash: honest government versus organized crime. Look deeper, pulling apart the bamboo grasses and smoke screens, and there are some fairly definitive answers as to: Why Nam? Nam was such a colossal failure, on the relatively recent heels of phenomenal WWII accomplishments all over the globe, it is only reasonable to wonder how, and why, it could even happen. Let's take another shot at it—because?

The internal national defense of a democracy to keep citizens from being misled, bribed, or cajoled to sleep by government, depends on an, ambitious, educated public. That educated public, as an aggregate, may have reached a peak post-WWII, in a time most critical to national, family and personal development, in a free enterprise economy. Since that time the general public has become less knowledgeable, less concerned and less involved in multilevel government workings, for multiple reasons. A less knowledgeable, less involved public, naturally lends more power to the elected. More power then begets more want of power until the process of natural government for the greater national good becomes ill, infected, and eventually lends to the LBJ's, Nancy Pelosi's, Dick Durbin's, and long, long lines of contemporary corrupted politicians and their associates, both Democrat and Republican. A less educated public, or a public living in fascination of the discovery of unending meaningless personal freedoms, lends to an all-powerful government, not able to restrain themselves from their own greed, self-adulation, or corruption, noting the busy public will not precisely discover the systemic decline of society in general.

Nam could and did happen because Nam occurred in the '60s, and it was the '60s when America changed into what is now a contemporary modern era. Initially, the "change" was merely creeping and tolerable, unsuspected by a society largely made up of people working and raising families, becoming career focused, educated and gaining experience in the work force, building their communities and lives in the communities. What happened in the '60s gave new life and credibility to uncharted segments of an irritated population, both at the core and the fringes, who began to distrust government. The more government is distrusted, the more goodies government has to give away to be trusted, or the more government has to lie about things they are doing or "will" give away later. Eventually, the goody giveaways and lies fade the lines of judgment and boundaries, and common human laws of decency and trust are sacrificed. Since the '60s a fairly substantial part of politics has focused on misleading the public at large, falsely cajoling and leading broad sectors of the population away from a basic trusted ideology toward vague and less understandable social ideological concepts. In addition, these forces seek to mislead and divide numerous segments of the populace creating as many subsegments as possible to drag from one political camp to another, as a public opinion fix for the next disaster, then the next disaster after that, as in the pending disaster of "global warming" caused by humans. Caused by *you*! How stupid do they think we are? Really, really stupid, apparently! (Thus, our current condition, trapped in Obamacare, to disrupt and tear apart the world's best national healthcare system, on whims and promises that the government can judiciously run our national health care system, if they just have enough control powers and enough of everyone's personal information.)

Several colliding, unique megastructures of the '60s encouraged actions and coalitions that had never before been a part of the American clashing subculture, factions, and general social landscape. Some of those many factors were as follows:

- Cold War concerns and the Cuban Revolution;
- a boundlessly growing CIA, building and nurturing powerfully influential assets;
- an entrenched American Mafia, especially in Tampa, New Orleans, and Chicago at a time when the head of the FBI, J. Edgar Hoover, denied there was a Mafia;
- Russia's growing fixed and military personnel assets in Cuba;

- a new US President JFK appointing his brother Bobby as attorney general, largely creating a dual presidency;
- the VP, good ole pliable, brainless LBJ was strictly a figurehead unattached to anything even marginally pertinent, in government, but cozy with the east-Texas mafia;
- growing camps of armed rebels in multiple Latin American countries including Costa Rico, Nicaragua, Guatemala;
- Kennedy's aggressive prosecution events against Mafia families: Trafficante, Tampa; Rosselli, Chicago; Marcello, New Orleans;
- the French Connection—global drug/heroin trafficking that hit the United States through the three Mafia organizations and bled influence into other institutional sectors;
- international CIA priorities to operate within the new standards of the Cold War via assassinations, human assets, gun-running, etc;
- a semi-shelved military/industrial complex, needing a good war, somewhere, anywhere, still eager to regain their diminished status from too much peace on earth;

(Bear with me, I know where this is going, you'll get it!)

- Kennedy's Bay of Pigs losses and ensuing national personal copresidency guilt;
- the Kennedy's formation and funding of a new Defense Intelligence Agency (DIA) perceived by some as an intergovernmental rival to the CIA;
- an active, aggressive Cuban exile population in the US;
- Jack Ruby, a Mafia midlevel player in Chicago, moved to Dallas to operate the western end of the Marcello Mafia family network out of New Orleans;

- Lee Harvey Oswald inducted into undercover spy work by circumstances in a U-2 spy plane incident in Japan, when his first low level "intelligence" assignment was reporting on Japanese bar girls inquiring about U-2 ops;
- the need for mob figures to find protection against the more aggressive Kennedy organized crime prosecution efforts;
- Wilson Street Boys and local draft boards;
- a population of patriotic core values, still believing in government;
- WWII propaganda techniques refined and modernized, technical field communication advancements;
- air, land, and sea assets sitting idle, needing.

All these issues and probably a thousand more, major and minor, blended in a period of 1962 through 1964, the period when America was held together by strings, national pride, city fathers and mothers, neighborhoods working together, history, but then, it changed. The results and untangling of that tight time span sent America into multiple levels of spinning, scheming, and general systemic misleading of the public. One of the results was a Domestic Nam. Nam was vaguely on America's map in the early '60s, in the early part of the Kennedy presidency. Nam was on the map because of aggressive Communist national concerns, the Cold War, the Domino Theory, and a quagmire of opinion and implementation in internal justice keeping. Right or wrong, Nam was lumped in with Indochina as a Cold War concern, a low-level military outpost to keep an eye on, influence if possible, at the very least to infiltrate in hopes of some form of vague, never explained American advantage that would put to good use our relatively new CIA international assets. Nam was a back-shelf, back-water part of a bigger chart of anti-Communist pieces to be dealt with in a still new unwinding post WWII atmosphere.

Why and how did something as innocuously vague in purpose as combat presence in Nam become such a gigantic gross national killing hairball, growing to impair a national treasury and infect millions of Americans for decades?

When Nam was such a vague confusing process, fundamentally wrong at any logical level, going nowhere: How did it continue and build to such gigantic proportions?

Nam continued and elevated in violence and asset commitment because of the following:

- The war in Nam was the distraction to what was going on in US politics, in the CIA, within the Kennedy Presidency, and within and surrounding the above bulleted issues.
- Nam went on because of a corrupted immoral President (LBJ), a president and his supporters who would take atrocious advantage of the general population and bleed them of their national patriotism, beyond any reasonable Pride of Service, in order to feed corrupt cronies and provide a distraction as to who killed Kennedy, why, and what national opportunities or discrepancies the first Kennedy assassination afforded.
- Nam went forward beyond any predictable imaginations to feed nefarious sources of many types in the mid-'60s and to present a public façade that American leadership was managing an ultimate national defense priority, stopping Communism.
- Nam was the floating empty shell of a gigantic illusion, while domestic peas were shuffled under different changing shells by America's blatantly corrupt of that era.

The subject of the War in South Vietnam will be forever debated. However, it is not too much of a stretch to find some intellectual solace, within the answers to the following:

> Who killed Kennedy?
> How?
> Why?
> What does the Kennedy assassination have
> to do with Nam?
> And Why Bobby?

Answer those questions satisfactorily, and we can more clearly see how it all led to a huge, unmanageable, national disgrace: the Domestic Vietnam.

Who killed President Kennedy?

JFK was killed by a team of international assassins. Oswald was the patsy, just as Sirhan would later be a patsy in the assassination of RFK. The plan to kill JFK had many sub and side plans, with many levels of knowing and unknowing contributors, including the Mafia, Cubans, French Connection Masters, and quite possibly complicit segments of the CIA. VP Johnson was not actively involved. LBJ would simply be the resulting heir to a tangle of sprawling open ends, with all the balls and bats, marbles, armies, and a treasury at his disposal. Johnson had a few other personal issues. He had no shame and no real sense of human patriotism other than as something he could manipulate and take advantage of. He also had a driving, hateful disposition toward the Kennedy's, especially toward Bobby who had superseded Johnson's VP status into virtually a dual presidency with his brother, leaving LBJ entirely out of all strategic discussion and decision processes. No attempt would ever be made to track the professional team of assassins who actually did the JFK killing, at least not by officials of the government. The whole incident was eagerly swept into a one-man assassin concept, with Oswald as the patsy and the next hit.

How was Kennedy killed?

Millions saw it. JFK was murdered in Dallas, at the Daley Plaza, no question about that. At least three trained assassins, from different locations, in a crossfire, were able to successfully kill JFK, in broad daylight, on live national TV. The actual shootings were merely the implementation.

Throughout the previous year, multiple levels of planning set in motion the many requirements to make the assassination possible. Timing was supremely important, and a patsy was essential. You can't go killing presidents without a quick easy patsy to arrest and steal a nation's attention, so Oswald had to be groomed and postured, plus other patsies in other locations had to be brought to their useful positions. Professional assassins had to be found and hired. Logistics of guns, ammo, and transportation needed to be organized as well as alternative assassination plans and locations. Assassination getaways are a big deal as is covering up the getaway trails, so that also had to be meticulously plotted.

A thousand "what ifs" would play into JFK's assassination, well in advance of the final opportunity and execution, what ifs that take influence, vision, know how, deep committed desires, and lots of money. (Oswald contained none of those essential ingredients.)

Why was Kennedy killed?

Kennedy was killed November 22, 1963, for two reasons. One, because of what the Kennedy Administration was doing, and the second being for what the Kennedy Administration was about to do. From the beginning of the Kennedy Presidency, JFK, with RFK, relentlessly, judiciously pursued organized crime, known to a general public as the Mafia (except for J. Edgar Hoover, head of the FBI, who repeatedly said no such organization existed). The JFK administration specifically targeted the Mafia families of Chicago (Roselli), Tampa (Trafficante), and New Orleans (Marcello). The Tampa and New Orleans families controlled organized crime from Miami to Dallas, which would then include most actions and underworld operations concerning Cuba and Latin America, Cuban exiles and their operations, all deeply involved in developing some of the early days of the drug trade, especially in heroin, and who would just as deeply develop the early stages of gun-running. The area would also include LBJ's electoral base.

Attorney General RFK was relentless in the pursuit if Mafia figures and actions, even to the point of capturing Marcello at one point and dumping him in the jungles of Latin America to find his way out. The Mafia, seeing no end to the legal pressures from the government, derived a solution to their government versus Mafia dilemma, first to assassinate the main instigator of their mounting legal irritations, RFK (Bobby). Eventually, mafia leadership decided RFK would merely be replaced by an appointment of JFK and thus to actually eliminate the assaulting legal pressures the Mafia must kill JFK, and that became the goal of the Mafia, a goal adopted about October 1962 after the Cuban Bay of Pigs disaster.

The Mafia's plan to kill Kennedy gained vast support from sectors of Mafia allies because of what the Kennedy's "were about to do," which was invade Cuba, again, and oust Castro, in December of 1963. Consequently, all assassination plans had to be designed, supported and set to implementation in the first half of December 1963. This was the target time for the launch of the new Cuba liberation movement, operationally organized and paid for within CIA ranks and field operations, which the Mafia had vigorously infiltrated. Such late '63 timing would give the Mafia several chances to assassinate JFK within consecutive public appearances in various US cities, including Dallas. The Mafia had become involved in the plans for a second invasion of Cuba when the failed Bay of Pigs disaster of October 1962 opened the door to a new invasion coalition requiring Mafia expertise in gun-running, payoffs, kidnappings, and assassinations.

Eventually, issues of security and planning would prevent assassination attempts in other cities and thus all killing assets would be poured into Dallas, which was the last chance before the early December second planned invasion of Cuba, to be led by trained units of Cuban exiles, followed by US military ground forces and air support. By assassinating JFK at that time, plans for this new Cuban invasion would have to be cancelled, and the government in general would be knocked back on their heels in ongoing Mafia prosecutions, while a corrupt LBJ, largely in the back pocket of the East Texas mob controlled by the Marcello family, would take over the presidency and rapidly become operational. Professional hit men killed Kennedy with many complicit supporting active interest groups assisting, some knowingly complicit, some complicit by unengaged association and circumstance.

Why did the Kennedy Assassination affect the escalations and killing in Nam?

This is the question that addresses: Why Nam? This is the essence of "Domestic Nam." Within the post-assassination environment of the JFK assassination, an honest, thorough investigation would reveal to the US public and world at large a multitude of devious, criminal, underworld, CIA operations, including the new planned and soon to be executed military actions from multiple fronts to invade and liberate Cuba, kill Castro, and lead the Cuban population to quick Government re-organizing options. Ordinarily for killing a sitting president the Mafia assassination team would be subject to the world's most intense investigations and thus could not be successful without an Oswald patsy, which would give any assassination investigation a one gunman theory to sell to the public and world waiting anxiously for an explanation, and a quick easy solution to assassination questions.

In addition, the Mafia's end game in the assassination plot for JFK was to make Ruby responsible for the murder of Oswald, which would provide the dead end to inquiries and ongoing investigation loose ends, giving the principles of the investigative Warren Commission a quick and easy way to bury the incident. Jack Ruby, Oswald's killer, was a lifetime midlevel Mafia figure, originally from Chicago, who then moved to Dallas to become involved in the west end of the New Orleans mob family growing heroin trade. These activities were in partnership with French connection mobsters who provided the international heroin source of product and distribution principally from Afghanistan. Ruby's main business was to corrupt law enforcement officials in Dallas by any means available, although Ruby was also instrumental in gun-running relationships to arm Latin American rebel groups.

The main international figure of the French connection operation, Michael Mertz, was in Dallas on November 22, 1963, surrounding the JFK assassination. Notably, he was congenially deported back to France on November 24. Mertz was untouchable, could not be arrested and was protected to the very top of the French government for several reasons.

Why would Ruby shoot Oswald, on camera, in front of the world?

He had to. He had already accepted Mafia payment to oversee the post JFK assassination with the hit on Oswald, the chosen patsy to take the JFK wrap. Officer Tippett was supposed to be the official gunman to knock-off Oswald as a part of official police business, but that didn't work out so well. That left the job to Ruby himself, who would then become dependent on mob lawyers and payoffs to have a chance to survive, that didn't work out so well either.

All of these actions and counteractions from coconspirators like the Mafia, complicit agencies (i.e., the Dallas police force) and others, left the US government and specifically the Johnson Administration with a gigantic requirement for a huge cover-up operation at multiple levels recognized and unseen. *Covering up* became the government's daily standard operation procedure, all in the midst of global Communist aggression in the dark, dangerous world of Cold War intelligence and counter intelligence.

War is profitable for a certain class of America. America's warring fixed assets were largely sitting idle, looking for a reason and a place to be used. The country's draft board offices were there but unchallenged by drafting and processing demand. Wilson Street Boys were numerous. Johnson was a senseless, conscienceless crook, and he needed a national diversion to the JFK assassination for multiple reasons derived from his own corrupt, self-interest, including the inner governmental adjustments to remove Bobby and others from central government influence at the time. Nam was a low simmering side show, diplomatic brew of mostly unknowable elements, on the map already, but of little concern in the whole Indochina/Domino/Communist puzzle. The Joint Chiefs had a changed structure in the JFK administration in that the leadership of General Maxwell Taylor no longer reported to and with the chiefs themselves. Taylor reported strictly to the president, first Kennedy, then Johnson, overlooking and circumventing the entire purpose of having the Joint Chiefs as a functioning body of intellectual military advisory assets. (General Taylor would later in mid-1968 replace General Westmoreland, having become the world's leading gun-running lap dog.) Gun-running and the heroin trade, with growing Mafia attention and control, were becoming megacorporate-style business processes through the 1960s, at a time when Jonson needed a major, national and international public distraction from the Kennedy investigation processes. Johnson and cronies found that distraction in a new war in Vietnam.

You see, Nam at its core was a *distraction*. "Hey, y'all don't look here [at this Kennedy assassination investigation backwash], look over there. There's a damn war that popped up. Big war too, a big war-thing goin' on, way over there, a big ole' new Communist fight'n war that needs all warrin' up," as in Johnson-speak.

Nam, a *distraction* from domestic issues. Nam was a surrogate location, practically in an unnoticeable, unreported, third-world population. The war, the entire mess, was simply and truly a "Domestic Vietnam." The real battle was at home in the United States. At the time of the JFK assassination, approximately 110 Americans had died within the conflicts of the Nam; soon, over fifty-eight thousand more would die. Quite a distraction!

Eventually, in the very early processes of escalating Nam warring, someone somehow had to finally legitimize the expenses, cost of lives, and growing intentions of Nam fighting, in order to justify the *distraction*. Easy for a snake-head like Johnson and military/industrial antagonists, so they invented the Gulf of Tonkin Incident May '64, where North Vietnamese patrol boats, kind of, maybe, almost, but sure would have, fired on US Navy vessels, in theory, they think, possibly, would have or could have fired on US Navy vessels. Massage that little "maybe" into a global Cold War Communist Stopping Concept of Falling Dominoes, and who wouldn't do the rumble in the Nam jungle? At least who wouldn't as long as it's someone else going and doing the fighting time, supported by public money and public confusion, and doubting but still steady public patriotism?

And that is what the Kennedy Assassination had to do with Nam! JFK's assassination *was* the first big domino. All the dominoes were in the United States, not in Indochina countries falling to Communism one leading to the other country's falling, as we were being told. The entire dreadful situation was and is the essence of looking in the mirror to find the culprits. The dominoes were US Dominoes all the time, largely diversions, conceptually disingenuous from the very beginning, and then once in the soup, in the soup it was. Obviously, there are much bigger episodes, links, concepts, and explanations within the entire mega-subjectivity of "Why Nam?" Most will remain silent, bent, or hidden conjecture forever. For those keenly concerned with the subject, it is only essential that you come to your own calm, confident landing zone of passion on the subjects of Nam.

That's why America changed in the '60s and will never change back. The dominoes are still falling; diversions became political standard operating procedure, entrenched in the preferred chicanery of political methodology. Once a sickness like that prevails, it spreads as a more convenient means of temporary public support than honest explanation. It is why a bombastic, self-consumed political yap like Hillary Clinton can boast "What difference does it make?" after watching four State Department associates murdered. The '60s, starting with the JFK assassination and Nam, injected the institutional politicized cancers now corrupting innocent areas of American life previously thought to be in sacred, blessed trust of country.

For those veterans and families really pissed, there is a mental place to go that is one step further. For over thirty years after WWII, Nazi leaders were hunted and occasionally apprehended and brought to trial, some were belatedly executed. Perhaps the thousands of Agent Orange victims from Nam should support some hunting. Perhaps Marines of the Tet-era in north I Corps, around Con Thien, at the edge of the DMZ should support some war criminal hunting. Perhaps McNamara should have been on trial for his Agent Orange, McNamara Line and others for equal global absurdities. Perhaps we should have a plaque of Johnson on trial, and if guilty, provide another *national distraction* for a posthumous place for the Johnson plaque at Guantanamo with other war criminals.

It is not difficult to draw multiple parallels between the stories and situations of Nam and the fundamental issues of Afghanistan or Iraq today, both destined to certain similar conclusions while wasting lives and US assets in another distracting cause. While America fights within itself for the goodies and powers of contemporary government, on a broader scope the same things plague social progress that gave rise in the '60s.

Why is the domestic and international illegal drug trade never reduced and seems to continuously grow? Why Afghanistan? To feed the payment end of the more important gun-running?

Why is gun-running, more sophisticated and internationally prolific than ever, generally accepted? Gun-running is so accepted that our own Obama administration is directly facilitating guns going into Mexico while professing tighter gun controls in the United States. How is that illegal gun-running behavior and activity possibly accepted? Are they just amateur gun-runners, not yet dealed up to be real gun-running associates through regular channels? Why was the news of four hundred surface to air missiles in Benghazi so overlooked, under reported, forgotten, washed away to nothingness. Four hundred SAMs!

Why in the hell can America deliberately choose not to control our own borders and then run off around the other side of the planet and try to close, control, or police borders of Afghanistan, perhaps the world's most well-known opium producing location?

Why does America take a little working capital, perhaps a few trillion of quantitative easing treasury funding, to fix things that then aren't fixed like highways and bridges, and no one speaks or insinuates the thievery of the funds? How do trillions of dollars, with a *T*, disappear through the treasury, only to show up later as a larger national debt number?

What is really going on in Guantanamo? Do we really own, patrol, and operate Guantanamo to isolate 166 terrorists? Shoot the bastards! No, that is not why we operate Guantanamo. Guantanamo is the listening post of the Caribbean, perhaps the central processing for guns and drugs and unimaginable other hard and soft goods traveling a crisscross of underground criminal labyrinths. Guantanamo is the free trade zone for the critical international gun-running business.

Why is the hungry American government never full, satisfied, solid, trustworthy, and always in the next conflict, like Syria? Is it because it's too unprofitable not to be involved? Countries used to ally because of ideology and shared global visions on behalf of better civilizations. Now, countries temporarily ally in the competitive spirit of profitable gun-running, as if part of three-year business plans, with new board members coming and going based on a probability of third-world flare-ups and weaponry demand.

The '60s changed social and government operating standards in America right up to the present and probably far beyond into our own trepid national future. The '60s made corrupt leadership standards not just possible, but practical, especially for the Democratic Party to shift from national short and longer term political interests, to pure criminal enterprising, dragging others from the political periphery of uncommitted intellectual honesty with them. Democratic leadership's demise went from Johnson, to Carter, to Clinton, to Obama, none with the back-bone, foresight, and fortitude to trade for one sturdy Wilson Street Boy. Yet Johnson aggressively traded his integrity and inner soul for fifty-eight thousand of America's young men, adjacently infecting hundreds of thousands of other families and friendships, while poisoning the soul of America to a new lower and lower collective unwearable behavioral depth. Apparently, LBJ and his cronies did this simply because they had the power to do so, and the inner evil to not recognize the process for what it was nor to recognize the inevitable eventualities for what would predictably be an embattled and torn apart America.

So on we go, basically with '60s criminal mind-sets as new operating standards, sucking more of the country into a blindly selfish, self-destructive funnel. Suddenly, today it is OK to lie repeatedly on national television to the public. It is OK to be a Senator Durbin from Illinois and compare the activities of the American military to that of common, nasty international terrorists. It is now OK, for high-level political yapping mouths to encourage the passing of legislation so we can see what is in the legislation. Now, it is OK for the State Department to abuse their responsibilities while American's die in the line of their service, and then profess, loudly, belligerently, "What difference does it make?" in answer to the questioning process about the incident, in an inquiry or legal investigation process. All these incredibly foolish and destructive exhibitions of government belligerence are OK in America since the '60s. Such political behavior is now normal and becoming more aggressive and shameless.

In baseball, "hitting begets more hitting." That is, a team can go through the motions of the game, within the game, within normal skills and rules, and then catch fire, as one hitter after another hitter blends in with higher levels of performance and new momentum. In government, corruption and criminal enterprising begets more corruption and criminal enterprising. Corrupt leadership mind-set, hand in hand with outrageous media "breakthroughs" advance corrupt circles by new means and methods of corrupting, a societal click at a time. Such was America in the 1800s as the desecrations of slaving infected more and more factions, mind-sets, and circles of influence until the inevitable clashes of a Civil War finally were necessary to reset some semblance of honest standards of leadership behavior, moving America back toward its founding center of honest core values for aggregate good of country, under God. This contemporary cancerous state of American government all started in the '60s.

But we had a way out in the '60s also. We had a determined emerging spokesman for setting the ship back toward being upright, afloat above the muck. And then, we lost that hopeful chapter, about as quickly as he arose and became noticed, as once again, as usual, the "surprise attacking of evil," conquers over more slowly evolving goodness, which takes time, explanations, with more measured steps to progress.

Why Bobby? Why was Bobby assassinated?

Bobby Kennedy is now largely overlooked in any historically comprehensive analysis concerning reconciliations surrounding Nam, amateur or academic. That oversight is rather easy to do in a government/media world more focused on distractions than analysis for reasonable solutions. The oversight is also easy to do because in a timeline of Nam events, Bobby's influence and actions were only a blip or two in the quagmire of one outrageous Nam concern after another. However, Bobby is absolutely central to the core concepts of Domestic Nam theorizing and central to how America has played it out, tottering today like an alcoholic stuck between a conscious resurrection, or more reasons for the alcohol.

As president, JFK lived a mere three years into the '60s, and that was almost with a copresidency, Bobby being the partner. LBJ started the '60s as an obscure, corrupted Texas legislator, chosen to be VP largely because of his obscurity, back in a day when presidents selected VPs to carry their home states. Bobby was central to JFK's election, operations, and demise. Bobby was the copresident, involved in every process and decision. It was Bobby who contributed to make Johnson irrelevant as a sitting VP. It was Bobby who understood "Who killed JFK?" It was Bobby who understood the depth of clashes and partnerships between the CIA and the Mafia. It was Bobby who knew of plans to support Cuban exile operations for a second invasion of Cuba, this time with strategic US military forces for a successful coup and organization of a new Cuban pro-American government. *It was Bobby who understood what it was like to send unsupported troops on an invasion commitment (Cuba or Nam) to a foreign shore and have them killed or imprisoned for years because of lack of promised support.* Thus, Bobby saw the corruption of the warring processes and was living with the guilt.

Bobby is reality 3, but first, who killed Bobby?

Sirhan may have shot Bobby, but he may not have. Sirhan was certainly there, as another patsy, just like Oswald. A good assassination of high-level social and government officials can only succeed with a patsy ready in the wings to take the blame and thus halt the investigation. So whether a lowest level, faceless Sirhan actually pulled the trigger is a bottom line of sorts, but not *the* bottom line.

Why and how would Sirhan want to kill Bobby or be in a hotel tunnel to kill Bobby when the hotel tunnel was not in any exit plans for Bobby after his June 6 LA speech in the Colonial Room of the Ambassador Hotel? A simple congratulatory speech, an acceptance announcement for public consumption, for winning the CA Democratic primary in a presidential race that would ultimately lend a conclusive direction to the Domestic Nam?

Bobby and his modest entourage had no plans to exit the Ambassador Hotel after his overwhelming, surprise primary victory, other than through normal public hotel exits and hallways. At the last moments of his speech in the colonial room, Bobby was immediately directed by a relatively unknown security guard, (who was a Cuban American, working part-time in the local CIA connected defense industry) to what was to be a quieter, private, safe exit from the hotel ballroom. That security guard with CIA/Mafia ties and with access to hotel events grabbed Bobby's arm, directing him down stairs, through a kitchen and out a little known employee tunnel, supposedly toward an exit, one that he would never reach. Sirhan waited, perhaps with the real assassins there also. *Bam! Bam! Bam!* Bobby was killed with three bullets to the neck and head. Sirhan was immediately arrested, and violà, another lone, faceless gunman to prosecute, put away, thus again eliminating the need for a broad national investigation.

There are Mafia related reasons that Sirhan would pull the trigger, if he did. There are certainly Mafia related reasons that Sirhan would be led to the remote underground passage as a patsy, at the exact time that Bobby would have changed his hotel, post-acceptance speech exit plans, and pass right by where Sirhan was positioned. The Mafia and expanse of partners had perfected their patsy strategies for major assassinations, as had the CIA, and controlled the connections to create the opportunity, which once again went to the depths of government, the CIA, and in Bobby's case, went to the depths of the Domestic Nam.

Reality #3—We had a way out, with Bobby, the Bobby speech.

Bobby Kennedy, RFK, is reality #3 because within Bobby, America had a leadership way out of Nam. With the probable election of Bobby Kennedy as president, America would have a direction that would likely lead to a concerted effort to withdraw from Nam rather immediately. He had said so, in a pivotal speech in Chicago on February 8 of '68. That time period sound interesting? It was ten days after the Tet Offensive began when Nam and all of America's Nam assets were clinging to lifelines, uncertain in everything.

Bobby, in his apparent role as copresident, had seen and felt the pressures of the office and understood national political pornography when he saw it.

Bobby understood that escalations in Nam were a Johnson Administration cover-up strategy of distraction to the real question of enough government-linked corruption to kill JFK.

Bobby understood that the real threat to America of Communist aggression was Cuba, not a remote far away, third world hamlet-connected ancient population, scratching rice paddies, riding water buffalo and raising ducks to survive.

Bobby felt the guilt and futility of the uncommitted invasion efforts of the Bay of Pigs, October '62, that would waste troop's lives to feed a military/industrial warring machine that was linked arm in arm with Mafia goals to reorganize Cuban operations back to the days of casino and gambling ownership that existed with Batista, pre-Castro.

Bobby had lived at the center of coalition building, arms delivering and payoffs in the JFK administration efforts to organize a second liberating invasion of Cuba. Bobby lived the corruption born in such processes firsthand, and the degenerative, institutional mind-set that it takes to create and prosecute such operations.

Bobby was killed for three primary reasons, with multiple other factors leading to these reasons. After the surprise, California Democratic politically impressive primary victory over a main rival Eugene McCarthy, it looked certain that Bobby would be the Democratic nominee and then likely president. Bobby suddenly had enormous momentum and felt right, his electorate star shining brighter than ever. Thus, old established rivalries would reemerge, to crush the momentum.

A contributing reason for Bobby's targeted elimination via assassination would have been his growing close relationship with Martin Luther King, but even that had a direct link to Domestic Nam. Bobby had begun to build an election platform related to America's disadvantaged, largely related to racial issues and the efforts of King. No question an electoral kinship was being built via King to the black voting population and other minorities. But the appeal to the "disadvantaged" did not stop there for Bobby and his campaign. Bobby's campaign began successfully to more specifically link whites of all locations and backgrounds as disadvantaged and thus drafted as bullet-bait for the growing atrocities in Nam. To America's warring minds in association with the Johnson administration, the military/industrial maintainers, gun-runners and bomb-makers, Bobby's growing relationship with King, was another potential problem to the military/industrial '60s undercover think tank style.

A second core reason for Bobby's assassination was again the Mafia. As attorney general and copresident with JFK, Bobby had relentlessly pursued key Mafia prosecutions, particularly focusing on Mafia families in Chicago, Tampa, New Orleans, plus the families' activities with Hoffa and the Teamsters, which then reaches further into America's gut. As president, it was a certainty that prosecution efforts would be revived with an increased vengeance, with the full force and backing of all assets of the US government. Early '60s prosecution memories were fresh in the minds of the Mafia and the general public nationwide, with the actionable confidence that what government prosecutors had done once, they could do again, perhaps even more efficiently, probably without wasting post-inauguration time.

The Mafia had prospered under the Johnson administration in the years when Las Vegas was their "Green Felt Jungle." Cuban casino building behind them, the Mafia moved to Las Vegas, big time, with help, and with Nam and race relations as the nation's codistractions. Las Vegas was an isolated fun place, regardless of the burning ghettos across fifty US cities and a growing hidden war in some place called Vietnam capturing more and more attention, headlines, and news feeds for a public becoming more and more interested in that far away warring commitment. The mob prospering, with a complicit President Johnson in charge of judicial methodic targeting and payback in general, would not tolerate a reemerging Bobby Kennedy, this time with all the presidential powers available. The 1968 presidential election was lining up to be a most pivotal time for America, providing new leadership to halt the criminal actions of Nam escalations.

The third and final reason Bobby was killed was his attitude on the war in Nam and because of an antiwar attitude flaunted in a speech delivered February 8 in Chicago. The title of the speech was "Unwinnable War." We have to look through the speech to understand the speech, appreciate what we lost at the time, and to appreciate the further corruptive declines that America was then allowed to sink within. If one understands this speech not just for what it says but also for what is between the lines, it becomes clear how the prosecution of Nam's criminal warring was so unopposed within official government, military, and industrial ranks. JFK, with Bobby at his side, had perfected the art of professing the obvious, while outwardly speaking to address the less obvious.

February 8, 1968, was the day of this forgotten speech, ten days after a national reality check, the recognized beginning to the Tet Offensive and, twenty days after the beginning of the siege at Khe Sanh. Battles raged all over Nam, in all forty-four provincial capitals, in a clear, undeniable message that what was thought to be reality by the US leadership, and so fed to the busy population as the war's reality, was not at all the truth. On February 8, because of Tet, Bobby knew America was at a Nam commitment crossroads, financially, morally, ideologically, and in Wilson Street-style public opinion. Not only did Bobby realize that Nam was the key electoral emerging issue to be on a correct side of on behalf of an irritated public, but he felt deeply against the immorality of the US government's escalation of a war that could never be won, or even compromised, while so many American young men had been committed.

Following are the key parts of this speech, with interpretations. While you read it, ask yourself this: although this speech is about another faroff, little understood Asian war in the late '60s, do these points apply today in Afghanistan?

This speech and the points made within it officially launched Bobby's presidential nomination aspirations. He was killed four months later.

This historically underregarded speech is about the War in Vietnam, which, at that time, no one called the Domestic Nam, in fact officially government went to great ends, not to refer to Vietnam as a war at all. Vietnam was a conflict, not a war! No one, certainly not institutionally, made an effort to identify Nam as a distraction, nor link the key elements within US borders as the key elements creating a need for a distraction war in Nam. Wars like Nam were still under the banner of fighting Communism, within a treacherous foggy Cold War threat, so ominous that it could not really be identified. Nam and the Cold War, like societal shifting and changes internally, could never be fought with any methods thought of that were even similar to historic traditional militaristic lines of battle. In the '60s, it all changed, and the ways and means of warring were wide open fluctuating conjecture. No specific warring target. No frontlines of battle. No specific population segment or standing armies to defeat. No timeline of progress. No limits to Wilson Street boys to throw into a fight. No military/industrial limits.

The June 6 speech contained four summary points that spoke directly to how a President RFK would regard the military and political situation in relation to Nam. Bobby speaking from Chicago to the nation:

- "we have concealed the war's true circumstances, even from ourselves";
- "reality of Vietnam, [we must be] freed from wishful, false hopes, and sentimental dreams";
- "it is an illusion that the last two weeks [the beginning of the Tet Offensive throughout South Vietnam], represent some sort of victory" (the Johnson administration portrayed Tet as a victory);
- "we have seen none of the population [Vietnamese] is secure, and no area is under sure control."

Tet was a massive defeat for American fighting investments and interests throughout Nam, and globally, while domestically spoken of by LBJ and staff as a victory. At the time of this speech, Tet had just begun, and while Johnson, with Westmoreland were spouting victorious war chants and tunes, troops all over Nam, air and land, were fighting daily for their lives (including yours truly). Bobby was the lone national voice of truth for the pivotal late '60s period of warring.

Bobby went on—"We have misconceived the nature of the war in five ways."

Examine the simple language of the five ways American leadership misconceived the war in 1968 and ask yourself, "Do these points apply today in our war in Afghanistan? What are the different circumstances of these two wars?" Ask yourself lots of questions. (If Assad of Syria is a war criminal, what was Johnson?)

1. Bobby continued, "We seek to solve the conflict [in Nam] by military might, while the issue depends on the will and conviction of the South Vietnamese people."

    This point could mean, no matter the might of the US military, and regardless of the bravery and intensity of young US troops in the fight, the South Vietnamese must win this fight for themselves because they want to win the fight for a homeland and way of life. This was spoken at a time when US leadership knew they were allied with a fleeting, corrupt South Vietnamese government, unlikely to have consistent, dependable, unified will and conviction on anything government or military. The early signals and circumstances of Nam were lessons supposedly rather commonsense and elementary, like putting one state department foreign relations foot in front of the other, unless the whole simmering pot is really about issues unrevealed. Does this simple statement of misconception number 1 apply today for the war in Afghanistan? Yes it does, the point would seem to apply perfectly!

2.   Bobby continued, "We have the illusion that we can win a war, that the South Vietnamese cannot win themselves. People will not fight and die to line the pockets of generals or swell the bank accounts of the wealthy."

Here is where we get into infamous Kennedy double-speak and language, possibly pointing more directly to a super sensitive presidential administration holding hands with an eager, mature military/industrial leadership, both calculating the various Nam long-term "returns on investments," or lack of. The Kennedy's national leadership tenure perfected the art of double speak in their brief era of coleadership. Who was Bobby referring to, speaking of "lining the pockets of generals" or "swelling the bank accounts of the wealthy"? Speaking in a general public genre, the assumption would be that Bobby was speaking of the South Vietnamese generals and wealthy. However, if the listener was complicit with the immorality of the administration prosecuting the Nam war, or within the ranks or peripheral ranks of the military/industrial complex, which would include occasional Mafia influences and other groups of all kinds, one could certainly conclude that Bobby was speaking directly to US citizens and certain leadership ranks, about US generals and domestic wealthy. Bobby could have easily been speaking to American families, sending Wilson Street Boys to war, for the generals and to line the pockets of the domestic wealthy that are prospering greatly in warring contracts and implementation. He is clearly implying that there will be a time when America itself rises up and says, "Enough." We will no longer send our boys around the world to die in a useless cause, and that time to rise up with "enough," would potentially be the first day of his new administration. Does this simple statement by Bobby, apply today, forty-five years later, in Afghanistan? Why yes, again, it does! For several coincidental reasons.

3. Bobby goes on, most intently, "The third illusion is that the unswerving pursuit of military victory, whatever the cost, is in the interest of either ourselves [the United States of America] or the people of Vietnam. We have dropped twelve tons of bombs for every square mile in North and South Vietnam."

    This is February 1968, relatively early in the Nam war, now submerged in the surprising intensity of the battles of Tet, and we had already dropped more bombs than the United States and allies had dropped fighting Nazi Germany. The key point here is the reference to "unswerving pursuit," meaning "hell bent," or no matter what, we are gonna drop a bunch of bombs and keep dropping a bunch of bombs. There could be a bit over a million square miles in North and South Vietnam, half north and half south. So if Bobby is even close (he was a New York senator at the time, so he may have been in the know), we, America alone this time without Europe's allies, the Cold War-fighting global leader, had manufactured, shipped, and handled twelve million bombs halfway around the globe, in order to unload, handle again, mount on or within guns or aircraft, fueled and staffed with trained gunners and pilots dropping the things in suspected points of enemy threats. Bobby's "unswerving pursuit" comment apparently meant more bombing is certainly the future, unless something happens to awaken a national public conscience.

Then, there is the question of the Vietnamese "will and determination"—such bomb dropping could embolden and make more determined those Vietnamese folks north of the DMZ, while demoralizing the folks to the south with some incremental will and determination shrinkage concerning the value and intent of the presence of the US military who manage such massive indiscernible bombings. Again, does this simple point apply today in the war in Afghanistan?

4.   A fourth illusion: "American national interest is identical with—or should be subordinated to—the selfish interest of an incompetent military regime. This is not the struggle for the beginning of a great Asian society."

Now he'd done it—"incompetent military regime"? Again, the general public would hear a statement about South Vietnam's "incompetent military regime" or at least most of the public would insinuate a direct reference to South Vietnam regime. Not so fast there American Tontos, we are analyzing Kennedy double-speak expertise, with which the politicians and military of that time had become accustomed and were obliged the leeway of their own interpretation. Bobby had lived the hands-on boondoggle Bay of Pigs operation, with an "incompetent military regime." Bobby also had a fresh memory of the incompetent military, infiltrated by a determined Mafia surrounding the second invasion planned for Cuba, December 1963.

As president, an "incompetent military" would be at the height of Bobby's conscious reasoning on all matters of national security, particularly the foreign conflicts currently in progress. To military/industrial leadership, supported by appropriate political Cold War brethren, Bobby was not referring to the South Vietnamese military. He was referring to the great waste and incompetent military plans being prosecuted in Nam by the United States. Remember, Maxwell Taylor was the chairman of the Joint Chiefs in the JFK administration but did not report to, for, or from the Joint Chiefs. Taylor worked directly with JFK and was still in the position in the Johnson administration. Thus, Bobby more than likely maintained that connection and attitude about how that structure was functioning.

This Chicago speech then became a clear message to some that, as president, withdrawing from Nam would be a high, perhaps even Bobby's highest, priority. One could also insinuate that the reference to a great Asian society had a much broader meaning—perhaps a meaning that Nam was not worth it, would never be worth it. Nam is not nor will it become a spot on the globe that needs such vast extensive American assets diplomatically committed and spent so recklessly. This point 4 was the heart of the speech with a rather clear message to domestic proponents of the war, just as JFK's Tampa speech in '63 to America was a direct speech to gathered forces waiting for the green light on a second Cuba invasion effort. Does this misconception 4 apply forty-five years later to Afghanistan? Why yes, I think it does, more certainly than ever. How unique and how utterly depressing. How do you explain this? Is it just a combination of greed and stupidity, with mountainous arrogance all woven into a deceitful hair ball attached to numerous land mines? But there is more.

5. The grandest illusion of the speech: "This war can be settled in our own way and in our own time, on our own terms. Such a privilege is only for the triumphant, those who crush an enemy."

    This is Bobby's announcement that America cannot win a ground war in Indochina, regardless of firepower or wave after wave of aerial bombing and elevated ground troop levels. Fighting this war with back-shelf restraint and political immorality would not ever result in any relative sort of satisfactory, recognizable victory. This speech was the first public pronouncement of the type, frightening the war's profiteers. Remember, this was ten days after the beginning of Tet. It was clear to Bobby that the war would not be settled in America's own way, time, or terms, and thus as president, ending the conflict and beginning the withdrawal would be an early priority of his administration. This was the Domestic Nam, the war was at home, within American shores, minds, and temperaments, and for a brief period in 1968, America had a way out. Does this fifth illusion fit today, forty-five years later, concerning our warring in Afghanistan? Most certainly, it does. What are the chances in Afghanistan of settling the war our way, in our own time, on our terms? Zero! In fact, we have already compromised our way, in our own time, on our terms, in several different defeating ways.

Bobby's speech was a national surprise announcement of his anti-Nam platform, at a time when all eyes and ears around the world were analyzing the affects that the Tet Offensive would have. The marines at Khe Sanh, on Hill 881 were wondering about the effects of Tet also, as were the brave pilots, Army Rangers, Green Berets in the Central Highlands, and Delta forces, so were the marines of the Twenty-Seventh Marines forming at Pendleton who would soon be in the Go Noi. Bobby seemed to be the lone voice of the obvious.

Bobby's February 8, 1968, speech went on, the latter part of the speech delivered in direct relation to the Tet Offensive, then just ten days into the fighting. Through the deflating experiences of ten days of Tet fighting, Bobby summarized "nine basic truths."

1) "A total military victory is not within sight, or around the corner. It is probably beyond our grasp."

> *Bobby had the vision to divide the battles of Nam from battles just fought in Europe and Korea. He understood in Nam there would be no visible fronts to fight for or within. To Bobby, Nam was the surrogate war to Cuba that he had worked on and planned, and thus not only had that experience, but had the Bay of Pigs defeat guilt. How would you win a faraway jungle war without the will and determination of the people for whom you fight? How long could the illusion of Nam as a Cold War front be sustained after the exhibition of Tet had proven there really had been no progress in nearly four years of escalations? Thus, if not "total military victory," what kind of victory is satisfactory in trade for the expense and body bags now being filled? Is there to be a half victory that is worth the effort and the sacrificing of national moral core values? Instead, do we just change the name of the type of victory,*

call it done, either diplomatically or in payoffs, declaring some new cosmic like force of American victory genius yet to be recognized or appreciated by the rest of the world? Change the attitude of victory?

Nam was where we learned to prosecute military/industrial war, declare it something else, rake the pot, and move on. Nam was the '60s, and the '60s changed it all. Will there be a "total military victory" in Afghanistan? Naw, not a chance! New deals will focus on rebuilding infrastructure contracts instead of arms and ordnance contracts, until that lesser phase of the gun-running flow chart runs its own material course. Then a remaining watch dog force, whose operations look at the operations of corrupt Afghan officials, who then are looking back at the watch dogs, while logistic lines are redrawn and reshaped to go several clicks east to Syria. We learned it in the '60s, largely in and around the Domestic Nam.

2) Bobby's next basic truth: "The pursuit of such a victory is not necessary to our national interest, and is even damaging to that interest."

The key words here are "pursuit," meaning the ongoing prosecution of the war indefinitely, and "national," meaning internal, domestic. The war was not even about Nam, it was about internal US interests and distractions. Bobby could see inside the process and understand how Nam was and would continue to demoralize America, contributing to increased new levels of corruption in all things connected to Nam. There really was no link between

Nam and national interests. Nam was a degenerate criminal quagmire on a global scale.

3) "The progress we claim toward controlling the countryside and the security of the population is largely illusory."

Until the beginning of Tet, the Johnson Administration professed great global leadership and progress in saving the poor third-world people of Vietnam from communism and then perhaps all of Indochina in the swooping communist cleansing. Johnson and his administration crew were all buying in to a delusion over time, to feed the American public whatever was necessary to cover-up the war's criminal bottom lines. I suppose that is easier to do if done from the States, in an office, with a lunch appointment highlighting the work day, rather than being a part of the fight. Tet shattered the propaganda fed to America about the war. Three years of inflated war-speak met reality at Tet, and Bobby was the first to speak loudly about it and thus uncomfortably stir those assisting to prosecute and then profit somehow from the war.

We make the same claims today in Afghanistan. We claim to control countryside and then claim to provide security for parts of the population. The Afghan countryside is just like the Nam countryside. We own the ground we stand on, and that's all. Half the population in Afghanistan can't wait to frag the first GI that turns his back, and in fact are doing so, and that will not change. It did not change in Nam and never would have. Dogs chasing tails have better results!

4) "The central battle cannot be measured by body counts or bomb damage: only by the extent to which the people of South Vietnam act on a sense of common purpose and hope with those that govern them."

The futility of the fight in Nam had no measure of success from '64 through to early '68, the time of Tet. Troop numbers doubled, then doubled from that, and kept on doubling—along the way doubling every real time aspect of troop support and the things needed to shoot more things and blow more things up at greater distances. Gargantuan supply lines from hand grenades to Wilson Street Boys were being urgently built in unprecedented warring ways. America had perfected getting to war with troops and the hard goods to make them potentially effective. Unfortunately, there were no real victories, no stories of progress to support sustaining losses and expenses. So officials in the rah-rah chain ramped up the enemy body count numbers first, then bragged about fighter pilot missions, and then tons of bombs dropped or shot from ships offshore or from hilltop artillery positions in support of some invisible grunt unit on the ground trapped in some lost jungle artery. Bobby was the first to speak of the uncertainty and false illusions of reporting such subjectively easy to manipulate numbers for public consumption and mind-bending. KIAs, WIAs, and bomb tonnage were just another distraction from the truth on the ground. Is that process SOP today in Afghanistan or even perhaps at Benghazi? Probably. It is the new way!

5) Bobby continued, "The current regime in Saigon is unwilling or incapable of being an effective ally in the war against Communists."

In the late '50s, one of two first senators then to meet future South Vietnamese President Diem was JFK. The Kennedy's had a lot of experience evaluating Nam through several years before JFK was elected president. It would be unlikely that even the dimwitted Johnson would say—those nifty tricky South Vietnamese are too unwilling or incapable to actually make sense of this costly effort, so Bobby had to eventually bring the basic truth to light. America had aligned with a low-life, third-world corrupt dictator, occasionally dressed as a perceptive diplomat. However, the truly important analysis of this basic truth is: Substitute Kabul *for* Saigon, *and substitute* the Taliban *for* Communists, *and— what is the current reality of this basic truth?*

6) Basic truths from February 1968 continued, "A political compromise is not just the best path to peace, but the only path."

America would come to that hard fought reality six years after Bobby's Chicago speech—six years. Perhaps the coffers were full by then, or full enough, simultaneous with the warring reality on the ground and in the diplomacy rooms, sensing the last of the propagandish wiggle room. This basic truth says, "Compromise is the only path to peace," "compromise." Bobby must have meant compromise on Nam and compromise domestically, with factions significant to the pro-warring effort in

Nam. This would mean multiple levels of internal domestic factions, certainly the military/industrial complex compromising with one another. This basic truth is almost a "domestic" peace offering to Bobby's political opponents. Regardless, this basic truth comment is now applicable, as Afghanistan is being compromised and when all of the compromising parts and dividends are divvied up, the implementation of actual military compromise can actually proceed. Compromise takes a business model, just like building a new plant, or structure, or process of any kind.

(There was a lesson on compromise about twenty years ago that is a unique American model for standard commercial compromise but works perfectly when applied to warring models of compromise also. The lesson was in downtown New Orleans right next to the Hilton Hotel and Conference Center on the river front and adjacent to the huge trade show and convention center. On one of my many visits, there was a new, fairly large casino popping up that was well under construction in downtown New Orleans. The business was to be a Harrah's, just a couple blocks from the infamous Bourbon Street threshold. The new casino might be fun someday, can't wait to visit, someday. A year later back in town and anxious to inspect, expecting to find a new open music/gaming filled casino, I found a halted construction site, surrounded and secured by multiple levels and walkways of chain link fencing with the appropriate stay the hell away barbed wire at opportune entry possibilities. The project looked 90 percent finished. What could be the story here? There's the big stretching beautiful building, right

where it should be. What could possibly be going on to halt this apparently perfectly placed, timely project? A local street corner inhabitant, hanging loose on his chosen corner, seemed a reliable source of inside info on the halted project. Sure enough, after some initial New Orleans style con-artistry, the accomplished Black street gentleman scooped the Louisiana media and told me, "They just ain't figured out the graft, skims and kickbacks yet. Soon as that's figured, they'll finish it, and open." Sure enough, a year later, about the time the Louisiana governor was sentenced to prison; the casino got finished and opened. That's the lesson, of Nam, and probably of Afghanistan. As soon as the contracts, graft, skimming and payoffs get figured out, and visions of the next probable conflicts appear reliable, the Afghan processes of declining intensity can be implemented, and political/military operations can join public opinion to end one worn-out conflict in favor of a new one, fresh to the misinformation process.)

More Bobby basic truths:

7) "The U.S. escalation policy in Vietnam is injuring our country, through the world, reducing faith in our wisdom and purpose, weakening the world resolve [just hard won in WWII] to stand together for freedom and peace."

  The United States, in Bobby's insightful view, was becoming no less cynical, no less misleading and destructive than the Communist forces so opposed. A costly, useless, expensive war in Nam would increasingly divide America's directions and willpower, sending degenerative signals globally. If America will waste its military and human assets on the Nam dung heap, how dependable will the new America be on relatively more needy and honest issues? Could America continue to stand for "freedom and peace," while dropping more bombs in NW I Corps alone in two months than they did on Germany? One then has to look and consider if it is the same in Afghanistan. Is America's "wisdom and purpose" dangling on display in Afghanistan? Is Afghanistan a model for "freedom and peace" that actually makes good sense, in an honest effort? Or is a presence in Afghanistan viewed in the world as a wise, peace-seeking national strategy?

8)   Bobby's next to last basic truth: "The best way to save our most precious stake in Vietnam—the lives of our soldiers—is to stop the war. The best way to end the casualties is to end the war." (It was as simple as getting rid of household dog hair—get rid of the dog.)

To many of the military/industrial main stream, the most precious asset of the Vietnam War was not the lives of soldiers. Soldiers were largely draftees, owing their time, no more than Hessians of the eighteenth century, expendable tools. Why would anyone want to end the casualties of expendable tools in favor of diminished cash flow from moving warring tools and assets? If and when Johnson ramped up Nam as a distraction, *posturing against a Cold War fog of a threat, there was no calculation of a sufficient number of soldier's lives to be sacrificed in various Nam meat grinders. Would the* distraction *and Cold War stopping effort be worth X number of soldier's lives lost? Is that when we quit and come home, or is it Y number of soldier's lives lost, or is the* sufficient *number of lives lost to be infinite as long as hard goods are moving and philosophical distractions are spinning? And would those soldiers be black or white Americans, urban or rural, some wanted, some just wanting? Wars for the purposes of distractions have no firm side boards. They have no plateaus of rejudging the real cause, cost, and implementation because they had no legitimate foundations to begin with. Ditto Afghanistan! When a leadership sees clearly that nothing can be gained or positively changed in a distant third-world war, does the leadership work to save the precious assets of soldier's lives? Nah, don't think so. Since the '60s the focus is military/industrial calculation until the next warring needs are identified and squishy "distraction-type" over reactions are fabricated and implemented into an actionable cause.*

9) Bobby came to his final point: "Our nation must be told the truth about this war."

Two powerful insinuations were left here for public, spiritual, and special consideration in this final point: First, Bobby was obviously saying, our nation is not being told the truth about the war in South Vietnam. Fast forward again, today, and it is obvious that our nation is not being told the truth about Benghazi? Nothing changes, or seems improved. Today it is more about a dumbed-down public than it is about leadership brilliance and accountability. Second, Bobby was unquestionably saying that in his campaign platform he was going to start to tell the truth about the war in Nam. It was that dedication to the truth that got him killed 4 months later, immediately after winning the California primary and looking like a shoe-in for the Democratic Presidential candidacy, thus becoming the likely Presidential winner in the late fall of '68.

Bobby Kennedy was the Domestic Nam bright shining truth teller at a time when America could grasp a way out before atrocities would really multiply and a nation's core moralities were to become destroyed from the top—down. Bobby saw there was nothing to win, nor a way to win anything of significance within a national interest, on a reasonable timeline.

On the day Bobby was shot and killed, taking with him any hopes of a reasonable, timely end to the Nam war, USMC Sergeants Rollie Cahill and Terry Emmerson were completing missions, and both on their way to meet up in Da Nang, June 8, 1968. For the Marines and thousands others in American uniform, Nam and Tet were still the overwhelming fighting reality. What no one would have, in an emerging politician like Bobby to end the atrocities, no one would ever miss. The whole Bobby potential vanished, like it had never emerged. Cahill and Emmerson would experience more and more of "looking through the Nam," some missions of their own mischievous nature, some assigned through rank and responsibility and deadly serious. Bobby, King and others simply faded into that fast-moving, uncertain '60s part of American history, just as hundreds of daily, tarmac staged dark-green body bags would fade into history, turning from body bags to American Legion graveside medallions without a voice or a whimper.

Bobby is never mentioned much in relation to Nam. Frankly neither are the other two million Vietnam Veterans who served and survived. Many Nam Veterans are dead now. More soon will be, perhaps not as silently as we thought. After 3 decades of business building, family tending, and community presence, two of Nam's Veterans eventually also disappeared, just as Fletcher and Stuebe had disappeared somewhere out of an Air America side door 35 years prior, just clicks east inside Laos.

In late 2001 Cahill and Emmerson would drop out of sight, pretty much at the same time. True to their working methods and unique relationship, the drop from sight would not be without continuing their unusual story building.

Afterword

"You all need singing to. You just don't know it yet."

E mmerson found his angel! Once a young soldier or pilot had been in the battles of Nam, especially surrounding Tet, life would often not fit casually for a while, or ever again. Big choices sometimes seem not as important as little choices, such as where to step, what route to take, when to answer a phone call, or when not to. A small choice to give something a try, an honest try, and follow one's own leaning instincts, bending, or yielding, often puts personal falling dominoes in a position to Win.

Nam fades reluctantly in emotions and consciousness, as if the inner feelings are a gluey stubborn mucous clinging to your boots as part of a thick red-mud bigger mucous. A veteran's questions or judgments start to arise cautiously for many years, especially in relation to ongoing American leadership and what a normal life is supposed to be like, in a normal town, with other normal people. The personal restraining breakthrough then may run its course when the Nam vet is weary of confusing himself with the uncertain load. An unusual, unexpected voice from some unexpected source can change everything, and suddenly, the barriers start to crack a little bit at a time, and a personal "breakthrough" from the veteran's past personal weighted baggage is allowed to flow gently out and away.

On a normal coastal Northeast Virginia October fall-feeling day, 1999, in a half kept garage backroom well-conceived man-cave, Emmerson routinely answered his shop phone. He did not recognize the soft angelic lady's voice on the other end making the call. The unknown voice was of a female, measuring her opening remarks gently as if tight rope stepping. The unknown lady caller made sure this Terry Emmerson was the Sergeant Emmerson, USMC, Nam, through '68, or close to that time period.

The soft, timid, but determined voice identified herself as Heather, and simply inquired if Emmerson had a few moments to answer a couple questions about some issues from the war in Nam that had concerned her for many years. Heather explained that she had gotten Emmerson's name from her brother several years ago, and it had taken these past few years to actually track him down a little bit at a time. Finding Emmerson really was about her brother, who was a Nam Marine Corps veteran, missing for near twenty years, suddenly returning home as if from the heavens, and then had died five years ago in '94. Heather further explained that her name was Heather Fletcher, previously from Arkansas, now living in Oregon.

Heather wanted to know if it was true. Was what she heard about her brother in the Marines Corps and in Nam in '67-'68 true, or near true? She explained that her brother had seemed to disappear in Nam and then strangely showed up, back in Searcy, Arkansas twenty years after everyone thought he had died. He was only reported MIA, so she and the family never really knew anything more. She introduced herself as "Heather," and went on to briefly recall some stories her brother had shared, stories that seemed impossible to have happened, and impossible to grasp a true feel for the stories listeners. She also explained that her brother seemed to have a strange, deep inner commitment to a Sergeant Emmerson. Was he Sergeant Emmerson? Would he talk to her about her Brother?

Nam stories mostly remain in Nam. Nam stories are emotionally expensive to resurrect for veterans and often too guarded to productively transfer a completed thought or meaning to most who would be largely unattached to the personal depths of the stories.

Emmerson, caught off guard, breathed in the intense, passionate angelic voice from the stranger. At first, he was so entranced and soothed by the soft voice that the actual stories of Fletcher and Stuebe seemed a distant second to Heather's surprise feminine reaching/ touching entrapment. Her soft soothingly intense introduction had stopped his motion, almost stopped his heart, as he spun his memory back to a guarded era, almost thirty-five plus years ago—an era from which most had been pushed mentally aside, except for the healthy subconscious with that closed gate. The voice was not a stranger's voice for very long.

> *Heather: Sergeant Emmerson, will you talk to me?*

Emmerson (gathering some thoughts then a breath): Terry, call me Terry, Sergeant is an old, gone Emmerson.

Heather (hesitantly starting over again): OK, good. Hi, Terry, glad to make your acquaintance. I have waited a long time for the day I could reach you, and say hi, and thank you. My brother, David, spoke heavenly of you. I don't know what you did for him, but want to know.

Emmerson: That was a long time ago, a lot of marines, doing a lot of things. Yes, I remember your brother, who could not.

Heather: Did my brother do those things? Did you save his life?

Emmerson: Your brother, David? In Nam, you don't know too many first names. He did a lot of things. But you have to understand, from Nam, you believe all the stories. You'd best believe his stories. Where are you calling from?

Heather: I live in Oregon, West of Salem, South of Portland, along the coast. And you?

Emmerson: I'm in Norfolk, as far from Oregon as I think you can get and still be in America.

Heather: Look you didn't know I was going to call, didn't know I existed. I don't want to interrupt or bother you. Is there a time I can call back? A time you might prepare for, so we can share some thoughts or ideas, maybe settle some thoughts and ideas also.

Emmerson: Sure, if you like, if I can help. What do you do in Oregon?

Heather: I do several things, mostly sing?

Emmerson: You sing? To whom? Where?

Heather: I sing to people who need singing to. When can I call you again, about David and Nam, maybe a little bit about Sergeant Emmerson, if he's not too far gone?

Emmerson: Tomorrow. I'm always in my shop here at home on Sunday mornings, this same number. Can you call tomorrow morning, 10:00 a.m.-ish?"

Heather: Yes, I certainly can, and will. Will this be uncomfortable for you? I don't want it to be. I feel like I should know you, know you a little bit anyway. You see, David and I were twins. In a way, when you saved his life, you saved part of my life also. We owe you so much, we think. David had a deep affection for you, for whatever it was you did. I just want to know a little more than he felt able to tell us. Talking about Nam was most uncomfortable for him, seems that way with all of you. I will call you tomorrow morning, Sunday, 10:00 a.m., EST. I'll practice calling you Terry, the rest of this day . . . Til tomorrow?"

Emmerson: Yes, tomorrow. I'll be better prepared to help. How long ago did your brother die?

Heather: Five years ago.

Emmerson: Look, I don't mean to be unpleasant, but how did he die. I ask for a reason.

Heather: He died in an interstate highway accident. A school bus had crashed into an overpass support, David was the first to come to the scene, stopped, and was able to pull over a dozen of the children from the crash, and then the bus just blew up, and David died inside the bus before emergency vehicles could arrive and put the fire out and save his life.

Emmerson: Sorry, very sorry. I'm glad you called. You know, there wasn't anything in the whole of Nam that could kill him, he seemed to try.

Heather: Talk to you in the morning.

Emmerson: Yes, look forward to it. You're a singer? Wow, I could use a singer! I may be one of those who needed singing to.

Heather: All of you need singing to. You just don't know it yet. Bye, love!

Emmerson: Bye! (Bye, love? Heather?)

The day passed slowly for Emmerson, that lazy 1999 fall day of one big throwback Nam surprise. Emmerson sat down as Norfolk breezes from the close shores enlightened then lifted the shop's normally dull atmosphere. Heather Fletcher, a singer, on the coast of Oregon!

Calvary, sit boy, just sit. I gotta think about this one. Heather sounds like singing just saying hello!

Heather and Terry talked the next day, the Sunday morning, at precisely 10:00 a.m., EST, on a perfect mid-Atlantic October day. They talked again in November, and made an appointment to talk again at Christmas time, both reluctantly eager to add a little singing adventure to their usual eventless holiday spirits.

In December, Heather and Terry agreed they should talk regularly, and they did, pretty much every time Heather's travels allowed her to settle into her coastal Oregon home for a while. Sometimes, she talked to Terry, and sometimes, she was certain she was talking to Sergeant Emmerson. Through the conversations of the year 2000, Heather sensed she was talking increasingly more to Terry than she was to Sergeant Emmerson. Heather thought she could actually feel Terry the person and couldn't get a handle on Sergeant Emmerson. As a surprise, she sent a picture to Norfolk, a gorgeous black evening dress picture, topped by the brightest blue eyes, strong shoulders, and a penetrating look of being right there, not afraid of very much. Sergeant Emmerson had no picture to send in response, nor would he ever have one—never the picture taken kind of guy.

The long distance from Oregon to Norfolk, Virginia, seemed to act more as a challenge than an obstacle for Heather and Emmerson as they continued to become better acquainted and share lives and stories beyond Nam and a past twin brother. Emmerson's shop soon had a few more Heather pics on the wall, some singing, some posing, but the same blue eyes adorning all and lighting to life the normally dim solitary man-cave shop, occasionally crowded with townie buddies, all inquiring about the new blue eyes Emm had posted.

The long distance relationship continued to be shared on a regular basis into 2001. Heather's travels and singing dominated everything that wasn't writing or on the phone with Terry. Emmerson said little about his life outside of his home shop, except for long beach walks on the eastern shore with Calvary and a few buddies with whom he seemed to share harmless surface moments, harmless surface happy hours and harmless surface local sporting events.

By fall of 2001, Nam finally had become a history more in the background than before. There is a *thing* with Nam vets that is very difficult to explain or comprehend. In Nam for one or more tours of duty, for Nam vets, life continues half Nam and half the future. Nam is always half through time; the impressions remain vivid, often until forced into a more diminished status by something worthy enough to take the place. Sometimes, that takes a couple years. Sometimes, it takes many more years. A point comes, when most of, or big parts of Nam break off and can be set aside. A "been there, done that" emotion seems reasonable, but that crossing point is different for everyone and generally takes a replacement inner stimulus of some sort. It takes the type of stimulus you have to get out of the personal box to let wash over you, to feel. A job and home man-cave shop don't normally stimulate the synergies to move from the Nam personal introspective box. Something else, perhaps starting with just a phone call, has to move the mountain and the baggage along another unknown route to good, open feelings previously too guarded. Just a small incident or tilt from routine can open inner passages to more inner gates of new visions that seemed so unlikely or impractical just a day before.

Like a decision to answer a ringing phone and finally say, "Hello." Then do it again and mean it.

What would stimulate and open personal spirits to make Nam way less than half of a past and make the future way more than half of lives that need moving on or perhaps sung to? Blue eyes and brave shoulders over a black evening gown definitely help. Slowly through 2001, a bravest, strong marine sergeant, bent with, instead of against, new personal breezes. Heather and Emmerson agreed to have another phone conversation, October 2001, marking a two-year anniversary from the initial call. Heather would be home in Oregon until February.

> *Heather: Hi, Terry. Hi, honey, been missing you. How are you and your Calvary?*
>
> *Emmerson: We're good, mostly.*
>
> *Heather: What's mostly? What's not a part of mostly?*
>
> *Emmerson: What's not a part of mostly is you. We've been talking for two years, I've studied the shop pictures from every angle a shop picture can pose and fake a conversation.*
>
> *Heather: I know, strange, like a novel one cannot fully separate from. I feel I know you better than these people here that I see every day. It's so far. You started here with me as a ghost who saved lives in a war no one could comprehend.*
>
> *Emmerson: That was a long time ago, gone, maybe finally gone. I'm starting to close up the house, sell things. Giving good stuff, to good friends, who have put up with me and my used-up, worn out war-ways for over thirty years here in Norfolk.*
>
> *Heather: Where are you going? When? What will happen to us? I've come to depend on your distant attention, your distant love and trust. It*

matters less and less we have never actually met. I feel you now, right now here with me, and you are no closer than you have ever been.

Emmerson: I'm gonna move to Oregon! (A deep sighing, timid breath.) Soon!"

Heather: Oh! How soon? (Heather's deep sighing, matching breath.)

Emmerson: I'd like to leave Monday morning, bring the Calvary, of course.

Heather: Hurry!

When Emmerson left Norfolk, he never looked back. He disappeared, almost like Heather's brother Fletcher did out the side of the Air America prop, back in '68, having crossed into a strange unknown jungle edge of Laos. Emmerson's balance of past and future finally tipped in a direction he could finally, confidently feel and embrace, although admittedly toward a strange unknown edge of an earned different kind. He would now be able to approach the strangeness personally unguarded.

Heather looked anxiously east for a week, finally seeing a new beige maxi-cab Ram pickup truck pull up to the ocean-side A-frame, with a Calvary wiggling in the back, sloppy tongue waiting for a first blue-eyed lick. Time had worked a way, as had Nam. A singer and a sergeant easily submerged, finally with more future and considerably less past.

Believe all the stories!

Late 2001, in the fall, Rollie Cahill also disappeared. No one made a connection between Cahill's disappearance and that of Emmerson. No one could have, there was no common network, no obvious connecting thread, or at least no one knew of a common network that kept the two Sergeants in continued rambunctious cahoots, except for Aunt Marge, and she wasn't tellin'.

Marge Cahill had escaped from the North Carolina Cahill's in the late '50s. Her husband Art Cahill had become a self-taught, self-made Hamm Radio operator as the new broad world of Hamm Radio had become essential as a part of various State Police distance communication operational requirements. The Hamm Radio technology having become perfected in WW II to cover communication needs in war operations over the vast Pacific Ocean was becoming essential to State Police needs, and various States were in search of professional Hamm operational engineers to manage a portion of their fast moving mobile communication needs. Art Cahill was one of the best, and best known for not only his work in North Carolina but also for training Hamm specialists for other State's mobile policing needs over greater distances.

The California State Police made Marge and Art Cahill an offer they wouldn't refuse, and by 1959, they were relocated to Coronado Island, across the bay from San Diego, in the stretching shadow of Pt. Loma, at America's furthest southwestern edge. Coronado was a small town amidst the growing San Diego metro area, a sliver of land that kissed the Pacific Ocean 24-7. The Cahill's settled into Coronado's civilian and small town rhythm easily, becoming a part of Coronado society, which at the time was mostly military families. Coronado is home to a large marine facility, home to the Southern Pacific aircraft carrier group and home to many other specialty training ops, such as Navy Seals, Special Forces, with a large airstrip locally called North Island, operational for all kinds of domestic and ocean probing military and government air assets. Across the bay and practically part of downtown San Diego is MCRD, Marine Corps Recruiting Depot, home to the west coast boot camp of the USMC. Just walking through Coronado sets a self-imposed marching cadence to a step, often with jet engines as back-round power music in their descending entry to North Island. Jets and props thunderous in taking off, or loudly hissing toward a landing, lend a constant military reality to beautiful Coronado Island.

From the modest Cahill home on B Street, two blocks toward the bay, and a couple clicks west is the gate to the very large, strategic North Island Naval base, where there is almost always one of the Pacific Fleet aircraft carriers docked, resupplying and waiting to disembark for a new mission and display of military superiority anywhere in the world needed for work, or just the show of military capability. The global strength and force of America's presence is quintessentially an Aircraft Carrier. Nothing on earth matches these beasts of power and mobility; they are the bulls in the globe's peacekeeping china shop, when ordered to be so. The large navy base further within the San Diego Bay provides a constant stream of the navy's war ships in and out of bay docking facilities for repairs and upgrades, often providing visitors with goosebumps of National Pride as the ships pass by Coronado, all hands at attention on deck, on their way through the narrow passage between Coronado and Pt. Loma, into the vast open Pacific. Carriers, having no equals, cruise through their own "shadows of death, fearing no evil."

Art and Marge Cahill were settled permanently into Coronado, leaving the North Carolina Cahill's far and away but not forgotten. In 1966, a call from the Carolinas informed Art and Marge that Rollie Cahill had joined the marines, and would soon, that early October, be on his way to San Diego, to MCRD for twelve weeks of boot camp. Ten weeks into Rollie's boot camp would be the one Sunday visitation for his training platoon, and the North Carolina Cahills wondered if the California Cahills would plan to visit MCRD, find Rollie, and see if life in the Corps was working for him, through boot camp anyway.

Rollie had never actually met Art and Marge but had heard of them and their brave move to Coronado more than ten years prior, when he was a North Carolina version of the Wilson Street Boys. Rollie met Marge and Art that sunny Sunday, next to the sprawling black top of marching parade grounds at MCRD, where the distant family members of many of the boots blended famously, naturally, lastingly into one another, all understanding that day's greetings, affections and feelings were now a permanent part of each of them, stuck to present and future personal spirits.

Ten months later, they would meet again as Rollie would return to California's west coast and the San Diego area for "staging" duties at Camp Pendleton, several clicks north from San Diego, at the edge of north San Diego County toward the metro LA spaghetti bowls of highways and American, west coast style ethnic blending. Camp Pendleton, the largest West Coast Marine Corps base, separates San Diego from the growing civilian chaos stretching in all directions from Los Angeles. "Staging" is final training before being shipped way west, so far west it becomes east, to the war in South Vietnam. Part of "staging" toward the end of training, is a weekend chit off base, and Rollie spent that last weekend in the World on Coronado, with Art and Marge, the family away from home he had not quite realized he would always have to embrace.

Rollie would see Art and Marge one more time, on the tarmac at Mira Mar Marine Corps air facility, at the boarding of his United, to be then on the way to Nam. Marge was a big woman, stout, German stout, with big reddish-bronze flowing hair plopped on her tall stature as if sporting her own moving flag. From the top of an airliner landing ramp, looking back to America, Marge seemed to anchor the whole scene of well-wishers and marine's families, wives, girlfriends, and fans, with her big broad shoulders and red lipstick, passionate smile and unique top-head flag. Then Rollie stepped into the plane's interior shadows and flew to Nam, early fall '67.

By 2001, Art had passed away, having retired from the California State Police to own and manage Coronado's first Hamm Radio and TV sales and service shop on Orange Boulevard that runs through the middle of Coronado from the edge of the Naval Base to the

Strand, which stretches a little further south into Tijuana, Mexico several clicks south of downtown Coronado. Marge remained on B Avenue after Art passed away, in the same house. Marge's world class talents were in playing the organ or piano as a local musical celebrity, even played special occasions up and down the coast, or played for guests in her home on the living room grand piano and organ, at the same time. She also spent her endless music, cheer and personal flag waving on and around the Coronado Naval and Marine bases when invited to participate in local musical events, which was often. Evenings and late restless nights she would tune up the back bedroom Hamm Radio system and talk with distant air wave friends from all over the Pacific rim, gaining notoriety as the "Fox of the Pacific Air Waves." Marge always had a confident, determined pace about her. Externally, she appeared as an anchor to whatever situation or event she attended. Internally, she was Coronado's human equivalent of Pt. Loma. Marge never forgot the special place she had kept in her heart for Rollie, the marine she sent to Nam on a sunny October day, over thirty years ago. In fact, she felt she could never forget that day as her commitment to Rollie always felt so full of deep love and hope that she in a way also made that journey through Nam's atrocities. Again, one phone call can shift a person's place and world and goodness!

> Marge: Hello, this is Margorie.
> Rollie: Aunt Marge, this is Rollie Cahill, from North Carolina.
> Marge: Oh, oh my lord, my dearest Rollie. Rollie, dear, I must sit down.
> Rollie: Marge, I'm so happy to find that you are still there. I'm coming to see you.
> Marge: Oh, gracious. Coming to see me? In Coronado?
> Rollie: Yes, soon. Are you OK? Is Art OK? I'll be in San Diego for just two days, maybe three but will see you and Art as much as I can.

Marge: "Art died . . . three years ago, but it's OK. He was ready, and so was I. I'll tell you more about that when you arrive.

Rollie: Sorry, I didn't know. Are you at home, on B, the same house?

Marge: Oh yes, right here, same darkened fading green paint that we put on about forty years ago, same 1950s kitchen. We just upgrade dogs every now and then. When will you arrive?

Rollie: I will pull up in front of your house, next Sunday, about 10:00 a.m., my flight lands about nine. I'll rent a car and be right over.

Marge: Oh Rollie, I can't wait. I still have the vision of the young marine on the jet ramp looking back to me. I wanted to go with you, keep you safe. Later, the strangest sensations told me over and over that you will live, live through Nam. An angel spoke to me that you would come back. You did! Why are you in San Diego after all of these years?

Rollie: I'll tell you when I get there. Keep the day open, Monday also if you can.

Marge: See you Sunday, Thanks. Thanks so much. I'm still big, not quite as strikingly beautiful.

Rollie: And Marge, be dressed to go out. We'll make a run across the bay for a couple hours.

Marge: Oh, goodness, OK, sure. Where to?

Rollie: Dat, dat. You just be ready; you'll see. See you Sunday. Love you! And thanks, thanks for being there, years ago, and one of my angels, many, many times since, or so I feel.

Rollie pulled up in front of the modest Coronado home, at 240 B Avenue, Sunday morning, 9:45 a.m., to see Marge at the front door, enough grinning lipstick to paint the front door red, arms out for a bear hug from thirty-five years at ease, flag waving, gleaming, reddened hair piece, unaltered.

Rollie had eventually realized "his Nam" kind of started with Marge, as part of his "staging" training, and send off. "Staging" was the outward, soldier training, physical, strategic: intended to position soldier certainty with human uncertainty, but it didn't. In '67, seeing, meeting, and being briefly with Art and Marge was the "human staging," the last reminder of Domestic love and commitment, an adjacent reminder of why we war, for love of family and country, theoretically. At the time, enough reason for a nineteen-year-old marine of why we war so frequently. Perhaps we have more love of family and country than peaceful countries that mind their own business and have less assets to waist. For Rollie and millions like him, Marge was then and would be forever that symbol of American stature worth defending, or at least that was the impression, perhaps for lack of any other impression worthy of a personal highest stature. What the heck, ranking impressions is a useless, wasteful exercise. "Impressions" are what they are, when you need or recognize them.

Thirty-five years after the California Mira Mar tarmac send off to the Domestic Nam, Marge was not that easy to get down the front steps, to the car, and with a massive "plop" into the rented front seat, mile-wide lipsticked grin never fading.

> Marge: OK, you got me captured. Where are we going? What is our mission today?
>
> Rollie: A fun mission, you'll love it, but it's too early for you to know, just sit, grin, behave, and spread your angel wings a bit. How long since you've been over the Coronado Bridge, looking at what your times built, seeing the US Navy in all directions?
>
> Marge: Too long, I don't drive any more, and no one my age does either.

Rollie: What fun, what memories, how good it is to capture you like this and selfishly squeeze more of your goodness in my direction.

Marge: Where are you taking me? You wouldn't do this if it weren't a big deal, important to us both, I know you wouldn't. I have no idea.

Rollie: What a bridge . . . There is South San Diego . . . Their day, maybe their week. . . . . The bay front restaurants . . . The divide to the airport . . . Lockheed . . . Cummins . . . General Dynamics . . . All strong-looking, American-busy.

Marge: Yep, all on the way to?

Rollie: Traffic quite light this Sunday morning, look, the harbor, families loading boats for the day, maybe the week, saluting Pt. Loma on their way past, saluting the navy, the Marine Corps base— saluting the USS Ronald Reagan, resting dockside at Coronado.

Marge: I'll salute you, if you tell me where we're going.

Half of downtown, San Diego is the streets and packed neighborhoods, the other half is inside the massive buildings surrounding the airport and stretching out into guarded industrial areas of the inner city. Bright, clean, sun-drenched, closed buildings, surrounded by parking lots, always filled twenty-four hours a day with moving shifts of workers. Five minutes around the corner from downtown, then just before the San Diego freeway north, drift left, then left more, into the neighborhood of dull yellow stucco, palm tree lined walks, red clay roofs, red and yellow signage, and serious American marines.

Marge: Rollie, this is MCRD. What are we doing here? This is where we met, that unusual deep-felt Sunday, 1966, another time, almost another life ago.

> *Rollie: Yep my Auntie Angel . . . MCRD. Let's go in.*
>
> *Marge: Great, fine! Why?*
>
> *Rollie: Why, because I lived, and perhaps shouldn't have. And because I want someone else to live, like I did, and you will help?*
>
> *Marge: Someone else? Who? Who may I bless, with you alongside?*
>
> *Rollie: My son, Casey. My son is here, in his tenth week of boot camp, and I wanted to bring him a special gift—you! This is their open Sunday visitation, his one chance for your blessing, before . . . well before his Marine Corps life really starts.*
>
> *Marge: Rollie Cahill! I don't know what to say. I can't even speak. I can hardly breathe. The marines will have to carry my battleship fainted body to a cool fountain."*

Passing through the front gates, directed by smart focused marines, the two attached Cahills were escorted to the shaded court yard behind the base chapel, where they would wait for Casey and his platoon to appear from an uncertain direction. And they soon did.

Whatever humans of all kinds are like in character before boot camp, ten weeks later, they are not like that anymore. Every move is calculated, every breath and notion is respectful, tightened and guarded. The activity of every site path is noticed. Marine boots in week ten are new people, newly focused, bravely grown, calm but ready not to be. Week ten, civilian/family visits are their first contact with the World they had grown up in, now an "otherworld" of sorts. Marine boots, ten weeks in, are ready, ready to graduate from MCRD and ready for an MOS, an assignment, an order, ready to carry new flags to new places, ready for all duties as assigned. Marine boots are the nation's warring assets, MVPs for the next beach, or hill, or perimeter. Their lights with grit are on, and they are ready, chomping, tuned.

Casey was a platoon's squad leader, a stature certain for promotion upon boot graduation, two weeks away. He was, of course, a quiet legacy, and seemed to carry that added weight effortlessly.

Rollie: "Hi, Case. You OK, holding up? Enjoying your stay?

Private Casey: I'm good, skating now, a little trouble a couple of weeks ago, but good now, ready to go, move on.

Rollie: I want you to meet your Aunt, Marge Cahill. Marge lives just across the bay in Coronado.

Private Casey: Please to meet you, Aunt Marge. Thank you for coming. Dad has spoken of you. Dad says you were his angel. Still are, he suspects.

Marge (suddenly stoic, now in official angel mode, a blessed statue of wisdom, pride, honor—a symbol of why we in America might survive our own greed and temptations): "Your dad surprised me. I had no idea, a most pleasant surprise for an elder lady no longer used to, or looking for surprises. You and your dad have made my day and year, perhaps have made my passing times. I may have been an angel to your dad in his time of needing an angel. Someone was. Angels are not self-made or self-appointed. They float and land where instructed. Perhaps that is why I am here today. I don't know, not sure, we are never sure. I do know my heart is bursting with pride of my own personal honor of service to my two marines. Rollie, Casey, hold my hands.

Dear Lord of ours, Bless this new young brave American marine. Bless his duties and travels across hills, through gaps, past America's enemies, deep into places and conditions never suspected by others. Add strength to his inner soul, packaged in muscle, bravery, and trained honest foresight. Lord, bless Casey within the causes and paths he will dutifully enter. Provide his angel, to always be present in times needed, always agile with his movements, and looking as one with him, as a guardian with his visions into the next Nam. Hold these blessings tight, never betting faith, so help us God!

A new faith arose from Rollie and Casey alike—the faith that once blessed by Aunt Marge, a marine stays blessed.

The hour of kinship and boot relief passed quickly. Casey described his squad leadership issue of a couple weeks ago, and described the remedy, sounding as if some sort of pre-Marge angel was already at work.

Looking around, in the shaded area behind the camps chapel, 111 other boot marines were quietly meeting with their respective friends or families or standing alone, at ease. Marines who had no families close enough to MCRD to visit their boots, were retrieved by other marine families and brought into their individual circles for introductions and sharing of the valuable visitation minutes left before orders barked for a formation commencing a strict regimen and more training for the final two weeks, then graduation, then orders, and a new serious life in the Corps begins.

Casey excused himself and fetched a boot buddy also from North Carolina, Pete. Pete was the flagman, tall, broad shouldered, pocked face as if shrapnel had already danced close into his life. If a pocked face can actually enhance a young man's outer appeal and looks, it was so with Pete. Somehow, the permanent scars from youth announced his determination, exaggerating his rugged appeal. Pete carried it well, leaving no doubt that later in life some lucky gal would see through the appearance test and take Pete to his new land.

Good-byes at boot visitation day can be clumsy, awkward, leaving loved ones and friends with more wishing to be said than having been said. That is often the case, but not in this case with the Cahills, not with Marge. Marge christened every passing wave brought her way with a touch of extraordinary grace.

> *Marge: Boys, hold my old hands one more time: Rollie, thank you. Thank you for thinking of me, and bringing me to this point of shared pride of service for us all. Your personal angel may pass on, pass to where it is now more needed.*
>
> *Marge: Casey, thank you. Keep your head up, see through your own Nam, keep your powder dry, and kick ass.*

With that parting inspiration, Casey returned to his forming unit, returned to his position, front left, squad leader, First Squad. Rollie and Marge silently observed, bursting with patriotic pride, as there was no more to say right then, no more to do, not that day. Fate, a new angel, and Semper Fi now were Casey's new wings.

> *SSgt. Servantes: Aaattennn-tion! Foooorward—Huu!*
>
> *Rollie: Aunt Marge, I think we are finished. How do you do it?*
>
> *Marge: Do what?*
>
> *Rollie: Do that!*
>
> *Marge: Do what, that?*
>
> *Rollie: You don't even know, do you? Well, among other things, the boy now thinks he's got his own angel, that's kind of what.*
>
> *Marge: He's gonna need one, an angel of his own. I suppose whether he actually has the angel or not doesn't matter right now, as long as he thinks*

he does. Hope it doesn't lead him to take too many
risks, be stupid about things.

  Rollie: It will, I know it will. Come on, I'm
gonna make you stay out of that house a little longer.
Let's get back to the Coronado side of the Bay and
have lunch in one of those fancy seafood places a spit
off the water's edge.

  Marge: How's my lipstick?

The drive out of MCRD, along the San Diego Bay front, through downtown and over the graciously beautiful, reaching toward the heavens Coronado Bridge was ten times longer than the original feelings of the drive to meet Casey and drink in the patriotic glories of MCRD. Marge and Rollie were full of the whole scene, the whole commitment, the whole part of America that stretched before them, the America they were lifelong contributing members of, the America they lived and fought for or angeled for or played the organ for or others sing for.

  Rollie (to a restaurant receptionist): A table for
two, as far out and as close to the bay water as your
waitresses can stretch their beautiful arms, please.

Rollie and Marge were seated, warming California sun flooding around them, the air refreshingly cool, the San Diego Bay in its perfect Sunday glory, calm, a deeply rolling majestic, with shade for lunch-a-teers, under the table's umbrella. Still mostly quiet, thoughtful, digesting the experience with Casey into the day, digesting his son's remaining two weeks of boot and next three, five, or ten years. How will he gain rank? What MOS will be assigned in two weeks? When will he be deployed to America's new next wars or conflicts not yet even known or charted strategically to maps? Certainly, he'll see the Middle East, maybe Asia. In a four-year enlistment commitment,

America can dream up lots of wars and conflicts for young men to survive through.

> *Rollie: What with 9/11, Bush will have us in the Middle East in no time. We won't be able to resist. Notice on the parade ground, certain platoons were marching in tan and brown instead of the tradition boot camp dark green.*

Rollie and Marge sat quietly, enjoying breathing each other's trusted company, Rollie mostly facing out into the Bay, Marge facing the other way, down the Coronado shoreline, onto the Naval Base, straight into the bow of the docked USS *Ronald Reagan*, America's newest Nimitz-class nuclear-powered supercarrier. Nothing in the modern world is more majestic than the view and reality of an aircraft carrier. So massive, they almost look like exaggerated, oversized animation. How can it possibly float? Three thousand two hundred Americans company the ship with five commanding officers. The USS *Ronald Reagan* has no specific range. The range is unlimited, cruising its nuclear way and displaying human and fixed warring assets for decades, deployed as part of Carrier Strike Group Nine, to where ever the next threat or conflict or freedom-saving or payback may arise in the world. The latest technology and best-trained, most-modern Wilson Street Boys enhance the structural carrier asset: fire control radar, air traffic control radar, air search radar, instrument landing system radar, Nixie torpedoes, missiles, Westinghouse A4W nuclear reactors, with 2,480 Naval Airmen on board to deploy ninety fixed wing fighter jets and numerous helicopters to duties as assigned. The USS *Ronald Reagan* deploys under the nationalized motto: "Peace through strength."

Northrop Grumman and numerous subcontractors built the USS *Ronald Reagan* in only seven years.

Marge: Rollie, I have never talked disparagingly about our beloved country and don't intend to again. Here's how I have learned to think of such matters . . . You may take this "opinion" as you wish.

I have lived in Coronado, as you know, since the '50s. In that time, I have seen it all. Coronado was pretty much strictly a military town, navy and marines, when we moved here. As you know, before they built the high-rise Coronado Bridge, most navy and marine personnel lived on the island. They had to. There was no way for easy daily commuting to live in San Diego or Chula Vista or surrounding communities and work on Island bases. Back then, through the '60s, through your time in the marines, and through the atrocities of Vietnam, Coronado was practically a closed society of military thinking and actions. Art and I were rather adjacent to it all, separate, but deeply attached just by being here. Almost all of our close friends were high-ranking military officers. In most cases, the wives and families of enlisted or officers remained on Coronado through numerous deployments. In the '60s, our whole lives were consumed by reasons for or excuses about or justifications of or blah-blah after blah-blah concerning the War in Vietnam.

With WWII and Korea fresh in anyone's minds and memories, Vietnam just seemed a next "circumstance" of defending freedom. Everyone thought of Vietnam in terms of more nasty global freedom spreading duties as befalls the emerged global leader of defending the ethics and moralities of global freedoms for everyone—the original "God-given basic human right." Freedom breaking through globally was the new rite of passage worth defending in some countries, worth extending to others. More wars simply meant more flags and more boys to send, more of everything—and Coronado, right here, right on B Avenue seemed to be the center of it all. While you were in God-awful places like Khe Sanh, the Battle of Hue or on some lost sand hill of a perimeter line or LZ, people here were still praising the efforts.

Then, it began to change, slowly, almost an oops-cover-up at a time, mostly after Tet, and the following one year. Too many dark-green body bags returned in place of broad-shouldered, proud, young marines. Too many American assets became wasted that were more honestly owed to moral national infrastructure, core ideologies of America's goodness were becoming obviously bent and twisted, confused, unreliable for sustaining an American way of life that Americans would be proud of. Around Coronado, a center pivot of naval and marine leadership, talk and attitudes slowly changed. Late afternoon cocktail parties became tiny pockets of angry frustrations when officers and wives could let their hair down a little, and talk more freely. These officers, perhaps led in reasoning by the logic of their wives who had the advantage of stepping back a bit with a wider lense to see Vietnam realities, began to quietly change positions, attitudes. It was a tough personal process for all of them, struggling between orders, military duties, and personal good judgment.

Bottom line Rollie, the '60s, your era, is when America slanted, tilted, leaned to corruptions and misgivings previously not tolerated in national leadership. Johnson and his cronies were war criminals, who rebuilt the waiting military/

industrial complex and skimmed millions from the processes of war, particularly in South Vietnam. In early '68, when Tet occurred, Coronado was a mix-master of moving troops, guns, war ships, and fighter jet training flights, with new pilots and Special Forces trainees filling Orange Boulevard. Art and I, with many other families of Coronado spent virtually every weekend feeding and entertaining, and then sending new young boys off to Vietnam. Our living room was full constantly with four, seven, or more marines, staging or just free from MCRD boot camp. We knew many of them would never return alive, and they didn't. I would shudder to think how many of the young marines that were one weekend in our living room, then soon became wrapped inside a dark, moldy, rubber body bag and sent home to friends and families who were wondering why. How is America in the evil clutches of such insane trappings?

Rollie, why do you think it is always us, always America, in a new war here, then there? Why do you think we cannot mind our own business, stay out of the stupidity of third-world struggles ancient in their origins, that are never resolved, nor will they be resolved? Why do you think that is?

Right there is why! Right there! The USS Ronald Reagan is the new massive, expensive symbol of why we have been and always will be aside positions of the challenged or just be the challenger. We can't help it. It is just too profitable in the dark halls of ways and means and fake diplomacies to refocus toward the original founding goodness of America's core values. In the '60s, it all changed. I fear it will never go back, certainly not in my lifetime. In my own speck of living, America has never, not been on the way to or in one war or another—and it all goes through right here, right here in Coronado. This is the wide lens of America's warring realities. Brave, smart young men walk through that restaurant door every day, all prissied in dress whites, dress blues, or dress greens, all determined looking, with equally beautiful, smart wives. Except the wives have a vacancy in their eyes, as if on a ride to an unknown threatening destination from which they have no control, and they don't, of course, have any control. The wives are correct in their feelings, you know. Except, military wives don't speak away from their unwritten codes. Their positions in life are to "sing," very loudly when they are called upon to.

Fifty years I've been here, living in the center of a half-military, half-civilian life, it has never changed. You did it, you came through, as tough and fit and determined as those before you, and those after you. Now Casey will come through, on the way to his marine-making and personal tests of survival and angel counting. It never changes. How can that be? I've seen it all. I was escorted on to the Enterprise *to perform an organ concert for diplomats and ranks of all kinds and for President Johnson. I saw the evil in the man, the look of pure evil obscenities like I have never seen before or since in a person. He was chilling in his personal characteristic obscenities. He died of shame, you know. His evil guts rotted from within for what he did in Vietnam, and for the evil standards he made into a free country's standard operating procedures for the military/industrial machines that still manipulate and operate within long lines of political whores. America's goodness alone will win some battles but all too often not the big important battles. The real question is, how long? How long can America survive in a down trend of government greed and deception? I guess we'll find out, or you'll find out. I'm rather pressing the envelope now with this pesky age issue.*

There, I've said it, finally said what I've been thinking for thirty-five years, since Vietnam, since your sacrifices and struggles for causes and duties as assigned. I think today brought it out of me, today with Casey and you of course, at the always majestic MCRD. Today struck me. That boy and his own angel will probably survive. He's tough, smart, also blessed. His walk is different, boots not quite touching the parade ground blacktop on the way to his platoon duties. It's the other thousands, not quite as blessed or agile that will pay the new American price, so that certain generals, politicians and back room industrial salesmen can reap and skim undercover, disjointed profits.

I'll shut up. Must shut up, I'm depressing myself, you too probably. Probably depressing all these good people here for a glorious, sunny Coronado-style late lunch, just by my angry, frustrated vibes spilling all over this beautiful lunch scene.

Rollie: Well, that's all? That's all you got, this Sunday? How old are you now my angel?

Marge: Old enough to say what I want! Eighty-six. I'm eighty-six. No, eighty-five. Oh, what's the difference.

Rollie: No real difference. Just thinking, I'm fifty-four. Trying to think how mad I'll get by the time I'm your age. You are right, you know. 100 percent correct! I wonder how many of us there are? What we can all do about it, if anything at all.

Marge: So what are you going to do, Rollie? I sense Casey's mom is long gone, out of the picture. What's next for my marine? I know you. I know whatever is next, is not normal. I can feel you are anxious, positive about a new chapter. You have something planned. Don't you? I sense you are ready to launch into something, and that is another reason you are here. I'm right, aren't I?

Rollie: Of course you are. You always are right. I'm going to deploy, again, kind of.

Marge: I can tell you are on an edge . . . going to deploy deeply, aren't you, in some sort of new jarhead commitment? I can see you have made up your mind about something. I sense you have returned to your original angel, for some sort of blessing.

Rollie: I have . . . and to see Casey, of course, and to see, feel, and drink in MCRD, which truthfully I mastered with eager ease. No one says that out loud you know? Those drill instructors hear that sort of thing, and they think they aren't being nasty enough to the boots.

Marge: So? So what now my Rollie? What is it that closes one chapter and opens this exciting new, probably dangerous chapter?

Rollie: Well, we'll finish lunch. See if a booming fighter jet launches our way off the Reagan.

Marge: Yeah, then what?

Rollie: Then, I'll take you four blocks home and kiss those big red lips good-bye. One more time!

Marge: You mean . . . really good-bye, don't you?

Rollie: Marge! Will you quit it! Just act for one short moment that you don't see everything before everybody else.

Marge: I'm shut—there—I'll lean back. It's yours. Take it.

Rollie: I feel just like you do. We all do. We all feel that way—that is, Nam vets, people our age who concern themselves with such things, feel it, underneath. We're pissed. We've had enough. Casey and thousands like him will most assuredly be on the way to Afghanistan, Iraq, or some other useless, faceless Middle East human compost, weaponry race track.

Rollie: I'm sick of it, sick of the lies and distortions, sick of the pompous politicians and their know-it-all "Trolleys" that bobble-head along as "Yes Men." Sick and pissed. We're gonna blow it, give it all away, what over two hundred years of freedom have built, that no other country in the history of the world could even begin to accomplish.

Marge: Yes, Rollie, I'm kissing ninety. I won't be going anywhere B Avenue and its passing traffic, and tons of memories is my destiny, like it or not. And you?

Rollie: I will now kind of, almost disappear.

Marge: There's a great hint, kind of, almost, disappear? What the heck does that mean? Well, when someone disappears. It's not fair to ask where to, or it wouldn't be disappearing. So drop me a hint. Tell me there is some beauteous, talent-filled, blue-eyed babe with her hands outstretched in your welcome direction. Tell me, you and she will disappear into a deserved harmless obscurity and hold one another blending with new angels. That it? Am I close?

Rollie: Marge, just for once behave. Amazingly close, again.

Marge: Aha, knew it. Who knows angel's ways? Who will be the best angel ever, riding coastal angel wave-things a decade at a time?

Rollie: You! You, Aunt Marge!

Marge: Will you be back? Will you ever be back? Even the USS Ronald Reagan *is gonna dock about every other year! Come back now and then! This angel stuff ain't free you know. To keep a good, tuned angel, you have to kiss the lipstick now and then. Where are going? Can you tell me that?*

Rollie: I'm going up the coast, staying out west. A Nam buddy of mine also has an angel. They say they will be singing up on the mid-Oregon coast. They have invited me to come up and do nothing with them. I've a friend who likes the idea. The four of us can do nothing together. Help each other through our nothingness, except for a few brief missions now and then. Hopefully, that also means staying out of trouble, which will be rather new for me. Plus, there is a low level mention of some sort of harmless mission that needs quick attention.

Marge: "OK, you have my angel blessings but will you be back? Back to see this angel? Right here, on this spot?

Rollie: I don't know. I'll see if my new angel wants to meet my old angel. I'll be up the coast a ways, not too far. I'll make you a deal.

Marge: Will you tell me about your new angel? Sorry! Make your deal. I need a deal. What's your

*deal? No, never mind . . . Rollie Cahill, you tell me
who the new angel is right now.*

*Rollie: She's a great babe! Smart, strong, might
even actually give a damn about me. Here's the deal!
When that big boat right there returns to Coronado,
so will I, and I'll bring the new angel. You can meet
her, touch her, mesmerize her, with angelic qualities.
Maybe Casey will be passing through. Deal? OK?*

*Marge: Deal! The best deal an old lady can
make right now, under the aging circumstances.*

*Marge: Rollie, hold my hand one last time
today. Dear Lord, again hear our humble prayers.
Watch over this marine, up the coast, with his new
angel. Protect our other young marine, Casey, as he
serves with pride, making his own way, building his
own character and stories, in a crossways world and
crossways America. And. Lord, bring us together
one more time, right here—with the USS* Ronald
Reagan, *any and all new angels, the newest with
older, if at all possible. Amen.*

*Marge: How's that? Can you top that? Give me
the check, come on. Let's go home.*

*Rollie: No, Marge, I can't top that. Never
would I try! Thanks again and always.*

Full of Coronado, full of Marge, full of Casey and MCRD,
Rollie proceeded with a lightened head and upbeat intentions, up
the California coast, toward Oregon, a long-awaited reunion with
Emmerson, topped off with an introduction to a singing Heather.
Typically, Emmerson, and Heather, perhaps had replaced the
mystique of Air America. For some, such a drive could be a normal
tripping, sightseeing pleasurable experience, for others the drive could
stimulate other long lost, set aside thoughts and feelings specific to
the history of inner consciousness. For Rollie, the drive would be a

majestic transformation, similar to the flight from Da Nang back to the World, in his defining fall of '68.

The driving mind-set would be to stick to the coastline, Highway 101. Drink in the scenery with the warm sun and cooled ocean air refreshing each breath and mile. Such a drive requires negotiating the crazy, congested traffic of LA, and later San Francisco—no matter on this drive. This was *the* drive of a lifetime, the drive we all wait for, have most likely earned in one way or another. Oxnard, Ventura, Santa Barbara, then on north through Vandenberg Air Force Base, the Pacific Ocean always just to the left. Beyond the Pacific was Vietnam also to the left, way out there somewhere still! On North through quaint, smaller California coastal stops and spots on 101, to Morro Bay for a wondrous evening walk, thoughts, and an overnight. On northward, further up a transforming coast to Oregon, passing through more California coastal towns, changing types of agricultural production displayed to the right. Past Big Sur, then through Monterey, where you think California can't get any better, more scenic, but then it does.

San Francisco busy traffic and wound-around, tied-up streets a pleasing new kind of driving fun to pass through on a second day of life-injecting coastal travel. The Golden Gate Bridge stands as the marker to northern progress, a place where a driver from the east can't rubber neck enough from the city to the right, to the vast open ocean to the left. Then north toward Eureka where the coastline changes to more of a rough Oregon-ish feeling! Crescent City now becomes the final California gateway into Oregon to travel the beautiful harsher coastlines on north to meet up with Emmerson, Heather, and a pooch named Calvary.

How would that first sight and handshake with Emmerson go?

What sort of ancient pushed-back feelings will arise?

War feelings that could never actually be explained?

What must Heather think of all of this post-Nam drama, from over three decades of simmering within a couple verily found souls?

How do veterans, humans with so many miles together, reblend once again, after so many years of other miles that have perhaps been miles just as significant in a life's journey?

Emmerson, of all people! "I couldn't figure him out then. No one could! What makes me think I can figure him out now?"

Soon enough on a second travel day, eyes now practically bulging from the drive, just as fingers are finally stuck to the steering wheel in a driving paralysis, just when the directions were supposed to conclude with a new kind of auto/highway destination LZ. There they were: Emmerson; woe-nelly blonde, blue-eyed, smiling Heather; and a tan wiggling big ball of dog slobber fur! There they were, right there! On the coastal highway, just as Emmerson said they would be—waiting!

"What should I first say?"

Doesn't matter. It's Emmerson. He always sets the pace, always. He probably sees into Oregon by now.

Emmerson will trap the situation to his liking! That's why he's Emmerson. That's why I'm here, probably why Heather's here, not sure about the Calvary.

>   *Rollie: Hi, Emm! Buddy, good to see ya! You must be the one and only dear Heather? My sincere pleasure. Allow me a first hug. And this must be Calvary!"*
>
>   *(That's it! That's all it took! Long, tight, passion-filled, full group hugs, and dog jumps with deep dog moan-a-things, marked the glorious precious reunion moment. Breaths difficult to manage! Manly tears suppressed in a strange twisted way. The moment was another long belated flight up and out of Da Nang.)*
>
>   *Emmerson: Rollie, just pull the car over. Come on, let's walk up to the house. It's right there!*

(Arms in arms, the three were speechless, too full of gut feelings, visions of each hour and day ahead in this new world of their patient making.)

Emmerson (at the small white fenced-in coastal front yard): Wait a minute! Almost have forgotten! Rollie, there is one thing I have always wanted to know—only one, then we can sit and look at Heather, look at the coast also if you want.

Rollie: What . . . what in the heck would that one thing be, after all these years?

Emmerson: Remember back in Da Nang? Our big payday poker night killing?

Rollie: Sure, how could I forget? I've gone over that fun night again and again. It's the best late night, can't sleep, fun thinking ever. You too?

Emmerson: Well? Kind of, parts of!

Rollie: Well what?

Emmerson: Well, that's the one thing . . . the one thing I wanted to ask about.

Rollie: Really! What about it?

Emmerson: Damn it, Rollie! Did you have the four Jacks, or not?"

Rollie: Heaaatherrrrrrrrr, could you come here a minute, please."

The Domestic Vietnam—
A Final Thought

"A Full Circle"

The original Wilson Street Boys came from a small Midwest town in the center of perhaps the earth's most productive farming country, rich flat prairie soils for livestock and commercial grain production. Like many small towns in the '60s, this town was well-kept, fundamentally patriotic, trustworthy by city father's high standards, and hard working. People and families all knew each other, generally shared in one another's cheer, victories, or burdens, certainly shared in pride of community. A small town where military experience is a given part of the American deal, practically within a rite of passage from the freedoms and open-minded ways of youth, to wider responsibilities of adulthood, toward careers and new joined families beyond. To have served in the military has always been a quiet badge of honor within community attitudes. The small town of the Wilson Street Boys was Monticello, Illinois, quietly unique, traditionally expansive, within itself as small towns go.

There are thousands of other small towns dotting the rural maps of America, all of which contain uniqueness within their landscapes, people's lives and accomplishments, and underlying values. America, by its very fundamental being allows for and encourages "unique." Some towns, with their vibrant citizens capture "unique." Others pass around unique, never collectively suspecting the investments, values, or rewards.

A short half-mile jog and click north of the downtown Monticello square and county courthouse, extending the town's main road of State Street from town to country is the community cemetery, a perfectly well-maintained and cared for cemetery, twenty-four hours a day, seven days a week, fifty-two weeks a year. The cemetery, on one of nature's gracious rolling landscapes dotted with the countryside's traditional sprawling giant oaks and other tasteful living backgrounds of nature, overlooks dense adjacent forested boundaries. There are now some Wilson Street Boys at the cemetery, permanently, and more are on the way. Strangely, beyond any preplans of individual families, grave sites of the Wilson Street Boys present and in the future are all rather lumped together in a very small section of the cemetery, right up by the frontage road, as if forever maintaining the kinships lived, shared and earned. Helton is there already, next to Bensyl, who also is prematurely already there, across from the Foxes family plot, which is next to the Parsons plot: strange, curious, existential, dramatic, authentic.

Typical of many patriotically stable small towns, gravesites of our country's military veterans are marked at the Monticello cemetery with small bronze American Legion medallions, supported off the ground about nine inches by a similar round bronze support with an unnoticeable small round fixture on the medallions backside.

Fifty-one weeks a year, all the cemetery gravesites are superbly kept, with the weather-faded bronze medallions always present, marking individual Pride of Service for deceased veterans and for their friends and family visitors to contemplate, then appreciate. Time fades the bronze medallions into the natural rolling beauty of the cemetery's fixtures and landscape through the changing seasons of Central Illinois. Fifty-one weeks a year, a visitor or passerby on the frontage road or on the winding paths within the cemetery, would typically not even notice the bronze medallions modestly marking the gravesites of Monticello's own veterans. Fifty-one weeks a year, the stately, underspoken medallions are generally taken for granted, easy to overlook within the trees and monuments of the solid appearing, stationary cemetery scene. Fifty-one weeks a year, the people of Monticello know the medallions are there, marking a military veteran's honorable stature, and the veterans with their medallions will always be there, with more on the way.

Then, there is that other one week of the year, within the spring months, when all things of nature's landscapes, particularly in the tidy cemetery, exhibit their own pride, popping out in floral display. One week a year, there is a most glorious week for the cemetery and all of its permanent residents to display a less modest celebration for the community's citizens and out-of-town visitors to acknowledge and contemplate. One week a year, the cemetery launches to life within the rolling landscape, breeze-driven waves of a new inspirational sort, joyously and continuously, in unison, cause a waving back from the cemetery itself, toward all visitors and passers-by. One week a year, the waving back from the cemetery to the general population never stops, and somehow, one week a year is just enough. That one week is the week of the Memorial Day National Holiday.

In this small, rural, Unique Monticello, that one special week each year a small determined group of the town's patriotic volunteers attach fresh new United States flags to the back of each of the veteran's medallions, at every individual veteran grave. The bronze medallions of the landscape that have likely not been noticed for fifty-one weeks come to life and become the front and center stage of the quiet cemetery scene. The whole cemetery is vibrant with a new waving "national pride" and display of unselfish waving service and patriotism, celebrating the extreme effort and dedication, given by these deceased for what we believe are the core values of the United States, Monticello, and thousands of other towns and crossroads. A cemetery's Pride of Service flag-waving exhibition, uninhibited in the continuous breezes given from the prairie.

One other startling cemetery impression is made at the Monticello cemetery surrounding each Memorial Day—an unavoidable impression, the type of underspoken impression that cannot be overlooked that special community week of the Memorial National Holiday. Although the individual stories of Service are forever silenced, the cemetery and community volunteers see to it that patriotic services given by these veterans will never be silenced.

From the energy of the beloved veterans' medallions and their waving flags, on the always perfectly groomed landscape, a new "live" energy is given one week a year. This special energy is a kind of free energy that typically lies untouched, overlooked, dormant in America's aggregate human spirit until there is a slight prompting toward that latent energy and promptings of local citizen spirit. The cemetery visitor cannot avoid noticing just how many of the veteran's flags mark the Monticello cemetery landscape and gravesites for one week a year. The flags are everywhere, numerous throughout the acreage, a waving glee club, disproportionate to the small population of the community. Often, there are several medallion-mounted flags within individual family sections. WWI veterans and WWII veterans are next to Korean veterans that are next to Domestic Nam veterans. The whole gloriously stoic cemetery scene waves, while overlooked by a special "Full Circle" section, on the highest grounds of Monticello's unique cemetery. The cemetery's highest ground, a sentry-like section, referred to as Military Circle, is populated by Pride of Service Veterans of the Civil War. Always Will Be!

Bibliography

I n the off-writing seasons, I would read Nam-related books, mostly to stay in the warring "mood." This is not technically a bibliography since I don't quote or borrow from these books but greatly appreciate the work of their creation. I let the ideas of these books mingle with my own. Following is a list of those books from which I could lengthen and deepen my own experience in preparation for writing a more complete work.

In no certain order, the helpful books are as follows:

A Grand Delusion: America's Descent Into Vietnam by Robert Man, copyright 2001. This is an objective historical review, much worth the time. Eight hundred pages to be read easily, a word at a time.

Fire in the Lake, by Francis FitzGerald, copyright 1972. Five hundred pages, this book was written before the American debacle had ended. It is a very valuable account of the French history in Vietnam and accounts analyzing the doomed efforts of American involvement following the same footsteps. In the reading, one wonders: Why doesn't President Johnson and/or military leadership just read along with Fitzgerald or even talk to him. Fitzgerald outlines everything about why America will be defeated, waste lives, eventually leave in disgrace and confusion. He was right-on, years before the dreadful reality.

Vietnam, A History: The First Complete Account of Vietnam at War by Stanley Karnow, copyright 1983. Seven hundred pages, it is a "complete" history, including ancient Southeast China societies. One can only surmise and see more clearly, why such a war undertaking by America could never, ever win anything. (Different terrain, different societies, but same scenarios as current Afghanistan.)

The Last Valley: Dien Bien Phu and French Defeat in Vietnam; The Battle that Doomed the French Empire and Led America Into Vietnam by Martin Windrow, copyright 2004. Seven hundred pages, this book is more valuable historical perspective, embedding the issue of, if so many journalists and such extensive reporting could pinpoint an inevitable defeat, why could not American leadership get that message? I sense the answer to that is world-class criminal!

The Cat from Hue by John Laurence, copyright 2002. Over eight hundred pages, my personal favorite. Starting with the Battle of Hue, right where I was, when I was there, the book is a fascinating account and perspective in a novel form. An entertaining must read for all I Corps Marines and their families.

The Magnificent Bastards: The Joint Army-Marine Defense of Dong Ha, 1968 by Keith Nolan, copyright 1994. Four hundred pages, Dong Ha was a latrine-hole, dirty, dangerous, a stone's throw from the south edge of the DMZ, so strategic it seemed. In the end, who cared? It was a bald knob of reddish dirt surrounded by booby-traps, decorated with barbed wire. Tough, tough neighborhood. Once controlled, then like everything else, given up.

Matterhorn: a Novel of the Vietnam War by Karl Marlantes, copyright 2010. Six hundred pages, compared as Vietnam's version of All Quiet on the Western Front, the famous WWI soldier's account of actions and progress from the front.

They Marched Into Sunlight: War and Peace, Vietnam and America, October 1967 by David Maraniss, copyright 2003. Five hundred fifty pages, another narrative of the era, making it a point to compare US homeland upheaval with those ten thousand miles away in Nam.

A Bright Shining Lie by Neil Sheehan. An early gripping review of the political/military fiasco directing a confused, misguided Nam war effort.

About the Author

D ick Fox is from a small, very productive farming community in East Central, Illinois, Monticello, where he once again resides. The writing of *The Domestic Vietnam* begins in Monticello and ends right there, insinuating or plainly stating all of the novelistic beginnings and conclusions that one might expect in such a classic review of the Vietnam Era and America in general in the contentious '60's and '70's. Fox is known locally as Coach Fox, for his lifetime of work, play, and coaching in baseball, now also coaching the ladies in softball. He characterizes his youth in three parts: Little League Baseball, American Legion Baseball, Marine Corps boot camp at MCRD, San Diego.

Within a busy career of writing many business plans, product reviews or merger and acquisition papers, Fox also completed three prior specialty books, one a classic on Coaching. Through his active '80's and '90's career, Fox delivered numerous public speaking event messages on various topics, coast to coast. In addition to writing projects, Fox is a radio host with his show "The Domestic Nam," produced by Radioactive Broadcasting, for the "Military Appreciation Channel," also available to various Armed Forces Radio programming, as a "spokesperson" for Veterans and their families and friends, about the Vietnam War. Current hobbies include wine making, personal training for baseball and softball, a specialty fitness program invented for Hitters, and gardening.

SEMPER FI!

V000006B.52P

CPSIA information can be obtained at www.ICGtesting.com
Printed in the USA
LVOW01s0949050615

441306LV00006B/52/P